P9-DWH-848

Schooling as a ritual performance
Second edition

When *Schooling as a Ritual Performance* was first published in 1986 it caught the educational community largely unprepared with its highly original and unusual approach to the analysis of contemporary schooling. This new fully revised edition has been published in response to demands from sociologists and educationalists. It contains a Coda which extends and deepens the author's original analysis. In addition, the revised edition offers a new Foreword by Colin Lankshear and an Afterword by Phil Carspecken.

Peter McLaren is Associate Professor at the University of California in Los Angeles, Graduate School of Education. Formerly Special Lecturer in Teacher Education at Brock University, St Catharines, Ontario, he became Director of the Center for Education and Cultural Studies at Miami University's School of Education in 1992, where he was also Renowned Scholar in Residence and Associate Professor in the Department of Educational Leadership. He is author of the Canadian bestseller, *Cries from the Corridor: the New Suburban Ghettoes*, and is well known for his ethnographic accounts of urban schooling and for his involvement in the struggle for educational reform.

Schooling as a ritual performance
Second edition

Towards a political economy
of educational symbols
and gestures

Peter McLaren

Foreword to the first edition
by Henry A.Giroux

Foreword to the second edition
by Colin Lankshear

Afterword by Phil Francis Carspecken

London and New York

First published 1986
by Routledge & Kegan Paul plc
Second edition published 1993
by Routledge
11 New Fetter Lane, London EC4P 4EE

Simultaneously published in the USA and Canada
by Routledge
29 West 35th Street, New York, NY 10001

© 1993 Peter McLaren

Typeset in Baskerville by
Mews Photosetting, Beckenham, Kent
Printed and bound in Great Britain by Mackays of Chatham PLC,
Chatham, Kent

British Library Cataloguing in Publication Data
A catalogue record for this book is available from the British Library

Library of Congress Cataloging in Publication Data
A catalog record for this book is available from the Library of Congress

ISBN 0-415-08265-X

To the memory of
Lawrence Omand McLaren and Frederick A. Carter

To Richard Courtney

To my mother, Frances
To my wife, Jennifer
To my daughter, Laura
And to my son, Jonathan Luke

To my four brothers
Henry Giroux, Joe Kincheloe, Colin Lankshear
and Donaldo Macedo.

Contents

Foreword

From time to time books appear in the educational literature that don't seem to fit – works so innovative in conception, yet powerful in their execution and far reaching in their implications, that they seemingly catch the educational community off guard. Their fates vary. Some are embraced at once, exerting a strong and immediate influence on the field. Others, however, slip through the net, making less impact than their strengths dictate. Their fates, so to speak, are in the lap of the gods.

Schooling as a Ritual Performance is such a book. It is intended to disrupt, challenge and 'irritate'. There is little about Peter McLaren's approach to educational inquiry here that could be described as orthodox or conventional. Rather, he presents us with a book which is as much a work of existential phenomenology and literature as an ethnography of school.

McLaren's insights demand, and are given, a new language. Indeed, the language is absolutely integral to the book's meaning-making activity: exploding common conventions, jarring, and infuriating.

While McLaren's alternative grammar has distressed numerous researchers exploring schooling and cultural life, it has compelled others to rethink the direction of their work. These extreme responses can, I think, largely be explained by McLaren's distinctive penchant for and success at rupturing existing analytical codes, occupying a space outside the current, and speaking to as yet latent or incipient audiences.

When *Schooling as a Ritual Performance* first appeared, in 1986, it was described by Stephen Ball in the *Times Educational Supplement* as 'Groundbreaking ... at once brilliant, cavalier, strange and irritating ... a tour de force'. Stanley Aronowitz said it stood at the pinnacle of ethnographic works. Michael Apple set it alongside Paul Willis's *Learning to Labour*, noting, however, that 'for all its brilliance Willis's volume remains outside the school [whereas] McLaren's work goes inside the institution [and] illuminates the interaction between the students and the rituals that organise day to day life in a working class school'. High praise indeed. *Schooling as a Ritual Performance* was widely reviewed and debated in diverse journals. Predictably, there were those who contested the book's credibility and status as a landmark work of critical research. Even so, the stage seemed set for it to become a major force in critical educational thinking, certainly among qualitative researchers.

This, however, did not happen. Within three or four years the book had largely disappeared from discussion, apart from sporadic comment in more arcane venues. The promise of a secure and central place in the literature, intimated by most reviews and by the book's sheer distinctiveness and topicality, went largely unrealized. Why? I think there are reasons beyond McLaren's capacity to unsettle and irritate those who feel more at home with familiar language and formulae. In short, there simply is nothing in the educational literature that invites sustained comparison to *Schooling as a Ritual Performance*. It is a strange hybrid: mixing anthropology, alchemy, ritual studies, and post-structuralism at a time when post-structuralism especially, and ritual studies as well (not to mention alchemy!), were virtually unknown to educationists. The book's very nature – which reflects McLaren's precocity and celebration of the different and quirky – militated against its becoming legitimate relative to conventional benchmarks.

Fortunately, history has intervened in its own way. Post-structuralism, and postmodern social theory more generally, have burgeoned in recent years, finding their way increasingly into educational discourse. Within theology the appearance of works such as Tom Driver's *The Magic of Ritual* has harnessed ritual studies to the theory and practice of liberation. And in *Alchemy of Race and Rights*, Patricia Williams has challenged no less a field than law to accommodate radically new languages and modes of analysis and synthesis.

These are important shifts which should help to redeem McLaren's initial mistake of publishing a book considerably ahead of its time. Happily, Routledge have chosen to run this new edition rather than let *Schooling as a Ritual Performance* lapse from print. This is good news for educationists, who are worthy objects of Bugsy Siegel's sentiment that everyone deserves a fresh chance from time to time.

Schooling as a Ritual Performance is a major contribution to the ethnography of school. It is a paragon of what has been called the 'new' sociology of education and provides important insights into the cultural politics of lived experience. Having said this, I hasten to add that McLaren has written a demanding book. Its intricate style, theoretical sweep, and depth of scholarly argument do not make for a quick and easy read. Not that they should. Interpreting and explaining the fine-grained workings of school within economies of power and privilege is a complex and serious business. The book is theorized accordingly and written in a way that creates new passageways to advancing an explanation through interpretation and analysis.

The mere fact that a work is demanding is not, of course, a sure guide to theoretical and practical advance. We need to be vigilant and discerning as to where we expend our resources of time and intellectual effort. It is important to distinguish between books that repay close attention and those that do not. I am reminded here of Paulo Freire's *Pedagogy of the Oppressed*, a demanding book indeed. Twenty years after it first appeared in an English translation it remains among the most important books on education, not simply, or even primarily, on account of its specific content, although that is important. Rather, *Pedagogy of the Oppressed* stretches intellectual and political horizons, forces readers to wrestle with sophisticated argument and unfamilar theoretical traditions, and helps them to think in a more rigorous way. Wrestling with Freire's work is a compelling and powerful discipline, in the progressive and expanding sense of the word. Friere also offers a new method for understanding and approaching the cultural world.

McLaren's work has important points in common with *Pedagogy of the Oppressed*. Although its focus is considerably narrower than that taken by Freire, *Schooling as a Ritual Performance* none the less stretches our horizons and takes us to depths of understanding everyday educational practices in a way equalled by very few contemporary studies. It is theorized in an exemplary way and offers a viable method for interpreting and explaining some of the most important symbolic and cultural processes that involve us on a daily basis and work to constitute us as subjects of history. It too has the capacity to discipline us in expansive ways if we engage with it seriously. While it is a demanding work it is eminently manageable, asking only the effort that should be accorded any text within teacher education programs intended to enhance our understanding of education as a complex social process that is inescapably political.

Schooling as a Ritual Performance amply repays the effort put into understanding and reflecting upon its content, and applying its method critically to our experience of schooling. It is a profoundly educative book, a model of critical inquiry and explication.

It is not, however, critical in the minimal sense of simply being negative. McLaren does not point faults or blame agents in classrooms merely to score points of criticism. At those rare points where adverse judgement of action or inaction is implied it is always admixed with compassion and an informed appreciation of the conditions under which classroom teaching is conducted. McLaren provides a consummate vantage point from which to understand the extent to which and manner in which our roles and deeds as teachers and learners are constrained by discursive structures, processes and ideologies, until such time as we grasp the 'limit situations' inherent in the classrooms and confront them with 'limit acts' (Friere).

Since I believe this book should be widely used in teacher education and educational studies generally, let me explain why *Schooling as a Ritual Performance* is the most compelling and insightful school ethnography I have yet read.

In recent years right-wing critics have mounted a highly successful attack on progressive education. They have kept things simple, employed sweeping generalizations, appealed to conservative prejudice through recourse to allegedly self-evident 'facts', and cheerfully – though unwittingly – confused causes with symptoms and effects. Unfortunately, progressive educators have failed to mount a persuasive challenge to the right's simple – *simplistic* – account of educational reality. Partly this is due to our lacking a clear and cogent account of the cultural politics of school.

Putting educational reality together clearly and cogently while at the same time expanding the parameters of our social vision is a very tall order. The task becomes more manageable if innovative ethnography is available. By unravelling details of cultural and economic reproduction within school we can, for example, obtain deep insights into school failure and classroom resistance patterned by ethnicity and/or social class. These insights provide a far stronger basis for envisaging and enacting educational improvements than do the 'critiques' of conservatives who point simplistically, and with prejudice, to 'soft' schools and falling standards. They are also a major advance on the recipes of education privateers, who bemoan the failure of state school systems to achieve desirable levels of efficiency. According to champions of privatization, desirable levels of efficiency will flow 'naturally' from the operation of a free market in educational provision. In place of superficial explanations and quick fixes born of economic blind faith, we need a rich vein of qualitative data which connects with people's everyday experience of schooling and which has been organized into a critical and accessible interpretation of that experience. Only then will we have an optimal chance of making inroads into 'common sense' with an alternative account of schooling that has genuine potential for educational progress and emancipation.

Schooling as a Ritual Performance makes a telling contribution to this end. It is based on an ethnographic study of three Grade 8 classes – 'the suite' – within a Catholic middle school (St Ryan) in Toronto. Seventy-five per cent of the students in the suite were Azorean Portuguese migrants, 15 per cent were Italian, and the remainder spanned a diverse range of ethnic minorities. McLaren investigates social reproduction processes within this setting, drawing on work from critical sociology, symbolic anthropology, liturgical studies and, most notably, from ritual and performance studies.

He applauds those who have used neo-Marxist, Gramscian, and reconceptualist approaches to schooling for taking up ethnographic field studies and critiquing micro-sociological studies of classrooms which ignore class, gender, and power dynamics. He chides them, however, for under-utilizing advances made by symbolic anthropologists and ritologists, claiming that

[a] focus on symbol and performance enables new light to be shed on the strong normative or hegemonic structures of classroom rituals that exist beyond the ken of our immediate perception. As a result, we have the beginnings of a critical approach for analysing the symbolic dimensions of the hidden curriculum.

McLaren explores structure and agency as interrelated aspects of 'the cultural field'. This has much potential for uncovering forms of enquiry and broad areas of cultural practice that can be taken up by radical and other progressive educators.

Culture refers to a system of symbols; more specifically, it is 'an historically transmitted pattern of meaning embodied in symbols, a system of inherited conceptions expressed in symbolic form by means of which [humans] communicate, perpetuate and develop their knowledge about and attitudes toward life'. Cultural productions have enormous significance within the social construction and maintenance of power and domination. Ritual is a key facet of cultural production, since culture is 'fundamentally formed by interrelated rituals and ritual systems'. Of course kinship, social structure, and production relations are also important, but the focus here is on ritual, the least analysed component of school culture. McLaren seeks to convince educators that they must adjust their perceptions to include symbolic dimensions of classroom proceedings.

Rituals are 'forms of enacted meaning' which enable 'social actors to frame, negotiate, and articulate their ... existence as social, cultural, and moral beings'. Rituals are embedded in the framework of private and institutional life, becoming part of 'the socially conditioned, historically acquired and biologically constituted rhythms and metaphors of human agency'. They arise out of the ordinary business of life, within secular as well as sacred activities. Rituals, in other words, are components of *ideology*, helping shape our perceptions of daily life and how we live it.

As a *process* ritualization helps 'create' the world for the social actor. Through such behaviours as formative bodily gestures, for example, ritual makes symbols, metaphors and root paradigms *incarnate*; into enfleshed enacted *meaning*. It is not as though rituals merely mirror or reflect meaning, however. They also *articulate*. Ritual – enacted – meaning must be seen as implicated in the very *construction* of reality and not simply as reflecting it. Moreover, ritual is ideological in the political sense, since 'the logic of autonomy and materiality of a ritual are always linked to the macro relations of power and privilege and to the logic of capital'.

It is educationally important to recognize and understand the cultural politics of ritual performance. Because rituals transmit societal and cultural ideologies, we can discover alot about 'how ideologies do their work' by examining 'the key symbols and root paradigms of the ritual system' of school. The potential of ritology – the study of ritual – for informing emancipatory pedagogies and wider political and ideological struggle derives from the role of ritual within ideology construction and the fact that ritual performance is situated within macro-relations of unequal power. Consequently, McLaren's study of ritual performance at St Ryan is political in terms of both its orientation and effect.

McLaren argues that classroom ritual in St Ryan worked to reproduce and reinforce existing patterns of class and ethnic dominance. Instructional, disciplinary, and religious observance rites collectively made up a system of lived practices and lived meanings which functioned mainly 'to sanctify the workplace, to hedge the cultural terrain with taboos, to shore up the status quo, and to create a student body conditioned to accept such a state of affairs'. How?

First, a *working* class is reproduced by rituals preparing Azorean migrant students for the world of labour:

> The sanctification of classroom experience reinforced the dominant epistemes of work as good and play as bad. To be busy at work was to be, in effect, in a state of grace. On the other hand, when students were engaged in play, they were chastised and disciplined.

Second, a working *class* is reproduced ritually. Azorean students who began life as working class were destined to remain there as adults.

> Ritualized classroom lessons tacitly created dispositions towards certain student needs while simultaneously offering to fulfil those needs. For instance, students were made to feel inadequate due to their class . . . status and hence the school offered to help socialize them into the 'appropriate' values and behaviours by tracking them into designated streams and basic level courses.

Ethnic dominance patterns were reproduced at the same time. The teachers were unwitting accomplices in this:

> Their failure to take into consideration the class/cultural differences and competencies of the Azorean students in the rituals shaped tacit messages which read: 'This is the kind of people *we* are, and to the extent that you differ from us, this is the kind of behaviour we expect from *you*.' These messages infused the ethos of the suite, shaped the ideologies behind the rituals, and constituted the alloy from which symbolic violence was forged.

Let us consider in a little detail how classroom rituals served to produce these outcomes, by reference to the dynamic between 'the streetcorner' and 'student' states within rituals of instruction, the 'root paradigms' of instruction, and teacher ideologies regarding Azoreans and how to educate them.

In the street, neighbourhood, or playground the students are maximally physical and emotional, even violent, as they act out roles, identities or statuses 'forged in the street'. They 'own' their time, 'control' their space, there is plenty of spontaneous activity. Speech and body rhythms are often 'irregular'. The mood of the street corner state is 'subjunctive': embracing 'fantasy, experiment, hypothesis and conjecture'. They experiment with different roles, but are 'most decidedly themselves in this state', the ethos of which is *play*.

In the student state, by contrast, *work* is the ethos. Emotional display is off limits. 'Work hard' is the major theme. Time is extremely structured, the mood 'indicative'. Movement is 'routinized and rigidified into gestures'. A wedge is driven between mind and body. Existential coherence is broken.

Students generally prefer the streetcorner state. As one put it, 'School can be OK but when you're outside you feel that you're back to normal. It's a happier time for sure.' There always exists within the classroom a pull toward the streetcorner. The states are in constant tension.

Teachers employ controlling rituals of reward, punishment, and prayer to compel students out of the streetcorner state and *make them into* students. But there is always the threat – and quite often the reality – of the street erupting into the classroom. McLaren details the myriad enacted meanings that establish and maintain the student state. During prayers heralding the morning and afternoon sessions teachers project an aura resembling the priest's. Lessons begin with teachers invoking authority with ritual gestures. Students are reined in by performative speech acts like 'This is a *Catholic* school' (where, by implication, such behaviour does not occur). Via an array of ritual gestures and performatives the duty to work in class is put beyond question and work effort literally *sanctified*. These establish a metacommunicative frame telling students their largely boring and drudging work is crucial to their future welfare, and part of a *sacred* task that mustn't be questioned. The sheer 'operational efficiency' of the instructional rituals 'was very striking'.

Of course the cultural terrain of the classroom is contested. McLaren does justice to students' enacted meanings which make up the antistructure of resistance. As with the instruction rituals, the data of resistance is given close theoretical analysis and interpretation. The integration of theory with data is exemplary. Moreover, by not intruding unduly on the data McLaren leaves it to speak with force and poignancy.

> *Student*: You can really get a teacher . . . make him go nuts. Sometimes you can get the vein in their foreheads to pop out. *Student*: I like to pretend I'm workin' . . . move my pencil . . . that kind of thing. But I'm really outside [of the class] in my head . . . I'm not movin' but my body can still feel the muscles workin'. . . . The teacher sometimes catches you. . . . Then she screams . . . 'Eyes on your work!'.

While overall students were compliant in the face of norms presented as salient, unquestionable or natural, teachers none the less faced complex resistance rituals daily. Following Victor Turner, McLaren treats resistance as a form of social drama. As instances of 'breach', acts of buffoonery, ribaldry, constant carping at classroom rules, making non-negotiable demands, looking and acting bored, and striking intimidatory poses are elements 'of the fight to establish the streetcorner state inside the suite'. McLaren establishes the cultural *meaning* of resistance, laying bare the political and moral elements of the situation. Gestures of resistance are not seen as *symbols* of student 'interiority', as weak translations of thoughts. Rather, gestures of resistance '*are* student anger, fear and refusal expressed in an incarnate form'. Plus:

> It was not difficult to understand why students resisted schooling in the student state . . . since [this] was the path to apathy, passionlessness and emotional and spiritual emptiness. It was . . . a denigration of their identity as a social class . . . Breaching the rules was a logical response to the oppressive conditions of the student state.

It is when McLaren draws together the threads of ritual in his account of the root paradigms of instruction that the full force of his analysis impacts. Root paradigms are consciously recognized cultural models for behaviour existing in the heads of the main actors in a social drama, representing for them the existential goals of humanity. The guiding root paradigms at St Ryan were 'becoming a worker' and 'becoming a Catholic'.

The ritual act of instruction became 'a dramatic representation and reconfirmation of the world-view that says, "life is hard work and the only way to lessen the agony of work is to be a good worker"'. Becoming a good Catholic worker *later* depended on developing good 'deportment', gaining 'basic academic skills', and 'appropriating the cultural capital of the teacher' *now*. Not to be constantly busy 'was tantamount to being anti-Catholic'.

> The drudgery of work was made emotionally acceptable to the majority of the students by the fact that everyone – both teachers and students – was involved in doing boring work. Teachers purported the hard life of the student to be homologous with the real world of work that awaited them when they left school. *This would appear to account for why so many students accepted the state of affairs that existed in the suite and why they projected such a dismal future for themseves once they left school.*

> *Student*: My uncle and brother say that you can't expect work to be fun but you can make it better by using the money to help out your family.
> *Peter*: What about the work you do in school?
> *Student*: It's OK. But it's not real work because you don't get paid for it. But it's like real work because . . . it's boring.

McLaren's explanation of these root paradigms is especially revealing, signalling important moral and political insights and exposing unpalatable contradictions. Three points stand out.

1. By confirming and deepening the students' conception of life and work under late capitalism, the school's ritual performances adjusted Azorean youth to a dehumanizing loss. In the Azores work was respected because participation was dignified and honourable. It was not merely wage labour. Rather, it was 'to keep the family going', or 'to sell vegetables and crafts'. While economic circumstances were often painfully difficult and widely resented in the Azores, workers could none the less affirm themselves as authors of their community. At home they could endow their privation with a sense of dignity and moral resolve. This was eroded, however, when Azorean migrants 'entered a new way of life based on certification, production, and the accumulation of wages through labour . . . To be dependent on wages was to lose one's self-sufficiency . . . dignity,

[and] sense of membership in the community'. To this must be added the destruction of memories and a vision of a more *human* relationship to work. Consequently, by enculturating migrant students to a new conception of work and relationship to it, the school undermined a final fragile basis from which to build informed struggle for more dignified relations and practices of labour. Even the potential 'gains' of enculturation are tenuous – a point grasped by some students.

> *Student*: [Teachers] say to work hard because it will get you a job. That's a joke. My Dad says that even high school graduates can't get jobs in this country. So we're supposed to work for nothing. This is worse than back home. Except for here you got TVs and more plazas.

2. The root paradigm of making workers intersected with teachers' extant beliefs about Azoreans to foster pedagogical values and practices virtually guaranteed to channel these migrant students into the lowest-level job slots (or else unemployment), whilst denying them any serious opportunity to develop critical rational acumen. Teachers 'objectified' Azorean students as 'level threes or fours' (i.e. below average), as rude, bad-mannered – 'delinquent' – products of 'bad sperm', and even as 'primitive'. Azoreans emerged in the teachers' perceptions as a 'low' or 'basic level' group in need of civilizing. Consequently, ' "basic level" programmes were created to fit an instructional paradigm for the "below average" student', reinforcing in turn the view of migrant students as dysfunctional.

> *Teacher*: Portuguese students learn best when discipline is strict and the work is drudgery.

Despite the fact 'that students are supposedly characterized by a wide range of different abilities', the teachers at St Ryan tended to lump all Azoreans under one description and teach to a single ability level.

3. The second root paradigm, 'becoming a Catholic'/'making Catholics', was subverted by the agenda of 'becoming/making workers'. Within school, Catholic symbolism appeared to be in the service of control much more than of liberation, and the ethos and practice of the classroom to owe more to the spirit of Calvinism than to Catholic spirituality. In the quest to make (Catholic) *workers*, ritual performance at St Ryan affirmed at best a strictly limited and one-sided range of Catholic values.

Catholic values such as denial of the body, endurance, deference to the authority of priest and Church, hard work and struggle ... paralleled the secular values inherent in ritualized instruction (e.g. hard work, endurance, sticking to the task, deference to the authority of the teacher). Together, these value domains simply mirrored each other at different symbolic junctures, or in different tacit dimensions of meaning. In fact they were practically convertible into one another. At the level of power they were functionally identical.

A concern to open students to values other than the work ethic either disappeared altogether or was hopelessly marginalized. Religion classes presented the only setting in which societal norms were ever questioned and students given any encouragement to take a critical look at the dominant culture. 'On several occasions Brock discussed with his class the ethical implications of owning too much land and money and exploiting the poor through wage labour ... [engaging] his students in ... discussion of the inherent moral dangers in capitalism'. These occasions, however, were minority departures from the dominant lived meanings of the suite.

McLaren asks what the instructional rituals of the religion class *mean* when they speak of equality and justice in a 'hived-off' manner and setting, while the rest of school experience is so strongly aligned with capitalist values that it becomes a repressive device for exploiting the poor. He invokes Rappaport in suggesting that, perhaps, 'rituals are parts of deceits if they lead the faithful into bondage while promising salvation ... When subordinated to the powerful and material, sanctity [becomes] false for [it falsifies] consciousness'. The efforts of Catholic schooling in helping the poor and oppressed 'are spiritualized away when Catholic values are themselves invisibly linked to a culture of domination and exploitation'.

At St Ryan the call to 'make Catholics' was domesticated; subordinated to the 'vocation' of preparing and serving up exploitable migrant labour for low-level jobs. McLaren passes judgement here.

> While I would argue that Catholics are called to experience the pain and humility that goes along with taking up the cross of Christ, the cross must also be witnessed as a symbol of joy and transcendence – a metaphor to inspire working-class students to surpass their hardships and fight against their lived subordination.

The medium was the message at St Ryan, and the news was not good for spirituality. Indeed, drudgery and endurance became the medium in highly inappropriate places, a fact not lost on the students. The Christmas Mass, says McLaren, 'was one of the shallowest [I have] experienced', failing to generate feelings noticeably different from 'the most perfunctory instructional rite'. He wasn't alone here.

Student: What a bore, man. We might just as well have been doing math.

Schooling as a Ritual Performance contributes to the development of an emancipatory theory and practice of education in three important ways. It contributes to the emergence of a more critically informed 'common sense' about educational matters; offers measured recommendations for classroom curriculum and pedagogy; and furthers the development of educational theory.

McLaren's ethnography of ritual performance is precisely a fine-grained account of typical processes through which patterns of success and failure correlating with social class or ethnicity are produced and reproduced in the dynamic between classrooms and the wider cultural politics of societies like our own. Close ethnographic detail and the depth of analysis and argument provide a valuable corrective to 'common-sense' views of the origins of success and failure, and expose the superficiality of quick-fix school reform and restructuring policies foisted on citizens as cures for 'inefficiency' and 'inequity' in education. *Schooling as a Ritual Performance* provides a basis for understanding more clearly the extent to which policies advocating increased privatization and market choice, or pinning hopes on basics, cultural literacy, or functionality, confuse causes with effects (or symptoms) and reduce complex structured social processes to individual pathologies or stereotyped group deficits – subverting democratic and social justice values whilst shoring up the status quo by generating pseudo answers to misconceived problems.

McLaren's practical suggestions, while cautious, are none the less helpful and point in a progressive direction. He calls for greater interdisciplinary collaboration in the study of classroom culture and recommends that school instruction 'becomes more of a celebration than a painful rite of passage and attempt to incorporate some of the cultural forms of the streetcorner state which, after all, belong to the phenomenal world of the students themselves'. This might involve making more time available for arts activities and for incorporating creative drama as a pedagogical technique, rather than merely relegating it to a timetable slot. Allowing more student-generated rituals might make for a more impersonal and flexible classroom control. At the level of 'micro ritual', McLaren recommends that teachers employ knowledge of unique ethnic and personalized interaction styles in developing the 'liturgical aspects' of instruction. Students should enjoy opportunities to plan their own time, find their own ritual rhythms, and discover ritual spaces in which they feel comfortable. Most important, perhaps, teachers should assume to a greater extent the role of the 'liminal servant'. In the new Coda to this edition McLaren situates his project in a more radical politics, addressing the development of a post-colonial pedagogy and a politics of difference, and advancing the concept of multiculturalism beyond its liberal assumptions.

In the final analysis, however, the book's major contribution is to the ongoing development of educational *theory*. By modelling its possibilities, McLaren makes a powerful case for developing classroom ritology as a necessary ingredient in any critical educational research agenda. He demonstrates the potential of ritual studies for charting previously unrecognized processes and mechanisms involved in the construction of learners' subjectivities. As educationists and teachers, we ignore these at our peril, for 'whether the path to knowledge is paved with quotes from Christ or Marx makes little difference if we fail to consider the systems of material and symbolic mediation that help create the learner'.

Moreover, McLaren taps the potential of ritual studies for illuminating the *political* role of schooling in producing patterned failure, reproducing relations of hierarchy and inequality, and maintaining a positivist–technocratic approach to educational practice that reinforces the logic of domination and subordination generally, and the logic of capital specifically. Of course this potential does not inhere in ritology *per se*. Neither does its application to emancipatory ends. For any development of ritual theory to be critical and emancipatory, 'it must be linked to a formal theory of hegemony and resistance'.

McLaren's approach is informed in precisely this way. Therein lies the key to its important and distinctive contribution to educational theory in the service of critical and emancipatory goals.

Colin Lankshear
Nindirí Literacy Project
Managua, Nicaragua

Foreword to the first edition

Peter McLaren is both a teacher and writer. As a teacher, he has spent a considerable amount of time working in urban public schools with economically disadvantaged students. As a writer, he combines the rare gifts of the astute theoretician with that of the storyteller in the manner celebrated by Walter Benjamin. That is, as a storyteller he is a person capable of providing a richly textured and illuminating protrait of the experiences and milieu of the people he is portraying, which in this case are the teachers and students of a predominantly Portuguese middle school in Toronto, Canada. Similarly, as a theoretician, McLaren brings to these experiences a set of critical categories and mode of analysis that allows him to perform the most important task of the storyteller, which is to provide a commentary on the nature of schooling that 'has counsel for his readers.'[1]

The major ideological concern that informs McLaren's story is one that has preoccupied radical educational work for the last fifteen years. On the one hand, it is a concern grounded in the political imperative to challenge through the language of critique the traditional assumption that schools are the major mechanism for the development of a democratic and egalitarian social order. On the other hand, it is a concern that expresses itself through attempts to develop a critical and emancipatory theory of schooling. These concerns have a history that is rooted in a variety of theoretical accounts, all of which have interrogated the nature of the particular relationship that schools have to the dominant social order while simultaneously attempting to explain how this social order is able to reproduce itself within the subjectivities, needs and experiences of teachers and students. Of course, the major task for radical educators has been one of trying to unravel *how* schools reproduce the logic of capital through the ideological and material forms of domination and privilege that structure the lives of students from differing class, gender and ethnic groupings. Needless to say, the challenges that radical educators have posed to traditional theories of schooling, along with their analyses of how schools contribute to the reproduction of capitalist societies, has opened up a new debate around the meaning of schooling and its place in the Western democracies. McLaren's newest book adds a significant theoretical dimension to this debate, while at the same time building upon its most important contributions. In order to gauge the significance and originality of McLaren's contribution, it is necessary to rehearse some of the strengths and weaknesses that are part of the legacy of left educational theory.

Left educational theorists have dealt a significant blow to the positivist and conservative notion that schools are primarily instructional sites involved in the reproduction of common values, skills and knowledge. Against the claim that school knowledge is objective and available to all students, radical critics have revealed such knowledge as a social construction embodying specific ideological interests. Radical critics rejected the notion that school curricula are merely functional to the demands of a democratic social order; and in doing so they illuminated how school knowledge and social practices were not only constructed within asymmetrical relations of power but were also expressive of struggles over orders of representation that ultimately favoured the economic and political interests of ruling groups. Another central contribution of left educational theorists centered around the insight that schools were more than instructional sites. They were also cultural sites, actively involved in the selective ordering and legitimation of specific forms of language, reasoning, sociality, daily experience and style. In this perspective, culture was intimately connected to power and fully implicated in the process of domination as its dynamics worked both on and within schols. By rejecting the positivist fixation on objectivity, its slavish preoccupation with the literal, and its fetish for quantifying and measuring human experience, left educators provided a profound insight into the workings of the hidden curriculum and the forms of social control it supported. Furthermore, by emphasizing the importance of the cultures of subordinated groups, advocates of theories of resistance pointed the way to honouring and appropriating the languages, lifestyles and histories of such groups.

While McLaren's work is strongly situated in many of the theoretical traditions that have emerged from left educational scholarship, it maintains a stance that is at once reverential and critical. He is theoretically indebted to the reproduction and resistance theorists, but he is not willing to emulate their mistakes. Instead, he appropriates their most critical elements and at the same time adds a new theoretical dimension to the emancipatory project that informs their works. In other words, while his research is grounded historically in radical educational traditions, it also provides a discourse that currently stands alone in its attempt to unravel how schools function as contradictory cultural sites engaged in the dialectical process of producing subjectivities and reproducing the dominant social order.

McLaren's ethnographic study is firmly rooted in the notion that schools perform the reproductive function of preparing working-class students for the lower rungs of the occupational ladder. But unlike reproduction theorists such as Bowles and Gintis,[2] he understands and demonstrates that the dynamics of reproduction take place within a cultural terrain marked by contestation and struggle. Furthermore, he begins with the assumption that subjectivities are produced in schools and have to be treated as an object of inquiry. The central question, of course, is how does one understand how schools attempt to produce such subjectivities, what interests underlie such pedagogical efforts, and how are such efforts mediated by the students themselves? It is these issues with which McLaren attempts to deal, and he does so in a way that represents a singularly impressive and original contribution to critical educational theory and practice. Let me be more specific.

McLaren's ethnographic approach has a number of strengths. First, it is eminently political in nature. It combines an attentiveness to detail with a mode of analysis that reveals how school experiences are organized within specific relations of power. Rather than provide the repetitive lull of a methodological approach intent on simply registering detail, McLaren begins with the problem of identifying and explaining how St Ryan Catholic Middle School organizes its classes and school day around the twin imperatives of producing workers and making Catholics. Second, McLaren develops his ethnography within a theoretical discourse that critically appropriates and combines the methods and insights of ritual and performance theory, on the one hand, and the new sociology of education on the other.

Utilizing this approach, McLaren provides a startling insight into the ways in which the ideologies embedded in the various rituals that inform all aspects of school life bear down on and limit the practices that give meaning and sense to the experiences of St Ryan's working-class Portuguese students. In effect, McLaren portrays how the multitude of significations that make up the ongoing ritualistic gestural displays of school life provide the cultural grounding for fostering moods of domination *and* resistance. By interrogating what McLaren calls the student state, the home state, the streetcorner state and the sanctity state, he is able to flush out the manner in which ideological messages and material practices come together in specific displays of icons, teacher talk, the use of prayer, the spacing of furniture and authoritative bodily gestures (i.e. the teacher who slits his eyes in order to get students to be quiet). Equally important, he is able to describe and analyze how dominant cultural capital comes into conflict with the cultural formations that students bring with them to the school.

In many respects, McLaren has developed a major theoretical insight into how power works through the use of performative and regulatory rituals, one that sheds new light on to the ways in which domination and student resistance work themselves out within the halls and classrooms of schools such as St Ryan. Domination is not simply reproduced in McLaren's ethnographic account, it is constantly being 'worked up' through the ongoing rituals and practices that constitute school life. Moreover, the ideologies born by such ritualistic practices and performances carry a material force that bears down on the bodies and minds of both teachers and students. In other words, such rituals embody a substantive force that functions to discipline, administer and limit the activities that students bring with them to the school. What becomes evident from this analysis is that student resistance, in many cases, is rooted in the need to dignify and affirm those experiences that make up their lives outside of school. What McLaren amply demonstrates in this book is that such resistance is as much a matter of self-confirmation as it is a reaction to oppressive ideologies and practices. And in doing so, he deepens our understanding of how power is implicated in the subjection of the body to school culture as well as in the refusal of the body to renounce its sedimented experiences and desires.

It is to McLaren's credit that his analysis of cultural domination and resistance is not situated solely with the discourse of critique. On the contrary, he employs the discourse of possibility as well by pointing to the many ways in which the dynamics of cultural production can provide teachers and educators with the tools for developing a critical pedagogy. This is especially evident in McLaren's call for teachers to interrogate their own cultural capital and how it mediates the way they structure and interpret classroom experiences. The discourse of possibility is further amplified in McLaren's call for administrators and teachers to develop modes of curriculum and teaching that appropriate and utilize the cultural capital of the students whom they service. This suggests that teachers not only be more attentive to the imposition of a dominant cultural capital that actively silences those who don't share its ideologies and interests, but also that teachers confirm *and* critically engage, rather than simply celebrate, those forms of lived and popular culture that provide the raw materials for student experiences.

In short, Peter McLaren has written an important book that will reward all those interested in analyzing the ideological and cultural dynamics that make up school life. It is a book for teachers, educators, parents and students. It is a book that one reads and rereads. It is a significant contribution from a scholar-teacher who cares.

Henry A. Giroux
Miami University, Ohio

NOTES

1 Walter Benjamin, *Illuminations*, edited, with an introduction by Hannah Arendt (New York, Schocken Books, 1969), p. 86.
2 Samuel Bowles and Herbert Gintis, *Schooling in Capitalist America* (New York, Basic Books, 1976). For a critical overview of theories of reproduction and resistance in the new sociology of education, see Henry A. Giroux, 'Theories of reproduction and resistance in the new sociology of education: a critical analysis,' *Harvard Educational Review* 53 (3), 1983, pp. 257–93.

Acknowledgements

I would like to thank Chris Rojek for his support for the revised edition of *Schooling as a Ritual Performance*. I am also grateful to Jayne Fargnoli for her encouragement. The attention that Basil Bernstein and Anthony Wilden gave to the original manuscript helped to hasten its publication. And I would be remiss if I did not extend appreciation to Henry Giroux, Colin Lankshear and Phil Carspecken. I benefitted greatly from the support and advice of a number of my graduate students, especially Marcia Moraes, Khaula Murtandha, Barry Nedeleman and Tom Oldenski. Colleagues in Latin America, without whose collaboration this new edition would not have been possible, also deserve credit. I will not forget the generosity of Alicia de Alba, Edgar Gonzalez and Adriana Puiggros, nor the kindness and wisdom of Nize Maria Campos Pellanda. A special word of thanks is given to Bertha Orozco Fuentes and her students in Xalapa City, Mexico, whose advice helped me to reformulate some of my initial ideas on multiculturalism. And thanks to Annette Street for her advice and assistance.

I wish to point out that, where possible, I have used 'she' and 'her' instead of 'he' and 'him' to counteract the tradition of using the masculine form.

The author and publishers are grateful to the University Press of America for permission to reproduce material from *Beginnings in Ritual Studies* by Ronald L. Grimes, Copyright © 1982 by University Press of America Inc.

Chapter 1

Education as a cultural system

THE NEGLECTED DOMAIN OF RITUAL

This book will argue for the primacy of understanding schooling from the perspectives of culture and performance. The major themes which inform this investigation have grown out of an empirical application of the concept of ritual in school settings, particularly the events and conditions which provide the context for classroom instruction.

The idea of bringing the concepts of teaching and ritual into a unified framework grew out of my fieldwork in a Catholic school in downtown Toronto, Canada. The school had been described to me as the 'toughest' Catholic junior high school in the city and had a school population which consisted primarily of Azorean and Italian students. I was invited there as an ethnographer who was undertaking some scholarly research in pedagogy. What I discovered was less than I expected (modern education can be quite disenchanting) and more than I had anticipated. I found that my ideas about ritual – and teaching – had been hidebound and simplistic and that as an academic I had grossly underestimated the significance of youth culture outside the boundaries of classroom life. What follows is an attempt to describe what I found, and concurrently, what I had overlooked during my own years as a teacher of working-class students. I was to uncover strange things made familiar and familiar things made strange: rites of passage in which bearing up under pain became the prevailing cultural drama; a curriculum in which distinctions between Catholic values and capitalist values were annulled; students who were exposed to the sufferings of Christ more than his teaching; and teachers who unconsciously made Christ into both a secular agent of social control and a spiritual corpse. In brief, I was confronted by relatively unexpected ramifications of what it means to acquire an education.

This explorative foray into the world of classroom symbols and rituals has been animated by the accumulative foolery of ritual scholars. To locate the roots of this present research in the context of foolery; to clothe the academic in a motley or foolscap; or to portray the student of performance as a knight errant, is not to denigrate the scientific utility of this study but to both vivify and enhance it. Fools, after all, frequently assist us in understanding the completely apparent – which, as Edward R. Murrow once informed us, is often a much greater trick than comprehending the obscure.

I use the term fool advisedly, sheering wide of Whitehead's adage: 'Fools act in imagination without knowledge' (1929, p. 140) in order to embrace the equally epigrammatic but eminently more revealing formulation posited by Enid Welsford: '[The Fool] is an amphibian, equally at home in the world of reality and the world of imagination . . . the Fool by his mere presence . . . throws doubt on the finality of fact' (1966, Introduction). In the spirit of the latter definition, Ronald L. Grimes offers us the following description of anthropologist Victor Turner, a distinguished and oftentimes brilliant expositer of the ritual process:

> Turner is an academic fool. He has stood on his head and told us that rituals are hot seedbeds of change; that rituals not only control process, they generate it; that rituals not only mark boundaries, they evoke phasic motion in a culture. (1982a, p. 202).

By drawing upon the scholarship of Victor Turner, Ronald L. Grimes, Richard Schechner, Barbara Myerhoff, Roy Rappaport and other 'engineers of the imagination', this work attempts to provide both researchers and teachers with liminal glimpses into everyday school life. With the help of such a confederacy of learned fools (sometimes known as 'ritologists'),[1] I am confident that educators will be able to develop and refine new and useful ways with which to survey the already well-trodden ground of classroom analysis.

My endeavour to give grounding to this investigation of ritual in a contemporary school setting is based on the following beliefs: that schools serve as rich repositories of ritual systems; that rituals play a crucial and ineradicable role in the whole of the student's existence; and that the variegated dimensions of the ritual process are intrinsic to the events and transactions of institutional life and the warp and woof of school culture. I shall argue that in order for the educator to speak intelligibly and tellingly about human behaviour in a school milieu, the concept of ritual needs to be examined in all its complexity and multiplicity; moreover, it must be reconsidered and re-examined from a different theoretical starting point, one that links gestural display and symbolic meaning to reality *construction* rather than simply reality *reflection*. I intend to take this investigation beyond what may be considered the prototypical classroom rituals (e.g. morning prayer, opening exercises, school assemblies) in order to locate the dynamics of the ritual process both in the performative characteristics of daily lessons and in various resistances to instruction.

An examination of schooling as a ritual performance provides a fecund basis for understanding the *modus operandi* of the pedagogical encounter. Germane to this investigation is the understanding that rituals symbolically transmit societal and cultural ideologies, and that it is possible to know how ideologies do their 'work' by examining the key symbols and root paradigms of the ritual system.

Following Geertz, this study attempts to connect action to its sense rather than behaviour to its determinants (1980, p. 178). Examined in the context of symbolic action, rituals may be perceived as carriers of cultural codes (cognitive and gestural information) that shape students' perceptions and ways of understanding; they inscribe both the 'surface structure' and 'deep grammar' of school culture. Rituals may also be understood as gestural and rhythmical models which enable students to negotiate between various symbol systems which have been nurtured by the wider society and augmented by the dominant culture. Such broad constructions of ritual can, I feel, be knit together to provide the educational researcher with a theoretically salutary model for examining how students codify and maintain their images of self and society.

To understand teaching and learning as a symbolic performance or ritual is to reject the common assumption that the categorization and meaning of behaviour is synonymous with a literal description of it. Certain assumptions in this study which pertain to the labyrinthine attributes of the symbol shift the analysis of classroom behaviour from the theoretical terrain of mainstream educational research to that of a semiotic, dramaturgical and phenomenological interpretation.

I have adopted a perspective of ritual which attempts to take seriously the concepts of power and domination and which addresses ritual as a cultural production constructed as a collective reference to the symbolic and situated experience of a group's social class. Accordingly, a ritual will be considered as a political event and part of the objectified distributions of the school's dominant cultural capital (e.g. systems of meanings, taste, attitudes and norms which legitimate the existing social order). I have also taken seriously Mac-Cannell's (1976) position that in modern societies cultural productions supersede economic productions as a basis of shared values, lifestyles and world views. Not only do social forces give rise to symbolic expressions (as Durkheim has shown us) but symbols and rituals are now in the process of creating social groups.[2] The position articulated by Aronowitz (1981) – that a critical theory of emancipation is needed that is able to move beyond the class and historical reductionism that plagues Marxist theory – has been adopted as an important advance in understanding how schools work. Hence, I would argue that the categories of ideology, culture, ritual, and the symbolic must compete with those of the economic sphere and class in order to understand present-day domination and struggle.[3]

Locating recent advances in ritual and performance studies within the practicality of the pedagogical encounter provides the reform-minded educator with a broad construction for unravelling and thereby decoding the obstacles and impediments faced by working-class students in acquiring an education. Given the recent work being done by ritual scholars and performance theorists, it is plausible to consider whether a ritual framework has some general applicability for making new sense of the bloom and buzz of classroom life – particularly in urban schools where prevailing instructional rituals are often contested by large groups of students. It is equally possible to anticipate that such a framework could potentially be adumbrated and refined should educational researchers and planners wish to bring such a framework into confrontation with mainstream research on classroom behaviour, organization and knowledge acquisition. If we are to consider ritual to be deeply entangled in the social and cultural particularities of school life – as part of the cultural equipment of the school, so to speak – we must be able to judge the extent to which classroom instruction shares common traits with the modes of symbolic expression which have been identified over the years by ritual scholars.

The axis of this investigation consists in demonstrating various examples of school-based ritual and examining their implicit relationships within the wider cultural system. Striking illustrative evidence is presented that confirms the existence within schools of a full complement of activities that bear a topographical and morphological filiation with ritual. In fact, ritual systems have been shown to exist in classrooms in a rich variety of proportions. An analysis of schooling from the dual perspectives of ritual and performance suggests important explanations for a wide range of patterned behaviours and transactions that exist inside the urban school. This book could be seen, then, as an attempt to bring educational research in *rapprochement* with some of the insights gained, both theoretical and methodological, within the rich disciplinary field of ritual studies.

The essence of this study lies in the ineluctable fact that culture is fundamentally formed by interrelated rituals and ritual systems. Indeed, any investigator's conceptual access to ritual and his approach to the study of social action will be greatly influenced by his metatheoretical approach to culture. Moreover, an understanding of ritual necessarily depends *ab initio* on a broad understanding of how culture may be conceptualized and problematized. Any critical analysis of culture (whether we refer to the exotic culture of a remote island paradise or the culture of the local elementary school) by dint of the model of perspective used, opens up a whole nexus of social, political and moral considerations.

Generally speaking, I will take culture to refer to a system of symbols in accordance with the proponents of the 'symbolic-system' school of thought exemplified in the work of Victor Turner, Clifford Geertz, Sherry Ortner, David Schneider and others. Geertz, for example, defines culture as 'an historically transmitted pattern of meaning embodied in symbols, a system of inherited conceptions expressed in symbolic form by means of which men communicate, perpetuate and develop their knowledge about and attitudes towards life'.[4] Culture is a construction that remains a consistent and meaningful reality through the overarching organization of rituals and symbol systems. Symbols may be verbal or non-verbal and are usually tied to the philosophical ethos of the dominant culture. I shall enlarge upon Geertz's definition by assuming the position that school culture is informed by class-specific, ideological and structural determinants of the wider society. My use of the term culture also includes a number of concepts which are intrinsic to the ritual process. These include: symbol, ethos, root paradigm, social drama and the pivotal concept of liminality.[5]

Classroom culture does not manifest itself as some pristine unity or disembodied, homogeneous entity but is, rather, discontinuous, murky, and productive of competition and conflict; it is a collectivity which is composed of 'contests' between ideologies and disjunctions between class, cultural and symbolic conditions.[6] It is, furthermore, a symbolic arena where students and teachers struggle over the interpretations of metaphors, icons, and structures of meanings, and where symbols have both centripetal and centrifugal pulls. To help discern a clear pattern from the turbulence of contested signs and symbols of classroom life, I shall adopt the role of a cultural cartographer and attempt to trace out meanings that exist on both the surface and beneath the manifest integuments of the pedagogical encounter; I shall likewise endeavour to tease out and hold some of the qualitative elements of classroom culture long enough to examine them from the perspectives of ritual and performance. This will permit me to posit a novel critique of school life through an interrogation of its symbol systems, ethoses, pervading myths and root paradigms. In this way the study of ritual and performance can assist me in exploring how the cultural field of a school functions, both in a tacit and manifest way, in the transmission of ideological messages. It will also provide a basis for a theoretical/critical excursion into the domain of ritual knowledge.

Within the parameters of this investigation, a number of questions will be addressed. How are rituals implicated in the day-to-day interactions and regularities of school instruction? Are rituals in some sense related to the organization and deployment of both the formal and informal corpora of school knowledge (that is, the overt and hidden curricula) which are found in various materials, ideologies and texts and actively filtered through teachers? Are rituals linked to the fundamental perspectives that educators use to plan, organize and evaluate what happens in schools? How do the rituals of everyday school instruction tacitly shape (by means of their dominant symbols and root paradigms) the learning process? How do these same rituals influence or impact upon the intentionality and lived experience of students?

Since our modern technocratic world has made for a wide and rapid diffusion of novel ritual systems which have been disseminated into the whole of contemporary culture, it is no accident that today we are witnessing a burgeoning of marginal sanctuaries harbouring youth subcultures whose resistances to the mind-numbing and spirit-deadening ethoses of institutional life partake of distinctive ritual characteristics with attendant ritual warnings. My emphasis on analysing schooling from the standpoint of ritual and performance has evolved out of the belief that a greater critical understanding of ritual and performance will enable educators to both pattern and repattern cultural symbols and thus mollify some of the negative symptoms of modern technocracy. An awareness of how rituals operate will also help teachers both modify cultural rules that otherwise would dictate the hegemonic patterns of classroom interaction and improve communication with students in today's often timorous educational climate.

Reformulating classroom activity under the illumination of culture and performance is not without its problems – the least of which centre around the problematic use of ritual terminology in connection with urban school settings. My task is to position ritual studies within a theory of educational praxis by finding a path between the ratiocinations of anthropologists, liturgists, performance theorists and educational researchers. To transform anthropological or liturgical assertions into educational statements becomes more complex than simply constructing a bipartite reading of school life into 'sacred' and 'profane' domains. We are dealing with symbolic proccesses that do not cleave into neat theoretical categories but which overlap and tincture one another with nuances of meaning.

In order to link the concept of ritual to the experience of 'being schooled', I have attempted to steer a course between the Scylla of a substantial lack of research connecting cultural performances with schooling and the Charybdis of transferring data already accrued in ritual studies to conform to educational settings. The work of Victor W. Turner has helped to set the keel of this fragile vessel.

VICTOR TURNER

Victor Turner is recognized as one of the leading anthropological exponents of symbolic analysis (which he describes as 'comparative symbology') and ritual studies. His work is epochal, inaugurating a new era in the understanding of both preliterate and contemporary cultural forms. Turner has signed the anthropology of his time with his own unique stamp by laying the groundwork for a new dispensation that connects the processual dimensions of Van Gennep's rites of passage to modern theatre, history, literature, and the performative dimensions of everyday life.

Like Marshall McLuhan, Turner was a true interdisciplinary scholar; both men had a penchant, amounting to genius, for opening up the study of humankind to eclectic disciplinary approaches that encompass the liberal arts as well as the 'hard' sciences.

Turner was trained in the school of British functionalist rationalism, and his early anthropological fieldwork reflected a structural–functionalist approach; eventually he steered away from attempts to understand culture as a functional or static moment frozen in time, preferring instead to conceive of cultural, literary and artistic genres as 'processes'. Continuing to assail the limitations of structural-functionalism throughout the remainder of his career, Turner stressed the concepts of indeterminacy, reflexivity and 'becoming' in his work. This change of direction for Turner was greatly influenced by Arnold van Gennep's work on rites of passage, the philosophy of Wilhelm Dilthey and the pioneering efforts of Gregory Bateson and his followers in the development of cybernetic systems theory.

Turner's concept of liminality (and its close cognates of anti-structure and communitas) has been avidly taken up by students in anthropology, liberal arts, religious studies and performance studies and is now quite commonplace in scholarly discourse. One of Turner's most audacious discriminations was his drawing of a distinction between the sensory (orectic) and ideological (normative) poles of the ritual symbol and his explanation of how these two poles mutually tincture one another, thereby conflating the normative with the sensory, and the moral with the material. During the interchange between these two poles, Turner maintained that the conceptual is given the power of the experiential (and vice versa), thus making the obligatory desirable. Turner is probably best known for his work on social drama and the role of metaphor in assigning meaning to social behaviour and conduct. Many scholars continue to find Turner's theories efficacious for examining contemporary social settings.

Turner ascribed a great deal of importance to analysing and understanding contemporary ritual forms in both religious and non-religious settings. His celebrated infatuation with symbols, rituals and social dramas eventually led to his watershed essay,

The Ritual Process: Structure and Anti-Structure – a masterwork which distilled most of his research on ritual and social drama and presaged some of the future directions of contemporary ritologists. Many years and many books later, we find the study of humankind broadened and illuminated by his peerless research.

Turner was an extraordinarily gifted fieldworker. He considered ethnography as something to be 'performed' rather than simply codified into a written text. His own fieldwork echoed his theories of play and subjunctivity as it took on a creative ludicity that was often pathfinding in both its expressiveness and insight.

Turner's Catholicism was strengthened by his fieldwork among the Ndembu in Northern Rhodesia (now Zambia) where he gained a new appreciation for the power of the ritual process. Liturgical scholars, including Mary Collins, continue to cite Turner's writings on ritual in their attempts to reform the Catholic mass. In his later works he examined the dynamics of the Christian pilgrimage, co-authoring several studies on this topic with his wife, Edith.

There are adumbrations of Turner's theories in the work of many contemporary drama and performance theorists. Turner disagreed with his erstwhile mentors, Max Gluckman and Raymond Firth, who claimed that dramatic analysis was too 'loaded' and not 'neutral' enough for scientific use. Turner argued that social dramas were evident on all levels of social organization. Canadian drama educator Richard Courtney and American performance theorist Richard Schechner owe an allegiance to Turner's innovative research. Few anthropologists strode so knowingly and with such perspicacity across the frontier of culture as Victor Turner. While Turner has effected a number of pivotal advances in anthropology, he has barely broached the topic of how rituals in contemporary culture are snarled in a web of mediating agents – class, cultural, and interpersonal – all of which are embedded in an ensemble of social relationships shaped by human labour and informed by the logic of capital.

The theoretical framework underlying this study, while Turnerian in emphasis, is unavoidably hybrid and constitutes a constellation of research from a variety of disciplines, some of which are only marginally or tenuously connected. That there is no one disciplinary focus under whose auspices and direction this study has been generated could be seen as a methodological deformity of specious scientific utility or at the very least, a form of rank, unprincipled eclecticism or theoretical woolly-headedness. While it is true that the majority of scholars I have cited throughout this work do not occupy a homogeneous tradition, I have attempted to find points of interconnection and cross-fertilization between their various perspectives. Furthermore, my rationale for selecting analytical data from such disparate sources is based on a number of common assumptions, namely: that rituals provide the generative base of cultural life; that a ritual is a subsistent relation whose nature is determined by the character and relations of its symbols; that the way in which we construe reality is linked to our perceptions which, in turn, are mediated through collectively shared symbol and ritual systems: and that we are subjectively located in the social order as agents and actors through engagement in particular ritual performances.

While not unmindful of the disputations between approaches to ritual in the various disciplines, the perspective of this study will be to highlight the similarities and the complements of theoretical models. To further treat ritual as a watershed division in the social sciences will only promote its further Balkanization within various academic disciplines and will do nothing to add to its importance as a research topic.

What could be described within these pages as a 'liberal arts' approach to ritual and schooling is a deliberate attempt to eschew disciplinary endogamy and steer away from what anthropologist Ernest Becker (1971) has described a a 'fetishist reaction' in the social sciences – a term that refers to work done by researchers who remain isolated in their respective disciplines, guarding their academic fiefdoms against the invasion of ideas from other scholarly domains. Fetishism in scientific analyses arises when one attempts 'to cope wtih an overwhelming problem of conceptualization by biting off very tiny pieces of it and concentrating on them alone, even, to push the analogy, deriving all one's sense of self, all one's delight in life and work, from the feverish contemplation of a ludicrously limited area of reality.'[7]

Disciplines are never discrete, and despite the best argumentation and back-pedalling of social scientists in our century, we are beginning to see more and more clearly that academic domains are largely syncretic; that the dog in the manger of separate university departments must be taught new tricks despite his advancing age. Although this study is far from realizing Hymes's (1972) goal of 'reinventing anthropology', it is within the spirit of his search for an integrated approach to culture that this work is undertaken.

I would like to make clear that by examining the process of schooling under the auspices of ritual and performance, I am not attempting to add new labels to processes already well understood by educators or to repackage or refurbish a familiar apologetics. In other words, I am not trying to play familiar educational themes in a new register; rather, I am attempting to drastically alter the score. Mine is a challenge which deliberately seeks the limits of our present methods of interpreting the schooling process. I believe that investigations which take seriously contemporary approaches to ritual and performance will be able to uncover critical ways of reconceiving and rediscovering classroom behaviour – ways which can enlarge upon established methods of understanding student behaviour so dearly beloved by Anglo-American education (e.g. behaviourism, genetic epistemology, ego psychology). It will be argued that a 'ritological' approach is vitally important since it attempts to free classroom research from the tyranny of the literal, the obvious and the self-evident. It is an approach that best fits with what has already been foreshadowed by reconceptualist and neo-Marxist approaches to schooling – approaches that have attempted to make educators aware of how cultural productions are distributed both in the classroom and wider society.

While neo-Gramscian, neo-Marxist, and reconceptualist approaches to schooling have popularized ethnographic field studies and have been unabashedly critical (and rightly so) of micro-sociological studies of classrooms which ignore categories of class, gender and power, they have often been guilty of either ignoring or disregarding advances made in symbolic anthropology, liturgical studies and ritual and performance studies. Generally missing from their pantheon of references are the important works of Abner Cohen, Roy Rappaport, Barbara Myerhoff, Sally Falk Moore, Ronald L. Grimes, Richard Schechner, and the doyen of ritual studies – Victor W. Turner. This study seeks to redress this gaping lacuna. A focus on symbol and performance enables new light to be shed on the strong normative or hegemonic structures of classroom rituals that exist beyond the ken of our immediate perception. As a result, we have the beginnings of a critical approach for analysing the symbolic dimensions of the hidden curriculum.

I would like to make clear, however, that by concentrating on rituals as signal elements in the formation of a cultural field,

I do not mean to suggest that all of classroom social behaviour is supposed to proceed exclusively from symbolic or indexical parameters, or that all of the pettifogging particulars of classroom activity can be accounted for by an appeal to various rites of passage, revitalization, intensification or resistance. In fact, to consider the classroom solely as a series of ritual enactments is to place oneself in a type of semiotic straightjacket. Ritual is but one dimension of a cultural system. Equally important are the concepts of kinship, social structure, and the relations of production. If this study gives inordinate attention to the concept of ritual it is because ritual has been – and remains – the least analysed component of school culture. However, to argue out a reconciliatory aesthetic of ritual is tangential to the main concern of this study and thus outside my purview. Rather, my interest is simply to alert the educator to adjust his or her perceptions to include the symbolic dimensions of classroom activities. The bias of tone in this investigation is in the direction of justifying the importance of everyday ritualized actions – the minutiae of classroom life, as it were – as against more elaborate ceremonies or celebrations. Yet while my focus dwells on 'ordinary events', this study does not preclude but rather invites the examination of more formal ceremonialized activities, if and when they manifest themselves naturally within the course of the school day.

The heuristic quality of this research looks beyond a mechanical 'fit' between a pre-ordinated definition of ritual and the data. The analysis is not cast to empirically advance one existing theory of ritual at the expense of others, but to use ritual and performance theory as a framework for interpreting the cultural grammar and lexica of classroom culture. The emphasis lies not so much with the vacuous generalizability of theory – e.g. with extrapolating insights pertinent at the pan-human level or pan-societal scale – as with the applicability of using ritual studies as a heuristic device to assist in the interrogation of classroom symbols. Thus, this study seeks to adumbrate rather than delineate; to illustrate rather than make grandiose proclamations. It should be seen as prolegomenous theorizing and a programmatic invitation for the further development of conceptual links between ritology and schooling.

PERSONAL BIASES

In any work that deals with the latent effects of school organization and instruction, it seems only fitting that the reseacher acknowledge his or her own hidden agenda. A strong emphasis on ritual as an articulating mechanism of social control colours the present work; concurrently, there is also an emphasis on the creative or socially reconstructive aspects of the ritual process. Not only am I concerned with how the potentially liberating forces of ritual become dissipated or depotentiated through attempts by schools to satisfy the demands of their corporate and hegemonic structures, but I also wish to explore the way rituals serve as seedbeds for social change.

Throughout this study the concept of the body is turned into a master symbol for the purpose of critical exegesis on schooling as a culture of pain. Pain, whether existential or physical, is intimately connected to the pedagogic encounter. In addition to emphasizing the corporeal predicament of the student, the 'semantic tension' (Geertz's term) which marks cultural meanings generated by classroom rituals, and the anomic breakdown of classroom life, I address the process whereby classroom instruction has been ritualized into root paradigms. Assuming a primal life of their own – a 'real-seemingness' (Whorf's term) – these paradigms became 'naturalized' and 'legitimized' and provided models for student learning and behaviour. A substantial section of this book is given over to articulating the latent and hegemonic effects of the root paradigms.

Much of my interest in the particular rites of Catholic instruction is motivated by a concern that the figure of Christ has been reduced to a silent accomplice in acts of symbolic violence and an invisible partner in the process of cultural reproduction. I therefore seek, as a Catholic and as an educator, to construct an approach to school reform that takes into account structure and symbolic agency.

SOME CAVEATS

Some caveats should be interpolated at this juncture. First and foremost, this book neither attempts to reconcile the notoriously controverted connections between myth and ritual nor intends to develop a comprehensive mythography or cosmology of school culture. Second, this book is not meant to be yet another assault on the problem of how the term 'culture' or 'popular culture' is to be defined. Furthermore, the problematic task of proving one definition of ritual over others is an intricate matter which I forbear to pursue. There is, so far as I can ascertain, no absolute 'right' or bona fide definition of ritual – some given unalterable meaning or brute intractable articulation by which to distinguish it antiseptically from other aspects of social life. Nevertheless, I shall attempt to make the term ritual less polymorphous by describing, as far as it is possible, its essential features, and by arriving at a synthesis which can function as a heuristic tool for examining classroom interaction. This, it might be objected, is the furtive narrowing of a wide cast net. One might protest that if there is no single comprehensive model of ritual which has achieved some official approbation – no Archimedean fulcrum by which to assess which of the many competing definitions is the 'correct' one – then there can be no scientific or analytic value in such a construct. However, I have no objection in adopting such a permissive stance. My challenge is to pinion pronouncements on ritual which have heretofore been feathered with flighty associations, and attempt to replace them with insights from the work of contemporary ritologists.

The theoretical approaches underlying this study, which have been drawn from the writings of scholars working within regions both directly adjacent to and considerably removed from symbolic anthropology, have all been subject to critical objections which I make no claim to resolve. This study does not attempt to confront all the epistemological ramifications of analysing rituals.

One final caveat. A nomothetic study of school rituals would inevitably require a larger sample of schools. Since this investigation is a case study of a single school, it is understandably idiographic in nature; that is, it attempts to establish particular factual propositions as opposed to more general ones.

Finally, it should be established that this study is but one conceptual 'lens' for viewing school culture. We interpret reality sieved through the particular lens, paradigm or model with which we choose to focus our investigative and analytical perceptions. In the present study, classroom rituals constitute the 'territory' of the investigation while ritual theory serves as the 'map', lens or interpretive model. A model establishes conceptual categories, defines theoretical parameters, and suggests correspondences between data that merit further research. Yet while models organize and select our perceptions in such a way that we make novel associations between phenomena, they also set bounds to our understanding and interpretation of the world. Models 'bracket' or isolate portions of the phenomenal world and invariably distort reality by emphasizing certain aspects of reality to the exclusion of others. No doubt this present model of classroom life could be further refined to include other previously overlooked domains of classroom culture.

MISPERCEPTIONS SURROUNDING THE TERM 'RITUAL'

The term ritual is tantalizingly ambiguous and has, over the years, engendered a welter of specious formulations. Few concepts are as pervasive and durable yet have been left to flounder for so long in a morass of teminological confusion.

Long hallowed by repeated liturgical and anthropological use, the meaning of ritual continues to provoke a cleavage of opinion among modern scholarly commentators. Conflicts still persist between various theoretical approaches to the understanding of ritual. Schools of thought include: the ritual-as-action (Tylor) and the ritual-as-belief schools (W.R. Smith); the semantic approach (Radcliffe-Brown) and the functional approach (Durkheim and Malinowski); the psychoanalytic approach (Freud) and the phenomenological approach (Cassirer); the system transformation approach and the structural redundancy approach (cf. Partridge, 1977); the positive theory of ritual and the negative theory of ritual (cf. Scheff, 1977); and the causal meaningful school and the causal functional school (cf. Nagendra, 1971). And while conflicting schools of thought remain at daggers drawn, the word ritual has not ceased to proliferate deeply embedded cliché images among laymen. A ritual, for instance, is frequently regarded as something an individual does over and over – like smoking a cigarette. Or else people tend to regard ritual as having to do with strange customs linked with ancient civilizations.

My introduction to the concept of ritual began during my adolescence and for years I persisted in holding a perniciously narrow view of the term. Fantasizing about life as an anthropologist (at approximately the level of the ethnocentric exploits of Hollywood's Indiana Jones), I would pore through copies of the *National Geographic* each month in order to find pictures of ancient ruins, burial mounds and gravesites which had been meticulously uncovered by picks, shovels and patient hands.

How I envied those dusty bone-jockeys, cradling their pickaxes close to their sweat-stained safari jackets, and standing triumphantly over the remains of some poor wretch who had been buried alive. For me, a ritual meant only one thing: a mysterious event from the past – some ancient and arcane ceremony which usually surrounded the death of a revered or infamous figure.

The long-standing problem of defining ritual continues to exercise scholars and is no doubt due to a strong oscillation between various poles of anthropological and lay explanations of ritual – poles which have often been merged, interrelated, intermixed or cross-referenced. What makes such an ephemeral concept so tenacious is difficult to say, except for the obvious ubiquity of ritual in every culture – past or present – known to man. The one word 'ritual' has frequently been substituted for what a number of commentators would distingish as a schedule, a meaningless repetition, or a form of superstitious behaviour. These misperceptions or misunderstandings of ritual stem, at least in part, from the restricted definitions of scholars and laymen alike who have overemphasized its picayune and superficial nature (e.g. as synonymous with meaningless artifact or empty routine) – a posture that has now reached popular consensus.

Because of the wide-ranging use of the term ritual, it is not surprising that we find a variety of definitions, or, as often as not, no explanation at all of what ritual means. As a 'catch-all' phrase for anything repetitive or habitual, ritual has been diluted and trivialized to such an extent that it has become both common cultural property and a conceptual encumbrance, and continues to present serious problems for the scientific examination of social relations.

Until recently, ritual studies have focused preponderantly on the religious or ceremonial aspects of 'primitive' cultures; hence, too often, the concept of ritual has become identified with those rapturous TV matinee depictions of frenzied natives sacrificing newborns before a steaming volcano. And psychoanalytic tradition has also proffered a rather distasteful view of ritual – conflating the term with symptoms of private pathology, idiosyncrasy, and neurosis (a view which first emerged from Viennese consulting rooms at the turn of the century). These conceptions have done little to enhance the reputation of ritual as a process of noteworthy social significance. We must guard against hoary stereotypes and ragbag and shopworn descriptions of ritual.

To this day, both ritual and myth remain widely misunderstood as either fictional, hypothetical or historical events, and this misunderstanding has resulted in the patent avoidance and obfuscation of these concepts in many cultural studies of post-modern settings. Indeed, the very sound of the word ritual is unpleasant to more contemporary ears. To those outside an anthropological or liturgical tradition, the term itself lacks resonance. Rituals are overwhelmingly regarded as existing today in putatively diminished, debilitated or denatured forms; they are looked upon as innocuous antiques, part of a bygone era – leftovers perhaps from some former vaunted age of ritual replete with the proverbial golden idols, smoking cauldrons and vestal virgins.

Because of the traditional assignment of ritual to the occult, the mysterious and the magical, the term ritual conjures up images of Rosicrucian adepts, magical prescriptions incanted in antique tongues, sacred anointings, spoon benders, joss sticks and other cultic paraphernalia – recrudescent symptoms of a spiritually impotent age where humankind is chained to a soul-less body, is steeped in restlessness and anomie, and is in need of some fancy symbolic props to assuage emotional emptiness. Ritual's trail of supernatural associations has surrounded the term in a miasma of mystification, as though ritual belonged on an altar with holy relics or vials of martyrs' blood. But rituals do not serve solely as some type of sacerdotal stilts or metaphysical prostheses that celebrants can spiritually strap on to assist them in their scramble towards the sublime. Anthropologically sterile misconceptions such as these perpetuate a puerile understanding of ritual, placing the term in conceptual shackles. Indeed, the concept of ritual has been mired in so many unwarranted assumptions that it creates more confusion than illumination. The halcyon days of discussing ritual have permenantly left us and it is the task of the ritologist of today to avoid both taking refuge behind a screen of conceptual biases or returning to an overly simplified or overly complicated use of the term.

Robert L. Moore *et al.* (1983) link the history of secularization in Western culture to a history of the 'decline and devaluing' of ritual. Ritual behaviours have been dismissed as 'archaisms' linked to the 'obscurantist forces of religion' from the Renaissance and Reformation right through to the Enlightenment (p. 209). Fortunately this attitude appears to be changing. We are entering a new era of ritual appreciation.

To summarize, the problematic of using the term ritual can be partially attributed to the vagaries associated with the contending definitions, the idea that ritual is a form of empty gesture, and the *ipso facto* disappearance of grandiloquent cremonialism (normally associated with the fanfare, pageantry and sacerdotal etiquette of patristic or medieval Christendom) in modern, industrial society. Fanning the anti-ritual flames are scholars and laymen who possess only a fugitive understanding of ritual and who have been trained to think of ritual dimensions as inevitably related to vital religions – a mystical forum full of formulaic utterances for tapping into the unfathomable and inexplicable mysteries. But rituals possess more than theurgic (or supernatural) qualities.

My approach to ritual will be more broadly embrasive of human behaviour than given credit by those outside anthropology and its varied theoretical affiliations (who hold restricted conceptions of ritual) and more earthbound than descriptions found in the current mystic/occult mindscape of popular culture.

THE TREATMENT OF RITUAL IN THE SOCIAL SCIENCES

General scepticism

Ritual is not one of the concepts that readily fits into the intellectual climate of present-day social science. It is a term that has not yet been recognized with sufficient determination by the scientific community – especially the community of 'normal' scientists (cf. Kuhn, 1962). Clearly, there is a noticeable lack of analyses linking ritual to social science explanatory models. The analysis of ritual – especially in industrial settings – has been damagingly narrow and continues to labour under various theoretical handicaps. 'Ritual', laments Mary Douglas, 'has become a bad word signifying empty conformity. We are witnessing a revolt against formalism, even against form' (1973, p. 19).

The analysis of ritual has been banished from serious scientific consideration by objections from anthropologists who are hostile to the ambiguity of the term, who have wilfully ignored the concept in their own research, and who are apt to dismiss it as 'useless' in that it fails to adequately articulate social activity in modern, secular society. To scholars of this ilk, investigations of ritual are tolerated as long as they are limited to anthropological studies of more compact and unified societies than our own. To suggest to critics of this persuasion that rituals widely exist in today's society would be taken as a cavalier assertion or a jejune attempt to mix religion and technology. Mainstream social scientists are prone to homologize a ritualist to a drab conceptualization of someone who performs external gestures mechanically and perfunctorily – without inner commitment to the values and ideas being expressed.

If opinions posed by the anti-ritual critics are correct, there is no useful purpose in studying ritual and we might as well permit the concept to fade even further into the background of scientific consideration. I believe it was Dietrich Bonhoeffer who once wrote: 'If you board the wrong train, it is no use running along the corridor in the opposite direction.' If I may use Bonhoeffer's statement as a spur, are those of us who choose the term 'ritual' as a conceptual category in our research really 'boarding the wrong train'? Anthropologist Jack Goody suggests that, to a certain extent, we are. With a certain measure of scholarly aplomb, Goody has recently set forth a stern warning against those researchers who do not use the term ritual advisedly in their research.[8] And although I have been pillorying the views of those who feel ritual is too vague a term to warrant serious use in conducting research, I must confess that I agree with a number of Goody's warnings. Some of his sanctions against using ritual as a theoretical tool are indeed reasonable. More importantly, however, none of them are insurmountable. Goody's attack on how ritual is defined – which is more autopsy than exegesis – has by no means exhausted the debate on the utility or richness of the concept. There exists to date no definitive refutation of ritual as a worthy conceptual instrument.

Pre-literate versus industrial society

Throughout much of the research on ritual there exists a theoretical scepticism regarding the appropriateness of applying conceptual advances gathered from anthropologists studying the rituals of preliterate societies to societies existing in complex industrial settings. It would not be surprising, therefore, to find some researchers raising as an objection what I offer as a statement (i.e. that rituals can be useful analytic tools in the study of contemporary society) because they question whether theories of ritual that have developed over the years from studies of small-scale, monolithic, subsistence level, or 'pre-discursive' societies can be applied to large-scale, pluralistic, technologically advanced, or 'hyper-discursive' societies where rituals have supposedly languished (except perhaps in such sociologically aberrant cases as youth countercultural movements, the Royal Wedding of Prince Charles and Lady Diana, or the spontaneous candlelight liturgies to mark the death of John Lennon). These commentators acknowledge the presence of contemporary rituals only to dismiss them as surface phenomena. Banalizing ritual by relegating it to a superficial feature, they continue to underestimate the primacy of ritual in contemporary society. Such a perspective, if not checked, could administer the very concept of ritual out of existence.

Ritual as anachronism

Another explanation for the disarticulation between positions involving the status of ritual in the social sciences rests on the argument that modern industrial societies are ritually bankrupt and denuded of their pre-industrial symbolic plenitude. Lurking around the edges of some sociological opinions regarding ritual is a penumbra of doubt in the efficacy – or even in the existence – of rituals in modern, mainstream life; rituals have supposedly retreated in our society to the periphery of culture to serve as ancillary appendages to the forces that created them. Over the decades, descriptions of pre-Christian or 'pagan' rituals have occurrred in lush profusion throughout the writings of cultural anthropologists. Yet today's cultural commentators are disinclined to concede that rituals play important roles in modern society. They would describe modern rituals as symbolic wraparounds that live in the cloakroom of culture – a place where anthropologists rummage through society's outer garments. Contemporary self-fulfilment in a beleagured and ritually deplete society such as ours appears the sole preserve of those poor de-symbolized souls insulated through superstition from the bold realities of the modern world – participants who bide their time in a milieu of make-believe: churches, synagogues, cinemas or theatres. Like alchemy, feudal lords or women's bustles, rituals are supposedly anachronistic in the twentieth century. However, any sociological perspective which dismisses rituals as anachronistic, as epiphenomenal, or as aberrational subcomponents of the social structure is less than an adequate explanation; it is at best a half truth and at worst falls short of a necessary understanding of modern ritual life. And it strips ritual of any epistemological nobility.

Qualitative versus quantitative research

Another explanation of why sociological inquiry has professed indifference to the rituals of post-industrial society and turned a myopic eye to studies of the symbolic dramas that pervade all levels of modern institutional life – that is, if they haven't already been rejected outright on *a priori* grounds – is the emphasis contemporary scholarship has placed upon quantitative research. Social scientists, it seems, have always been idolatrously fixed on the measurable. Within the authoritative wings of social scientific research, there exists a grievous imbalance in favour of pre-ordinate studies. Quantitative research design is still upheld as the methodology that best guarantees and legitimates scientific objectivity. It should therefore come as little surprise that a hypothesis that conceives of ritual honorifically, as more than a cultural artifact, dependent variable, or peepshow in an anthropological circus, tends to ruffle the academic feathers of those who couch social process in algorithmic terminology, who flinch at the sound of the word 'symbolic', who betray a constitutional aversion to emic accounts, and who regard the term 'interpretive' as the *bête noire* of contemporary social science. This situation not only has deterred researchers from deferring to the conceptual richness of ritual studies, but has impaired respect for associated disciplines as well. Thus mythology, dramaturgy, thaumaturgical arts and folklore – which are not easily studied in quantitative terms – have, up to and including the present day, frequently been abjured as topics of serious inquiry, branded as unnecessary scholarly accretions, shunned as otiose relics or peripheral additions to serious 'hard' research, and consigned to the realm of social insignia – cultural gargoyles perched upon the structural foundations of the social order. As Guy Davenport so sardonically puts it: 'The arts can look after themselves, they are used to neglect and obfuscation (1981, p. 134). Debilitating and perturbing as these anti-ritual trends may be, they have not gone unanswered. For example, anthropologist Abner Cohen (1974) believes that the trend to quantify data in many sociological studies has become an end in itself rather than a means to an end. Because rituals have a symbolic dimension as well as utilitarian and instrumental dimensions, they cannot be examined *solely* with regard to the material, the palpable, the tangible. They cannot be fully captured in correlational tables, T tests or regression analysis. A ritual must be understood as a 'phasing process, not as a set of systemic grids' (Grimes, 1982a, p. 151). Nor does a ritual simply reflect measurable societal values but 'holds the generating source of culture and structure' (Grimes, 1982a, p. 150).

Cohen writes that 'the analysis of the political significance of a specific ideology, of a public ceremonial, or of a religious drama, cannot – at least at the present state of our knowledge – be done quantitatively' (1974, p. 52). He echoes these sentiments further when he argues that the process of institutionalization can best be understood in *dramatistic terms* – terms which he deems imperative in any undertaking of social analysis (1974, p. 7).

Max Gluckman (1963) – a leader of the so-called Manchester School of social anthropology – and like-minded critics of contemporary ritual argue that in primitive society, where relationships are multiplex, ritualization is intense as it serves as a necessary mechanism for role, and hence institutional differentiation. In modern society, on the other hand, roles, and hence institutions, tend to be formally differentiated and therefore there is no need for ritualization (Cohen, 1974, pp. 49–50). In simple terms, industrialization appears to have given the *coup de grâce* to ritual. *Exeunt* ritual.

Cohen takes considerable issue with the logic of Gluckman's perspective, assailing the self-deception and parochialism of contemporary social science, and arguing that sociologists and anthropologists have exaggerated the qualitative difference between the nature of primitive society and that of industrial society. In Cohen's words: 'they [sociologists and anthropologists] have tended to emphasize the rational and the contractual and to minimize the significance of the symbolic in the structure of modern industrial society' (1974, p. 52). Trapped by their own scientific propositions and epistemological premises, which tend on occasion to serve as intellectual blinders, mainstream social anthropologists have overlooked the subtleties of the process of institutionalization and symbolization. Part of the problem was that many of the great sociologists at the turn of the century saw a qualitative difference between the sociocultural nature of primitive society and that of industrial complex society (1974, p. 50). Hence, social anthropology concerned itself with the study of primitive society and sociology focused on the dynamics of industrial society. However, Cohen does offer us a more comforting prognosis for the future of social science by reporting that researchers 'committed to the social anthropological approach . . . are now probing into the potentialities of their concepts and techniques for the study of contemporary industrial society' (1974, p. 13).

Gemeinschaft versus Gesellschaft

Another supposed explanation for the impoverishment of ritual in modern society is the idea, prominent in contemporary sociology, that society is evolving from a *Gemeinschaft* community to a *Gesellschaft* community; in other words, from a social aggregate in which individuals remain relatively united in spite of separating factors – as in European feudalism – to a community which superficially appears united but which essentially remains separated in spite of all the uniting factors – as evident in modern, technological societies (Bocock, 1974, p. 57). There appears today to be a distinct shift from the 'mythological to the religionless, from the sacred to the profane, from the folk to the urban' (Greeley, 1972, p. 32). The old primordial forces (such as blood and land ties) are on the wane and rapidly being replaced by contractual ones. If primordial ties survive, it is only in the private or 'leisure' sphere that one would find them (p. 32). Rituals in a *Gemeinschaft* society are pictured as having a depth of communal feeling which is often felt to be lacking in rituals carried out in *Gesellschaft* conditions (Bocock, 1974, p. 58). It is no wonder, then, that rituals would appear to be on the retreat.

Andrew Greeley has forcefully challenged this position, arguing that it is a sociological fallacy to assume that mankind's primordial ties no longer persist. On the contrary, argues Greeley, the vast network of *Gesellschaft* relationships is actually a superstructure based on an infrastructure of persisting *Gemeinschaft* relationships (Greeley, 1972, p. 31). Greeley's cogent argument stresses that 'the large corporate structures which constitute the *Gesellschaft* technological society represent *additions* to the pool of human relationships and not substitutions for the old relationships' (p. 31). Greeley does not deny that there is often stress and strain between these two structures; nor does he claim that there are no tendencies towards dehumanization and depersonalization in much of *Gesellschaft* society. But he asserts, none the less, that 'the basic ties of friendship, primary relationship, land, faith, common origin and consciousness of kind persist [today] much as they did in the Ice Age' (p. 35). They merely operate in different ways and in different contexts. The same could certainly be said about today's interactional rituals and their multiple 'liminoid' progency of mime, theatre, film and sports. Given the arguments presented by Cohen and Greeley, there does not appear to be any incontrovertible evidence that would compel us to abolish the idea that rituals are the prime building blocks of our industrial – or any other – society. In fact, their commentaries proclaim the indispensability of ritual to the continuation of contemporary social and cultural existence.

THE TREATMENT OF RITUAL IN EDUCATIONAL RESEARCH

Quite independently of recent developments in ritual studies, educational research is undergoing prodigious changes; it currently exists in a state of ferment that shows little sign of abating. A growing interest among educational researchers in qualitative research methodology and ethnographic portrayals of classroom life has sparked a developing awareness of the value of anthropological theory used in an educational context. So far, however, scholarly forays into the domain of ritual and schooling have, in most cases, amounted to no more than excursive essays which are either shockingly ill-informed on the nature of ritual or else convey a rather complacent pedantry. Regrettably, attempts to link ritual and the pedagogic encounter have been, up to the present time, signally tenuous and undifferentiated.

The classroom ethnographer, drawing on conventional sociological wisdom, has so far failed to realize the potential value of utilizing ritual as an explanatory concept in classroom analysis. The symbolic self-awareness and sheer verve that Victor Turner has brought to the study of the ritual process has been slow to filter through to the investigation of classroom practices. In fact, most questions pertaining to symbolic action and gestural embodiment have hidden behind a cloud of non-discussion. Predictably, where ritual has proven itself most applicable to studies of classroom settings has been in examinations of the singing of the national anthem, open house, caning, the Lord's prayer, school assemblies and opening exercises. Nevertheless, misconceptions still surrounding the term ritual in the social sciences have deflected researchers from considering *classroom instruction itself* as a ritual-ized transaction. That there is a definite lack of well-articulated links between the theoretical foundations of ritual and educational ethnography cannot be seriously denied. It is certainly no understatement to claim that connections between schooling and ritual process are in need of further exegesis.

OVERVIEW OF THE LITERATURE ON RITUAL AND SCHOOLING

The long history of anthropological and theological association with ritual contrasts with the relatively short history of interest to educators. A great deal has been written about education as the transmission of cultural knowledge; yet the way in which culture, as ritual action, constitutes and fosters ideology and behaviour remains largely unexplored in the context of school settings.

To the educator, it might appear as if the secular and osten-sibly profane life of school instruction bears a superficial affinity to ritual. Such is not the case, however, as ritologists have made abundantly clear. Lessons, exams and trips to the washroom are only inimical to the concept of ritual if we entertain a definition of ritual so narrow as to exclude all functions less formalized than the Catholic mass.

Over the years educators of various stripe ranging from Ivan Illich to Richard Courtney have commented upon the existence of rituals in educational settings. Schooling as a type of rite of passage has been discussed from the perspective of the experience of novice teachers (Eddy, 1969) and inner-city teachers (Foster, 1974). Lancy (1975) and Meyer (1977) prefer to look at schooling as an oftentimes painful initiation rite. Applying some of Goffman's concepts to the ghetto classroom, Moore (1976) uses the terms 'avoidance rituals' and 'presentation rituals' to discuss student-teacher interaction. Lutz and Ramsey (1973) connect rituals to belief systems operative in schools, describing them as 'non-directive cues' which schools frequently employ to reinforce policy assump-tions. Weiss and Weiss (1976) describe Christmas gift giving between teachers (the 'secret-pal' ceremony) as an indigenous rite of intensification. Durka and Smith (1979) stress the importance of ceremony as an educational experience while comparing ceremony to Dewey's five conditions of the aesthetic: conservation, tension, cumulation, anticipation and fulfillment. Clifton (1979) sees the concept of ritual as inextricably related to the performance of teaching itself; rituals are thus linked to classroom instruction, teacher organization and 'pedagogical style'. Using the term 'routinization' as a rather limp substitute for ritual, Willower (1969) maintains that it is usually employed by schools as a protective device. Jacquetta Hill Burnett (1969) uses an adaptation of Goody's definition of ritual to articulate connections between the high school ceremonial system and the student economic system. Rituals are seen to serve primarily an 'integrating function'. Connelly and Clandinin (1982) link the term ritual (which they formulate after Jennings) as a process in the development of a teacher's 'personal knowledge'.

It has been argued both by Illich (1970) and Kapferer (1981) that school rites have an inherently political, 'hegemonic' or mystificatory function that encourages students to accept and support the dominant school culture. Kamens (1977) also sees rituals as serving a political function – especially in higher education where students become 'certified' members of the corporate elite. Knight (1974) perceives school rituals to be 'gatekeeping' devices which regulate the social and economic reward system of the dominant culture. Describing rituals as a form of 'restricted code', Bernstein *et al.* (1966) maintain that their primary function is that of social control. The work of Bernstein *et al.* (which is influenced by the writings of Durkheim) deals mainly with the instrumental and expressive domains of school culture. McLaren (1982b) looks at violence and disorder among working-class schoolgirls as ritualized resistances which are unconsciously marshalled against an oppressive social order. While Gehrke (1979) acknowledges rituals as a type of 'hidden curriculum' which socializes students into the dominant order, she also stresses that rituals have a propitiatory function of soothing conflict and promoting harmony among students.

Clancy (1977) sees schoolwide ritual as a form of protection against individual indoctrination by charismatic and subversive teachers. Similarly, Shipman (1968) conceives of school rituals as important sources of academic motivation, involvement and identification.

Studies of Everhart and Doyle (1980) and Johnson (1980) stress the importance of both the symbolic and material aspects of school culture (classroom displays, posters, slogans, etc.). Grumet (1978) uses the theatrical metaphor ('All the world's a stage') in a fascinating articulation of curriculum as a ritual mode. Courtney (1980, 1982) extends the theatrical metaphor through his use of the dramatic metaphor ('We are such stuff/As dreams are made on; and our little life/Is rounded with a sleep'). The work of Richard Smith (1979) is exceptionally faithful to the anthropological literature in its very promising discussion of ritual, myth, metaphor, metonymy and teacher education. Both O'Farrell (1981) and Courtney (1980, 1981) have linked the concept of ritual to creative drama, school programming, and the work of prominent expositors of ritual such as Victor Turner and Barbara Myerhoff.

Part of the stock-in-trade of practising anthropologists and ethologists, the term ritual is not part of the everyday lexicon of the classroom educator. It is rarely found among the in-house slogans in the school staff room. And as far as traditional educational research is concerned, the study of ritual has enjoyed a desultory engagement. With the exception of the studies cited above, researchers have attended but dimly to the symbolic and mythopoetic dimensions of schooling. Many of the educational researchers who have discussed ritual as a variable in classroom interaction could be described as living in the shoals of ritual studies – away, as it were, from the major waves.

Most of the educational literature on ritual echoes the general tenets of Durkheimian structural-functional theory (e.g. that rituals bind groups and society together, creating a kind of primordial unity). Studies by Illich, Gehrke, Kamens and Kapferer suggest ritual brings about social unity through its mystificatory power – that of perpetuating social life in such a way that it is perceived as natural. This mystificatory power can be understood as a process in which rituals, as cultural forms, are objectified into a symbolic medium which supports an existing social order.

With few exceptions, investigations of ritual and schooling have been speculative and vague. To what extent do these investigations correspond to the lived experiences of the students? In many cases, they represent examples of what Glaser and Strauss (1967) characterize as ungrounded, speculative theory because the concepts propounded in these articulations of ritual do not directly emerge from concrete qualitative data under investigation; and many of the formulations which have been put forward have not been derived from actual observations of teachers and students. The assumptive background from which the majority of these studies emerge tends to reflect schools as politically neutered sites which, along with their lack of culturally reproductive power, exist unproblematically in society-at-large. In this context, a ritual appears to function as a comforting narcotic or else a symbolic emollient whose purpose is to smooth over the rough and fissured surface of communal strife. Seldom do these researchers link rituals, as cultural events, to forms of rupture and resistance that emerge among class, economic and cultural forces. P.G. Clancy, for instance, argues for the return of traditional rituals in schools. He calls for the reaffirmation of conservative mores and rigorous standards of *civilité*. While he underscores the importance of the role that ritual plays in school instruction, his arguments revolve around a rather ill-conceived, unilinear theory of ritual – one in which rituals simply provide a mirror image for the collective virtues of society (although he chooses not to expand on what those particular virtues might be). That rituals and ritual symbols often function as powerful transmitters of the manifest values of our society cannot be questioned; however, Clancy's theory of ritual totally neglects any discussion of how particular rituals work, how they often embody contradictions, or how they can be used to foster not only positive values, but hypocritical ones as well. Furthermore, this work is beclouded by the specious conviction that traditional rituals will somehow counteract the improvised, self-generated rituals of charismatic and independent teachers. Indeed, his whole argument sounds like a rallying cry to bring back the days when all teachers were 'men of stature' and when students slavishly venerated school escutcheons, crests, cups, honour boards, badges, pennants and school ties – the standard supporting insignia during the days when Mr Gradgrind used to crack you on the knuckles for failing to memorize your ten lines of Cicero. More disturbingly, Clancy does not appear to be particularly troubled about the exploitative aspects of ritual – the possibility of manipulating the collectivity into a false consciousness.

Recent work by Henry Giroux, Michael W. Apple and Rachel Sharp suggest that any analysis of school rituals must be placed in a context of culture that problematicizes the relationship between schooling, power, conflict and class. For Giroux, 'School culture is really a battleground on which meanings are defined, knowledge is legitimated, and futures are sometimes created and destroyed. It is a place of ideological and cultural struggle favored primarily to benefit the wealthy, males and whites' (1984, p. 133). What must be critically uncovered are the latent connections between educational rituals and the ways in which inequality is maintained in school settings. Michael Apple, for example, raises the issue of how 'the routines and rituals' of classroom life influence the role of the school as a social and economic institution (1978, p. 485). Rachel Sharp declares that 'A political program which does not recognize the unconscious elements of ideology and its embodiment in social routines and rituals at all levels of social existence, and which relies simply on cultural critiques at the level of ideas, is doomed to failure' (1980, p. 86). She maintains that an understanding of bourgeois ideology involves 'examining the forms of self-representation through the rituals and practices and myths which pervade every day existence' (1980, p. 108) and adds that 'pervasive representations of man and society [as part of liberal democratic ideology] are not merely abstractly stored in the head but are materialized in social practices and rituals which have explanatory power' (1980, p.109).

It would appear that the majority of the writers on ritual and education have derived their scholarly warrant and their programmatic impetus from a perspective which is exemplarily removed from the pressing questions raised by radical educational theorists such as Sharp and Apple. Outside of the work of Bernstein *et al.* and a few other commentators, it would appear that the concepts of class and power are considered to be potentially disruptive categories. Spellbound by the sheen on the outer tissue of classroom culture, most researchers, on the rites of schooling appear reluctant to penetrate into the social organs of deceit and privilege that exist in the larger society and which ultimately influence the shape and meaning of the classroom rituals themselves. In addition, few, if any, of the authors cited attempt to examine ritual as a symbolic 'process' (Courtney is one notable exception); indeed, they often exhibit a staggering propensity to ignore existing writings in liturgical studies and symbolic anthropology. For the most part, researchers responsible for the existing literature on education and ritual remain uninformed by Turner's anthropological *doxa* and singularly untutored with respect to the relationship between rituals, symbols, and root paradigms. To this day, these complex articulations of ritual remain relatively unexplored. Our present state of knowledge surrounding the relationship between ritual and schooling is appreciably less than definitive.

THE BIRTH OF RITOLOGY

Through decades of anthropological and liturgical inquiry, we have inherited a rich legacy of studies involving ritual. While this already voluminous literature has been rapidly expanding in recent years, ritual studies has only just emerged as a distinct discipline, or sub-discipline of religious studies. It is at once exhilarating and dangerous to work at the boundary of a new *Wissenschaft* or 'science of religion' that is striving to grow – exhilarating, because of the wide expanse of scholarly terrain to be charted – and dangerous, because of the absence of any imprimatur from the Ecclesia of Social Science.

A burgeoning group of scholars working in the field of ritual scholarship (which Ronald Grimes calls 'ritology') are ascribing a great deal of importance to the analysis and understanding of contemporary cultural forms in non-religious settings. They are taking the sociological spotlight from the study of tribal ceremony and focusing it on contemporary secular events. Holding the crystal of culture up to the light of recent advances in comparative symbology, they twist it slightly so that the image of the proverbial sacred grove gives way to that of the secular city.

In a state-of-the-art introduction to his book, one of the foremost ambassadors and patron spirits of ritual studies, Ronald L. Grimes, describes its evolution:

> 'Ritual studies' is a term initially used, as far as I know, in 1977, when the first Ritual Studies Consultation was held during the American Academy of Religion's annual meeting. So ritual studies, or 'ritology,' is a new field, not because doing ritual or thinking about it is new, but because the effort to consolidate methods from the humanities and social sciences for the study of ritual in a context that is free to be cross-cultural and comparative is new ... So there is an immense need for annotated bibliographies, field studies of specific rituals, typologies and taxonomies, and more fully developed theories. In addition, there is a need for studying connections between ritual and therapy, theatre, theology, political science, kinesics, and psychosomatic medicine. The time for beginning ritual studies is ripe.
>
> (1982a, Preface)

Nowhere have studies of ritual been mobilized more abundantly and with such erudition than in the research done by Grimes.

Working in the interstices between the anthropology of ritual and liturgics – between analytic and normative approaches to the investigation of ritual – Grimes proffers a critical validation of ritual studies. He defines ritual as enacted metaphor and embodied rhythm that includes both an ultimate 'high' type (liturgy) and a tacit type (interaction ritual), as well as a 'low' type (ritualization).[9] He writes that ritual studies can be conceptualized in basically three ways: 'as an interdisciplinary task, as a subfield of religious studies, or as a fundamental reconceptualization – in action-oriented terms – of religion itself'.[10] Ritologists are 'trying to offset the theological predilection to perceive only the "high" end of ritual performance, since the bias blinds us to less differentiated "interaction rituals"'.[11] Accordingly, Grimes sets out the three major goals of ritual studies as follows:

(1) to mediate between normative and descriptive, as well as textual and field-observational, methods; (2) to lay the groundwork for a coherent taxonomy and theory that can account for the full range of symbolic acts running from ritualization behaviour in animals, through interaction ritual, to highly differentiated religious liturgies and civil ceremonies; and (3) to cultivate the study of ritual in a manner that does not automatically assume it to be a dependent variable.[12]

Through his work at the Ritual Studies Laboratory at Wilfrid Laurier University in Waterloo, Ontario, Grimes has begun the important task of consolidating studies of ritual; and in his careful articulation of the relationship between ritual, rhythm and gesture, he has taken a field of scholarship which has been doggedly parochial and expanded it into a protoscience of its own. Recently, he has exactingly traced and perspicuously classified investigations of ritual into an index comprising ten ritual categories, sixteen ritual types, various ritual descriptions and a number of general works in various field clusters. Just to glance at one of Grimes's categories – that of ritual types – the reader is confronted with such ritual variants as rites of passage, marriage rites, funerary rites, festivals, pilgrimage, purification, civil ceremony, rituals of exchange, sacrifice, worship, magic, healing rites, interaction rites, mediation rites, rites of inversion and ritual drama.[13]

The last few years have witnessed a groundswell of reevaluation of ritual. The most notable controversies and concerns have arisen from a new awareness and interest in symbol and metaphor.

The field of contemporary ritual studies is profoundly inclusive and open to numerous theoretical entry points from a wide range of social scientists – researchers who are made kindred by their common interest in contemporary cultural forms. It is currently developing at the interface of hitherto discrete or only marginally connected disciplines: social and cultural anthropology, microsociology, sociolinguistics, folklore, literary criticism, semiology, kinesics, liturgics, dramatic sociology and proxemics. Conferences and colloquia organized in these fields are now becoming trysting places for sharing ritual dicta. To illustrate the sheer diversity of ritual studies, one need only refer to the work of scholars who are frequently quoted in the field, e.g. Jerzy Grotowski (a Polish theatre director), Victor Turner (a symbolic anthropologist), Erving Goffman (a dramatistic sociologist), Ray Birdwhistell (a kinesicist), Gregory Bateson (an anthropologist and one of the founders of cybernetic systems theory), Konard Lorenz (an ethologist), Mary Collins (a liturgist), Johann Huizinga (a cultural historian), Richard Schechner (an avant-garde theatre director and performance theorist) and Richard Courtney (a drama educator).

Although ritual studies is making serious inroads into the traditional preserves of cultural studies, Grimes warns us that, at this juncture in time, there are *only* students of ritual. In addition, he writes that there 'is no "ritual studies viewpoint" but rather a field upon which are focused multiple viewpoints' (1982a, Preface).

As theoretical trajectories from various academic terminals continue to converge around the topic of ritual, creating an atmosphere of intellectual ferment, there is an increasing pressure to unify the field. This will not be an easy task.

Grimes writes that

> What is needed presently is what literary critics call an 'anatomy,' religionists a 'phenomenology,' and anthropologists a 'taxonomy' of performative actions. We must sketch the shape of the field. To do so is a pre-methodological task, though not an 'objective' one without presuppositions. Such an undertaking requires what in Zen is called 'beginner's mind' (*shoshin*) and in phenomenology 'bracketing' (*epoché*). Theology is always being rewritten by each generation, and philosophy, as Husserl reminded us, is always returning to its roots to begin again. (1982a, Preface)

Victor Turner reports that anthropology is shifting from a stress on concepts such as structure, equilibrium, function and system to terms such as process, indeterminacy and reflexivity – from a 'being' to a 'becoming' vocabulary.

However, because taxonomies of action are not so nearly developed as generic studies of literary modes, Grimes reports that current ritual terminology is often makeshift. He presents us with a list of surrogate terms presently in use which include 'opus-process' (Grotowski, 1978); 'paratheatrical event' (Mennen, 1976); 'restored behaviour' (Schechner, 1981a); 'ethnographic drama' (Turner, 1979a); 'liminoid phenomena' (Turner, 1978); and 'parashamanism' (Grimes, 1982a) as well as many ritual derivatives such as 'ritual exploration', 'meta-ritual,' and 'ritual exercise' (1982a, p. 54). According to Grimes, the proliferation of hyphenated terms and coining of neologisms are indications that a nascent genre of action, which Grimes labels 'ritualizing', is precipitating a new view of ritual itself (p. 54).

Having attacked the limitations of structural functionalism, Turner indicates that 'the potentiality for a major breakthrough [in anthropology] exists today' (1977, p. 74). Turner's perspectival view interprets the direction of change as moving towards the role of metaphor in assigning meaning to social behaviour and conduct. Sociocultural systems are pictured as oriented through the cumulative effects of their performative genres, to what Turner calls root paradigms (1977, p. 74).

For Turner, it is imperative that the major disciplines begin to move towards a form of ludic interdependence. Such disciplines include cultural anthropology, symbolic anthropology, ecological anthropology, biocultural anthropology, phenomenological anthropology, structuralist anthropology, biocultural ecology, legal and political anthropologies, 'plus the many hybridizations between anthropology and other scholarly approaches' (1977, p. 75). These 'other' approaches include anthropological linguistics and ethnography of speaking; the uses of systems theory in archeological research; Marxist approaches in anthropology; and applications of the sociology of knowledge to anthropological data (p. 75). Turner suggests that

> instead of working in blinkers, anthropologists and scholars in adjacent disciplines . . . should make an earnest (and 'ludic') attempt at mutual empathy – earnest in the sense that the

disciplines mentioned above, and significant others, might be treated at least as a unified field whose unity might have something to do with the systems theory view ... (p. 75)

The work of Victor Turner stands as the centrepiece of the ritual studies enterprise. Contemporary ritologists are largely symbolic consociates of Victor Turner, since many of them work under the influence of the Turnerian vulgate (whose doctrines are directed at a 'processual' explanation of ritual via symbolic anthropology). Probing the cultural core of ritual, stripping it of its derisory connotations, making the concept relevant to a wide variety of disciplines, and creating an unprecedented interest in comparative symbology, ritologists have begun to pen highly significant studies of ritual which are advanced enough to be considered more than a journeyman's footnotes or adjuncts to Turner's peerless work. Scholars such as Barbara Myerhoff, Richard Schechner and Frank Manning have entered fully into Turner's heritage and tradition. As Turner's intellectual heirs, they have lifted the analysis of ritual out of the circumscribed 'liminal' context of traditional pre-literate societies and placed it in the wider 'liminoid' context of our diversified modern metropolises.

Unwilling to wall off a separate province of rituals from events of everyday existence and ordinary (normophrenic) states of consciousness, these new progenitors of ritual theory seek to explore numerous areas of human life and relate them to ritual. They have taken the study of ritual out of cold storage and located it within a more contemporary intellectual climate. Some bridges from ritual to the secular world constructed in detailed and perceptive studies include, among others, accounts of the ritualized life of a hippie commune, journal writing, the rituals of a Canadian theatre company, and rituals in a Jewish old folk's home.[14]

Findings from the fledgling field of ritology are tightening the once tenuous theoretical link between secular and religious symbol and metaphor. What distinguishes the work of these investigators is not an attempt to forge an unholy alliance between priestcraft and social science, but rather a success at bridging the yawning chasm between the sociologist's understanding of ritual and that of the anthropologist and liturgist. In addition, ritologists are committed to synthesizing anthropological approaches to ritual and advances made in semiotics, literary criticism and performance theory – scholarly strands that continue to be braided into the

contemporary fabric of social science – what Geertz (1980) refers
to as 'genre blurring'.

It is eminently clear to ritologists that there exists, in secular-
ized form, more than just vestiges of rituals whose popularized
genealogies date back to prehistoric caves, Dionysian revelry, sacred
groves of Druidic worship or the highly mythicized centuries of
ornate medieval church masses. Modern rituals are more than the
solemn or festive appurtenaces of mystical events that have all but
disappeared. That rituals appear to persist in contemporary
society, in some fashion or another – despite growing forces
of secularization, institutionalization, the retreat to privatism
and the overall complexification of society – is overwhelmingly
acknowledged by these writers. Citing evidence of contemporary
rituals is undertaken, however, not to emphasize that man's
primordial ties persist, as much as to point out the ongoing importance of the symbolic and expressive dimension in human culture.
Linked to the ritologists' concept of expressive culture is the
important recognition that formal celebrations are but one extreme
on the ritual continuum (the other extreme is animal ritualization) and are not to be taken as paradigmatic of most ritual
activities.

While the fraternity of ritologists is small, it easily makes up for
its few academic coteries by the pioneering spirit of its members;
some well-built epistemological walls had to be levelled in order
to accommodate some of their scholarly advances. It redounds to
the credit of these researchers that they have enlarged the concept
of ritual to include many ordinary, pedestrian events; as a conse-
quence the field of ritual inquiry has been broadened and illuminated. And great though the contribution of this group has been,
little in their expanding corpus of work has, to date, provided the
necessary connection beween ritual and school culture. There is
still much room for a reexamination of important issues in this area.
This study represents, in part, a valorization of, and building upon,
the work of contemporary ritologists. As the currency of the word
ritual rises in the social sciences, it is hoped that more emphasis
will be placed on educational studies of a symbolic nature. Thanks
to the work of modern ritologists, the door to explorations of contemporary ritual remains ajar despite continued attempts by some
social scientists to shut it.

WHAT A RITUAL IS

A ritual is not simply an arcane idea or pious abstraction preserved in the breviary of the parish priest: it extends beyond man's religious heritage kept alive by antiquarian interest and the august weight of tradition. Nor is it necessarily linked to noetic experiences that are ineffable or to mysterious gestures, invocations, or lustrations surrounding the consumption of wafers and wine. Contemporary ritologists have dissolved the mystical halo with which the liturgists have managed to keep the term ritual surrounded and have told us that rituals are constitutive of everyday human life, including secular activities.

We are ontogenetically constitued by ritual and cosmologically informed by it as well. All of us are under ritual's sway; absolutely none of us stands outside of ritual's symbolic jurisdiction. In fact, humanity has no option against ritual. To engage in ritual is, for men and women, a human necessity. We cannot divest ourselves of our ritual rhythms since they penetrate the very core of our nervous systems. The roots of ritual in any society are the distilled meanings embodied in rhythms and gestures. They vary enormously from culture to culture yet they are imperishable. Older than written history, they are what remains once the stones and columns have disintegrated and the ruins have been cleared.

Rituals are natural social activities found in, but not confined to, religious contexts. As organized behaviour, rituals arise out of the ordinary business of life. In opposition to the widespread opinion among many scholars and laymen that rituals have generally disappeared in contemporary society, rituals are always and everywhere present in modern industrial life. They are not just part of the mausoleum of society; they remain as alive and vital today as they did in ancient Greece or Babylon. Their orbit of influence permeates all aspects of our existence.

We are all inveterate ritualizers and ritual-employing beings. We do not have to wait for ecclesiastical edict or royal or school board fiat before partaking of ritual actions. Rituals are not confined to a compact proscenium, church chancel or government office; in fact, the modern 'global village' is full of novel and highly intricate ritual systems. Added to today's complexity of ritual systems is the vagueness of the term ritual itself.

This present research is guided by a perspective surrounding the term ritual that is more concerned with the mythic and

symbolic repertoire of our common metropolitan existence – with
the liturgy of the everyday – than with doctrinal pronouncements
litterae divinae, reliquaries containing particles of the 'true cross',
moral temper, denominational affiliation, or the ecclesiastic politics
of organized bodies of religious worship. Many scholarly perspectives on ritual sheer away from recondite questions pertaining to
ultimacy or revelation – to some *unio mystica* or '*der Dinge tiefer
Inbegriff*' – or involvement with ancient artifacts, figurines,
inhumations or middens. Instead, they refer to the sacrality inherent
in mankind's own ordinariness and everyday life (Grimes, 1982a,
p. 36). My concern, then, is not with rubrics set forth by ecclesiastic
codifiers or with museum-housed relics unearthed at the site of some
ancient temple. My interest lies with the practical and the mun-
dane and how these domains become sanctified inside schools.
Skorupski remarks that we need 'to be set free from the strait-jacket
of "ritual = sacred = symbolic" versus "practical = profane =
instrumental", and the contortions to which this simple-minded
opposition leads' (1976, p. 173). The concept of ritual 'may
surround any field of behaviour and itself does not give birth to
religion any more than it gives birth to art or to social organization' (Benedict, 1934, p. 396).

Lincoln suggests that, as I research and acknowledge the sources
of this study, I engage in a ritual process: that of footnoting or 'the
invocation of the ancestors'. Footnoting is, in effect, 'a way of
demonstrating anamnesis, the conquest of forgetfulness, for in the
footnote we preserve the memory of our forebears and pay honor
to their achievements' (1977, p. 155). The results of engaging in
a ritual are also evident in my fieldwork. 'The fieldworker,'
Schechner informs us, 'like the theatre director, like performers
in workshop-rehearsals, goes through the three-phase process Van
Gennep mapped out as the preliminal rites of separation, the liminal
rites of transition, and the postliminal rites of incorporation' (1981a,
p. 43). Even the words on this page, which have been chosen to
develop the themes and ideas for this research, are themselves part
of a ritual event. For, as Richardson notes, the graphic form and
power of the word 'is as much a power of our profession
[anthropology] as is the shaman's spirit helper' (1980, p. 2). Ronald
L. Grimes writes that 'Pen and paper are power objects, fetishes;
theorizing and observing are ritual gestures laden with ideology'
(1982a, p. 12). Following a formulation by Kenneth Burke, Richard
J. Martin suggests that the very practice of sociology is a ritual

form of secular prayer. He writes that: 'It is through secular prayer that a sociologist builds his character – his integrity of style, his consistency of purpose, his identity as a sociologist' (1974, p. 24).

Rituals are more than mere signs or symbols in some kind of sociocultural semaphore. On the contrary, they form the warp on which the tapestry of culture is woven, thereby 'creating' the world for the social actor; they are indispensable to our allegories, our fables and our parables. A group or community's rituals become, *inter alia*, the symbolic codes for interpreting and negotiating events of everyday existence. Psychological, sociological and anthropological investigations have uncovered various dimensions to ritual which locate it at the very nodal point or nerve centre of human organization (Worgul, 1980, p. 224).

Rituals suffuse our biogenetic, political, economic, artistic and educational life. To engage in ritual is to 'achieve ... historicocultural existence' (Sullivan, 1975, p. 23). Our entire social structure has a pre-emptive dependence on ritual for transmitting the symbolic codes of the dominant culture (I use the term 'codes' after Jeremy Campbell to refer to forms of stored information or sets of rules governing information). It is no exaggeration to claim – as the perdurability of rituals attests – that ritual serves as the pivot of the social world: the hinge of culture, the linchpin of society, and the foundation of institutional life such as that found in schools.

Notably, rituals are both part of the natural order of things (as in the ritualization of animals) and the consequences of human action (as in the rules and routines of classroom life). The way we ritualize our lives is culture somaticized – culture incarnated in and through our bodily acts and gestures.

Rituals are not created *ex nihilo*. Nor do they exist in some ornate vacuum. The seeds of ritual do not float about in some sanctified ether or waft of incense; the roots of ritual do not tunnel through the cultural soil of an idyllic mythical garden or emerge from the sterile moisture of a laboratory petri dish. Rituals thrive in the world of lived experience; they germinate in the loam of human foibles and a desire for survival and transcendence; they grow conjuncturally out of the cultural and political mediations that shape the contours of groups and institutions serving as agencies of socialization.

Rituals are not ethereal entities distinct from the vagaries of everyday living, as though they are somehow perched atop the crust of culture as a bundle of abstract norms and ordinances to be enacted apart from the concrete constitution of individual roles and relations out of which daily life is built. Rather, rituals are inherently social and political; they cannot be understood in isolation from how individuals are located biographically and historically in various traditions of mediation (e.g. clan, gender, home environment, peer group culture). Ensconced in the framework of both private and institutional life, rituals become part of the socially conditioned, historically acquired and biologically constituted rhythms and metaphors of human agency. And while rituals tend to sprout anywhere people gather in groups, their fluorescence becomes the most intricate and textured in the religious life where individuals adorn their experience with the rich symbols of transcendence and cultivate their rituals as dramas of the divine.

Although the concept of ritual stretches from Canaanite priest-kings, to Cargo cults, to the Catholic mass, rituals remain as inalienable a fact of modern secular society as the proliferation of high-rise buildings, crowded freeways, neon lights, acid rain, 'born again' televangelists, or family trips to McDonald's. Anthropologist Conrad P. Kottak's brief ethnography of the Big Mac offers us stimulating evidence that eating at McDonald's is a ritual event – one that is grounded in the 'clean cut' value system of suburban churchgoers.[15] (The fact that McDonald's is America's symbol of suburban family solidarity only intensifies the evil surrounding the worst mass murder in America's history which took place in a small town McDonald's restaurant near the Mexican border.)

Rituals serve as both the pillars of support for urban social structure and the substratum which supports those very pillars; that is, rituals are attributes of both the infrastructure and super-structure of society. In their absence both familial and corporate structures would collapse. Rituals are imperishably rooted in man's search for transcendence. They provide for contemporary man and woman dimensions to their existence which have been termed symbolic, holy, mythic or poetic. However, they do not appertain exclusively to the domain of the *logos*; rather, they are situated more specifically in 'the realm of gesture, of external and corporeal manifestation' (Panikkar, 1977, p. 9). Ritual 'belongs to the domain of incarnation, of the visible, the temporal and the spacial' (p. 9).

The human personality is born out of and sustained by ritual (Erikson, 1966). A ritual transforms itself into a type of psychosocial vessel in which the catalytic action of symbols and root paradigms promotes the fermentation of world views. Rituals are the generative forces by which we, as social actors, adjudicate our instinctual conflicts with our surrounding culture –with both public and private symbols providing the *mise-en-scène*; at the same time they are the articulating mechanisms of social control which literally 'put us in our place'. Ritual lies in the motional world; it 'thematizes' its milieu through 'mindful' bodily gesture. Ritual symbols often point beyond themselves and yet participate in that to which they point (Brenneman *et al.*, 1982; Tillich, 1956). However, engaging in ritual is not a process that just happens to us; it is a process in which necessarily we are actively and daily involved. Rituals constitute, to a great degree, the major semantic networks, cultural contexts, and ideational domains through which attempts are made to regulate social life and keep it from slipping into what Sally Falk Moore calls 'a flux of indeterminacy' (Moore and Myerhoff, 1977, p. 19). Rituals are semiogenetic: they frame, punctuate and bracket the flow of social life, thereby assigning meaning to events. Rituals are the 'corporate re-membering by the whole community' (Sullivan, 1975, p. 19). Rituals frequently serve normative functions, governed by categorical imperatives or 'oughts' that are rooted in the psychic structures of social actors through the process of continuous socialization. The cultural forms which constitute our industrial life are tacitly shaped in terms of, and therefore dominated by, the parabolic and discursive contexts provided by ritual symbols and metaphors. Yet regardless of how copiously human nature lends itself to the ritualizing process, we seldom become consciously aware of its structuring effects on our perception and behaviour.

RITUAL AND SYMBOLIC MEANING

According to Grimes (1982a), a ritual is a form of symbolic action composed primarily of gestures (the enactment of evocative rhythms which constitute dynamic symbolic acts) and postures (a symbolic stilling of action). Ritual gesture is formative; it is inescapably and integrally related to everyday action and may oscillate between randomness and formality. The apparent simplicity of this conception of ritual is deceiving. For instance, the critic of ritual may be tempted to see a tautology embedded in the assertion that ritual is a symbolic act. The more astute and indefatigable critic, claiming that my position on ritual begs the question, might arguably retort: 'If ritual is a form of symbolic behaviour, and if all behaviour

is symbolic, doesn't it follow that all behaviour is ritual behaviour?'
The question itself is double-edged. For the philosopher it is perhaps
rhetorical but for the ritologist it has fundamental significance.
Ritual so conceived serves as a type of blank cheque on which almost
any explanation of social and cultural process can be written – a
way of refining the concept to the vanishing point and out of
existence. Moreover, I may be accused of skirting a theoretical abyss
by using circular logic to advance my argument, resulting in an
explanation of ritual which achieves little theoretical rigour but
which possesses an evocative rhetorical appeal. I would begin to
untangle this Gordian knot by claiming that not all symbolic
behaviour is ritualized behaviour. Symbols, in order to be considered ritualistic, *must evoke gestures* (Grimes, 1982a, p. 61). Next,
I would argue that not all ritual meaning is symbolic. Within a
ritual, the relation between a signal and its referent may also be
indexical or self-referential (Rappaport, 1979, pp. 179–83). Finally
I would point out that, in searching through the dossier of ritual
behaviour, we discover that rituals do more than simply inscribe
or display symbolic meanings or states of affairs but *instrumentally
bring states of affairs into being*. To argue that a ritual simply reflects
or mirrors meaning in an *ex post facto* manner is to trip philosophically
over the same stumbling block that has, over the years, impeded
many students of ritual. Furthermore, to sponsor such a view is
to separate the medium of ritual from its message. Rituals do not
merely reflect – they *articulate* (Delattre, 1978, p. 38).[16] By ignoring this aspect of ritual, we are mortgaging our understanding of
contemporary cultural forms.

Ritual gestures are always concerned with the genesis of action;
they 'constitute a class of mediating actions which transform the
style and values of everyday action, thereby becoming the very
ground of action itself' (Grimes, 1982a, p. 61). Rituals may be considered as gestural embodiments of the inner cognitive or affective
states of the performers. Grimes claims that gestures are metaphors
of the body: they display the identifications which constitute the
performer. A 'virtual' gesture may generate corresponding thought
and feeling patterns as well as reinforce particular values. It may
be equally argued that rituals constitute, at least in part, the gestural
embodiments of the dominant metaphors of the social structure.

The tendency to perceive ritual simply as a routine or habit is
a bowdlerization or corrupted usage of the term ritual which has
invaded public discourse since the advent of high technology.

Properly speaking, however, a routine or habit may be a genuine form of ritualized behaviour. That is, a routine is more than a ritual surrogate; a habit, more than a psychoanalytic stepchild. But while routine or habitual actions do in fact fall under the morphological umbrella of ritual, they must necessarily be considered as paler, less authentic, more 'wraithlike' forms of ritualization. 'Habituation', says Grimes, 'is the bane of ritualization . . . imposed in the form of ought-filled, unmindful heteronomy, and then the secret of this imposition is glossed over' (1982a, p. 38). Some scholars treat routines and habits as subspecies or subrealms of ritual. Barbara Myerhoff, for instance, distinguishes rituals from habits and customs by their utilization of symbols; rituals are said to possess a significance beyond the information transmitted. While they are described as accompanying routine or instrumental proceedings, ritual symbols are said to point beyond themselves, endowing routines and customs with a larger meaning (1977, pp. 199–200).

WHAT A RITUAL IS NOT

Though we long for permanence, social life is always mutable. The same applies to our ritual systems. A ritual may be conceived as a series of encoded movements that must oscillate between excessive randomness (high entropy) and rigid structure (high redundancy). High entropy means that there are a wide variety of ways that an energy system may be arranged (cf. Campbell, 1982). This echoes Turner's concept of antistructure. Rigid structure or redundancy means that there are few possible ways of arranging a system; Sally Falk Moore (1975) refers to this feature as the process of regularization. Sullivan describes ritual as 'the "rescuing" of possibilities from the flux of life' (1975, p. 25). Ritual gestures with high redundancy amplify the uniformity and symmetry of social process; they draw together and catenate various symbolic events into a meaningful pattern. Ritual actions high in entropy tend to draw our attention to the tenuousness and arbitrariness of social life (as in the carnival or rites of inversion).

Non-ritual action may be described as a form of 'gestural noise' in which entropy is so high that all possible meanings for the gesture are equally probable. Gestural noise results from random movements lacking in predictability, syntax, codes or patterns of meanings. Gestural noise is similar to Brenneman et al.'s 'first-form of bodily awareness, a form in which body consciousness is so close to itself that, like the serpent eating its own tail, it consumes itself' (1982, p. 112). Such movements are 'self-possessed', 'premeaningful', and 'presymbolic'; they are also 'sporadic, compulsive, and lack the rhythm that is the basis for a symbolic, and later, a meaningful gesture' (p. 112).

Ritual gestures, on the other hand, are more self-reflexive; they 'possess within themselves a tendency to place greater stress upon the "pointing beyond" function of the symbol. That which is pointed to soon becomes the "meaning" of the gesture and gains greater importance itself' (p. 113).

Nascent rituals, which betray a greater randomness or variance than formal liturgies, carry with them a greater freight of information – that is, they allow a great deal of uncertainty to be resolved by participants. Nascent rituals are composed of gestures which are frequently encoded by the performers themselves; the codes are made up or improvised as the ritual transpires. Nascent rituals are more idiosyncratic and less static than formal liturgies. In the more punctilious formal liturgy, participants conform to a series of acts which they themselves do not encode (Rappaport, 1978). Actions which transpire at both poles on the continuum of gesture – pure entropy (gestural noise) and pure redundancy (invariance) – convey no information (that is, if we agree with the communications theorists who say that information is the reduction of uncertainty between two equally likely alternatives). Unlike gestural noise, a formal liturgy may still be considered ritual because (following Rappaport) although it contains little or no information, its informationlessness due to invariance conveys a sense of certainty, unquestionableness and sanctity.

TOWARDS WORKING DEFINITIONS OF RITUAL

The term ritual is a diffuse and often impalpable concept – one that has been beset with problems of definition that have haunted it for years. Strong misunderstandings interfere with its conceptualization as a coherent process. Most contemporary descriptions are inadequate, needing to be superseded by ideas which locate ritual in an emergent epistemology of gesture, symbol and metaphor. Since ritual is the principal protagonist in the most simple and complex of cultural dramas, we must attempt the prodigious task of providing it with some epistemological anchor points – some determinant character and meaning. And we must detach from the term 'ritual' the more derisory connotations with which it has been saddled. A careful determination of the meaning we wish to assign to ritual is essential to the conduct of this enquiry.

The task of defining ritual poses similar problems to that of defining dance (Grimes considers dance a 'first cousin' of ritual). Hence, one can only remain sympathetic to the remark made by Isadora Duncan: 'If I could tell you what it [dance] meant there would be no point in dancing it.' The conceptual quagmire or definitional dyscrasia in which the term ritual appears interminably trapped bespeaks the need to develop a perspective that is both broad in scope, yet concise enough to grant the concept potential to interpret student and teacher behaviour in classroom settings.

The scope of ritual scholarship is vast. Even a fleeting examination of the sweep of the ritual literature is enough to deter the most diehard scholar from attempting a definitive pronouncement on the topic. For instance, ritual has, over the years, been treated as a theme (Eliade, 1961, 1963); symbol system (Geertz, 1966); gestural grammar (Birdwhistell, 1970); metalanguage (Bateson, 1972); articulation (Delattre, 1978); distancing device (Scheff, 1977); regulating mechanism in a biotic community (Rappaport, 1971a); type of logic (Langer, 1957; Cassirer, 1955) and deep structure (Leach, 1968; Lévi-Strauss, 1967). Additionally, a ritual has been described as a social function (Durkheim, 1965); co-variant (Douglas, 1973); restricted code (Bernstein et al., 1966); standardized behaviour (Goody, 1961); primordial human need (Jung, 1953); developmental stage (Erikson, 1966); neuroreductionistic description (D'Aquili and Laughlin, 1975); role (Schechner, 1982; Goffman, 1974); mazeway (Wallace, 1970); compulsion (Freud, 1953); process (Turner, 1969, 1976); and form of play (Callois, 1961; Neale, 1969; Huizinga, 1955a). A ritual has also been considered as a mechanism for both understanding reality (Ricoeur, 1969; Gadamer, 1976; Palmer, 1969) and experiencing ultimate reality (Tillich, 1960; Berger, 1967).[17]

It is often difficult to gauge the depth and scope of the ritual process, how it encompasses desacralized as well as religious dimensions. This is not helped by the fact that the literature on ritual often reveals a concatenation of paradoxical and contradictory assessments bristling with such juxtaposed polarities as sacred and secular, structure and antistructure, rituals of resolutions, and rites of rebellion. Thus, the problem of defining ritual becomes a daunting task and especially acute on the epistemological level, particularly if one wishes to trap precise units of analysis distilled by ritual forms. Because of the spate of approaches in the literature and the often kaleidoscopic complexity of various ritual theories, it is just as difficult to develop broad units of analysis as it is to develop precise ones. Consequently, the process of ritual remains refractory to any overall proclamation. There is virtually no one conceptual organon that has achieved the agreement of all and sundry: no formulation of ritual that exercises a powerful untrammalled authority; no unimpugnable statements pronounced *ex cathedra* by an unquestionable, definitive authority. For now the issue cannot be solved, only cozened into a theoretical truce.

Part of the problem of understanding ritual goes beyond both the vagueness of the concept and the staggering array of perspectives within the literature (does the ritual tail wag the mythic dog or vice versa?); it resides in the problematic status of its central unit of expression: the symbol. To explicate ritual is, unavoidably, to examine the symbolic dimensions of social life. Rituals are best fathomed through an understanding of symbols. That rituals consist of clusters of symbols is the one unifying tenet that prevents us from merely offering quick and unambiguous answers when we are questioned as to ritual meaning. The new interest in symbol and metaphor has, to a great extent, stimulated a new interest in ritual.

It is exigent that we obtain from the vexing disputes of ritual scholars a perspective of ritual that is at least generalizable enough to apply to institutionalized school life. We must construct a baseline provisional conception – or at the very least provide some type of bench-mark or yardstick – against which a definition of instructional ritual can be cogently conceived.

PERSPECTIVE ON THE DEFINITIONAL PROBLEM

Victor Turner has called for a reevaluation of the way ritual is defined. He is particularly adamant that the 'flat view' of ritual must go (1980, p. 162). By 'flat view' he means the perspective of ritual used by functionalist anthropologists who refer to rituals as mere 'reflections' of aspects or components of the social structure. Turner, on the contrary, attributes a paradigmatic function to ritual; as a 'model for', he claims that ritual can anticipate, even generate, change'; as a 'model of', he argues that ritual 'may inscribe order in the minds, hearts, and wills of participants' (p. 163).

Grimes attempts to correct limited or 'flat' perspectives of ritual by drawing our attention to the important fact that there are both *hard* and *soft* ways of defining ritual. He distingishes between the two types of definitions as follows:

> A 'hard' definition is an abstractly stated consensus established by a tradition of usage and calling attention to what is in bounds. A 'soft' one typically congeals around nascent phenomena and calls attention to the bounding process itself or to the spaces *between* boundaries. It operates like a naming rite and develops largely on the basis of images. A hard definition of ritual is a 'model of' (Geertz, 1966: 7) properties of known rituals. A soft one is a 'model for' attending to what is yet relatively unknown about them. Hard definitions attempt to establish a clear figure. Soft ones aim at surveying and connecting adjacent fields. (1982a, p. 55)

A hard definiton creates the questionable assumption that ritual is only – or mainly – a bounded, circumscribed and somewhat frozen act. Traditional 'hard' definitions define ritual in terms of its middle phases and neglect both the emergent and incubatory phases or rituals – or the decaying ones. Unlike hard definitions, which tend to become trapped in an Aristotelian view of causality, soft definitions enable a researcher to 'catch' the processual dimensions of ritual as they transpire in the fieldsite.

In attempting to arrive at a definition of magic, Daniel Lawrence O'Keefe was reminded of the proverbial Durkheimian double-blind concerning the problems posed by the development of initial definitions before undertaking fieldwork. Durkheim had advised researchers not to begin investigations of raw, unfamiliar subject matter with a minimal hypothesis in order to avoid the creation of premature theory. Yet at the same time Durkheim insisted on a clear advance definition in order to avoid 'picking one's cases' (O'Keefe, 1982, p. 11).

I have tried to follow O'Keefe's suggestions for escaping from the Durkheimian double-bind by choosing to operationalize two types of definitions: a definition in the 'strict sense' and a definition in the 'weak sense'. The 'strict' definition (similar to Grimes's 'hard' definition) is a summary of twenty-two characteristics of ritual culled from a detailed survey of the ritual literature. The 'weak' definition (similar to Grimes's 'soft' definition) is designed to allow meaning to accumulate during fieldwork and has been modelled after definitions used by Delattre and Grimes.[18]

O'Keefe maintains that one way of avoiding equivocations on a subject that is real on several levels is to use several definitions. He claims the 'category errors' can be avoided 'by making sure that any sentence which designates phenomena in more than one of these definitions asserts a functional relationship between the two' (1982, p 11). Thus, where references are made to ritual in both the 'strict' and 'weak' sense, some kind of functional relationship is assumed to exist between the two.

The concept of ritual (in the 'strict' sense) to be used in this study is heteronomous and includes twenty-two basic elements (and a number of sub-elements) which have been ferreted out of the ritual literature – some of which conflate several discipline-specific uses of the term. The summary that follows, which I have advanced as a series of assertions, will serve as a backcloth of theoretical assumptions and descriptions surrounding ritual to be used in this study.

THE 'STRICT' DEFINITION OF RITUAL

Properties of ritual

1   A ritual has a distinct *form* in which its medium (morphological characteristics) is part of its message. The form gives the social structure a subjunctive or 'as if' quality (Myerhoff, 1977; Van Gennep, 1960; Myerhoff and Metzger, 1980; Rappaport, 1979).

2   Rituals are primarily clusters of *symbols* and can best be understood using symbolic analysis (Turner, 1969).

3   Rituals are inherently *dramatic* (Courtney, 1980).

4   Rituals are important aspects of psychosocial integration leading to personality development (Erikson, 1966; Worgul, 1980; Kavanagh, 1973; Schechner, 1982).

5   Language codified into texts may possess an inherent ritual *authority* over readers (Olson, 1980).

6   Many rituals may be termed *secular* and exhibit the formal qualities of repetition, 'special behaviour' or stylization, order and evocative presentational style or staging (Moore and Myerhoff, 1977; Turner, 1982a).

7   Rituals embody a repertoire of choices or 'tokens' which centre around specific rules or 'types' (Lewis, 1980).

8   Ritual codes (restricted and elaborate) are related to family structures and may grow out of social class divisions (Douglas, 1973; Bernstein *et al.*, 1966).

9   Rituals invariably partake of six modes (ritualization, decorum, ceremony, liturgy, magic, celebration). While these modes overlap, one mode generally dominates (Grimes, 1982a).

Functions of ritual

1   Rituals serve as a *framing device*. Framing establishes a centre/periphery or figure/ground relation which is metacommunicative; the characteristic of frame enables the ritual participants to interpret what occurs within it (Turner, 1979b; Myerhoff, 1977; Handleman, 1977).

2   Rituals encourage holistic involvement in the form of *flow* which implies a 'willing suspension of disbelief' (Turner, 1979b, 1982a).

3   Rituals communicate by classifying information in different contexts (Da Matta, 1979).

4   Rituals have the ability to *transform* participants into different social statuses as well as different states of consciousness. This is usually achieved in ritual's liminal state (e.g. communitas or antistructure) (Moore and Myerhoff, 1977; Turner, 1979b; Partridge, 1972; Myerhoff, 1975; Holmes, 1973b; Myerhoff, 1978; Bilmes and Howard, 1980).

5   Rituals *negotiate* and *articulate* meaning through distinctive *rhythms* (Delattre, 1978, 1979).

6   Rituals provoke an aura of sanctity through their morphological characteristics and by addressing themselves to supernatural entities which are not necessarily spirits but which are synonymous with aspects of 'transcendence', 'ultimate importance', or 'unquestionability' (Nagendra, 1971; Moore and Myerhoff, 1977; Panikkar, 1977; Turner, 1982a; Goffman, 1981; Smith, 1979; Rappaport, 1976, 1979, 1980).

7   Undergoing a ritual experience endows the participant with a unique type of 'ritual knowledge' (Wallace, 1966; Jennings, 1982).

8   Ritual language possesses a *performative force* which is capable

of bringing about *conventional effects* (Worgul, 1980; Rappaport, 1978, 1979; Ray, 1973; Bloch, 1974; Gill, 1977; Tambiah, 1968; Finnegan, 1969).

9 Rituals are capable of *reifying* the sociocultural world in which they are embedded (Dolgin *et al.*, 1977; Munn, 1973).

10 Rituals may *invert* the norms and values of the dominant social order (Babcock, 1978a; Yinger, 1977; Moore and Myerhoff, 1977; Gluckman, 1963; Ortiz, 1972).

11 Rituals enable participants to reflect on their own processes of interpretation as well as their location in the dominant culture (Geertz, 1966; Turner, 1974e; Rappaport, 1980).

12 Rituals have a *political* aspect to them and may embody and transmit certain ideologies or world views (Lukes, 1975; Piven, 1976; Bennett, 1980; Edelman, 1964, 1971, 1974, 1977; Cox, 1969).

13 Rituals have the capability of *fusing* polar domains of experience, such as the physical and the moral (Turner, 1982a; Worgul, 1980).

The characteristics listed in the above definition represent both structural elements of ritual and theoretical perspectives about ritual. The extent to which these features are present in any ritual will depend to a great extent on the context in which the ritual is enacted. Moreover, to state that all of these characteristics of ritual are manifest (to a greater or lesser extent) in every ritual is to imply that the conclusions of ritual are built into its very concepts. These descriptive characteristics and their functional attributes are neither foreordained nor omnipresent in the enactment of every rite. For instance, when defining a broad entity such as 'games', Wittgenstein agreed that it would be impossible to find a criterion that would fit every game. Rather, he showed games to be characterized by clusters related by 'family resemblances' whose borders are not always highly defined (O'Keefe, 1982, p. 13).

Thus, the characteristics in the above list should not be looked upon as dyed-in-the-wool descriptions but as reference points for discussion. The importance of the latter looms large if we are to focus on the heuristic usefulness of the term ritual in our discussion. These characteristics can prove fertile both in defining certain social actions as ritual and in the interpretation of ritual meaning.

THE WEAK DEFINITION OF RITUAL

I shall now include a more compact view of ritual in the form of a minimal definition (in the 'weak' or 'soft' sense). Such a definition is concerned with process and not pre-specified behaviour or extrinsic outcomes. It is designed to capture ritual *in statu nascendi*. It is framed at a level of generality in order to allow meaning to accumulate within a particular context. Yet because it bears a functional relationship to the 'strict' definition, it avoids the 'looseness' that could lead to overgeneralized descriptions and interpretations.

All definitions are mutable and subject to modification and reassessment in the light of continuous research. Definitions should not be employed as though they conferred some form of indisputable, omniscient facts. Thus, in offering the following definition 'in the weak sense', I share with Delattre his perspective that 'definitions serve best as relatively compact points of departure for systematic inquiry rather than as conclusions, and that they will therefore call in time for redefinition' (1979, p. 36).

Ritualization is a process which involves the incarnation of symbols, symbol clusters, metaphors, and root paradigms through formative bodily gesture. As forms of enacted meaning, rituals enable social actors to frame, negotiate, and articulate their phenomenological existence as social, cultural, and moral beings.

The above definition is coincident with the perspective of Marsh *et al.* that 'in addition to rule-governed patterns of conduct [rituals consist of] . . . a distinct and identifiable system of symbols which communicate particular meanings within a microsociety, and in so doing accomplish certain social acts . . .' (1978, p. 121). Defined as such, rituals must not be seen as transparent vehicles that house prepackaged signifieds. Ideological aspects of ritualization reside in the relationship and interdependence of symbols (signifiers) and signifieds. The logic of autonomy and materiality of a ritual are always linked to macro relations of power and privilege and to the logic of capital.

Chapter 2

The setting

WEDNESDAY, 21 OCTOBER

A student knocked on the door. 'Sorry I'm late but I had to take my mom to the unemployment office.'

'Okay', said one of the teachers. He then added, 'I feel sorry for that kid.'

CATHOLIC SCHOOLS

In 1867, the British North America Act empowered the Provinical Government to make laws in relation to education, with the provision that 'nothing in any such law shall prejudicially affect any right or privilege with respect to denominational schools which any class of persons have by law in the Province at the Union'. Thus, the BNA Act protected the educational rights of the Catholic minority in Upper Canada and the Protestant minority in Lower Canada. However, in 1915, Department of Education regulations prohibited any elementary school in a high school area from offering programmes beyond grade 10. Catholics were therefore prohibited under the existing tax regulations to send their children to Catholic schools after grade 10. This regulation was challenged right through to the Privy Council in 1924. However, the courts ruled that there was no grievance under law but no justice either.

As of 30 September 1981, the total enrolment of students in both public and separate schools in Ontario was 782,000 and 430,000 respectively. Today in Ontario there are approximately 1,100 Catholic elementary schools; twenty-seven Catholic junior high schools (7–10); and seventy Catholic high schols (9–13). In 1980 the total separate school per pupil revenue was 96.8 per cent of the public school per pupil revenue. In Metro Toronto, 95,000 students are enrolled in Catholic separate schools. There are 2.4 million Catholics in Ontario – about 35 per cent of the province's 8.5 million residents. In general, Catholic parents feel that it is their democratic right to educate their children in the separate school system. The primary objective of Catholic Education has been put forward as 'concerning itself with the whole truth of man and God. Catholic education should teach children to think, judge and act consistently in accordance with the example and teaching of Christ.'[1]

The Catholic school community insists that each student be taught to the maximum of his or her potential, which includes 'the opportunity to grow in Christian revelation so that some day he/she may make a mature, free and personal commitment to Christ.'[2] Reverend Laurence K. Shook argues that Catholic education is relevant today because it accepts the sacred 'and carries out its educational objectives in this context . . . Secular education seems . . . to fail for Catholics because it has no contact with the sacred lived'.[3]

The Catholic position on religion classes is very clear. Catholics do not feel that a religion lesson at the end or the beginning of the day in non-Catholic schools would be sufficient to ensure that Catholic children are properly prepared in their religion:

> A formal class in religious instruction could and should be an important segment of the life of every Catholic student. Such classes, if taught in the Public School, could assist Catholic girls and boys who attend these classes in updating their religious knowledge and in pointing out some of the things which the Catholic religion means in today's modern world. The point to remember, however, is that it is not primarily in the one period a day devoted to religious education that we find the difference between the Catholic schools and the Public Schools. Other differences are even more significant.[4]

The formal distinction between Catholic (separate) schools and public schools is articulated as follows:

a   The Catholic School Faculty must be basically a group of Christians, academically and professionally qualified to be sure, but with a Christian consciousness about themselves, a Christian sense of community, a Christian purpose and a common Christian life.

b   These teachers attempt to offer this experience of meaningful
    Christian community with their students who have the same
    religious consciousness and purpose. The Christian students
    themselves are able to deepen their own spiritual convictions
    and values by sharing common faith experiences with others
    of their peers in the normal setting of their school life and at
    a time in their own lives, when such are most necessary and
    helpful.
        The sum total of all these influences, many of them intangible
    in themselves, give the Catholic School its distinctively Chris-
    tian character.[5]

Until the landmark decision by the Ontario government to fund
Catholic schools to grade 13 (a ruling which occurred shortly after
this research was conducted), the law permitted Catholic school
boards to administer schools only to the end of grade 10. Therefore,
many Catholic students were never given the opportunity to acquire
a sense of continuity within their own educational system. Only
those students whose parents could afford tuition fees for grades
11, 12 and 13 were able to obtain their required twenty-seven credits
in the Catholic school system.

    Catholics justify the use of public funds for the purpose of
furthering their religious convictions by arguing that

a   Separate Schools were established because of the religious con-
    viction of the Catholic parents. These schools are a part of the
    Public School structure and thus we are entitled to operate with
    public funds. In today's materialistic society the importance
    of religious and spiritual values cannot be negated; on the con-
    trary, these values must be cherished and nurtured through
    the schools that uphold them.
b   The Separate School Trustees are elected by the people and
    hence are completely separate from the financial operation of
    Catholic Churches. Thus, public funds used to operate Separate
    Schools are not used to subsidize the church.[6]

In June 1984 the Premier of Ontario agreed to give Catholic high
schools full government funding by 1988. However, he asked, in
exchange, that Catholic high schools hire non-Catholic teachers
for the next ten years and stop giving priority to Catholic students
in favour of universal access for all students. While there has been
discussion in the ranks of Catholic officials, it appears likely that

the Separate School Board will make some concessions to the government request. Money means survival – even if it means survival in a different form. (At the time of writing, debates surrounding Catholic funding continue to appear in the nation's press.)

Catholic education is very different from that offered by many Christian evangelical schools, avoiding the simplistic, fundamentalist fervour of the latter. That the Catholic Church has moved away from a narrow, literal biblicism is nowhere more evident than in the comments of Pope John Paul II at CERN physics laboratory in Geneva:

> I say to the Christians . . . May you create an existential unity in your intellectual activities between the two orders of reality (science and religion) which tend to be opposed to each other as if they were antithetical; the quest for truth and the certainty that you already know the source of truth.[7]

THE COMMUNITY

Toronto's Portuguese community was generally unfamiliar to me. Initially, there seemed to be little to distinguish this particular part of the city from other 'ethnic' enclaves – except perhaps the colourfully painted homes and the profusion of rust-splotched cars that drove by with crucifixes and colourful medallions of Senhor Santo Cristo dangling from the rear-view mirrors. After a few days of exploring the streets, a number of distinctive features pressed for attention: the baskets of plastic flowers that hung on verandas; the aluminium doors that featured full-colour replicas of St Francis and the birds on the centre panel; the front yard gardens that were decorated with small shrines made from bathtubs turned on their ends and buried half way into the ground; the plaster statues of the Virgin, entwined with strings of blinking coloured lights, that stood near the entrance gates; the houses painted in cotton candy colours: pistachio green, bright red, orange, pink and coral (individual bricks were usually outlined with white paint); and the fences constructed from concrete blocks and decorated with pottery shards, broken glass and pop bottles. Angel brick, wrought iron fences and porch railings also appeared as popular decorative items.

The Portuguese community is fairly self-contained – an attempt to create a microcosm of Portugal or to extend some characteristic Azorean village beliefs and customs to the heart of the city. Most

Metro Toronto Portuguese immigrants are from the Azores (about 65 per cent), an archipelago consisting of nine volcanic islands and the Formigas rocks which is located in the Atlantic (strategically important from a Western alliance and military standpoint). The southeastern portion, comprising São Miguel and Santa Maria, lies approximately 900 miles west of Lisbon, Portugal. Most of the inhabitants are Portuguese Roman Catholics. The Azores are part of the archbishopric of Lisbon. There were 31,000 Portuguese in Toronto in 1971 and in the ten years that followed the number tripled.[8]

Canada's accessibiilty as a land of promise and haven of opportunity has been a major symbol that has drawn Azorean immigrants to Toronto since the Second World War. The concept of immigrating to the land of plenty – a place where the belly is always full and the unfettered spirit is allowed to soar – is undeniably magnificent, the reality inevitably less so. The Portuguese exodus to economically richer Canada has not made for an easy cultural transition. The extent to which Portuguese (and Azorean) culture has been compromised through immigration to Toronto is an issue of considerable concern to Portuguese leaders.

Canadians are apt to describe Azoreans not as the exploited poor but as an exotic race who would add to the Canadian stock a much needed element of 'colour' and 'industriousness'. Yet, among some Canadians there exists a growing paranoia about being 'outbreeded' by darker-skinned nationalities. Not all Canadians accept the concept of multiculturalism with equanimity.

Many of Toronto's Azorean immigrants were farmer-gardeners and possess few urban skills. They generally distrust the more 'sophisticated' Portuguese from the mainland – a fact which was confirmed by a number of informants including a Portuguese teacher and a priest. One explanation for the Azorean hostility to the mainland Portuguese was traced back to the Second World War, when mainland soldiers were sent to defend the islands. Bad feelings were engendered during the soldiers' stay (supposedly having to do with the soldiers' treatment of Azorean women) and have not been forgotten up to and including the present day. Portugal has a legacy of historically sedimented oppression, ruthless dictatorship and economic hardship. The socialist government of Mario Soares is Portugal's fifteenth government since 1974, the year democracy was restored during the 'revolution of carnations' (when a group of reform-minded army officers, sporting red carnations in their rifle barrels, took over the government). Portugal is western Europe's poorest nation with a per capita income of approximately $2,000 per year. The inflation rate currently runs at approximately 20 per cent while the unemployment rate is estimated at 16 per cent and on the rise. Industry has traditionally been poor and is presently operating at two-thirds of its potential.[9]

Since the overthrow of the Salazar-Caetano dictatorship in Portugal in 1974, more than ten political parties have merged. (Of course in 1974 Salazar was already dead and buried, but his style of dictatorship was continued by his successor, Marcello Caetano.) Free elections were held in Portugal in 1975. A year later, General Antonio Ramalho Eanes was elected and he appointed Mario Soares as Prime Minister. Under an agreement that allows them to hold dual citizenship, Portuguese immigrants are still permitted to vote in their homeland. Voting may take place in Canada for candidates running for office in Portugal. Consequently, politicians sometimes visit Toronto to court more support.[10]

Portuguese immigrants are often ill-equipped to face their new world. After their arrival in Toronto, they frequently secure unskilled blue-collar jobs as, for example, welders, office cleaners, dish washers, piece workers in garment factories, and mail room operators. However, some are able to open their own stores, churches, social clubs and auto repair shops. The stereotype runs that the men wield shovels, trundle wheelbarrows and lay bricks while the women scrub the floors of affluent WASP mansions.

It has been reported that when you walk down a street in a Portuguese neighbourhood, it is rare to find children playing who are unsupervised. I did not discover this to be the case. I frequently found groups of Portuguese students – including girls – hanging around the streetcorner and at the plaza at all hours of the day.

At home, Portuguese parents still appear strict disciplinarians despite the generally more 'liberal' culture in which they have chosen to live. In many cases, both girls and boys are encouraged to leave school early to help support the family. Unemployed Portuguese immigrants are often prey to bureaucratic scourges: the unemployment insurance office, the welfare office, the Manpower office; they are sometimes forced to go on welfare, but welfare carries a strong social stigma.

Newspaper clippings from a decade ago discussed complaints from Portuguese immigrants who accused the Canadian immigration authorities of misrepresenting Canada by telling prospective Azorean immigrants that there was no unemployment in Ontario. Toronto often appeared as a ticket to Xanadu or Eldorado for many Portuguese immigrants.

John Slinger writes that when

> the Portuguese lands at Toronto International Airport he believes the streets of Toronto are paved with gold. When he steps out of the terminal he learns three things: First, the streets aren't paved with gold. Second, some of the streets aren't even paved. And, third, he is the guy who is going to have to pave them. . . . Teachers tell stories of children's grades slipping, in fact of elementary-school youngsters dozing off in the morning because they spent the night with their parents picking dew worms for sale as bait.[11]

Some Portuguese are worried that the old traditions are slowly fading. During one Portuguese carnival, a barker was reputedly heard saying: 'Come see the bright, bright houses, folks. See them while you can.'[12]

In a recent report, Elaine Carey notes that new organizations such as the Portuguese Business and Professional People's Association and the Portuguese Interagency Network are starting to gain support.[13] In addition, women from the Working Women Community Centre are attempting to provide language classes for women – especially women who work in factories or cleaning jobs and are being denied access to government-sponsored language classes because they are sponsored by their husbands. The women from the Centre are also lobbying for changes to the National Training Act that will open language classes to women who are not sole support mothers.[14]

In the area immediately surrounding the school, there were no bright-coloured houses. Children did play in the streets unsupervised. Occasionally girls were seen tightly girded in leather skirts or designer jeans, walking arm in arm with boys. The school was not located in the heart of Toronto's Portuguese community but in an adjacent area that was also heavily populated by Italian Canadians. However, as one informant pointed out, the Italians were slowly moving out as the Portuguese were moving in. One area resident told me that when the Portuguese began attending one of the local churches, they successfully pressured the priest to remove the statue of the Virgin of Lourdes (hands outstretched) and replace it with a statue of the Virgin of Fatima (hands clasped in prayer). The Virgin of Lourdes reportedly still rests in the church basement.

One of the major events of the Portuguese community is the Santo Cristo festival during which time 40,000 Portuguese immigrants crowd the streets to witness a procession carrying a statue of Senhor Santo Cristo (as the Portuguese call Christ).

The Portuguese community at present is marked by the absence of a powerful unified and articulate grass roots movement that could serve as a collective advocate for Portuguese equality in the school system.

THE PORTUGUESE IMMIGRANT

There is not much literature available pertaining to the transition of the Portuguese family from their homeland to Toronto. Ethnographic materials about Azorean youth are even less readily available. What does exist – and much of it relates to the Portuguese experience in the United States – will give us an initial insight into Portuguese youth and an entrée for examining the relationship between the school and the Azorean student. These existing studies will be supplemented – and modified where necessary – by surveys conducted by the Toronto Board of Education and by interviews undertaken during this investigation.

According to the Toronto Board of Education *Every Student Survey* (which was completed by 98 per cent of the Board's 96,000 students on 30 May 1975), children born in Portugal and the Azores are now the largest group of foreign-born students in Toronto public schools. The survey reveals that the better the job held by parents, the more likely the child is to succeed in school. It reports that

> for Portuguese children, there is a 74.2 per cent chance that the head of the household will be in the lowest occupational group (which includes laborers and factory workers). For children born in Canada and whose home language is English, this percentage is only 25.5. At the top end of the socio-economic scale, Portuguese children had only a 0.3 per cent chance of the head of their household being in the highest (mainly professional) occupational group. 13.3 per cent of English-speaking household heads are in this top category ... the survey [shows] that for 72 per cent of working mothers whose children's first language was English, this figure is 27 per cent. And only 1.7 per cent of working mothers

whose children's first language is not English are in the highest occupational category (mainly professional jobs). 7.6 per cent of English-speaking working mothers are in this category.[15]

The survey also showed that 42 per cent of Toronto students were found in the lowest socioeconomic group and that they had a 20 per cent chance of ending up in basic level programmes (non-university stream) whereas students whose parents were in the highest occupation group had a 3 per cent chance of ending up in such a programme. It was discovered that a higher proportion of students for whom English is a second language are in vocational classes because it is more likely that their parents are in low-income jobs. Socioeconomic status was found to be a greater predictor of student success than either country of birth or mother tongue.

A 1982 report conducted by the Toronto Board of Education entitled *Post Secondary Plans of Grade Eight Students and Related Variables* isolated two groups of grade 8 students: those who were considering university and felt they had the ability to succeed; and those who were not considering university and felt they did not have the ability. Over 20 per cent of the Portuguese students surveyed fell into the latter group, compared to less than 5 per cent of East Indian, Ukrainian, Chinese, Polish, Jewish, Japanese and Korean children. Portuguese children were the least likely to be found in the first group, most likely to be found in the second group, and likely to rate low in socioeconomic status.

Not all Portuguese immigrants are inwardly adjusted towards industrial life: they often arrive in Toronto devoid of the inner resources to become what our society demands: industrious, self-promoting and obedient workers. And once they do manage to secure a job, they must learn to make even greater adjustments. Part of this adjustment involves understanding a new management hierarchy with its associated positions and symbols. Crespi (1979) comments that

> Instead of inferring a stranger's social position from family name and reputation, which in Portugal represent 'social credit cards,' immigrants must learn to interpret and act on subtle differences in dress, speech and other symbols that distinguish 'big and little bosses' from co-workers, potential friends from adversaries, and so on.[16]

Within the Azorean community, work is highly respected but is most often restricted to 'manual work'. Accustomed to the survival skills of life in the country, both children and parents 'excel in concrete operations rather than abstract ones, in visible and touchable evidences rather than in rational logic, in facts rather than theories.'[17]

Because of their large families, Portuguese families find it inconvenient to rent apartments. Flats or apartments are often perceived as restrictive because the mother feels pressured to keep the children quiet. So the Portuguese family usually purchases a house. But in order to help pay for the mortgage, mothers and older children are encouraged to go out to work.

Most families are brought to Canada by relatives, and they usually enter communities almost wholly composed of Portuguese immigrants, many of whom persevere in the old customs – country and consanguinity being highly valued attributes of Portuguese culture. Children find it much easier to learn the new language than the parents who are usually too busy and too tired to go to night school to learn English. Despite their willingness to fit into their new country, Portuguese parents try ardently to preserve the values of the 'old country' against change.

The generation gap among the Portuguese is very wide. In some agrarian areas of Portugal, dating is a 'highly ritualized and formal behaviour' which is wholly incompatible with the informal dating of Canadian teens. In Portugal, boys and girls rarely date since stringent courtship patterns, which leave little room for ambiguity about matters of sex-role comportment, dictate that boys have to wait a considerable length of time (often years) before being invited to the girl's home. During the initial visits, the boy and girl

> are allowed to talk, the girl from the window and the boy outside. When both families agree to let the courtship continue, the boy may come to the home on days designated by the father and the boy can go out with the girl provided they are accompanied by a chaperone.[18]

Da Cunha maintains that the unconscious ideal model for dating is the 'namoro à janela' (dating at the window). He writes: 'From this ideal to the informal, short-term and sometimes simultaneous dating of more than one person there is a gap that many parents don't want to bridge.'[19] Family breakdown is more common in

Canada than in the Azores. Breakdown often occurs as families become estranged through long separation. In recent years men came to Canada as visitors; they could not send for their families until they had obtained landed immigrant status. Once they managed to bring their families to Canada, the parents began to work at jobs at different hours and this also served to separate the family.

There are many adjustment difficulties for Portuguese immigrants related to education and occupational skills: differences in family patterns, transition from rural to urban life and transition from a conservative to a putatively freer sociey. For instance, Portuguese workers, a large percentage of whom are unskilled, find frequent job changes inevitable and very difficult. They are often rejected for jobs because they lack 'Canadian experience'. Boys who had left school in Portugal to work to help support their families are now, in Canada, forced to attend school until they are 16. When Portuguese students start following the 'Westernized' practices of Canadian youth, the mother usually acts as a buffer between the children and the father.

Portuguese workers who are lucky enough to find jobs are often exploited. Numerous instances have been recorded in which Portuguese workers were paid less than other workers and often worked long hours without overtime pay. In addition, when Portuguese workers find themselves in straitened circumstances they find it difficult to seek social assistance:

> They are referred from one office to another in different parts of the city and are very diffident about talking to officials because of their language handicap and their ignorance of the services provided. They feel they are often treated in an unfriendly manner in government offices.[20]

Elaine Carey has noted that the reluctance of the Portuguese to apply for social assistance has led to a lack of community support services for other ethnic groups. Only now, she contends, are those services beginning to get established. A Portuguese community worker is quoted as saying:

> The last thing they [the Portuguese] do when they get laid off is to go on unemployment insurance ... they are entitled to apply right away but they don't. They go around looking for another job for many weeks first. They don't like to exploit and they don't like to be exploited.[21]

Wallace Lambert has compared Portuguese immigrant parents with their counterparts in Portugal, and has uncovered an interesting set of 'value changes' attributable to new life experiences in the United States and also a set of 'value persistences'. Relative to American parents, Portuguese parents 'are harsher in their reactions to outbursts of social temper or aggressivity and are more inclined to discourage independence gestures; at the same time they are more lenient on requests for guest privileges and on displays of insolence.'[22] The sharp contrast suggests that Portuguese homeland parents are more concerned with managing the aggressive impulses of their children than American parents; they are less concerned with punishing insolence directed at them by their children. And while Portuguese parents encourage their children to invite playmates home, they discourage their children to visit other homes. Lambert maintains that, in contrast, American parents place more value on having their children work out interpersonal squabbles on their own; they encourage gestures of independence and discourage dependence on playmates. Moreover, they demand respect from their children and are more apt to react strongly against any display of insolence towards them.[23]

Portuguese mothers and fathers were also found by Lambert to react more in unison than American mothers or fathers. For example, American fathers are more inclined than their wives to withold gestures of comfort and they expect more sex-role differentiations. The Portuguese families do not exhibit such parental diversity.

Lambert accounts for a number of instances of 'value change' on the part of Portuguese immigrants who are now settled and bringing up their families in America. They appear to be more lenient on guest privileges and have moved away from old-country norms with regard to sex-role expectations.[24]

Lambert informs us that the single most important influence on parental reactions turns out to be the social class backgrounds of parents, not their ethnicity. In addition, we are told that the values of Portuguese parents are generally more in line with American working-class values than American middle-class values. Value changes are, in fact, consistently in the direction of working-class norms. In the cases where the values of the Portuguese immigrant parents did not change, these values were already very similar to those of American working-class parents. Lambert remarks that a simple rule . . . seems to guide Portuguese immigrant parents in their attempts to adjust to the American host society: in cases where one's values are off the norms, modify values in the direction of the norms; where values are not at odds with local norms, hold fast. This would mean that the Portuguese immigrant parents have focused mainly on American working-class rather than middle-class norms, and reasonable as this may seem it is fascinating to us that this was apparently not the strategy followed by Italian and Greek immigrant parents who, although of the same socioeconomic background as the Portuguese immigrants, set their sights more on midle-class than working-class norms.[25]

During my fieldwork at St Ryan, I was able to talk to a popular young Portuguese priest (I'll call him Father Eldorado) from a near-by church who spoke very candidly about some of the problems that he saw facing the Portuguese immigrant.

Peter: What are the Portuguese festivals like?
Priest: When they go to a wedding, the children drink, dance with parents. People enjoy to see the young kids dancing and having a good time. Everybody is relaxed. There is not that atmosphere that you have to be 18 to drink. You social drink; you don't get drunk – that counts as part of the meal. If you go to a Portuguese family they always have wine or beer at least once a day with meals. If a child comes home from school wet, I remember back home when I was a kid, it was raining and my mother took a towel, dried my hair, and gave me a little brandy and a hot cup of tea. I didn't like it but she thought of it as medicine. It was a simple way to avoid colds; it wasn't anything to get drunk – it was prescribed by my mother.
Peter: There isn't a conflict between Italian and Portuguese students, then?
Priest: Not that much. The only conflict will be a Portuguese mother or Italian mother would say to her son and daughter, how come you're going to marry an Italian? How come you're going to marry a Portuguese? I can never talk to her or him because she doesn't speak my language. Because they love to talk to their daughter or son-in-law every day. Portuguese mothers call every day on the telephone, how are you doing, how are the kids?
Peter: What about the public rituals?

Priest: The Portuguese now are having different celebrations than they did five years ago. There is a very strong attitude among some priests and lay people to rethink and rework them in order to purify them. For instance, in Portugal everybody from the town got together for a procession; they sang high mass, give to the sick, old and aged. Now here, in Canada – now what you have is the cops, Miss Azores or Miss Lisbon in the procession; the mayor wants to come, the local politicians want to come as a way of winning sympathy for the next election, business men want to advertise in the procession, so there has been a use of the Church by people who don't even belong. . . . Even Joe Clark has been there – put stickers on the kids.

Peter: What about the church here?

Priest: There is a great shortage of Portuguese priests in Toronto. There is a Canadian priest for every four dozen people. There is a Portuguese priest for every nine to ten thousand people. Sometimes an Anglo priest will say two masses on Sunday. A Portuguese priest will say four or five.

THE EDUCATIONAL MILIEU

MONDAY, 2 NOVEMBER

The first thing that struck me when I entered the school was a picture of His Holiness John Paul II that stood about eye level at the end of the hall. This was, indeed, a Catholic school.

Although I had made a profession of faith as a Roman Catholic over seven years ago, this was one of the few times that I had been inside a Catholic school. At the main office the vice-principal, looking chipper in a Donegal tweed suit, pulled up a chair beside me and beckoned me to sit down.

He told me that there were three teachers who were willing to let me observe them. Initially, he had asked two other teachers but was told that they would feel too intimidated. I thanked him profusely for the opportunity of doing research in his school. Perhaps I was too profuse. At any rate, he seemed pleased that I was pleased. I felt strange sitting there in a pair of ill-fitting pressed slacks and a shirt and tie. I felt like a salesman from Radio Schack. The vice-principal confirmed what the head of the research Department at the Separate School Board had told me on the telephone that this school was a 'problem' school – one of the big 'problem' inner city schools.

After class, I went into the planning room and ate lunch with Peggy, a supply teacher, and a teacher from another suite. They were talking about the previous day. All of them claimed it was the worst day of the year. They said that it was due to the rainy weather. Weather, they said, affects the students' behaviour. Brock came in and joined the discussion. Brock said that when it rains, the students can't 'escape outside'.

I was told that last year the students would congregate in the nearby park where forty girls at a time would 'go at it' against rival gangs.

One teacher said that she enjoyed teaching at St Ryan because the teachers stressed strictness.

'These kids appreciate it when you come down hard on them,' she said.

The same teacher had once taught in a school where a pregnant teacher was kicked in the stomach by students ('who were looking for a good laugh') and lost her baby. 'And you know what?' she said. 'The principal didn't do a thing about it!'

Brock and some other teachers confessed that they had been threatened with beatings by students at St Ryan. They described a fight that had occurred the previous day.

'One student damn near had his head taken off,' Brock said, in a half-bragging manner.

THURSDAY, 12 NOVEMBER

As a doctoral candidate, I was participating in the second phase of a three-phase rite of passage, the rubrics of which were laid down by previous generations of scholars: (1) the successful formulation of research proposal; (2) collecting research data in a fieldsite; and (3) withdrawing from the fieldsite to reflect upon and analyse one's data. (Participating in fieldwork is really a subrite in the overall passage to becoming a scholar.) At one level, I had the support of the teachers: they expressed a genuine desire that my fieldwork should run smoothly: at another level, they were aware that my research put them at risk: to what extent would I sacrifice them in

order to sharpen the critical edge of my study? Doctoral disserta-
tions have frequently been critical of the status quo; moreover, many
scholars have been known to build their reputations at the expense
of their informants, or by deconstructing the social order. To what
extent did the teachers consider themselves potential victims of my
scholarly ambition? The teachers were trapped in a double-bind:
On the one hand, if they agreed to be observed, they opened
themselves up to be criticized by the researcher; if they refused,
then they risked provoking animosity from the principal (who understandably wanted to co-operate with the Research Department of
the Board); or – perhaps more threatening – they may be suspected
of attempting to hide their incompetence. Yet even when the
teachers agreed to be observed, they still held power over the
research. They could, for instance, disagree with the interpretation of the study and thereby erode some of its credibility.

During the beginning of my fieldwork in the suite I was a
'floater': I wandered around the room at will, recorded lessons and
listened to conversations. I left the suite whenever I felt like going
to the washroom or having a drink. Then I decided to go through
the very same motions as the students – sitting at a desk, listening
to the teacher, and even trying to sketch out and work at some
of the assignments in my note pad.

Overall, I tried hard throughout my fieldwork to be more than
just an academic sharp-talker dressed in the stereotypical tweed
and denim uniform of the learned researcher – the type of observer
who, stuffed into a student's chair (to show that he's just 'one of
the boys'), would sit at the back of the room and scribble incessantly
into an ominous black binder (trying to appear dutiful and
scholarly). I wanted to win the confidence of the teachers and
students and encourage them to react to me as an individual first,
and an observer second. Yet at the same time I was cautious not
to tamper with the 'natural script' of the suite. The rewriting of
reality would come soon enough – in my analysis. It wasn't easy
in practice to avoid the ethnographic pitfall described by Janulin:
that anthropologists 'conduct research like colonial barbers; they
cut the hair (of their subjects) in *their* own style' (Janulin, 1970,
p. 274. Quoted in Stoller, 1982, p. 2).

Before entering the fieldsite, I attempted to undergo a certain
askesis, an *unlearning* in which I was able to prepare my mind for
receiving the phenomena under investigation – that is, without being
clouded by the writings of Turner, Grimes, Rappaport, etc.

I reminded myself of a juror, who, having heard some opinions of the trial leaked through the media, nevertheless tried (perhaps in vain) not to let the information prejudice his judgment.

TUESDAY, 17 MARCH

Tony stopped me on my way out the door, pointed to an attractive girl in tight jeans and said:
    'Hey sir, she's sellin' sheiks to the guys!'
    'Come on,' I said. 'Really?'
    I walked down the hall and Tony followed me.
    'Hey, sir, she's selling sheiks!'
    'Well, that's interesting,' I said.
    'Ain't you gonna buy some, sir? They're half price because they're already used!'

MONDAY, 23 NOVEMBER

I attended the staff meeting after school (after first securing permission from the principal). I was amazed by all the 'administrivia' the teachers were expected to deal with: they were given the dates when they were being evaluated by the principal or the two vice-principals: they were told when their report cards had to be finished: they were informed when they had to have their 'suite promotion meetings' complete; they were given dates for the parent-teacher interviews. They were also informed of the latest curriculum memos and workshops they could attend. I found it almost impossible to keep track of all this in my fieldnotes.

WEDNESDAY, 25 NOVEMBER

Today I spoke to a teacher about aggression in the halls between periods.
    'Oh, that's easy to figure out,' she smiled. 'We got a bad crop of kids this year. I just blame it on bad sperm.'

MONDAY, 30 NOVEMBER

I talked with two teachers about the suspension of Billy for fighting. One teacher asked if Billy was getting transferred. The other teacher replied that Billy's mother insisted that her son stay in the school.

'You mean we can't get rid of him!' the teacher exclaimed.

'That's right. In this case, the parents have the ultimate say. We're powerless here.'

'But even if the kid brutally attacks other kids?'

'That's right. The school has to serve him, unless, of course, we want to get involved in a court battle.

'Well, I think that's ridiculous. Really insane.'

Another teacher broke in laughing. 'I guess that Portuguese mother is pretty strong-minded.'

I could hear a teacher mimicking an accent. 'Good mornink Mrs So-and-so. Mine name is Carlos.'

TUESDAY, 1 DECEMBER

Brock, Barbie and Penelope had a forty-minute spare and I joined them in the teachers' planning room. We discussed discipline. Brock told me that last year there were few school rules so the suite had to make up their own. This year there were a great deal of school rules so the suite didn't have to make many up. The previous year there had been a lot of fights between Portuguese and Italian students. That was when the area was predominantly Italian. Now it's mainly inhabited by Portuguese immigrants. He said that the high school (which the teachers refer to as 'Brother') is even stricter. The high school is located in the same building as the junior high. However, they put up walls in order to turn the open-plan school into single classrooms. 'We go over there and drool,' Barbie said. Barbie wasn't happy teaching in the open-plan. Brock said that not many students want to go to a high school that's in the same building as their junior high school because the school is so small. 'Small schools lack spirit,' he said. I asked about the school uniforms that the high school kids wear. Brock said that the uniforms, although they're just material, serve hidden disciplinary roles. 'And they make the "monsters" look like angels!' Barbie chimed in.

MONDAY, 7 DECEMBER

After lunch one of the students approached the drinking fountain and was scolded by a teacher: 'No drinking!'

The students noisily took to their seats, placed their coats on the backs of chairs, and slumped into their desks. The entire suite grew silent as the teachers stood at the front of the room and gave them a special 'look' that read: 'Prepare yourselves quietly for the morning offering.' It struck me that the important moments of the day were always framed by silence. All the students stood up and faced the crucifix and began the morning offering.

FRIDAY, 11 DECEMBER

Two figures of the crucified Christ peered down at the students from their positions over the blackboards.

'Ya see those guys,' one of the students remarked. 'If the teacher don't catch you, He will.'

ST RYAN

St Ryan (not the school's real name) is a relatively modern school and quite pleasant in appearance. The grounds are clean and attractively landscaped. The well-kept appearance of the school contrasts sharply with the dingy smokestacks of the surrounding factories, the broken windows of the abandoned warehouses and the deserted lots full of debris which were once used to store sheet metal and auto parts.

The interior of the school is also kept in good condition. The only evidence of wear and tear is in the boys' washroom where your eye catches bits of graffiti and the ceiling betrays puncture marks made by objects of various shapes and sizes. In terms of its appearance, the school did not strike me as being, in the words of one of the teachers, 'one of the toughest Catholic schools in the city'.

One of the predominant features of the school was the visibility of religious symbols. Although one teacher reported to me that St Ryan had fewer religious symbols than many Catholic schools, there was nevertheless a distinct Catholic flavour to the school's surroundings. Discussing the importance of visual symbols in Catholic education, Raymond F. Bronowicz (1982) writes:

a school and any other institution is Catholic if its entire philosophy, thrust, and *modus operandi* reflect the life, mind and teaching of Christ as handed down by the apostles and as preserved and explained by the Holy Catholic Church.

If religious symbols do not make a school Catholic, then what purpose do they serve? At the very least, they serve as visual aids in the teaching of Christian truths and values. The Church and its schools realized the value of visual aids in the teaching of the gospel and of religion long before other educators became aware of their value in secular subjects. Beyond their educational value, religious pictures and symbols give an institution a clear, unmistakable and necessary Catholic identity.[26]

St Ryan shared space with a Catholic high school named Brother Regis (not the real name). The students from Brother Regis are distinguishable from the students at St Ryan by the Nile-green uniforms and colourful crests worn by the former. There was very little reported conflict between the high school and junior high students.

Teachers at St Ryan sported an irredeemably bland wardrobe: men usually wore polyester sports jackets and shiny dress slacks (although a daring staff member or two sometimes risked jeans or a track suit), while women donned lacklustre print skirts and wool sweaters. Students dressed according to a distinctive class/cultural code: 'cool guys' wore their hair long, sometimes under peaked caps. They favoured leather jackets and open shirts which permitted a display of criss-crossed chains about the neck. Girls had their hair styled in a 'feather' and were totemistically attached to tight, designer jeans.

Portuguese students preferred not to be 'overcoded' in their manner of dress; their sartorial styles were not nearly as untamed or unsober as those which one frequently encounters in some of the more middle-class public schools. There was no anti-fashion punk aesthetic of ripped shirts, spiked hair and movie style horror make-up; no new hippies wearing floppy leather hats, embroidered cuffs or dashikis; no mods with their green army parkas with Union Jacks or bullseye targets fastened to their backs; no blitz new romantics with their puffy sleeves, crystal earrings, or pirate belts; and no skinheads with their suspenders and Doc Marten's boots. While the Brother Regis students stood out in their conservative school uniforms (jacket and crest, creased slacks or kilts), the St Ryan students appeared rather ordinary and bland. And whereas some of the high school students had 'modernized' (via Lévi-Straussian *bricolage*) their uniforms, adding buttons advertising rock groups, turning their shirt and jacket collars up, or slicing back their hair in semi-punk fashion, the students at St Ryan were satisfied with remaining distinctive in their indistinctiveness: they could have been placed nearly anywhere on the street and still looked invisible. Their leather and denim uniforms became, in a sense, the sartorial equivalent of an ethnic subculture trying hard to assimilate into the mainstream working class.

The school has an enrolment of approximately 610 students and an overall staff of thirty-five teachers. In addition to the primary and junior grades, there were one and a half grade 7 classes, eight and a half grade 8 classes and three special education classes serving the intermediate division.

The principal – an athletic-looking young man who is almost totally bald, but who possesses an engaging smile – admitted that the morale among the staff had been strained by rumours of what would happen to St Ryan the following year: the possibility that it would eventually become a full-time high school. Not even the school administration could clarify this situation with the Separate School Board. There was an uncomfortable confusion as to which teachers might be moved – and where – and a concern among many of the staff members about whether or not they would be at St Ryan the following year.

Peter: Do you know what is happening next year at all?

Staff member Here? It will be either one of two things: either we will be moved to another school to reestablish, or we will stay here with approximately 200 children from Junior K to grade 8 and have to move the next year.

Peter: OK, so there may be one grade 8 class. . . . Everything would stay the same?

Staff member: Pretty much. We really dropped in our kindergarten registration this year. We had over forty Junior K last year. We had ten – I think it's up to eleven now – and after inquiring around we found that people felt there was no sense in putting their child in for one or two years and then have to move them, so they sought out another school.

Peter: I guess there is a bit of ambivalence among the teachers about what is going to happen . . .

Staff member: Yeah, like where am I going to be next year?

One of the major concerns among many staff members revolved around the fact that grade 7 and 8 students were transferred to St Ryan from feeder schools and were expected to fit into the school programme for only two years. The main problem appeared to be a lack of consistency.

Staff member: Up until this year there has always been 800 to 1,000 grades 7 and 8s that have come from the other feeder schools and they come to strange teachers and are thrown into open areas for two years. Compare this to Kindergarten to grade 8 schools where problems are usually identified around grade 3 or 4. What would have happened in the feeder schools is that by the time they identify the problems, they think: 'Oh well, they are leaving here in another year or two anyway so they can be handled at the senior school.' So here you have a school that might have 200 students from their own community, living around here ... and you've got all these others from feeder schools with problems coming into the open areas which they know nothing about. In both cases, teachers never got to work more than a year together. I would think that the burn-out rate must have been grave.

Peter: That's been a real criticism of the junior high schools – that whole notion that there really isn't enough time.

Staff member: There's never been a consistency in administration here; nobody stayed. One person stayed for five years and outside of that they have either a new principal or vice-principal every year. So there was no rapport built for teachers. Teachers withdrew from their support in the workroom. Last year the staff room was never used; there was no community here whatsoever. You would have staff meetings with no feedback, no nothing. You knew that the people went back and it was discussed, chewed out, and people misinterpreted what the message was. It was only gradually throughout this year that I began to talk to people and realize this was terrible. The whole thing was wrong ... It's been very hard knocking down doors.

Peter: And the kids from six different feeder schools?

Staff member: Last year when I arrived there were 400 grade 7s coming in and there were 400 grade 8s going out at the end of the year and this is where you deal mainly with your problems.

Peter: That's where the lack of spirit is at fault?

Staff member: I can see why people have built up a team spirit if you had to have something to call your own. In most schools they have a staff, and a staff room, and have staff functions and things, but last year that staff room was never used so I tried initiating one morning every couple of weeks having coffee and doughnuts but still everybody didn't come. They still won't come ...

Perhaps the most effective way of delineating the setting would be to quote directly from the principal's school report for 1981–2. I shall quote sections which are still relevant for the school for this academic year.

Description of community: The students of St Ryan School are nearly all of an ethnic group, the most prominent being Portuguese and Italian with some Spanish, Polish, Lithuanian and West Indian. . . . The majority of the families are low or lower-middle economic groups. In most cases, both mother and father work doing shift work. Because of this fact, a great deal of responsibility is put on to the older children of the family. Most families live in single dwellings, but the multi-extended family makes the situation congested. The school boundary area also includes three major public high schools within close proximity . . . and a large shopping plaza . . . all present factors that influence the overall climate of the school atmosphere.

There are three parishes that are affiliated with St Ryan. Meetings have been held to develop common ground for all to work on, especially in terms of preparation for sacraments and mass celebrations. Teachers present the religion program of our Board and facilitate celebrations with the parish priests. The priests in turn are affiliated with two suites each but for sacraments they meet with the children of their parishes.

Teachers attempt, on a daily basis, to realistically point out to the students the importance of sound moral decision making in their everyday life with people. In addition, a concentrated effort was made to develop in the children a more comprehensive awareness through actual activities of the many liturgical activities that are a part of our lives.

The religious aims and objectives of the present school year were written out as follows:

1 To continue to bring about a co-operative spirit between parishes to bring about activities and celebrations compatible with the students and the religious education programme.
2 To examine and develop specific priorities especially in the area of Family Life and Guidance in order to organize a more comprehensive and practical programme.

3 To make the parent committee more aware of the spiritual and religious dimension of our programmes and school activities.
4 To encourage students to make a more independent commitment to the religious programme through example.

THE SUITE

I was placed in a 'suite' consisting of an open area that housed four classes: three grade 8 classes and one special education class. Classes (of approximately thirty-five students each) were separated by makeshift partitions consisting of study carrels and cupboards on rollers. The partitions in no way hindered anyone observing what was going on in the other classes; they simply circumscribed the territorial boundaries of the classes. Desks were arranged in rows and the teachers taught lecture-style at the front of the room. There was always a great deal of noise and teachers were all forced to shout (to some degree, at least) their lessons.

The teachers estimated that 75 per cent of the students in the suite were from the Azores. They also estimated that 15 per cent were Italian and the remaining 10 per cent constituted Asian, Spanish (from South America), Irish, Polish, Croatian, North American Indian and British peoples.

All my observations were carried out in the three grade 8 classes (e.g. the suite). Two of my teacher/informants were female, one was male. The male (I'll call him Brock) and one female teacher (I'll call her Barbie) were in their late forties. The other teacher (Penelope) was in her early twenties. All three were extremely competent instructors, each excelling in certain subject areas. Located on the second floor of the school, the suite was separated by doors and a short hallway from another suite. Teachers from both suites shared a common space called 'the teachers' planning room' which housed their lockers and study carrels. The teachers would congregate in the planning room in the mornings, during breaks and after school. Many of the teachers ate lunch there and participated in occasional informal team planning meetings. All the teachers (six regular teachers, two special education teachers, and one French teacher) who shared this communal space appeared to get along very well. One male teacher from the other suite was Portuguese and one teacher was a nun or 'sister'.

The following description of the intermediate division (grade 8) for the previous school year was documented by the principal as follows:

The grade 8 students are taught the curriculum subjects based on the Ministry and MSSB [Metropolitan Toronto Separate School Board] guidelines. The instructional level at which the majority of these students are taught is approximately one year below grade level. Students are grouped according to ability for Language Arts and Math.

The students are motivated in increasing numbers to the attainment of higher levels for High School. . . . Specialists in Family Studies, Physical Education and Visual Arts provide a significant contribution to the programme.

The school's overall manifest intentions for the grade 8 students for this year read:

1 To implement better grouping situations for the benefit of the children.
2 To provide input into evaluation processes.

PORTUGUESE STUDENTS AND THE SCHOOL

Despite the fact that some Portuguese immigrants are beginning to acquire characteristics often associated with upward mobility, there is a high drop-out rate among Portuguese students. Pedro da Cunha (n.d.) writes that

the Portuguese as a group have a very cohesive and stable family life, they are hard workers, religious, law-abiding and ambitious. Nevertheless, at sixteen a great number of Portuguese boys and girls drop out of school – some glad to leave, others wanting to stay; many having lost hope of graduating close behind their peers; others leaving despite good grades and encouragement from teachers to continue.[27]

Da Cunha attributes this drop-out rate to three factors: individual maladjustment, family culture shock and academic programming.

Many Portuguese students have already been working before immigrating to Toronto and find it difficult to conform to the discipline and 'immediate irrelevancy' of school. Even after many years of school, some students can barely read in their own language.

Therefore the task of 'mastering another language is realistically too much for them, and perhaps the best option is still the world of work.'[28]

Da Cunha reports that many teachers are puzzled to see Portuguese students who are well adjusted in school, 'with good potential and motivation', quitting school at their parents' insistence. He writes that

> Such behaviour is totally inexcusable for many teachers and administrators. Recently a school administrator typically summarized the reason why Portuguese parents take their children from school: the Portuguese are materialistic and exploitative – materialistic, because they use their children to achieve this goal. What they want is just another cheque coming into the house, and are not concerned with the long-range benefits that education could bring to their children. The only way to help these students, the administrator continued, is to protect them from their parents, or to forcefully change the parents' values.[29]

We have, according to Da Cunha, a situation in which Portuguese parents are accused of moral deprivation for wanting their children to earn a living rather than to continue in school. It would appear to be incumbent on the teacher, therefore, to appreciate the values of the Portuguese parent within the context of his or her agrarian society homeland. In the Azores, all family members contribute to the support of the 'house'. It is the Portuguese custom for sons and daughters to work for the parents until they marry. When the peasant family emigrates to the city,

> this whole structure continues more or less the same, with some obvious minor adjustments. The collaboration is still the value, and the custom of working for the parents as soon as possible is taken for granted. The only difference being that, instead of working in the fields, the children will work in the factory, and will bring home a cheque instead of a cow.[30]

Da Cunha argues that this custom must change if the value is to be preserved. That is, in this new industrialized setting, the parents don't provide for the future of their children through inheritance but through education. Education would serve as a type of 'survival value'. To change the parents' values would, according to Da Cunha, be a 'new kind of colonialism'. What is effective 'is not moral preaching, since it utterly confuses the family who was acting on the basis of their moral values.' For Da Cunha, 'understanding and translation' is the answer.[31]

When parents do give permission for their children to continue their education, opposition often comes from older siblings – despite the fact that family co-operation is one of the fundamental values of the culture. Da Cunha posits three reasons for this:

1 Working children give the money they earn to their parents, as we have seen. In a sense, therefore, the working children are supporting the studying ones.
2 For a non-educated person from a rural area, studying is considered a leisure activity. Only manual work is perceived as real work – something that fatigues the body and dirties the hands.
3 For these rural families, to study is also a sign of hubris (i.e. an attempt to escape the social conditions of the family) and, therefore, an insult to those who accept those conditions.[32]

Another factor leading Portuguese students to leave school is related to the relationship between boys and girls and the different patterns of dating. Parents sometimes take their daughters out of school because they are afraid they will start dating boys.

The following candid description summarizes the plight of the Azorean student in Ontario's education system:

'I've seen it happen so many times,' says Mrs Aroujo, a counsellor and interpreter at the Community Information Centre on Adelaide Street.

'Portuguese kids are shunted into vocational schools at an early age because people assume they'll never make it academically.

'I think it's terrible the way they're punished for no good reason. Portuguese children are no more stupid than the kids of any group.'

. . . 'Immigrants and their children are discriminated against because they can't speak English. And everyone thinks all Portuguese work in factories or as office cleaners because they can't do anything else.'

. . . 'It takes a long time, maybe three generations, before Portuguese assimilate totally. But they are hard-working, good people. They just need to be treated fairly.'[33]

Maria Rodrigues, a Portuguese counsellor at the Working Women Community, is quoted in the following report:

'In a lot of cases, parents still need economic help and they're pushing their children to leave school at 16 to help out ... Portuguese children have the second highest dropout rate in the city's school system.'
    As well, many of them are streamed into vocational programs, a system the parents don't understand, she [Mrs Rodrigues] said.[34]

Leo Pereira, past president of the First Portuguese Canadian Club, offers the following criticisms of the educational system:

Parents think every high school is the same. . . . They rely on the schools to educate their children as they did at home. They don't have the facilities to communicate with the teachers in English. There are counsellors to help them out but they don't even know that. . . . People are waking up to the fact that our children are not going to stay with a broom in their hand for the rest of their lives. . . . But I think that the community has to start applying pressure to get their children into the good education programs that exist in this country.[35]

The school system in Portugal is vastly different than in Toronto – or, for that matter, the rest of Canada. Controlled entirely from Lisbon, there is no local autonomy with respect to locale or community. Portuguese elementary schooling generally lasts six years. Children begin at the age of 7 and attend school for a gruelling eight hours a day (from 8 a.m. to 12 noon and from 1 p.m. until 5 p.m.). Students are expected to attend school on a regular basis, six days a week, from 1 October until the end of June. There are few Kindergarten or pre-school classes.

    After elementary school there are three streams of secondary school education (much the same as in Canada): the academic, the commercial and the technical. School discipline is strict – perhaps even harsh – in comparison to Canadian standards. And programming is highly structured. Few young people manage to attend secondary school, particularly in the Azores where the schools may be located far from their homes. But distance is not the only factor that accounts for a small number of Azorean youth enrolling in high school; many boys seek full-time employment at a very early age (usually after elementary school) to help out their families.

Girls, too, are expected to help out in the home after elementary school. Anna Maria Coelho writes that 'The high structure and discipline often creates a feeling of resentment towards the system, in many students.'[36]

Father Eldorado sums up his feelings about the Portuguese student in the following remarks.

Priest: We have things [in Portugal] like the Holy Spirit, processions and crowns and parties, many things that are typically Portuguese – especially in the Azores – and these teachers do not know what these are. In school they are never talked about, the Feast of Santo Cristo – although a teacher may say something about St Patrick's Day . . .

I know these kids, later on when they leave school, they aren't going to be praying four or five times a day. If they actually can take a few minutes and pray when they are waiting for the subway I think it's great. They get a sense of the Divine. We just have to be open to those experiences. The Portuguese, for instance, have been geared for a number of years to vocational schools instead of going to colleges or universities but that has been a manipulation of the educational system. We have been having Chinese doctors and Spanish and Italian doctors for a number of years while we use a Portuguese girl with grade 12 to translate between the patient and the doctor. Sometimes there are grave consequences. Mistakes have been done simply because we should have by now a number of lawyers and doctors. I know the Portuguese who came here, with large families, little education, little money, and they want to pay their mortgages, see the kids get more education than they did. The parents had four or five years of school and now the kids get twelve. Hey, that's great to be able to speak two languages and finish high school with a high standard. But in the past few years it has become not enough. I remember when I went to St Mike's [university] there were very few Portuguese students and now there are a few hundred.

Peter: How could this system help Portuguese students more?

Priest: To encourage those with potential to go to university. To go and make them leaders. As long as we have someone else to make decisions for us, we can't get ahead.

Peter: Are schools looked upon as threatening the Portuguese family's core value systems because the students come back home and perhaps question what's going on their homes?

Priest: I don't think the schools are threatening the Portuguese kids, I think the schools are threatened by the Portuguese. I think the teachers are threatened.

Peter: What do you mean?

Priest: Look . . . most teachers of Catholic schools and public schools look at teaching as a job first. Most of the teachers live far away from this area. At 3.30 when school is over, they run home and they don't know the things that happen. Sometimes they hear stories that come to their ears – if someone dies – but they don't feel the experiences, the celebrations, the mournings – they don't know anything about the background. Even if there are Portuguese teachers in the school – they don't want to be taken as Portuguese because so much is expected of them. They are expected to translate for the Board . . . and not be paid for it . . .

Peter: Yes, and do you perceive other problems?

Priest: As long as the schools do their meetings in English and you try to explain yourself but the person says 'What do you mean?', 'Do you mean this or that?' – after you do it two or three times the parent feels humiliated. I believe that a school with 80 per cent Portuguese children should have 50 per cent Portuguese teachers.

Peter: What about celebrations in the lives of the students?

Priest: At puberty we should have beautiful celebrations in the Church. To celebrate becoming a man. The tribes of Africa celebrate when girls become women – dances and rituals and beautiful clothing, and a big feast. We should celebrate that.

Chapter 3

The structure of conformity

THE RITUAL SYSTEM

The cultural field of St Ryan was an intricate ritual system consisting of various symbols, world views, ethoses, root paradigms and forms of resistance. One of the key features of the cultural field was the way in which instruction was organized and carried out by the teaching staff. I have analysed classroom instruction as a ritual system and, in so doing, have constructed the following typology.

RITUALS OF INSTRUCTION

The micro ritual

The micro ritual consists of the individual lessons that took place on a day-to-day basis in the classroom.

The macro ritual

The macro ritual consists of the aggregate of classroom lessons observed over a single school day (including the periods between lessons and immediately before and after the lessons).

The micro and macro rituals may be understood primarily as variations of the rite of passage scheme (cf. Van Gennep, 1960). While the rite of passage model may be loosely applied to a micro ritual or a macro ritual, it is more readily applicable to the overall passage of students through the school system. For example, at St Ryan students may pass from the status of grade 7 students in September to that of grade 8 students in June, provided, of course, that they do not fail their year. Academic failure is a risk all student initiands face both on a daily random basis (e.g. through homework assignments, 'spot' questions, and 'surprise' tests) and at more formally allocated times over the school year (eg. pre-specified term tests and final exams).

Rituals of revitalization

A ritual of revitalization may be described as a processual event that functions to inject a renewal of commitment into the motivations and values of the ritual participants (cf. Wallace, 1966). Staff meetings frequently served as revitalization rites during which time authority figures such as the principal or vice-principal would attempt to boost staff morale and strengthen commitment to the values of Catholic education. Classroom rituals of revitalization usually took the form of emotional discussions between teacher and students which revolved around the importance of mastering coursework and school objectives. For some students, the school-wide masses and confessions served as rituals of revitalization, formally linking the values of the school and Church.

Rituals of intensification

Rituals of intensification comprise a subtype of revitalizaton rituals serving mainly to recharge students or teachers emotionally – to unify the group without necessarily reinforcing the values or goals of the ritual participants (cf. Wallace, 1966). Rituals of revitalization and intensification may take the form of micro or macro rituals.

Rituals of resistance

Rituals of resistance emerge as a series of both subtle and dramatic cultural forms which partake of many characteristics of 'symbolic inversion', and invariably prove refractory for the dominant authoritative tenets and pre-established codes of conduct established by the teacher. Rituals of resistance may be aptly described as a type of ceremonial 'destructuring' (cf. Grimes, 1982b). That is, they are rituals which turn our view towards the dark side of the cultural landscape. Rituals of resistance are 'agonistic' – that is, they are rituals of conflict. Within such rituals we find the seeds of Turner's third phase of the social drama: redressive ritual and symbolic action. As I do not wish to deploy here the full range of Turner's theory of social drama, suffice it to say that students are transformed into combatants and antagonists: hidden grudges and tensions are mobilized for the purpose of rupturing the cultural axiomatic rules of the school and subverting the grammars of mainstream classroom discourse. Rituals of resistance are often attempts at 'purifying' the contaminated and fragmented world of institutionalized social structure. Rituals of resistance partake of two distinct forms: active and passive. Active resistance rituals are intentional or conscious attempts by students to subvert or sabotage teacher instruction or rules and norms established by school authorities. Passive resistance rituals unconsciously or tacitly subvert or sabotage the normative codes of the dominant school order. These rituals are less overt and less demonstrative than active resistance rituals. While rituals of resistance are included as part of the overall instructional system (as a form of ritualized feedback), the term 'rites of instruction' generally refers to the macro and micro rituals. The term 'ritual' will serve as a generic term for all the variations of instructional rites.

CRITERIA FOR EVALUATING THE RITUAL SYSTEM

Instructional rituals do not exist in a pristine state, uncontaminated by the contexts and juxtapositions of which they are necessarily a part. Similarly, no interpreter of a ritual stands ideologically naked or is immune from the political ramifications of his observations. A political perspective enters any study as soon as the researcher begins to frame the research question. We are, to be sure, all wrapped in our predilections and personal biases and our evaluative criteria are bound to suffer – if not through a warped defensiveness, then through a welter of rationalizations.

Any assertion that a ritual performance is a politically or ideologically neutral event, purged of political considerations, is pure pomposity and amounts to nothing more than a spurious, contrived chimera. What constitutes a seemingly objective fact gleaned through observation of or enactment in a particular rite may, in reality, be a suggestive mystification or a proffered representation: in short, a hegemonic definition of reality designed to prevail over others.

It is exceedingly difficult – if not impossible – to attempt any interpretation of ritual without first understanding its relational aspects, that is, without examining the contexts (historical and situational) within which the ritual is enacted. Furthermore, a substantive evaluation of the ritual system of a school is more than undertaking a sign hunt or a symbol hunt; rather, it is to locate the parameters of the hunt itself in the sociopolitical milieu of the wider society – one in which notions of power and cultural distribution are taken seriously.

With these considerations in mind, I have created an index by which to adjudicate the symbolic and performative characteristics of instruction – apart, that is, from their efficacy and aesthetics. What is important is to be able to evaluate whether or not the ritualized exigencies of instruction mediate in favour of or against the intellectual prosperity of Portuguese students and whether or not they enhance their self and social empowerment and the development of a critical class consciousness.

Since, properly speaking, instructional rituals can only be evaluated relationally, that is, in the context of performance, I have eschewed a rigid or hidebound set of principles in assessing what characteristics a good ritual of instruction must possess. My evaluative criteria by which a given ritual performance may be faulted or accredited consists of a number of general questions which reflect the extent to which these performances become culturally hegemonic.

The hegemony of instructional rites not only refers to how they reinforce or reproduce the political and economic dominance of one social class over another, but also considers the success with which the dominant class is able to project – through symbolic meanings and practices that structure daily experience – its own way of interpreting the world to the extent that it is considered natural, universal and all-inclusive. Hegemony refers to the dominant system of 'lived' meanings which becomes an important factor in mobilizing spontaneous group consent within social institutions; it is a process which creates an ideology pervasive and potent enough to penetrate the level of common sense and suffuse society through taken-for-granted rules of discourse (cf. Apple, 1979, pp. 1–25).

Thus, rituals may be considered 'bad' if they constrain the subjectivities of the students by placing limits on oppositional discourse, reflective dialogue and critique. And rituals may be considered 'good' if they create an alternative to hegemony (counter-hegemony) which will enable participants to critically reflect upon the way reality is perceived and understood. Considerations such as these are reflected in the following questions which may be asked of the instructional rites of classrooms in general: Whose interests (from the perspectives of class, culture, gender and power) do the rituals ultimately serve? Are they keeping certain groups of students in basic level courses or are they providing the necessary opportunities for entrance into university stream courses? Who benefits most from the ritual structures remaining as they are? Who is marginalized as a result? What virtues or vices are embedded in the media and morphology of the rites themselves? How are power and control invested and mediated through the ritual symbols, ritual paradigms and ritual codes? How is consciousness 'locked' into the messages of the rites? How do the instructional rites inform the values and behaviour of the students? In what ways do school rituals uncritically transmit the dominant ideology? The key word here is 'uncritically'. Instructional rites are generally criticized in this study because they have provided at the level of common sense little room for ideology critique, or some form of counter-hegemonic or liberatory dialogue. Likewise, they are criticized if they fail to permit the students to affirm their own class/cultural identities, recognize their own experiences, and evaluate them on a scale of merit which has dialectically emerged out of collective reflection and constructive dialogue.

STATES OF INTERACTION

The ritual repertoire of the classroom at St Ryan did not accommodate, as do many educational settings, both derisively unspontaneous and unapologetically improvisational teaching patterns. It was the tendency to hold on to the former protocol that, at St Ryan, sanctioned such a positivistic approach to schooling. Teachers worked predominantly within an ultra-conservative 'old school' pedagogical format. The majority of instructional forms could aptly be linked to a 'museum mentality'; there was a noticeable lack of newer and more innovative teaching procedures and styles despite the fact that classrooms were of the 'open area' format – usually regarded as an ideal milieu for progressive and innovative teachers.

The typological axes of the rites of instruction were composed of four interactive states: the streetcorner state; the student state; the sanctity state; and the home state. By use of the word 'state',

I do not mean to suggest some type of trance or state of consciousness in the clinical or psychological sense of the term. Rather, I mean to suggest styles of interacting with the environment and with others which could, perhaps, be appropriately labelled behavioural clusters or complexes. The states of interaction are not simply congeries of abstract events. They consist of organized assemblages of behaviours out of which emerge a central or dominant system of *lived* practices. The four states of interaction are mutually embedded in the dominant ritual system in so far as they constitute the major modes of ritual sensibilities.

The streetcorner state

Prior to 9 o'clock students enter into particular roles and statuses and engage in certain distinctive behaviours which I have termed the 'streetcorner state'. Heralded by the physical setting in which students find themselves, the streetcorner state, as the name suggests, is evocative of behaviour students exhibit on the street (e.g. hanging around the local neighbourhood). Yet this behaviour does not remain in the street but extends into enveloping areas such as the school playground, the nearby park, the vacant lots, the video arcades, the plaza and the abandoned buildings. The student state, in contrast, characterizes most of the student behaviour inside the school building (listening to a lesson, taking notes, writing an exam, etc.).

The streetcorner state is composed of a cluster of attributes which, when lumped together, constitute a particular *manner* of relating to settings, events and people. Seldom do actions in the streetcorner state conform to a predictable scenario. While engrossed in or in the thrall of the streetcorner state, students 'own their time' as a collectivity. They play out the roles and statuses that predominantly reflect the dynamics of their peer relationships and identities – those relationships and identities which are forged in the street or playground. The schoolyard or street, therefore, becomes the state where the individual acts his or her drama of apotheosis, revenge, resistance or revitalization. When in this state, students frequently and characteristically unleash and give vent to their pent-up frustrations. The streetcorner state is therefore cathartic – ritual forms are often underdistanced (cf. Scheff, 1977).

Student 1: Yah, you got to wait for before school or lunch time to get at somebody. I wait until before school – before the teachers are there – to punch somebody out. You can't do it in class or you'll get in trouble.

Student 2: Or you can wait until after school if the guy doesn't run home.

Student 1: Yah, but you can mostly catch the guy if he don't leave early before the other kids.

[Laughter. Student 1 sticks out his tongue and makes a noise simulating flatulence.]

While in the streetcorner state, students are indulgently physical and exhibit an unfettered exuberance. Activity in the streetcorner state sometimes bears a close approximation to primary experience: bodies can often be seen to twist, turn and shake in an oasis of free abandon, as though locked within some experiential primordium or primal state of non-differentiation. There is often a great deal of physical contact. Behaviours have an *ad hoc* and episodic characteristic to them, often appearing unbound and ungoverned. Yet it would be a mistake to think that their lack of formality renders them innocuous as a ritual mode. On the contrary, the streetcorner state comes closest to ritualization (associated with biorhythms and psychosomatic patterning) and its tacit ritual elements – personal habituations or interaction rituals (cf. Grimes, 1982a).

Bodily movement, some of which carries overtones of merriment, revelling, and disportings, generally lacks the demarcations of precise gesture (cf. Brenneman *et al.*, 1982). The boundaries between spaces, roles and objects are more plastic, adaptive and malleable than in the student state. Students also appear more unpredictable, boisterous and obstreperous in the streetcorner state than they do in the student state.

Students frequently exhibit exaggerated instances of kinesthetic activity; there are more aperiodic sequences of action while postural configurations are more pronounced. In addition, there are greater instances of irregular speech and body rhythms (e.g. spontaneous and ejaculatory expressions of feelings and emotions). There is often the stimulation of an abundance of furtive sensual pleasures. Relationships between individuals frequently approach unmediated intimacy.

Time in the streetcorner state is relatively unstructured or polychromatic (cf. Hall, 1973). That is, various activities happen simultaneously and consequently overlap. Individuals are often able to 'create' their own schedules.

> *Student*: Here [the playground] you can do whatever you want as long as you watch out for the tough kids. You can play soccer or football. Or just goof around. Nobody does work, not even the browners.

The behavioural correlates of the streetcorner state emphasize personal functions – those which are usually controlled in the student state but which are not considered taboo in the streetcorner state (e.g. bodily emissions, idiosyncrasies and eccentricities). Students are frequently motivated by archetypal symbols such as those of the bully, the clown, the weakling and the slut. These symbols often shade into one another.

> *Student*: The cool guys like to fight. They pick on the guys who think they're funny or the wrist guys, the fairies. The cool guys like to make out with girls. But they're usually sluts who carry sheiks.
> *Peter*: What other kinds of girls are there, other than the ones that carry the sheiks?
> *Student*: The decent ones. You got the sluts but you also got the decent ones. Cool guys like the sluts.

Culture has its distinct 'moods'. The mood of the streetcorner state is 'subjunctive' (in the sense described by Turner); it is one that embraces fantasy, experiment, hypothesis and conjecture. In this mood of 'may-be', metaphors flourish and promote novel cultural forms (cf. Paine, 1981, pp. 187–200). There is apt to be more 'flow' (after Csikszentmihalyi) in the matching of skills and abilities since students do things at their own pace. Students spend time experimenting with different roles – playing 'as if' they were others. Yet students are most decidedly themselves in this state.

> *Student*: Sometimes Nestor pretends he's Gretsky. . . . I like to pretend I'm with Benfica and Nestor with Juventus and I score five goals. Or else I'm Mike Palmateer.

If the students are in a state of turmoil or under intense emotional stress (e.g. due to the death of a family member, an argument with a parent or friend or family problems at home) they are better able to confront their emotions directly and have a greater opportunity to share their emotions with select friends and peers while in the streetcorner state. Consumerism constitutes a prevailing theme. For instance, students frequently talked about buying cars, colour television sets, motorcycles, leather garments and ghettoblasters.

Individuals in the streetcorner state bathe in the ambience of working-class and distinctively ethnic cultural forms and remain unencumbered by the obligations and values which are officially lauded in the student state. For instance, Portuguese is occasionally spoken and students listen to rock music and engage in recreational activity. Spontaneous communitas is frequently present and this state could be said to possess a liminal or liminoid dimension. The ethos of this state is ludic or of the nature of play.

THURSDAY, 17 DECEMBER

I arrived early today, about fifteen minutes before the bell rang. As I entered the schoolyard, I noticed a middle-aged man with a pot belly and stubble on his chin standing across the street on his front porch, leering at the students. It was amazing to see so much activity among the students so early in the morning. Movement was pronounced, even exaggerated. After searching in vain for a handkerchief, a kid about 12 sporting the moustache of an 18 year-old, blew his nose directly on the pavement. I was worried that someone might slip on his invention. A group of students played football at one end of the yard. Groups of younger female students were skipping and singing in the central area of the yard. The most boisterous groups played 'murder ball' on an elevated portion of the yard. The ball was flung lightning fast at the heads of the students. A few of the players barely avoided getting hit on the head and some did get injured by the ball. I had a feeling that because the kids were aware that they wouldn't be using their bodies very much inside the school, they were vigorously compensating before the bell rang. Two teachers on yard duty nodded good morning.

I was chilly, so I decided to head into the school after only a few minutes of observing. I tried a central door, but it was locked. I tried another. Locked. Several more. All were locked tight with no one waiting inside the halls to open them. I decided that, like the kids, I would have to wait for the bell. Finally it sounded its usual loud, metallic, oppressive ring, and in a matter of moments two teachers appeared in the hallway to open the doors. The students remained gathered about the doors and slowly, listlessly, they formed rough lines and waited to be admitted. The teachers stood by the doors silently, staring hard at the students. Then they slowly led them to their lockers. Once inside, the students' body rhythms changed substantially. Gone were the looping gaits, the swaggers, the animated arms forming complex arabesques. Gone, too, were the shouts, and hollers. Now came the groans, the sighs and the cynical laughter.

FRIDAY, 18 DECEMBER

Today's lesson was about the painter, Lawren Harris, one of Canada's famous Group of Seven. The students sat there motion-less, in a kind of mechanical stupor. Some appeared interested, others appeared bored and restless. Brock would catch a student not paying attention and say, 'Do you have a problem?' Brock looks like a benign Rasputin or a mystical Jesuit. He has an imposing beard and clear sparkling eyes.

I watch three classes simultaneously. Barbie is teaching a lesson on verbs; Penelope is teaching about anthropoids. A student in a New York Yankees sweater belches. Another student leans back in a chair too far and crashes on to the floor.

The student state

Following their entrance into the building, students realign and readjust their behaviour, shifting from the natural flow of the street-corner state to the more formal and rigidly sequestered precinct of the 'student state'. It is here that the students give themselves over to the powerful controls and enforcement procedures available to teachers – controls which allow teachers to dominate students without recourse to brute force. Students move 'offstage' from where they are more naturally themselves to the proscenium of the suite where they must write their student roles and scenarios in confor-mity to the teacher's master script; they move from the 'raw' state of streetcorner life to the more 'cooked' or socialized state of school existence. Actually, within both streetcorner and student states, students are already 'cooked' (i.e. their roles are informed by their social experience in the sense that they sustain a set of social standards expected of them by both their peers and the authorities). While it is safe to say that the streetcorner state is much more 'raw' when compared to the student state, this is not to suggest that individuals exist as *tabulae rasae* – but that they enter a more 'visceral' and informal state of interaction akin to what is colloquially referred to as *au naturel*.

The student state refers to an adoption of the gestures, disposition, attitudes and work habits expected of 'being a student'. Emotional display on the part of students is viewed by teachers as 'antisocial'. The major theme of the student state is 'work hard!'. The teacher's control mechanisms constitute the *boundaries* between the streetcorner state and the student state. These boundaries are seldom permeable – and only during prescribed times (such as between classes or at the end of the school day). Most often, the students are compelled to enter into the student state through a highly ritualized and institutionalized punishment and reward system which serves to guy the hoopla, gibing, kibbitzing, ribaldry, scurrilous bantering and general effervescence of the streetcorner state.

> *Teacher*: OK. Settle down. You heard the bell. Into your seats and start getting ready for the first class. Vinnie! Did you hear what I said?!

Youngsters in the student state are generally quiet, well-mannered, predictable and obedient. There is a pronounced systematicity of gesture. The mood of this state is 'indicative' – meaning it prevails in the world of actual fact (in the manner employed by Turner). Metonymy is prevalent and helps to produce predictable and restrictive cultural forms (cf. Paine, 1981). Symbolization is primarily through the use of signs and religious symbols (in Courtney's terminology). Time is segmented and monochromatic (cf. Hall, 1973). Movements are often resolutely routinized and rigidified into gestures (see Brenneman *et al.* 1982). There is little physical movement unless on the cue of the teacher.

> *Teacher*: Come on, Nestor, wake up. Sit up properly. Where's your exercise book Tony?
> [Tony sits up and removes his exercise book from his desk.]

In addition, there is a distinct separation between mind and body with a stress on the work ethic.

Teacher: Look, you guys can wait for lunch to do that [look at a car magazine], all right? Right now I want you to work on your assignments. Did you hear me? Would you move away from him, please! And take your feet off the desk while you're at it. [Student frowns, glances around the room, moves his desk and plants his feet underneath it.]

Ritual forms are, for the most part, invariant and conventionalized. Communitas is rare – as are elements that partake of liminal or liminoid ritual genres. Lessons are often overdistanced (Scheff, 1977).

The sanctity state

The day is further punctuated by prayers which bring about a third state which I term the 'sanctity state'. Ideally students in the sanctity state are filled with a realization of something greater beyond themselves which cannot be explained in rational terms. This state occasionally evokes a sense of the numinous although it is rarely felt as a direct and unmediated experience of the ultimate – as in some mystical epiphany. This state is evoked when students entertain meaning in excess of common sense and known limits – something that transcends the students' usual sense of finitude. There is an acknowledgement of unknowable supra-existent entities or forces from another dimension discontinuous with this one. The mood of this state is one of reverence and *subservience* although the actions and gestures associated with this state (e.g. sign of the cross, clasping one's hands in prayer) are often carried out in a quick and perfunctory fashion. The major theme of this state is 'we are Catholic'. This state begins as students assemble in their home rooms in the morning and repeat the following offering:

Teacher: [stands with arms crossed, legs firmly planted on the ground] I'm still waiting, Juliana!
Teacher and students: [together, with heads reverently bowed] O Jesus,
through the Immaculate Heart of Mary, I offer you all my prayers, works, and sufferings of this day. For all the intentions of Your Sacred Heart. In union with the Holy Sacrifice of the Mass throughout the world. In reparation for all my sins. For the intentions of all our associations, and, in particular, for the general intention recommended for this month.

[Students then break into laughter and conversation and wait for the teacher to settle them down before moving to their designated classes.]

The home state

While I cannot speak of this state from direct observation, it can none the less be inferred from conversations and interviews with the students. The home state refers to particular types of interactions between students and family members (e.g. mother, father, grandparents, siblings). During this state, parents partake of authority roles similar to those of teachers, priests, etc. However, students have ready access to the streetcorner state (for instance, when they go to the privacy of their rooms or when they are playing with friends in the nearby yard or corner lot). The normative rules governing the home state appear, in many cases, to be similar to those of the school (e.g. respect of the authority of the priest, teacher, school administrator, belief in God and adulation of the sacraments). However it is safe to assume that the normative rules for some individual homes will, in many instances, be very different from those of the school.

In reality, these four states do not cleave neatly into analytic categories but are mutually inclusive of one another. That is to say, they overlap and interlock. However, I shall draw sharp contrast between them in order to present them as ideal-typical states. While there does not exist a truly unbridgeable antithesis between the robust and carnivalesque ethos of the streetcorner state and the repressed and 'tense' ethos of the student state, a radical disjunction beween these states must be made for the purpose of further discussion; in practice the edges of these categories remain somewhat blurred. Although there may be cultural gaps between these states, there are no existential gaps; all four states are rooted in the need for students to engage rhythmically, gesturally and meaningfully with their immediate surroundings. I suspect that these states are only vaguely perceived from time to time by students as self-conscious behaviour.

Table 3.1 Forms of student interaction

Streetcorner state	Student state
tribal	institutional
emotional, non-rational	cognitive, rational
random, imprecise gestures	non-random, precise gestures
ludic	serious
forms of symbolization (icons, symbols)	forms of symbolization (signs)
play (ritual frame)	work (ritual frame)
spontaneous action	teleological
tapping own inner resources (right lobe emphasis)	imitation of teachers (left lobe emphasis)
away from formality	formal, technical
sensuous	mechanical
multi-signifiers (hyper-intensity)	multi-signified (low intensity)
cathartic	frustrating, tension-inducing
whimsy, frivolity	task-oriented
status determined by peers	status determined by institution
liminal/liminoid	hierarchical
communitas (repartee)	anomie, anxiety
subjunctive mood	indicative mood
flow	flow-resistant
ritual forms (elastic, flexible haphazard, improvisational)	ritual forms (conventualized, stereotyped, formal)
motion	gesture
p-time	m-time
informal space	fixed feature space
pediarchic	pedagogic
analogue	digital

RITUALS OF INSTRUCTION

The macro and micro rituals are more invariant and forma-lized than the rites of intensification and resistance and are thus the most amenable to systematic analysis. Macro and micro rituals embody a regular, repetitive and prescribed format which follows, with very few exceptions, the rubrical mandate of the Metropolitan Separate School Board set forth in its curriculum guidelines.

The macro ritual

The macro ritual is composed of a variety of micro rituals and ritual segments which span the entire school day.

SEGMENT 1

Between 9 o'clock and 9.10, the students undertake a transformation from the streetcorner state (which is manifested by the students in the schoolyard before the opening bell) to the student state. This latter state lasts throughout most of the day. During this segment, students lose their possession of time, space and street roles, transferring them over to the hierarchy and control of the school authorities. However, there is still some opportunity during this segment to enter back and forth from the student state to the streetcorner state. Gradually, as the clock winds down to 9.10, the students also begin to wind down – if ever so slightly – some of their talking and body movements. As the teacher looks out across the class in preparation for the morning offering, the students prepare themselves for another transition.

SEGMENT 2

At 9.10 the students make their morning offering prayer. With heads slightly bowed and turned towards the crucifix on the west wall, the students enter the sanctity state by repeating the morning offering prayer.

SEGMENT 3

The sanctity state ceases once prayers have been repeated. Students either stay in their home room or transfer to another class and teacher, depending on their timetable. They have about two minutes to make the transition from the state of sanctification to the student state. During this time, students may enter into either the streetcorner state or the student state. While in the streetcorner state, students may, on occasion, experience liminal feelings such as communitas and well-being, depending on the circumstances. (Only occasionally will students feel a surge of communitas in the student state, and this, if it happens, usually occurs among the students who are most comfortable in the role of student, e.g. the academically well-adjusted students.) We will generally refer to the transitional states beween periods as streetcorner states since most of our observations confirm that this is the predominant state during these times. While in the streetcorner state, the students are the most threatening to teachers. Often the students recognize their collective strength in this state and purposely resist making a quick transition back to the student state or sanctity state. I call these instances 'symbolic stalling'.

SEGMENT 4
Students pass from a streetcorner state to a student state as they prepare for their first class of the day. They remain seated from 9.13 to 9.50. (Some students may excuse themselves to get a drink or go to the washroom but this kind of behaviour is encouraged to take place during home room periods only.) During this segment students either listen to the teacher expound on some topic, answer questions or work on various assignments.

SEGMENT 5
Students move from a student state to a streetcorner state for approximately two minutes as they change classes or prepare for a change of subject area.

SEGMENT 6
Students are instructed in a particular subject and remain in the student state until 10.45 (this includes time for some follow-up work).

SEGMENT 7
Students move from a student state to a streetcorner state for two minutes as they change subject areas.

SEGMENT 8
Students remain in a student state for one period. The duration of this period varies because this segment is sometimes one long period in one subject area, or two shorter periods dealing with two subject areas.

SEGMENT 9
Students move from a student state to a streetcorner state as they move from or remain in their home room and prepare for the transition to a state of sanctification.

SEGMENT 10

A transition is made from the streetcorner state to a sanctification state just before the lunch period. This is achieved through the recitation of a prayer, normally called 'grace'. Students return to their home classrooms and repeat, in unison, with their respective teacher: 'Bless us, O Lord, and these Thy gifts, which we are about to receive from Thy Bounty, through Christ our Lord, Amen.'

SEGMENT 11

Students move from a state of sanctification to a streetcorner state as they make their way to either their homes, the cafetorium or a nearby restaurant.

SEGMENT 12

From 11.45 to 12.30 the students have lunch. Students who do not eat lunch at the school may make a complete transition to the street-corner state. A favourite place for students to gather is the Chinese fast food outlet a few blocks away. Students who eat at home must make a further transition to being a 'son' or 'daughter' (during the home state). Students who remain in the school for lunch are rigidly supervised in the cafetorium by patrolling teachers. These students remain in a state of limbo – not quite in the streetcorner state and not quite in the student state. After twenty minutes, students are marshalled out of the doors to spend the remaining lunch hour outside. These students must remain in the schoolyard, supervised by patrolling teachers. However, once they are outside the school building, the students can enter more readily into the streetcorner state.

SEGMENT 13

Students again make the transition from the streetcorner state to that of student state as they are met at the doors and ushered up into the suite by teachers. However, the student state is not quite achieved until after the forthcoming state of sanctification.

SEGMENT 14

The state of sanctification is achieved through a post-lunch prayer of gratitude. Students assemble in their home rooms and repeat together: 'We give thee thanks for all Thy benefits, which we have received, through Christ, our Lord. Amen.'

SEGMENT 15
Students either stay in their home rooms or move on to other classes. In either case, as the students prepare themselves for another subject area, there is brief transition from the sanctity state to the streetcorner state, lasting about two minutes.

SEGMENT 16
Students shift subject areas, remaining in their respective classes in the student state for a period of instruction.

SEGMENT 17
A transition occurs from the student state to the streetcorner state as students once again change classes. This streetcorner state lasts approximately two minutes.

SEGMENT 18
Students spend this segment in the student state receiving instruction in an academic subject.

SEGMENT 19
Students make a transition to the streetcorner state and prepare for the next period of instruction.

SEGMENT 20
Students spend the last period of instruction in the student state.

SEGMENT 21
Students move from the student state almost directly to the sanctity state, foregoing much of the streetcorner state that usually serves as a prelude to the sanctity state. The reason for this is that students are about to be dismissed and are most anxious to leave the building. Students enter the final sanctity state as they repeat the closing prayer of the day in their home rooms: 'O my God, I am heartily sorry for having offended you, and I detest all my sins because

Table 3.2 The macro ritual

Ritual segment	Transition	Activity	Time
Segment 1	streetcorner state to student state	schoolyard to home room	9.00–9.10
Segment 2	student state to sanctity state	morning offering prayer	9.10–9.11
Segment 3	sanctity state to streetcorner state	move to or prepare for class	9.11–9.13
Segment 4	streetcorner state to student state	class instruction	9.13–9.50
Segment 5	student state to streetcorner state	move to or prepare for class	9.50–9.52
Segment 6	streetcorner state to student state	class instruction	9.52–10.45
Segment 7	student state to streetcorner state	move to or prepare for class	10.45–10.47
Segment 8	streetcorner state to student state	class instruction	10.47–11.45
Segment 9	student state to streetcorner state	preparation for grace	11.45–11.46
Segment 10	streetcorner state to sanctity state	grace before meal	11.46–11.47
Segment 11	sanctity state to streetcorner state	move to lunch location	11.47–11.50
Segment 12	streetcorner state continues	lunch	11.50–12.30
Segment 13	streetcorner state to student state	line up outside to enter school	12.30–12.38
Segment 14	student state to sanctity state	grace after meal	12.38–12.39
Segment 15	sanctity state to streetcorner state	move to prepare for class	12.39–12.41
Segment 16	streetcorner state to student state	class instruction	12.41–1.30
Segment 17	student state to streetcorner state	move to or prepare for class	1.30–1.32
Segment 18	streetcorner state to student state	class instruction	1.32–2.30
Segment 19	student state to streetcorner state	move or prepare for class	2.30–2.32
Segment 20	streetcorner state to student state	class instruction	2.32–3.15
Segment 21	streetcorner state to sanctity state	act of contrition	3.15–3.16
Segment 22	sanctity state to streetcorner state	dismissed and leave school	3.16–3.18

of your just punishments, but most of all because they offend you my God, who art all good.'

SEGMENT 22
Students undergo the final transition from the state of sanctification to the streetcorner state as they are quickly escorted outside the building by their home room teachers. Once outside, the students again express themselves in a random and carefree manner, released from the former stagnation of the student state.

The students spend approximately seventy-six minutes of the school day in the streetcorner state, four minutes in the sanctity state, and 298 minutes in the student state.

The macro ritual so described constitutes a bastard version of Van Gennep's rites of passage – a mutant similitude or refined variant of the classical ritual process. The performative sequencing of separation (preliminal), threshold rites (liminal), and rite of reaggregation (postliminal) is effectively altered both structurally and qualitatively. As in Van Gennep's tripartite schema, transformation from one state to another entails a 'separation' and a change of status and behaviour on the part of the students. But the change from streetcorner state to student state is a change from a more natural state with characteristics of spontaneous communitas to an institutionalized state constituted by uncomfortable, painful and oppressive characteristics often associated with initiatory rites. One could, in effect, argue that the streetcorner state also has its initiations (e.g. being vigorously pummelled by a street gang as your initiation into a new neighbourhood), but at least in the streetcorner state students usually know what they're up against (the law of the jungle) and possess greater options for retaliation against oppressors (if in trouble, one can always fight back or run away). In any case, there is a distinct 'aliveness' associated with the streetcorner state. (Later on I shall argue that some students prefer this 'aliveness' conferred through the pain of school punishment to the slow, institutionalized death of being a student.)

The passage from the streetcorner state to the student state is a move across a threshold into a qualitatively different cultural realm accompanied by a parallel passage in space (from street and schoolyard to school building) and a parallel passage in time (from polychromatic to monochromatic time).

The liminal initiands (the Azorean students) are often feared by the generally white, middle-class instructors (the Azoreans are dark, exotic, physical; they are gypsies, outlanders, relegated to a pariah status). In school they must be tamed, stripped of their unpredictability and mystery. They are immediately slotted into hard, plastic chairs (behind desks which hide their bodies from the waist down). They are forced to sit still for hours, made to listen to boring lessons, and are assigned tasks which many of them consider irrelevant. Furthermore, they are given few washroom breaks or class spares (more will be said about the levelling process of students in a later section entitled 'the culture of pain').

The rite of passage model breaks down in the final phase of incorporation in which the initiands are supposedly returned to a relatively stable, well-defined position in the social structure. Incorporation or reaggregation is never complete either way (i.e. from the streetcorner state to the student state state or vice versa), and rarely occurs in such a way that preritual ties become irremediably broken. Some students may be temporarily incorporated into the student state – but not all. Furthermore, the tendency towards incorporation occurs in two directions at once: there are two simultaneous 'pulls' on the students – a force pulling the students into the streetcorner state, and a force pulling the students into the student state. Those students whose identities and statuses are bolstered significantly in the streetcorner state will struggle – often vigorously – to extend such a state in class. Yet even for those students who give themselves over, mind and body, to the student state (more than likely the most successful students), there still exists a pull towards the streetcorner state. A possible exception to this (other than in instances where students are lucky enough to have a teacher that can inspire learning by utilizing cultural forms from the streetcorner state) is the student who has such an extremely ambiguous status in the streetcorner state that he prefers even the rigid control of the student state (where at least he knows who he is) to the streetcorner state (where he literally feels like a 'nothing'). However, the streetcorner state is generally preferred by students because knowledge is acquired more organically and there are greater instances of spontaneous communitas.

> *Student*: Most people like it better when we go for lunch or go home. School can be OK but when you're outside you feel that you're back to normal. It's a happier time for sure.

The streetcorner state is more seductive and symbolically tantalizing than the student state. Symbols encountered in the streetcorner state – the bully (villain), the hero (who defeats the villain), the champion (sports hero, breakdancer, etc.), the Madonna (often an attractive female teacher), the slut (a girl who is known for having sex with boys), the coward and the rebel – are alive and 'lived through' by the students. The informally sanctioned symbols of the student state (the browner, the teacher's pet, the good Catholic worker) become mere ashes to the fire that forges the debilitatingly patriarchal ritual symbols in the crucible of the streetcorner state.

Movement from the streetcorner state to the student state often embodies a distinct paradox. While the students are undergoing ritual instruction that attempts to bring them in symbolic concordance with the strictures of the student state – the rubrics of 'being a student' – they may in fact become reconfirmed back into the streetcorner state either by resisting the instructional rituals or making the most of the streetcorner state between periods or during lunch – if, in fact, they ever really leave the streetcorner state at all. When a ritual is missing its most distinctive ingredient – liminality – you can sometimes attempt to fake the passage (i.e. pretend you are in the student or streetcorner state). However, a counterfeit rite of passage in the strict sense of the word is a contradiction in terms. It is easier to make your passage from the student state to the streetcorner state (because you are pulled along, sometimes even against your will, by the liminal ingredients of the streetcorner state) but it is never easy to fake your passage from the streetcorner state to the student state (unless you have mastered the codes, the indexical clues, symbolic cues and kinesthetic routines that are representative of the student state).

Again, a reminder: there are no 'absolute' student, streetcorner, sanctity or home states. The real-world distinction between these states is not always as pure as the simplistic description just presented. In reality, each state is interdigitated or tinctured with one another to varying degrees. Nevertheless, it is my claim that student behaviours do tend to cluster in the fashion just presented.

The micro ritual

Each school day consisted of a battery of instructional 'micro rituals', or individual lessons. Serving as the component and constituent elements of the macro ritual, the micro ritual offers us a model whereby we can isolate and catalogue various processual characteristics of ritual. A fixed number of micro rituals (six on the average) are nested in each macro ritual (e.g. six lessons per school day). I have presented the opening lesson of the day as paradigmatic of all micro rituals – not in terms of content, naturally, but in terms of structure, sequence and numerous performative characteristics. The following description will therefore be considered the epitomizing ritual of instruction.

SILENCE AND THE EVIL EYE (1)

Initially, teachers attempt to bring the students into a state of reverence for the opening prayer. In their attempt to project a certain gravity of bearing, to emphasize their authorial role, and to enhance their redoubtable presence, the teachers stand motionless at the front of the class. Sometimes a tinge of anguish breaks across their brows as if they were trying to appear noble and disinterested sufferers. With eyes narrowed, arms akimbo, and legs spread out slightly to give the impression of a firmly balanced body that is capable of repelling any struggle or attempted subversion (a kind of dressed down 'horse stance' that you find in the martial arts), the teachers move their heads in a steady, rotating fashion, much like the automatic surveillance cameras in department stores. This self-conscious and mechanical posturing tends to reinforce the mien of seriousness of the occasion and contributes to the artificial aggrandizement of the teacher-as-mentor or teacher as an unfathomable, mysterious, and all-powerful being. Brock's requisite 'commanding' appearance included a Rasputin-like beard.

The teacher's eye, like the Eye of God, becomes invested with menace and dread, and at times can assume the agency of divine wrath. The ability to structure and enforce the protocol of the occasion is inextricably woven into the status of the teacher as an instrument or arbiter of punishment. (Brock admitted to me privately that he grew a beard to give himself a more formidable and imposing appearance among his students; yet the question of whether or not there is an ideal physiogonomic and sartorial paradigm for this type of conventional teaching is a moot point.)

As soon as a few students begin to settle down, other students follow. When silence has been achieved, the teacher begins the prayer in an unhesitating tone.

PRAYER

Prior to the opening lessons of the morning and afternoon, prayer is recited. Prayer serves as a symbolic prologue for each lesson, linking the student body to the sacred body of Christ, and identifying what is to be taught with the Holy Family and community of saints as well as serving the more practical function of keeping the students quiet and motionless before instruction begins. In other words, through prayer the teacher attempts to insulate the affective self of each student against the boisterous, visceral reality of the streetcorner state. During the prayer there is an ambiguity evoked between the teacher as a dispenser of secular 'everyday' knowledge and the teacher as priest.

> *Student 1*: In a way a teacher is like a priest because when the priest says something you got to do it and the same with the teacher. They both are supposed to know what the right thing to do is.
>
> *Student 2*: Yeah, teachers are like priests but there's still a big difference. You don't go to school to confess your sins; you go to school to learn.
>
> *Student 1*: When you do something wrong, you confess your sins to the teacher.
>
> *Student 3*: She never gets anything out of me.
>
> *Student 4*: Sometimes she forces it out of us – to tell us if it was true or not.
>
> *Student 3*: She makes you do it; the priest doesn't make you do it.
>
> *Student 4*: He tells you to try to do it. The priest is more sympathetic towards your problems. The teacher just tells you what . . . the priest, he gives you advice and helps you make up your own mind. Like if you want to be good or not – it's up to you.
>
> *Student 1*: He also gives us prayers to do after Confession.
>
> *Student 3*: Well, she gives us lines! She gives me five hundred. There's a chart on the wall, saying 'happiness is.' Well I wrote happiness is not having a teacher like ____. She got angry at me and said: 'OK, mister, you got five hundred lines.' After three weeks I finished it.
>
> *Student 1*: They both help us to love God but the teacher can help us better to get a job.

In the minds of many students, the teacher projects characteristics of the priesthood – those qualities which prepare the students for both the workaday world and the sacred life of a Catholic. (This is further emphasized by the fact that the teachers periodically consult with three priests from the nearby parishes in order to prepare the students for their upcoming Confirmation. In addition, the priests schedule a number of classroom visits per year in order to chat with the students.) Therefore, by representing 'hooks' upon which students link the sacred and secular aspects of their scholastic cosmology, the teacher is very much the plenipotentiary of the priest. The teacher (as a representative of Christ) becomes the normative symbol of Catholocity and moral consensus. There exists a metonymic relationship between the teacher/priest and the embodiment of the good Catholic worker.

> *Student*: The teacher knows what the proper things are that you have to do. We learn about God and get ready for Confirmation. Most of us know the prayers off by heart. And we also learn math and reading and all the other stuff that will help us when we leave.

As a member of the educational clerisy, the teacher leads the students both in prayer and in school work. In a certain sense the opening lesson – and all subsequent lessons – can be looked upon as an extension of the opening prayer. The opening prayer is therefore the nodal point or hub of the entire sequence of instructional rituals. It is interesting to note that the morning orison is said in conjunction with the national anthem. It is in the conflation and conjunction of these two symbolic activities that the official forging of the sacred/secular instructional paradigm begins to emerge.

After the opening ceremonies the teacher transfers the group focus from the 'sacred' to his opening remarks and then to the 'work' at hand.

SILENCE AND THE EVIL EYE (2)

The teacher begins each lesson by invoking a characteristic authoritarian gesture – such as folding the arms (in the case of Barbie), standing behind the lectern (in Brock's case), or standing totally still by the side of the desk (in Penelope's case) – which abruptly signals the foreclosure of the streetcorner state. Once again, the eye contact is extremely pronounced. In fact, eyes are sometimes narrowed to tiny slits in order to signify displeasure at any lingering remnants of the streetcorner state. Again, the teacher waits for silence to ensue before beginning to talk – a ploy which Goffman would refer to as a 'bracket ritual'. Silence before and after the lesson sets off whatever the teacher has to say as important.

SACRED TALK

Teachers are montagists who use gestures, verbal intonation and rhythmic methods of ritualized expression. While a great deal of classroom life is ocular (in the sense that the focal instructional points revolve around silent reading and writing), the teacher *talks* throughout most of the instructional rites. Talk (which is often incessant to the point of painful monologue) is used by the teacher to define the situation or context of instruction. Occasionally the context is so ambiguous that it must be defined numerous times by the teacher so that students know exactly what is expected. However, there must always be some ambiguity if the sacred aura surrounding the instructional ritual is to be effective. That is to say, there must be a broad enough scope when setting the parameters for the lesson so that a number of interpretations are possible; otherwise, there is no room for the instructional system to evolve (although it is clear that the teachers are not directly aware of the connection between ambiguity and evolution; cf. Rappaport, 1971b).

Talk also allows the teacher to establish the scale or frequency of student responses. If a student is suspected of not following instructions, the teacher may call upon him to present some evidence that he has understood the proceedings. Failure to provide such evidence may result in a strict reprimand or a detention.

Teacher: Can you tell us Frankie?
Student: What?
Teacher: Maybe you can tell us the answer.
[Silence]
Teacher: Well what were you doing, talking to Juliana if you don't have the answer!

The initial speaking on the part of the teacher serves to focus student attention on himself. The teacher's own pedagogical presence becomes an instrument for organizing group identity. The students are placed immediately in the context of 'we are all students here under the leadership and direction of the teacher'.

Teacher: OK take out your notebooks and pencils and open your text books to where we left off last.

Teacher talk makes use of declarations and proclamations – what are sometimes called 'performatives'. A performative (after J.L. Austin) is an act or utterance which brings a conventional state of affairs into being. (For instance, when an authorized official states 'I name this ship the *Queen Elizabeth*', he does not describe a mere act of naming. Rather, the utterance itself constitutes the act of naming and therefore 'does something' – it performs a deed as well as says something.) A performative statement or illocutionary act is not subject to the same verification procedures as a referential remark; it is not subject to falsifiablity. We can question the conditions surrounding the performative utterances but not the beliefs underlying them. A performative may be judged ineffective – but only by using normative criteria such as valid, or invalid, appropriate or inappropriate. According to Rappaport, 'The performative constitutes a criterion in terms of which states of affairs are assessed as 'right' or 'wrong'.

The performative force of the teachers' instructional language played as much a part – if not more – than the actual informational content of instruction. Performative-like utterances often 'controlled' the communication during the pedagogical encounter. For instance, when a teacher made an announcement such as 'we are Catholics when we are behaving this way', and then proceeded to describe the behaviour of the students, she did not simply describe a state of affairs but actually brought a state of affairs into existence: she composed the 'charter' that inscribed the appropriate attitudes that Catholic students should exhibit. In essence, the teacher defined – in fact, *created* a moral order. The parameters that defined Catholic behaviour were thus drawn up and the students now had a criterion with which to judge subsequent behaviour as right (Catholic) or wrong (non-Catholic).

Teacher: We [Catholic students] don't act that way during class. You wouldn't act that way in your own homes, would you? You try to be polite when strangers come into your house, don't you? Then why can't you behave properly when guests come into the school? We try to show our neighbours from the other school that we respect others, that we care about others. From now, we shall always respect others, and treat others as we would have them treat us.

Once, when students were working hard at a task, and a teacher stated '*Now* this is a Catholic school,' she not only described something, but *did* something. A conventional effect was created: that of pronouncing dedication to a particular classroom exercise as 'Catholic'. The teacher thus helped to 'create' a spiritual and value laden domain through a certain performative-like utterance. In the example cited above, the students became part of Catholic cosmology by collectively engaging in an assignment. Presumably if the students, through laziness or defiance, chose not to work at the prescribed task, they would no longer 'be' in a Catholic school but in a marginalized, perhaps even pagan institution.

In addition to performatives, teachers used various indirect speech acts such as 'I hear fussing', 'I see slouching', 'I hear whispers', or 'somebody is not listening'. Indirect speech gives the impression that the source of the statements is permanent and sacred and not to be questioned (cf. Olson, 1980). Teacher talk also betrayed characteristics of formalization (cf. Bloch, 1975) and persuasion (cf. Paine, 1981). According to Clyde Kluckhohn, our subject/predicate form of speech creates the illusion of an immutable world of fixed relations between substances and their qualities (Bowers, 1984, p. 61). In actual fact, of course, the map (spoken word) can only approximate the territory (the reality behind the word), as Korzybski and Whorf have shown us.

Brock usually conducted his lessons behind a lectern at the front of the room. The lectern itself seemed to increase the importance of what Brock was trying to say. The format was typical of the traditional 'lecture'.

Student: . . . I don't know what it's called but it's [the lectern] the same sort of thing that the priest stands at and talks to us at on Sunday.

Barbie and Penelope did not use the lectern when addressing the class; nevertheless, they still delivered their declamations 'lecture style', usually standing in front of their desks and reciting factual information before the entire class – information which the students were expected to recite back, in condensed form, on request. Teacher talk often took the form of redundant epithets that had lost their original power through over use. Enthymemic appeals such as 'hard work pays off' and 'what you do now can influence your future later' – or varitions of these – were repeated often enough to become stripped of meaning yet nevertheless took on the liturgical power of the incantation, the rhythmic chant.

Constant talk on the part of the teacher was a way of achieving a synchronization of affect and overall group cohesion. Talk became, in effect, an autonomic tuning device. That is, the rhythmic drone of the teacher helped to decrease personal space and increase communal space (cf. Chapple, 1981). During a lesson, the teacher became, in Chapple's terms, a pacemaker intent on eliciting responses from a large number of 'uncoupled oscillators' and entraining them as rapidly and intensely as possible. Coined by William Condon, the term 'entrainment' refers to the process that takes place when the rhythms of two or more individuals become engaged and are able to synchronize (cf. Chapple, 1981; Hall, 1984, pp. 17–93).

The entrainment of the class was often affected by the spacing of the furniture, the seating arrangements of the students, teacher pauses and student responses.

Teacher: You have to project your voice so that everyone picks you up. While I'm giving a lecture I can also hear the other teachers so I'm often forced to shout my lessons. You have to get into a certain rhythm but if it's too smooth it can put kids to sleep. So you have to pick up the pace. You get to know the kids and the pacing after the first few months. The big trick is to wait until the kids are all settled down first. The prayers help with that.

In a similar fashion to the mass, instructional rituals revolved around recitation and response. Successful lessons appeared to possess a natural rhythm that provided for student reaction. They also possessed Csikszentmihalyi's characteristic of *flow*. That is, they were 'autoelic' and required no rewards or goals outside of themselves. Unsuccessful lessons were mostly teacher monologues. During the latter instances, students became increasingly restless or else fell into states of consciousness perilously close to sleep. Students generally found it difficult to forbear a sustained student state for forty minutes without 'goofing off'.

Student: The best lessons are when things are smooth. The teacher doesn't talk that much and gives the class a chance to talk. When the teacher talks too much it's like being in a car and listening to the engine hum. You get tired.

A major problem associated with the micro ritual was the spatial arrangement in the room which contributed to the oppressive sonic environment. The noise in the open area setting was, at the best of times, intolerable. The noise would routinely fluctuate from ear splitting pain, to decrescendo, to silence, to arias of jolting whispers, and back to a bedlam of voices. During the first lesson of the day the students' voices intoned a low, whispered hum. By lunchtime they had become an upper register chatter. Since it was hard to ignore the noise, teachers found it difficult – if not impossible – to establish a frequency capable of entrainment.

Total silence was present in the suite only during prayers. Brock once remarked that the only way he could think while he was lecturing was to shout his words. Otherwise, he couldn't string his thoughts together. Entrainment – when it did occur – rarely lasted very long because of the competing frequencies from the other classes.

Brock had the fastest frequency and greatest 'coupling power' of the three teachers. This was, no doubt, related to his deep, sonorous voice, his charisma, and the air of intense involvement in which he delivered his lessons. Consequently, Barbie's and Penelope's classes often listened to Brock's lessons, even though Brock's class was in another part of the suite. Students found Penelope's German accent obtrusive and were frequently discourteous to her on this account. In written exercises, students made curt remarks:

'Mrs _____ is a good teacher but she talks funny. I can't make out what she says.'

'She talks with an accent. People at the back of the room can't hear her.'

'When she is teaching, I can't make it out so I listen to the other teachers. So I get detention for not listening.'

Lessons were most rhythmically 'catching' when they were orchestrated by Brock – which probably accounts for the fact that I spent more time observing Brock's class than any other.

THE WRITTEN WORD

On the average, talking took place for about three-quarters of each lesson. Students were then expected to do 'follow-up' work consisting mostly of writing and reading from textbooks. Follow-up assignments often took the form of homework to be completed by the students that evening.

Students very clearly respected their textbooks. Perhaps this was partially attributable to the fact that one frequently used text was the Bible. The fact that students possessed little opportunity for challenging information from their texts increased the authority of the written word (cf. Olson, 1980, pp. 192–4). Is it any wonder that Catholic students (contrary to what some Protestants might think) revere the written word? After all, at the completion of the second reading during the mass, the priest reverently kisses the Bible – the 'written' or 'archival' God.

Written work also helped to objectify, reify and sanctify the contents of the lessons. C.A. Bowers holds that

> As much as the reality sharing process of the curriculum is dependent on written language there is a greater tendency for reification than if socialization were dependent entirely on interpersonal communication. This does not mean that interpersonal communication is free of reifications; what is being stressed . . . is that the nature of our language contributes to the transformation within the communication process of subjective intentions and interpretations into statements that often appear to denote an objective reality. . . . The appearance of facticity – that things are as they are named – is achieved by the inadequacy of our language to communicate context, intentionality, and subjective meaning. (1984, p. 61)

During follow-up assignments, students set their own rhythms for the duration of the period. Teachers attempted to ensure a smooth synchronization of this last activity by upbraiding students who were not writing.

THURSDAY, 12 FEBRUARY

I told Brock that he looked religious and that he reminded me of a picture of an early Jesuit missionary – one of 'God's Dobermans'. He said that no matter who you are, beards give you an 'intellectual' appearance. He thought about his teaching performance in two contradictory ways: as disciplinarian and as animator. He said that he would adopt either role according to which class he taught. With brighter kids he became the animator. With 'lower' students he became a disciplinarian. Brock said that he feels more like a 'protector' with his home room class and he relates to them on a more personal level. With his other classes, he feels more like a 'professional'.

I talked to Brock about the incredible eye contact the teachers in the suite use with their students. He said that his beard was effective in 'accenting his eyes'. I told him I was thinking of call-ing a section of my study 'The Evil Eye'. He laughed, thinking I wasn't serious. I was serious.

Brock was absolutely convinced that there are more beards among male teachers than in the population in general: 'They do it for control!'

For Brock, beards were devices to create a persona, a symbolic 'mask'.

FRIDAY, 20 FEBRUARY

Brock's geography lesson was interrupted by a voice from the PA. The class watched Brock talk to this voice coming from a grey, square grating. The scene struck me as bizarre.

I began to explore the notion of every teacher having his or her own 'power spot' that is, a place where he does most of his instructing and where he most often retreats when feeling unsure or threatened.

Brock's power spot was approximately five square feet behind his lectern. Barbie's was about three square feet in front of her desk. Penelope's was to the left of her desk. But she also taught in a variety of locations, usually in a seated position.

When Brock and Barbie changed classes, I noticed that each would go to the other's power spot almost instinctively. Later during the day, Brock asked me to take over his class (Barbie's home room) while he threaded a film projector in the other room. I wandered around the room, watching the kids do their seatwork. As soon as I approached Barbie's power spot the noise began to dim. But when I actually entered the power spot, one of the kids shot up his hand:

'Are you the teacher now?!'
'Well, not exactly,' I said.

'Cause I wanna know if I can get a drink.'
'Sure, go ahead.'

TUESDAY, 14 APRIL

I was amazed at how similar the days seemed, even though the content of the lessons never remained the same. I suppose there was a certain amount of security knowing the format of each day almost to the exact minute but then there was also the great risk of boredom. I found that after about an hour I would go almost into a trance state, unable to concentrate on my field-notes. The voices of the teachers didn't vary much and served almost as con-tinuous drone – veritable monotones – broken only by the deathlike silence before prayers.

On the average, teachers would pause in their lectures about three times every period, bringing a student into line with various remarks:

'Chris, why can I hear you up here?'
'There's a voice coming from the back of the room.'
'I don't care whose pencil that is. Whose pencil it is is not the purpose of the exercise. The purpose is to do the exercise.'

PERFORMANCE TYPES

As in the case of the macro ritual, the micro rituals were successful to the extent that the liminal pull of the instructional sequencing served to compete with the liminal pull of the streetcorner state. This occurred very seldom during my observations as teachers were generally reduced to presiders, mere functionaries. Seldom did teachers – as 'senders' of meaning – adjust their frequencies to the students. As passive 'receptors', students were expected to adjust their frequencies to the teacher. But the term 'frequency' does not just refer to pitch and rhythmical expertise in speaking or presenting information; a frequency also relates to the communication of particular information. This requires that the teachers become aware of the symbols and subject matter which the students find interesting and meaningful. Teachers must know what the students need to know.

Three variant teacher types were identified within the micro ritual: teacher-as-liminal-servant; teacher-as-entertainer; and teacher-as-hegemonic-overlord. When students responded with a sense of immediacy or purpose, either verbally or gesturally, to the teacher's performance – when, for instance, they became the 'primary actors' – then they engaged in an authentic ritual of instruction: the surroundings were sanctified, the students became co-celebrants of knowledge with teacher (who had adopted the role of liminal servant), and the class was transformed into a congregation. As in religious ritual, where the meta-congregation is God, the meta-congregation of a successful instructional ritual is the Logos (in Christian theology the Logos is equivalent to the second person of the Trinity and its functions are associated with the creative activity of Christ). In this sanctified curriculum 'moment' during which students bore witness to the universal wisdom embodied in the rites of instruction, the teacher's role partook of shamanic dimensions.

When students were actively engaged by the instructor, but – due to various obstacles inherent in the ritual structure and performance – remained isolated viewers of the action, then the students were being entertained. The classroom was transformed into a theatre and the students became an audience. In this instance, the teacher lost her shamanic function and encountered students in a number of roles: as a priestly pedagogue or propagandist – or even worse, an evangelist – for the dominant culture.

When, however, the students were not provoked to respond to the teacher's instruction – either verbally, gesturally or silently in their heads (e.g. when they ceased to think at all about what went on) – then the students no longer figuratively sat in a church or a theatre but in Max Weber's iron cage. The teacher was reduced to a hegemonic overlord and knowledge was passed on perfunctorily – as though it were a tray of food passed under a cell door. In such a situation – one that is all too common in our classrooms – the few feet surrounding the student might as well have been a place of solitary confinement: a numbing state of spiritual and emotional emptiness.

THE LIMINAL SERVANT

The following section on the liminal servant is a composite description of what I consider to be the best attributes of a teacher working within a liberatory pedagogy.[1] These attributes have been collected from observing teachers both formally and informally for over a decade. Some of the characteristics of the liminal servant were evident in teacher performances at St Ryan.

When a teacher possesses the attributes of a liminal servant, an added vitality is brought to the rites of instruction: figurative significance is given to the learning process, and the context of lessons is transformed from the indicative (a stress on mere facts) to the subjunctive (a stress on the 'as if' quality of learning), from resistance to undifferentiated human kindness, and from within the confines of social structures to the seedbeds of creativity located within the antistructure (a receptive mode of consciousness in which we exist in a state of human totality).

The liminal servant is both a convener of customs and a cultural provocateur – yet she (or he) transcends both roles. She does not subordinate the political rights of students to their utility as future members of the labour force. She is a social activist and spiritual director as much as she is a school pedagogue. The liminal servant, as the name suggests, is able to bring dimensions of liminality to the classroom setting where obligations that go with one's social status and immediate role are held temporarily in abeyance.

The liminal servant does not shy away from the ambiguity and opacity of existence. She/he is androgynous, drawing upon both feminine and masculine modes of consciousness. Much depends on her personal charisma and her powers of observation and diagnosis. She becomes aware of the strengths and weaknesses of her students by observing and diagnosing their ritual needs. The liminal servant views working-class students as members of an oppressed group. Not only does she fight for the equality of her students outside the classroom, but she also attempts to educate her fellow teachers to the dangers of false consciousness.

The liminal servant presents an array of symbols which have a high density of meaning for the student; she creates a 'felt context' by promoting conditions which will allow the student to internalize both exegetical (normative) and orectic (physical) meanings. By thus creating a particular posture towards symbols, she is able to ensure that symbols possess a fecundating power and are adequately encountered by students through both cognition and affect.

The liminal servant is the bringer of culture and is ever-cognizant of her shamanic roots. She is a mystagogue rather than an ideologue. She does not eschew theory (which would be a form of pedagogic pietism), nor does she avoid intuition that comes with practice (where avoidance would amount to a moribund intellectualism or 'siege mentality'). The *métier* of the liminal servant is the clearing away of all obstacles to the embodiment of knowledge. She abjures making excuses for the deficiencies of her students; rather, she proclaims the academic equality of all her charges.

The liminal servant is wary of too much ratiocination and leans towards divining myths, metaphors and rhythms that will have meaning and purpose for her students – not just as abstractions, but as 'lived' forms of consciousness. Modes of symbolic action are employed that do not betray a cleavage between the passive reception of facts and the active participatory ethos of 'learning by doing'. The liminal servant encourages students to enact metaphors and embody rhythms that bypass the traditional mind/body dualism so prevalent in mainstream educational epistemology and practice. The liminal servant is a vagrant, a tramp of the obvious who becomes the tramp of demystifying conscientization (Freire, 1984, p. 171). The ordinary becomes the object of critical examination and reflection.

The liminal servant does not put a high priority on structure and order (although her classes may be highly structured and ordered), and she is able to 'conjure' conditions amenable to the eventuation of communitas and flow. She knows that she must not merely *present* knowledge to students; she must *transform* the consciousness of students by allowing them to 'embody' or incarnate knowledge.

As in the case of the teacher-as-entertainer, the ontological status and personal characteristics of the liminal servant are intrinsically ambiguous. However, there are essential differences between these two pedagogical types. Whereas the teacher-as-entertainer is intent upon conditioning for sameness; the liminal servant nurtures counter-hegemonic forces through the formation of an alter-ideology. It is through this alter-ideology that the liminal servant is able to educate for individuality, distinction and eccentricity. She is closer to her students than to her profession.

The teacher-as-entertainer often fails to see the value of unique human experience whereas the liminal servant is never blind to the significance of collective values and class struggle. The teacher-as-hegemonic overlord follows her lessons entirely by the book. On a more abstract level, she serves as a conditioned reflex of the culture's consensus ideology.

All three teacher types are 'cultural practitioners' who produce, orchestrate, integrate and distribute cultural meanings, offer their incantations of various educational mythologies, and help to suffuse the classroom with particular orders of experience. To a far greater extent than the other pedagogical types, the liminal servant is able to help students crack the prevailing cultural crust and discover alternative meanings.

The liminal servant understands teaching to be essentially an improvised drama. To fully understand the subtext of the student, the liminal servant must 'become' the student as part of the dramatic encounter. While in the thrall of such a drama, the liminal servant knows that the results will often be unpredictable; that understanding, like play, has a spirit of its own (cf. Courtney, 1982). Feelings and attitudes become the matrix of learning for the liminal servant; thus the rational processes of her students must be placed in an emotive context.

The liminal servant often challenges the presuppositions embedded in the left hemisphere of the brain. Moreover, she is acutely aware of the distinction between abstract and objective truth. Aesthetic truth is prized as much as objective truth, for truth can only become 'real' when a student acts with it (cf. Courtney, 1982).

The liminal servant is a parashaman (cf. Grimes, 1982a), she is performance-oriented and enjoys working in small groups rather than with an entire class. She teaches in order to discover meanings for herself, not because she wishes to share available answers. Teaching is a form of 'holy play' that is more akin to the drama of hunting societies than to the theatre of agricultural societies (cf. Grimes, 1982a).

The liminal servant is a potentially dangerous role to enact; it could easily 'blow up' in the teacher's face, leaving both teacher and students emotionally scarred. The liminal servant is a role to which teachers should aspire only so long as the values they desire their students to embody are productive and beneficial for intellectual, moral and emotional growth.

Never did any teacher I observed at St Ryan possess all of the characteristics of the liminal servant at any one time. But when these characteristics did present themselves to some degree or another in the orchestration of an instructional rite, it was usually during religion class when the students were encouraged to discuss events related to their own lives and inner concerns as well as to reflect on sacralized images.

During religion class, students discussed fables, parables and biblical themes, built icons to hang on the Jesse Tree, constructed an Advent Wreath, lit candles and reflected on the meanings of sacred symbols. Once Brock discussed the concept of Christ as a social activist and students related stories of their own that dealt with issues of poverty and hardship.

> *Student*: Religion class is boring sometimes. But sometimes you get a feeling that God is real because the teacher asks you to look inside yourself for your own feelings. And then he explains those feelings using the Bible or talking about mass. Then when things happen we understand why they happen to us because of what God wants.

During a successful 'liminal' lesson, students dropped their 'student' personae and participated spontaneously in the lesson. Their 'actions' were not so much 'pretending' as 'doing'. Most of the time, however, teachers distanced their lessons to such an extent that what they had to say did not make much of an impression on the students. There was little stimulation and tension and therefore little catharsis. Too often there was no immediate discussion or portrayal of events which students could recognize as being vitally important. As lived bodies of authorized precedent, the micro rituals served mainly as sacred shields behind which teachers could hide from the incessant attempts by students to create their own personalized streetcorner culture inside school walls.

> *Student*: Most of the lessons are boring. Same old thing all the time. Why can't teachers make things interesting? They never ask us what we think is important.

As a part of the instructional process, teachers consciously – even self-consciously – manipulated ritual symbols and gestures in order to both entertain (in the sense of keeping the students interested and occupied) and control the students (keeping student behaviour within predictable limits). Teachers usually spent a great deal of time 'being in one's head' while 'acting' the role of teacher. Their gestures were dissimulative, were acted out for the sake of the spectator, and were often hidden behind the trappings of various 'official' facades and personae.

> *Teacher*: Sometimes I can see myself in different roles. Sometimes I'm like a parent. Other times I'm more like a sergeant. But

you can't be too friendly or the kids will take advantage of you and you'll lose some respect and suffer the consequences for the rest of the year.

In contrast, many students regarded the heteronomy of imitating 'the good student' with a certain amount of disdain. Some students were able to collude in search of appropriate gestures and decorum to fit the values and attitudes perceived to be those held by the teachers. Hence, there were those students who had mastered the art of 'acting middle-class' and reaped the rewards of a good evaluation and a chance to enter or remain at a level 5 or 6 programme.

Student: I hate trying to act like a browner. But you can get away with it. If the teacher thinks you're trying to be a browner before exams, then you'll get better marks. But you might lose your friends if you stay a browner too long.

Generally speaking, the micro rituals were of the teacher-as-entertainer or teacher-as-hegemonic-overlord model rather than the liminal servant paradigm. The pretence that learning is primarily a product of individual student volition – despite an ineffective performance on the part of the teacher – inured the student to the absence of real, active, participatory experience. Students were reduced to the role of pure spectators who assimilated knowledge *about* things rather than knowledge *of* things in relation to other things or knowledge as lived experience. Ostensibly, the paroxysm of the micro ritual occurred with the teacher's smiling reception at the recital of a student's correct answer.

Teacher: Good boy, Danny. You got it! Can you tell the class what the other fables in the chapter were about?

However, the latent consummation of the micro ritual did not occur with the successful recital of the correct answer, but through the accolades from teachers in response to the students' collective 'busy silence' during the seatwork exercises.

Teacher: I'm glad to see you all at work. You've all got the right idea.

In many ways, it was more important to be busy than to be correct. Instruction was often reduced to a time-and-space filling expediency.

MONDAY, 16 FEBRUARY

I was given permission to talk to the students about my research. It wasn't difficult for me to slip into the role of teacher. I had been speaking at a number of conventions and professional development days over the last few years and felt confident that I could win over most audiences – at least for a limited period of time. Because I felt that most of the work assigned the students was designed primarily to keep them busy, I tried to show – through my gestures and motions – that I cared about both the topic I was discussing and my audience. I wrinkled my brow and nodded my head. I also moved about the room. The metaphor I was trying to express with my body was: 'The time frame in which we are now engaged is important and serious.' I felt phony and sincere at the same time. I let my hands rest in my pockets to appear relaxed, informal, but I kept an anxious look on my face as if to indicate I would be disappointed if there wasn't a great deal of interest in my presentation.

I felt more sympathetic to the teachers when I put on the role of the pedagogue myself. My expectations and obligations were then framed in a similar manner to the teacher. Suddenly, I had to elicit certain responses from the students. I had to command attention, keep the students quiet, and make them appear interested. I had to prove my worth to the students and the teachers.

TUESDAY, 24 FEBRUARY

Today, as I was explaining my research to the students, a group of boys started to 'goof around'. One of the students was knocked off his chair and on to the floor. Students laughed. The other teachers watched me to see what I would do. Immediately I felt a rush of old sensations from my teaching days sweeping over me. My face felt flushed and I started feeling threatened. I had never been forced to 'discipline' a student since arriving in the suite. First, I waited for the boys to stop on their own. But the situation grew worse. So I finally exploded (to my horror) and directed my anger at the most obstreperous student:

'Hey, what the hell are you doing!'

My eyes darted to Brock as I let go of the remark. I think he was smiling but I couldn't be sure. The class was stone silent. I started to swagger, to get into the role of 'Don't mess with me any more – or I'll take your head off!'

Afterwards I apologized to Barbie for getting 'heavy' with her kids. She smiled: 'Hey, no problem at all. I enjoyed it. It only reinforces my own authority!'

THE STAFF MEETING

Staff meetings were held periodically throughout the school timetable (approximately once every week). The meetings were used to discuss problems of morale, to provide information on forthcoming workshops and events, and to serve as a collective forum to signify unity. One senior staff member – a verbose gentleman who was quite popular among the staff – perceived staff morale to be a serious problem. There were rumours that the school was going to be made over completely into a high school the following year – with only a small coterie of teachers remaining from the current staff. The fact that many teachers weren't sure at what school they would be employed the following year hardly contributed to a positive school climate.

One staff member criticized as 'ridiculous' the Board's present arrangement of sending students from neighbouring 'feeder' schools to St Ryan for grades 7 and 8. He questioned how you could build morale among students – or teachers – when you are working with large groups of grade 7s and 8s who would be together for only two years.

In such a climate of uncertainty, staff meetings offered an arena where frustrations could be voiced and support compassionately extended. Teachers would enter the staff room shaking their heads and complaining, only to be rescued by other teachers inquiring what was wrong – and then encouraging them to 'hang tough', and 'stick it through'. In this sense, a staff meeting could be looked upon as type of ritual of revitalization since it served to regulate the discharge of collectively accumulated anxiety and emotional distress. Apathy was temporarily dissolved. And while every staff meeting consisted of a practical exchange of information (e.g. the simple sharing of facts), it also symbolized and affirmed the 'rational' nature of teaching itself (e.g. what the teachers referred to as their 'Socratic' style of teaching through questioning and answering).

During one meeting, a staff member exhorted those present not to expect too much from this year's crop of students, claiming that teachers couldn't be expected to fill sixty-ounce bottles with

ninety ounces of wine. By this he meant that Portuguese students
– presumably because of their language and cultural differences
– couldn't be expected to learn as much as middle-class Anglo-Saxon
students. Staff meetings thus became occasions during which the
tacit categories that located Portuguese students as academically
inferior were credentialized and made legitimate. The paradigmatic
status of cultural deprivation theory was therefore enhanced through
the imputed consensus that Portuguese students were 'inferior' to
middle-class students in manifold ways – the most pronounced
deficit consisting of poor academic achievement. Through informal
gossip on the part of the teachers, the Portuguese student was made
into a type of subcultural underdog – a member of an underclass
or *Untermensch*.

> *Teacher*: When I talk to other teachers about the problems they
> face with immigrant students, it makes your problems seem all
> the less troublesome because you know others are facing similar
> situations. The problem as I see it is that students don't get the
> same type of stimulation at home as non-immigrant students
> from better areas of the city. Their vocabularies are weak to begin
> with and they don't have the social skills to interact in a
> reasonable and independent way. You've got to be on their backs
> all the time.

Under the shibboleth of 'cultural deprivation', the concept of the
Portuguese student as an 'alien' from a subaltern class became part
of the ideological ensemble or set of canonical categories of teacher
thinking and therefore part of the teachers' corpus of classroom
knowledge. Through informal teacher dialogue over sandwiches
and coffee, the stereotype of the Portuguese 'deviant' was able to
invade the lexicon of professional chitchat.

In addition to communally confirming categories of deviance
with regard to students, staff meetings also had a determinate effect
on the school's hidden curriculum. Meetings such as these were
part of the unstated pedagogical plot of redeeming Azorean students
from the horror of their 'medieval' culture-forms, their 'vagrant'
attitudes, and their 'primitive' raw being.

Expectations of teachers by Board and Church officials were clari-
fied on these occasions as recent conciliar, papal, curial, or diocesan
directives were discussed in relation to their possible influence on
educational decisions. The power of the school administration was
affirmed and a sense of social solidarity was created.

THE OBJECTIFICATION OF THE CLASSROOM CULTURE

The rites of instruction constituted one of the primary means by which the cultural world of the school was objectified or reified. Reification in the suite impinged on how the instructional rituals enabled the teachers and students to decode reality through socially acquired stereotypes, pre-definitions, and ideologies that made up the explanatory system or cosmology of the suite.

Reification is an extreme form of what Berger and Luckmann refer to as 'objectification' – part of the process of the social construction of reality. They define reification as

> the apprehension of the products of human activity *as if* they were something else than human products – such as facts of nature, results of cosmic laws, or manifestations of divine will. Reification implies that man is capable of forgetting his own authorship of the human world, and further, that the dialectic between man, the producer, and his products is lost to consciousness. The reified world is, by definition, a dehumanized world. (1967, p. 89)

Both students and teachers unquestioningly internalized the cultural operative in the school milieu in their reified forms. Through the ritualized interactions of classroom life, the school was able tacitly to mediate the conceptual development of the students. Rarely did students encounter the culture directly. They were trapped in a puerile catechism of lococentric discourse.

Instructional rituals were linked to reification in a number of contexts. For instance, from the teachers' perspective, students were looked upon as 'level threes or fours'. Many of them were described as 'rude' and 'bad-mannered'. They were simply 'kids from the hills'. Collectively they were described as a 'low' or 'basic level' group. Some of the students were even reified as 'clowns' and 'delinquents' during informal teacher discourse. On one occasion, a senior staff member used the term 'wolves in sheep's clothing' to describe a group of students. A definite feeling was evoked that the Portuguese student was 'primitive' in some fundamental way. Thus, the emergence of the feral stereotype:

> *Staff member*: When something violent happens in the schoolyard, generally, it's usually the Portuguese for some reason or another.

In addition, the Brother Regis students (who share space with St Ryan) were occasionally described as 'hoods' or 'toughs'.

Staff member: They're all hoods! We've got tough, problem kids. But . . . they walk smartly, even try and behave smartly because they're wearing smart uniforms.

Italian students were thought by some teachers to be less honest but more sophisticated than the 'primeval' Portuguese students.

Staff member 1: I find the Portuguese are more honest in their emotions. I think the Italians have got all sorts of twists and turns to something.

Staff member 2: The Italians are culturally more sophisticated. The Portuguese student comes from basically a more primitive environment that's mostly agricultural and he is still influenced quite a lot by the superstition of the Church there which tends to carry over a lot of superstition from Europe.

One of the consequences of this reification was that 'basic level' programmes were created to fit an instructional paradigm for the 'below average' student. This further reinforced the perception that immigrant students were dysfunctional. In educational parlance, this is called the lie of 'cultural deprivation'. Students were reified as lacking in socialization or as pathologically deficit in cultural graces: in short, they were regarded as constitutionally disposed towards academic retardation and atavistic behaviour – the Lockean view of children as unformed adults in need of civilizing taken to a hideous extreme (cf. Postman, 1982). One smiling teacher tried 'humourously' to sum up the situation by describing the students as products of 'bad sperm'.

This particular use of nomenclature – frequently called 'labelling' – which affirms Azorean students as culturally deprived and therefore pathological – acquires an objective legitimacy by virtue of its association with esoteric or pedagogical opinion. It becomes a pejorative – yet sedulously promoted – typification that is all the more powerful because hiding behind the veil of 'professional' status is the pathologizing of the darker-skinned Portuguese body.

Students were physically separated into unevenly distributed groups and moved from class to class within those groups. Teachers generally geared the contents of the lessons to one level only, despite the fact that students are supposedly characterized by a wide range of differing abilities.

Managerial practices were emphasized and there was a strong stress on disciplinary tactics. Students were taught to consider themselves not simply as students, but as qualitatively distinct types of students: namely, level three, level four, or level five students. The criteria that were used to determine these levels were perceived as ambiguous by the majority of students.

> *Student*: My teacher said that I could easily be a level five but I fool around a lot. I know I could but it would be hard for me. I think I'm a level four now and I want to be a level five because I want to go to Central Tech and take some subjects there and they're sort of hard. I asked the teacher one time, I said, 'What level am I?' And he said 'Oh, you could easily be a level five.' I thought, 'Oh, I guess so.' He expects more, sometimes less – like my French teacher. I hate that. Like I got 27 out of 100. She said, 'That's very good; that's a beginning.' Like, my math teacher would say, 'Oh my God, is that all!'

In an interview with a senior staff member, the remark was made that Portuguese students learn best when discipline is strict and the work is drudgery.

> *Staff member*: They [the Portuguese students] basically see life as tough, harsh, and unrewarding. That's one aspect of their life. You can see that in the country from where they come from. They have to work hard at the land. They have to eke out a living from the cruel sea all around them. And in that environment there's nothing that really comes easy.

The same staff member also mentioned that the school must be 'ardently sensitive to the cultural differences of the students' by making schoolwork dull. His general remarks about Portuguese students conveyed the opinion that the students at St Ryan were future delinquents; he also betrayed an uneasiness about whether or not Catholic education could survive mass participation:

> *Staff member*: I think Catholic schools in the city are really lucky because they're level five . . . this is the exception [St Ryan]. We're the one with all the level threes. All the others are exclusively level five . . . I think it's unfortunate in some ways that now we're taking children for the hospital service, we're

taking children for the penitentiary service. We're bringing so many other dimensions into what is essentially an academic institution.

There was an attempt, then, to concretize the culture of the school so that it conformed to the putative culture of Portugal – at least by what was regarded by teachers as an emphasis on hard work and drudgery. While one could, superficially at least, consider the staff member's objectives as an attempt to implement a 'multicultural' sensitivity into school programming, one might, on the other hand, question whether it is not pedagogical treason to reify the social world through classroom rituals into a puerile cultural fiction where life is boredom and drudgery. According to Robin Williams,

> A cultural fiction exists whenever there is a cultural description, explanation, or normative prescription that is both *generally accepted as a norm* and *is typically followed* in conduct but is at the same time markedly at variance with the subjective conceptions or inclinations of participants in the pattern or with certain objective scientific knowledge. (1970, p. 432)

Cultural fictions are created by a ritual 'framing' of events – a demarcation, remarking upon, or bracketing of slices of social life. A ritual frame is essentially a fiction; it claims that the world is as it seems instead of invented or made up (Myerhoff, 1977, p. 200).

The organizational properties of the instructional rituals made it easy to regard the students as one body lumped together and composed of either 'achievers' or 'underachievers' (also referred to as 'dull-normals'). Except for mathematics and language, in which students were tracked into three groups (levels 3, 4, and 5), there were no ability groupings whatsoever (e.g. in geography, history, French, industrial arts, health, current events, family studies, religion). Every student was expected to do the same amount of work, the same assignments, within the same time span. This overall situation was reponsible for some feelings of unity and presence of homogeneity throughout the suite: the world operated on everyone basically the same way. Nevertheless, considerable pressure was put on those students who weren't able to keep up with the others (although some students preferred it to being tracked into a low-level maths or language group). Of course, the possibility was always open for the teachers to structure their classroom rituals in a more individualized manner (perhaps even encouraging more self-generated rituals) so that students with different levels of cognitive ability would be more prudently served. However by keeping the patterning and sequencing of events and ritual formats uniform and predictable throughout the suite, the teachers were able to create the effect of wielding more power and control.

THURSDAY, 9 APRIL

Thinking that I would miss the beginning of mass with the students, I went directly to the church after disembarking from the subway. The church doors were locked. I had gone to the wrong church. So I went back to the school.

I passed the office on the way to the suite, and overheard a teacher chide her class:

'You children are grade threes! Grade threes! If you can't behave now, you're in big trouble. You should be able to behave perfectly. Perfectly! Because everything goes downhill after grade three. Downhill!'

THE SANCTIFICATION OF THE SUITE

Rituals do not possess a neutral opacity; they are invariably trace-ridden with ideological residues which point to the existence of a ritual substructure that reflects various social and cultural logics. The reification or objectification of classroom culture points to one of the logics of ritual production; but the rituals of classroom instruction also fuel the hegemony of yet another logic: the sanctification of pedagogical practices.

The following section attempts to portray how classroom rituals are able to sanctify and legitimate certain configurations of time and space as well as certain relationships of power (*pouvoir*). The broad challenge of this portrayal will be to develop a curriculum of cultural politics that runs athwart the logic of capital and the hegemonic hold of Late Capitalism. What is imperative here is the deconstruction and displacement in our classrooms of the centrality of symbolic manipulation and moral violence – a task which is necessary in order to promote the insurrection of sub-jugated student voices and the creation of a pedagogy of self-empowerment. Accordingly, educators are called to adopt a adversarial position to normative ritual practices and their repressive and displacing forms.

So far we have used the concepts of objectification and reification to help discern how material and symbolic practices are constituted through rituals of instruction. A useful way of thinking about instructional rites, at this point, would be to view them as discursive practices which constitute a discourse. To understand the ritual process as a performative discourse – one which has a preferred reading within the dominant signifying system – is to confront the hidden and unrecognized codes that operate in the everyday world of classroom signifying practices.

Classroom rituals represent a field of discourse or dominant mode of representation which naturalizes, sanctifies and privileges certain forms of knowledge and symbolic practice over others and, in so doing, shatters the force of other discourses. A discourse theory of ritual constitutes a means of understanding how symbols are related to other symbols in a field and how they serve as strategic articulations that assign students to their place in the moral economy of the school by making maleness and whites an invisible culture marker against which they are judged.

A discourse is a cultural-political configuration of signifiers through which ideologies are inscribed. A ritual event constitutes a discourse that is both constitutive of and a product of power (cf. Foucault, 1980). For instance, the ritualized discourse of school instruction at St Ryan presents to students a realist notion of the world in which there exists a privileged ground of reflection (e.g., Catholic religious teaching) from which students are encouraged to organize their temporal existence. Within this discourse, knowledge and power are understood as essentially direct and unmediated.

Classroom life is lived within a multiplicity and plurality of shifting discourses which are anchored materially and symbolically by ritual performances. Within the discursive fields and contested cultural spaces of classroom and streetcorner cultures, various discourses war for dominance. In the classroom, rituals do their work of privileging particular renderings of how everyday life should be understood and physically engaged. However, within the discourse or rationality of streetcorner rituals, instructional rites constitute a false epistemology.

Ritual discourse is set in train through particular juxtapositions of symbols, the commutative properties of root paradigms, and the various morphological characteristics of the rituals themselves. Since there is never a one-to-one relationship between ritual symbols and their referents, interpretations of ritual are infinitely extendable.

While one can never fully dismantle or unravel the plurality of classroom and streetcorner discourses, we can gain some purchase on ritual's articulating mechanisms by examining the symbolic and morphological characteristics of the rituals. The following section attempts to sketch out the 'rules of formation' of ritual sanctity and power.

One way that the instructional rites of the suite were able to contribute to the reification of the classroom culture was to create an envelope or net of sanctity surrounding the ritual transactions of the day – what Peter Berger (1967) would call a sacred canopy of the socially constructed world. Sanctity here is referred to as 'the quality of unquestionableness imputed by a congregation to propositions in their nature neither verifiable nor falsifiable' (Rappaport, 1980, p. 189). It is important to keep in mind that unquestionableness is not necessarily related to religion; in fact, unquestionable tenets exist in many facets of secular society. As Moore and Myerhoff remind us:

> That which is postulated as unquestionable may but need not be religious. It may but need not have to do with mystical forces and the spirit world. Unquestionability may instead be invested in a system of authority or a political ideology or other matters. (1977, p. 22).

Since school work was fequently boring and drudging, the undertaking of tasks set by the teachers had to be located within a metacommunicative frame which read: 'What and how you are required to perform in the suite is important for your future welfare. Regard your work and behaviour as part of a *sacred* task that must not be questioned.'

Whether or not the teacher or the social system was the true author of the instructional rituals is debatable. Perhaps it is more accurate to consider them as co-authors. Nevertheless, most students participated in the rites of instruction with few questions asked. When one student asked Penelope why she had to 'get to work', Penelope bluntly replied: 'Because you have to, that's all.' When a student questioned a visiting representative from one of the high schools about why high school students were forced to wear uniforms, the visitor answered: 'Because it's tradition'. When Barbie told some restless students that their behaviour was 'inappropriate', there was no material referent given in her reply (i.e. no concrete reason given as to 'why' their behaviour was inappropriate).

Many of the routine remarks and elicitations used by the teachers during instruction possessed performative and illocutionary power. The metafactive quality of the performatives allowed conventions to be established through the creation of criteria from which states of affairs were judged as Catholic and non-Catholic, as sacred and profane.

Students realized that there was some logic to school rules and conventions. A number of respondents maintained that without school rules there would be confusion and chaos. However, students were also aware that many of the rules were 'unnecessary' – even 'stupid'. It is significant that no class time was allotted to discuss the rules, procedures, or the compostition and dynamics of the classroom environment.

What was very striking about the instructional rituals was their operational efficacy. A sense of certainty was created by the monotonous, ineluctable invariance of instructional forms. Rappaport has described the power of ritual in terms of its invariance, defining ritual as 'the performance of more or less invariant sequences of formal acts and utterances not encoded by the performers' (1979, p. 175).

Lessons were ritually articulated through a series of postulates and directives which remained unquestionable. Most were delivered verbally in lessons (which were nearly always lectures), or from standard texts. Much of the content disseminated by teachers was not amenable to verification; but neither was it vulnerable to falsification. Propositions, we have said, do not necessarily have to be religious in order to be surrounded with a sense of sanctity. Secular knowledge acquired by students by participating in the instructional rituals was considered just as sanctified as postulates delivered in church. A sense of unquestionability was invested in the cadences of the teacher' voice, the invariance of the instructional format, and the ideological dimensions embedded in the root paradigms.

Regardless of the monotonous repetition, the invariance and the formality of classroom instruction, most students conformed to what was required of them, although this conformity did not, in most instances, entail belief. While student conformity did not necessarily symbolize students' belief in the values of the school, it did serve as an 'index' of accepting those values. Going through the motions of school rituals, no matter how perfunctorily, brought conformance into being.

The mere conforming to the 'form' of the ritual (i.e. going through the motions) was perforce to conform to the culturally postulated codes, conventions and values of the school (cf. Rappaport, 1979).

Student: The school rules are bad. But you have to have them. But I don't know why we have to put up with boring work. You've got no choice, though.

Student: I don't believe everything the teacher says. But you have to respect your teacher. If you show disrespect you can get expelled. . . . So you go along with the rest of the kids.

Teacher: We can't suspend a student for not believing. But we do try to help a student resolve his or her own doubts about their faith.

Teacher: All that we ask is that a student learns enough social skills to get along with others in his class.

It appears that what is required of the students at St Ryan is compliance in the rituals, not necessarily belief in the information or values transmitted through the rituals. This echoes anthropologist Roy Rappaport's idea that conformance does not necessarily imply belief – but is instead a meta-meaning which attempts to blur the distinction between map and territory. At this point it may prove worthwhile to unpack some of the literature on how ritual enables 'sanctified' messages to be communicated through its morphological characteristics.

That the major messages of ritual are recurrently transmitted through its form, is now accepted as a fact by a growing number of ritologists. Victor Turner has been quoted as saying that rituals are to symbols as is a metal container to a radioactive isotope (Myerhoff, 1977, pp. 199-200). In addition, Turner states that:

The work of ritual (and ritual does 'work', as many tribal and post-tribal etymologies indicate) is partly attributable to its morphological characteristics. Its medium is part of its message. It can 'contain' almost anything, for any aspect of social life, any aspect of behaviour or ideology, may lend itself to ritualization. (Turner, 1979b, p. 87)

Rappaport has bequeathed to us the foundations of a theory which accounts for the sanctity of ritual as being inherent in the morphology of the ritual itself (the 'cybernetics of the holy'). He points out that if the order of acts performed and utterances voiced by the actor is not encoded by him, his performance perforce conforms to that order. In other words, by simply performing a ritual, the participant subordinates himself to that order. For a performer to reject whatever is encoded in the ritual in which he is performing is a contradiction in terms and therefore impossible. While performance of a ritual does not always entail *belief* (the act of the private, subjective 'I') or *faith* (the dialectic between 'I' and 'me'), it does entail *acceptance* (an outwards visible act of the socially constituted 'me') and therefore *obligation*. According to Rappaport, it is the acceptance by the participants of the invariance of a ritual which is the form of the sacred. In ritual, the transmitter-receiver (the participant) becomes one with the message she is transmitting and receiving. Rappaport writes:

Thus, *by performing a liturgical order the performer accepts, and indicates to himself as well as to others that he accepts whatever is encoded in the canons of the liturgical order in which he is participating*, that is, of which he has become a part. This message of acceptance is the indexical message – or meta-message – that is intrinsic to all ritual, the self-referential message without which canonical messages are devoid of force, mere theological or philosophical speculation or opinion. The message of acceptance is not a trivial message because men are not bound by their genotypes to the acceptance of any particular order and have the choice, a least logically, of participating or not. (1978, p. 84)

Thus, *acceptance is intrinsic to performance*. Again, Rappaport clearly distinguishes between 'acceptance' and 'belief'. Belief is 'an inward state knowable subjectively if at all', whereas acceptance, in contrast, is not an inward state but a *'public act* visible to both witnesses and the performer himself'. Rappaport elaborates:

Acceptance is . . . a fundamental social act forming the basis, as unknowable and volatile belief cannot, for public social orders. Acceptance not only is not belief, it does not even imply belief. While the private processes of individuals may be persuaded by their participation to come into conformity with their public acts this is not always the case. Men may have their doubts. But doubt does not vitiate acceptance. Indeed, a number of theologians have told us that acceptance may be more profound than uncritical belief, for in his participation the performer may transcend his own doubts by accepting in defiance of them . . . (1978, p. 85)

Following the theoretical lead of linguistic philosopher J.R. Searle (1969), Rappaport holds that 'even in the absence of belief and faith the act of acceptance in ritual is not hollow because . . . acceptance entails obligation . . .' (1980, p. 188). Morality is thus *inherent* in ritual, argues Rappaport, if obligation is entailed by acceptance and acceptance is entailed by participation.

Searle himself writes that 'when one enters an institutional activity by invoking the rules of the institution one necessarily commits oneself in such and such ways, regardless of whether one approves or disapproves of the institution' (1969, p. 189). Myerhoff comments that

rituals are innately rhetorical. Doing is believing, and as Mircea Eliade puts it so well, one may become what one performs. Rituals call for belief, but not through the cognitive mechanisms that allow critical thinking to interfere with conviction. (1982a, p. 28)

Rappaport goes so far as to claim that sanctity is a part of *discourse* itself. Sanctity or unquestionableness is related to both the *acceptance* entailed by performance of the ritual and the *invariant characteristics* of ritual. Interestingly, Rappaport suggests (following Anthony Wallace) that if ritual is a mode of communication it is one that is *devoid of information* (if we take information to mean that which reduces uncertainty). He notes that 'the informationless of ritual's invariance asserts that that which it encodes is certain, which is very close to saying unquestionable' (1980, p. 189). He also follows Bloch (1974) in maintaining that the *punctiliousness* animating ritual utterances is virtually a concomitant of invariance and therefore evokes the notion of sanctity (p. 190). Rappaport's work thus elucidates the bi-directionality of ritual: in the self-same act of ritual the performer is (1) incorporated into an order and (2) establishes that order (p. 187). While sanctification does not necessarily entail faith, individuals are much more willing to accept sanctified than unsanctified messages as true (1971b, p. 30).

Rappaport's theory has a profound potential for uncovering the power of instructional ritual in school settings (to the extent that the rituals of the classroom exhibit invariance, participation and performative force). Following Rappaport, we can see how students going through the stilted motions of a 'good learner' *embody* the protocols of the dominant culture rather than merely display them.

As Anglicanism holds that *lex credendi lex orandi* (one believes what one prays), it could be said about school ritual that one conforms to whatever symbol or paradigm one enacts or embodies. Engagement in ritual, therefore, does not necessarily affect the participant's ultimate values, but is more of a function or political power. Students' subjectivities are shaped through conformance to the classroom liturgy. At age 14 students have, after all, no choice but to attend school. Compulsory attendance has been decreed by those who neither know nor understand the students but who nevertheless have an investment in their conformance.

The rituals of instruction ultimately established classroom conventions (G.K. Chesterton once referred to convention as 'the democracy of the dead'). In their questionnaires, students indicated that they accepted most of the classroom conventions. And in their daily behaviour students showed (with some exceptions to be discussed in the next chapter) relative conformity to those rules – despite the fact that, in creating those rules, teachers betrayed an almost slavish dedication to the banal. In reality, of course, conventions for establishing procedure, instructional settings and teaching styles are entirely arbitrary (cf. Rappaport, 1971b, p. 32).

Interviews with several school administrators revealed that there was considerable latitude with respect to establishing classroom conventions, provided discipline was maintained and the required content was taught. However, there was pressure on the teachers in the suite to keep their conventions uniform. Similar philosophies of teaching and compatible teaching styles were cited by Brock, Penelope and Barbie as the major reasons why they worked so well together. Working well together meant effective behavioural management and increased surveillance capacity. The advantage of a uniform pedagogical approach was that it prevented the outbreak of random and unpredictable events. Rituals were carefully – though perhaps unconsciously – orchestrated to mask the arbitrary nature of classroom conventions even if those conventions proved to be objectionable to the students. Two conventions frequently cited as objectionable by students dealt with the short time allotted for lunch and the fact that permission was not always given to students wishing to use the washroom.

The sanctification of classroom experience reinforced the dominant epistemes of work as good and play as bad. To be busy at work was to be, in effect, in a state of grace. On the other hand, when students engaged in play, they were chastised and disciplined. Offenders and culprits became 'polluters' of the sacred workplace. Sometimes they were 'excommunicated' and transferred to a different school entirely. One grade 8 student was placed in a grade 6 class because, as one teacher told me, 'he acted like a grade 6 so we put him into a grade 6 class. Besides, he's small for his age.'

What seemed to transpire frequently throughout enactment in the rituals of instruction was the wielding of power for its own sake. Power – moral force ritually legitimized by organizational fiat – was often antipathetic to the marketing of sanctity throughout daily classroom transactions. The blatant exercise of power often punctured the canopy of sanctity surrounding the negotiations between students and the teacher. This would usually occur when the students felt that their best interests were not always among the first and foremost priorities on the teachers' agenda. For example, when a student had to go to the washroom, teachers would often say 'no' when there was clearly no reason for it except for the unseemly and gratuitous wielding of power on the part of the teacher.

Student 1: School rules are needed to control the school but not needed to control our lives. . . . School rules should not be like prison rules.

Student 2: I think that some of the school rules and routines are too much for us to take. ... The lunch hour is so short that we have hardly no time to do anything. We're not even allowed to go to the washroom after we're finished eating our lunch. We're not allowed to go to our lockers if we forget something. I hate these school rules.

The way that power was wielded in the suite conformed significantly to Rappaport's idea that sanctity can become eroded by an inordinate exercise of power. Sensitive to the possible degradation of sanctity by power, Rappaport points out that when acceptance of a ritual is coerced, it is transformed into a lie: the 'lie of the coercer'. Collectively, these lies become 'lies of oppression'. Rappaport adds that:

> In lies of oppression the coercer is not only the liar but also the ultimate victim of his own lie, for if, as I have just argued, both acceptance and its waning inform the regulatory operations of society then for an authority to coerce acceptance is for it itself to distort the information by which it is guided. (1976, p. 99).

Thus, power not only becomes inhumane and threatens truth, but it also becomes *maladaptive*. Sanctity, 'the foundation of truth and correctness', is turned into a deceit at the hands of those interested in manipulating others in the interests of power and materialism. Once this occurs, the 'act of ritual acceptance, once more profound than belief, becomes a paradigm of hypocrisy' (p. 99). This often results in the falsification of consciousness, neurosis and alienation among the ritual participants.

Analysis of the instructional rituals of the suite afforded some corroboration of Rappaport's concept of 'oversanctification' (1976, pp. 96–7). Oversanctification existed in the suite to the extent that petty rules such as the times afforded to do work and to eat lunch were non-negotiable and therefore absolutized. Oversanctification occurred when the messages embodied in the school rules were taken to be *true in themselves* (i.e. specific with respect to regulatory mechanisms rather than perceived as sanctified by virtue of sacred propositions which are non-specific and thereby open to reinterpretation). When this was the case – as it often was – the central hierarchy of the suite became all the more resistant to adjustment through reinterpretation. This form of oversanctification had deleterious effects, provoking instances of open hostility towards the teachers. For example, when students were incessantly exhorted to 'keep busy' at some specified task, the exhortation often took the form of a sacred proposition in itself, rather than as an acknowledged management technique designed to help the teacher survive. Little room was left for the students to interpret the meaning of busyness or the value of the assigned tasks.

As Rappaport has noted, oversanctification can be found in the resistance of the Vatican to birth control and insistence on clerical celibacy. It is possible that, without oversanctification, both clerical marriage and birth control could be made acceptable without challenge to sacred dogma through reinterpretation (1971b, pp. 71–2).

THE ROOT PARADIGMS OF INSTRUCTION

Ora et labora (Work and pray): early Benedictine motto

Two guiding root paradigms emerged from the multistranded fabric of classroom life: 'becoming a worker' and 'becoming a Catholic'. These root paradigms (close cognates of Stephen Pepper's 'root metaphors' and James Fernandez's 'ritual metaphors') formed the governing design and primary ritual nodes of the suite and constitued the germinal forms of world views. Root paradigms serve as culturally induced scripts that exist in the teachers' and students' heads. They can be further conceived as types of master compasses that guide cognition or automatic pilots that programme – or at least delimit – behaviour. 'Becoming a worker' and 'becoming a Catholic' represented two of the most prevailing motifs that emerged from the Gestalt of daily classroom life and the collective treasury of classroom meanings.

Although root paradigms are considered here as isolable processive forms which characterize the generative themes running through the cognizable world of teachers and students, it must be acknowledged, in reality, that these paradigms represent only a small parcel of the students' and teachers' systematized beliefs and values. They do not encapsulate the whole of an individual's 'life script'. To characterize their functions in yet another way, root paradigms may be said to comprise the *primordial disclosures of the dominant pedagogical themes – the chief exemplifications of the ritual scenarios of classroom life*. Admittedly, however, not all classroom life can be reduced to the polysemic ramifications of root paradigms.

The root paradigms were often surrounded by a nest of attendant symbols – the former delineating major educative themes, the latter either reinforcing, rendering ambiguous, or countermanding the root paradigms.

BECOMING A WORKER

The observations and theoretical sorties that follow support existing research on the 'hidden curriculum' which suggests that the school serves as a form of 'workplace' where students rehearse role behaviours and develop competencies essential to participation in bureaucratic work settings (Bowles and Gintis, 1976; Dreeben, 1968). They also lend support to the notion that school functions to allocate students within the sociocultural system from the perspective of ascribed traits (Carnoy, 1974; Katz, 1975). The view that schools are created to process good workers is hardly a seminal insight and not an even particularly novel one. Yet while this view makes no claim to originality, it is re-presented here because, as patently – even flagrantly – obvious as it is in itself, the concept that schools are designed to create competent and obedient workers takes on a number of hitherto unexplained implications when we introduce a cultural focus and begin to question the manipulation of students through symbolic and ritualistic enactment. It is in the exegesis of rituals and root paradigms in particular that the process of cultural reproduction spreads itself out for careful and detailed scrutiny.

A prevailing root paradigm – the one which guides and orients a large portion of the activity of the suite – has been termed 'becoming a worker'. This dominant theme reveals itself most often throughout the instructional rituals. While it is almost too obvious to state that school is geared to programming students to churn out 'work' in the form of assignments, tests, projects, reports, etc., what is often not so obvious is how the process of schooling manages to both inculcate certain dispositions and ideologically constitute student subjectivities in favour of 'the good worker' – a process which is necessary for the maintenance of the daily round of events. It is this process to which this analysis is now directed.

Teachers regarded the determination to work hard and complete all assignments, despite whatever obstacles, to be a cardinal virtue

– one that was instrumental for future success in the adult world of work. To be busy at work became one of the dominant themes of each day. In fact, the nature of school work was such that it would accord nicely with a stock description of the Calvinist ethos, i.e. spiritual salvation through toil and labour. In this respect, work (labour) was felt by the teachers to be sacred.

The ethos (pervasive values of the school as exemplified in symbols and teacher/student relationships) of the school-sponsored student state emphasized values associated with good workers, e.g. dedication, punctuality, docility, reliability. The ethos could thus be termed *ergic*, 'of the nature of work', while the ethos of the streetcorner state could be described as *ludic*, 'of the nature of play'. The ritual 'act' of instruction or 'curriculum moment' that took place during the student state became a dramatic representation and reconfirmation of the world view that says: 'life is hard work and the only way to lessen the agony of work is to be a good worker.'

The ethos of the student state could be further described as industrious and sacrificial. Indeed, there was a ring of soteriology about work – as if Dante's inferno awaited a misstep or an unfinished assignment. As the ethos helped to sustain the overarching world view which was transmitted to the students via instructional rituals, its tacit message communicated the fact that the future and status of a good Catholic worker, once he left school, depended on good deportment, the acquisition of basic academic skills, and the appropriation of the cultural capital of the teachers. Students were implicitly taught that not to be constantly busy or to appear to be busy was tantamount to being anti-Catholic. The mood was frequently – if not predominantly – serious. 'Sit still, copy your work, and be silent' were the watchwords.

Observation of the instructional rituals would appear consistent with Geertz's (1957) assertion that ritual possesses the capacity to fuse ethos and world view. That is, the concept of 'the way things are' (world view) embedded in the instructional rites (e.g. life is hard; work is dull but necessary; always appear busy) was made emotionally acceptable by reflecting an authentic expression of life as lived on a day-to-day basis by the students and teachers through their interaction in boring instruction (ethos). Similarily, the tone, character and aesthetic style (ethos) of instruction was made intellectually reasonable by representing a way of life implied by the state of affairs that the world view articulated. The drudgery of work was made emotionally acceptable to the majority of the students by the fact that everyone – both teachers and students – was involved in doing boring work. Teachers purported the hard life of a student to be homologous with the real world of work that awaited them when they left school. This would appear to account for why so many students accepted the state of affairs that existed in the suite and why they projected such a dismal future for themselves once they left school.

> *Student*: My uncle and my brother say that you can't expect work to be fun but you can make it better by using the money to help out your family.
> *Peter*: What about the work you do in school?
> *Student*: It's OK. But it's not real work because you don't get paid for it. But it's like real work because . . . it's boring.

Written responses from 100 students to the question of 'What kind of job do you think you will have when you leave school?' resulted in 38 per cent of the boys responding that they would probably be auto mechanics; 58 per cent indicating that they would be working in some form of manual labour (as mechanics, factory workers or carpenters); and the remainder choosing computer programming or professions (e.g. teachers, doctors, lawyers). Responses from the girls indicated that 30 per cent felt that they would be hairdressers while the rest predicted that they would be working in a profession or doing computer work.

Few teachers seemed to be concerned with presenting students with alternative values to the work ethic, since a strict adherence to the values inherent in the work ethic was reputedly more conducive to immediate survival:

> *Teacher*: The kids have go to go out there on the job market with everyone else and learn to compete. So we try to teach them good work habits.

Presumably, the education values associated with self-actualization, individuation (in the Maslovian or Kohlbergian sense), or holistic approaches to learning, appeared too frivolous. Who, after all, had time to teach personal growth or generate peak learning experiences when you were trying to provide a student with enough skills to acquire a job – enough, at least, to put the meat and potatoes on the table? However, there was an inherent danger in totally ignoring self-development as a teaching objective – a dilemma which resulted in the continued reification of the cultural order (through the lack of alternative visions) and the cleavage of mind and physicality. There remained too great a disjunction between streetcorner states and student states – a disjunction which was manifested in varying degrees during instances of student resistance, subversion and rebellion.

To orchestrate the intructional rites so that they would engender a liminal state (similar to aspects of the streetcorner state) is not without its risks. And perhaps it is an intuitive awareness on the part of the teachers concerning these very risks that explains why the lessons remained predominantly linear, indicative and boring.

> *Teacher*: If the kids get too happy, or too confident, they'll want to take over the place. Make them feel good – yes. But within reason.

For the Portuguese student, the concept of work was, prior to immigration, a form of 'sacred play' – indispensible to the well-being of his family and the community. Work was fecund of religious cosmology and placed the individual in an order larger than himself which was represented by the Church. Moving to the industrial terrain of Toronto substantially changed values and attitudes surrounding work.

> *Student*: You did work [in the Azores] with your father and your brother. You did it to help out so you felt okay about it. Here [in Canada] it's not the same because you have to wait to learn a trade like at Central Tech [school] or something like that.

While school labour was seen as intrinsic to employability later on in life, it was deemed oppressive and irrelevant by students who lived in the 'now'. Consequently, Portuguese students refused to conform 'now' in the hope that their efforts would yield power and encashable knowledge 'later'. The reason that work was respected in the Azores was that it was honourable and dignified to participate in it. Work in the Azores was not always 'wage labour' – it was work to keep the farm going, to sell vegetables and crafts. Economic pressure was indeed great and monetary rewards were dismally – often painfully – poor yet the Azorean worker could at least affirm himself as an author of his community. And although many Azorians resented their poverty, they were able to endow their privation with a certain sense of dignity and moral resolve – a resolve that was eroded once the Azorean entered a new way of life based on certification, production and the accumulation of wages through labour. Work in downtown Toronto was linked solely to wage labour and to be dependent on wages was to lose one's self sufficiency and dignity – let alone one's sense of membership in the community. It was difficult for both students and parents to see school work – which didn't immediately profit the home – as dignified, despite the Calvinistic-like promises of eventual financial salvation through long hours of mental exertion and obedience to the teacher. And there was no way that the Azorean student was going to respect school work just because it was hard, practical and drudging.

Students were torn between what they felt was the irrelevancy of school work and the necessity of obtaining enough education to permit them to enter the workforce with a reasonable chance of securing a job. They regarded the certification by schools to be a useful commodity – but one that had its price.

> *Student*: They [the teachers] say to work hard because it will help you get a job. That's a joke. My dad says that even high school graduates can't find jobs in this country. So we're supposed to work for nothing. This is worse than back home. Except for here you got TVs and more plazas.

In the workplace of the school, the students' assignments were evaluated from some abstract rendering in the form of a written report of what constituted academic achievement. Yet even the teachers admitted that they would be more prone to passing or giving a good grade to a student if they liked the student and felt he was well-behaved:

> *Teacher*: Well . . . if I was on good terms with the kid, then it would probably influence my decision. Also, if the kid was generally sincere in his desire to get his year . . . if he didn't cause trouble or get in the way.

The arbitrary nature of giving good grades for good work was never explained to the students. To them, what constituted good marks was something that was decided according to some unquestionable code etched in stone by teachers and administrators – sacred tablets handed down from the Catholic mountaintop (the offices atop the Separate School Board). Evaluation was both a fact of life in school and a fact of life in the outside world.

Student: When you're in school you gotta do good or else you fail. In a job later on you get fired if you can't do the work.

The one noteworthy exception to the divinization of the work ethic was found in religion class where prevailing societal norms were often questioned, and individual values were relativized in terms of what could benefit humanity as a whole. Religion classes constituted the only occasions during which the students were encouraged to adopt a critical stance towards the dominant culture. For instance, on several occasions Brock discussed with his class the ethical implications of owning too much land and money and exploiting the poor through wage labour. Furthermore, he engaged his students in a protracted discussion on the inherent moral dangers of capitalism.

WEDNESDAY, 4 MARCH

I watched Brock teach a religion class. The topic for the day was the Sermon on the Mount. It was one of the most powerful lessons I had witnessed in a long time. Brock spoke of the pope's call for the common rights of man to be clothed, fed and sheltered. Moreover, he stressed that this was a right that was more powerful than the right to property. Brock went on to criticize the consumer society we lived in and I was amazed at how politically astute the lesson sounded. The kids were noisy, but many of them showed a growing interest in what was being said.

What happens when a student discovers that his or her religion speaks of equality and justice but that selfsame religion is so aligned with capitalist virtues that it becomes a repressive device for exploiting the poor? What do the instructional rites of religion class mean? Perhaps Rappaport provides part of the answer when he writes that

to the extent that ritual participation alleviates the anxieties of the faithful without alleviating the causes of their anxieties it bears formal resemblance to neurosis as Freud (...) claimed, and to opiates as Marx (...) claimed, and rituals are parts of deceits if they lead the faithful into bondage while promising salvation. Sanctity . . . and the numinous . . . when subordinated to the powerful and material become false, for they falsify consciousness. (1976, p. 99)

Chapter 4

The antistructure of resistance

MONDAY, 23 MARCH

A small number of students and teachers joined hundreds of protesters from all walks of life in order to converge en masse on the Litton factory in Rexdale, an industrial complex that was – and still is – making parts for the US nuclear missile euphemistically known as the 'cruise'. The march outside the plant, which was organized by a variety of anti-nuke groups across Canada, constituted a rite of revitalization by reinforcing the growing Catholic position (as exemplified in many recent statements made by the Catholic bishops) against nuclear weaponry. During the march, the students walked in a circle outside the plant, armed with a huge banner of the Virgin Mary. Also on the banner were pictures of miniature cruise missiles with Xs crossing them out. The words HAIL MARY were written in block letters on one side of the banner.

There was a tremendous surge of spontaneous communitas throughout this powerful symbolic protest. An unmistakeable feeling of solidarity among the protesters made them seem invulnerable. Freed temporarily from structural constraints and legislated encumbrances of role, class, reputation, gender and status, the students shed the institutional armour of the student state and talked openly and animatedly with other groups who had gathered to protest. Some students even defied the police – who were present in a startling display of force. I watched as several students, arms akimbo, stood before the police and insisted on knowing why they supported nuclear armament. Walking arm in arm to display their solidarity for a common cause, teachers and students chanted anti-nuclear slogans, their voices rising in confidence as the march progressed.

The march on the Litton factory was equally a rite of intensification since the direct confrontation with the police served to stimulate and motivate the students as much as the anti-nuclear sentiments that they were espousing.

Student: I really got nervous when we shouted at the cops. My heart started to pound. It was fun. I wish more St Ryan students showed up.

After several hours the students took a bus back to the school. During the ride home, I overheard teachers from Brother Regis discuss animatedly how they planned to follow up on the protest march in their forthcoming lessons.

The ideological hegemony of school life was not monolithically impregnable – an iron-clad system which held captive students' subjectivities and agency. There were considerable resistances on the part of students to engagement in the macro and micro rites. The very existence of school rules and shared symbols intimated their profanation or violation. The classroom, with all its hydra-like symbolic dimensions, became a highly contested territory – a Homeric battlefield where struggles were continuously waged over existing power relations and symbolic meanings. The seeming harmony that pervaded life in the classroom existed at the imaginary level only; when one began to scratch the surface of this apparent solitude one quickly realized that ritual meaning often lurks in subtle negation, opposition and resistance as well as affirmation of the status quo: it is conflictual as it is consensualist.

Despite the fact that, on the whole, students were compliant and acquiesced to teacher-sponsored rules which were presented as salient, real and natural, teachers were faced each day with a spectrum of resistances and reprisals to their instruction – a series of ineluctable acts of ritualized disjunction and reritualization (Erikson's terms) designed to rupture and erode the authority of the teacher. In fact, student resistance in inner city schools has been one of the largest sustained guerrilla warfare campaigns since the advent of mass literacy.

By the term 'resistance' I refer to oppositional student behaviour that has both symbolic, historical and 'lived' meaning and which contests the legitimacy, power and significance of school culture in general and instruction in particular (e.g. the overt and hidden curriculum).

Organized resistance to school policy in the form of student unions or grievance committees is largely the preserve of the children of the ruling class, not the children of the dispossessed. Resistance among working-class students rarely occurs through legitimate channels of checks and balances that exist in educational organizations. Rather, resistances among the disaffected and disenfranchised are often tacit, informal, unwitting and unconscious. This is because they are resisting more than just a formal corpus of rules and injunctions: they are resisting the distinction between the 'lived' informal culture of the streets and the formal, dominant culture of the classroom.

Resistances were, in Turner's idiom, 'liminal' experiences; they occurred among students who had begun to traffic in illegitimate symbols and who attempted to deride authority by flexing, as it were, their countercultural muscles. The provenance of resistances was located in the antistructure where contradiction and conflict competed with the continuity of ritual symbols and ritual metaphors – and where students attempted to disrupt, obstruct and circumvent the incumbent moral demands of the instructional rites. The terrain of resistance was the world of Burroughs and Genet. It was a world devoid of approved symbolic arrangements – a world filleted of traditional meanings and associations. Here students would scoff at and deride the accepted syntax of communication. The antistructure of resistance was a dialectical theatre in which meanings were both affirmed and denied simultaneously. Whatever sense of identity was stripped from the student during class time was returned through the torn seams, fissures and eruptions of the resistant and liminal self. In both subtle and overt ways, recusant students exhibited actions which undermined the consensually validated norms and authorized codes of the school – norms and codes which made up the bric-à-brac of constitutional life. The performances of resistance in the suite consisted of ritualized acts of *sparagmos* or dismemberment which comprised a spectrum of modes: from the stirring frenzy of a class 'going wild'; the carefree abandonment of students at play (which generally moved through prescribed limits); the lugubrious whining of students who felt 'cheated' or 'hard done by'; to the orderly resistance of collective struggle. Added to these resistances were various other ritualized modes of conflict, dramatic confrontative performances, and the release of anarchic behaviour – all assaults on the established order. During times of acute distress, teachers would occasionally suspend the rules (e.g.

the class would be given a period of 'goof off', engage in a game or read a book). This type of teacher ploy served as a steam valve effect which diffused growing frustrations in the class against assaults on their identities.

It was not difficult to understand why students resisted schooling in the student state through rites of transgression since the student state was a path to apathy, passionlessness and emotional and spiritual emptiness. It was, furthermore, a denigration of their identity as a social class. The norms of how one related to life in the student state was drawn from the requirements of the culture to maintain the status quo – a situation found by the students to be overwhelmingly oppressive. Breaching the rules was a logical response to the oppressive conditions of the student state and occurred most often when the naked authoritarianism of the teacher became too much to bear.

But resistance went beyond reactions to bureaucrats high on the aphrodisiac of power: it was a reaction to the separation between the lived cultural meaning of the streetcorner state and the thing-oriented, digital approach to learning of the student state – an approach in which thinking skills were stressed over political and moral values and individual feelings.

It is important to understand school resistance as a form of what Turner calls 'social drama'. The four cultural markers of the social drama are: breach, crisis, redress, and either reintegration or recognition of schism. Rituals traditionally associated with breach are those dealing with life crises, marriage and death. Redressive rituals include divination, curative rituals and initiatory rites.

The breach in the classroom social drama became manifested through subtle and not-so-subtle acts of subversion undertaken by a group of students known as the 'cool guys' and 'class clowns' – acts which I refer to as 'working the system'.

> *Student:* The cool guys wear the leather jackets and act tough. They like to talk back to the teacher. The guys who like to work are the browners. Lots of them are wrist guys.
> *Peter:* What are 'wrist guys'?
> *Student:* You know – fairies, fags.

Student breaches were typical reactions to the anti-incarnational characterisitics of school instruction. Consisting of a variety of behaviours which were marshalled in opposition to the *pro forma* curricular declarations of the suite, resistances often took the form of buffoonery, ribaldry, raillery, hoopla, and even disputation, the occasional affray, a plethora of anti-teacher verbiage (usually muttered in muted or whispered tones), the thwarting of a lesson through brusque remarks, constant carping at the classroom rules, non-negotiable demands, sabotaging lessons by taunting teachers, incessant jabber, insouciant slapstick, engaging in conversations with peers unbeknownst to the teachers, marvellously inventive obscenities and general intransigence – 'streetcorner' characteristics which threatened to make hay of established codes of classroom propriety.

TUESDAY, 20 JANUARY

I was tired at the end of the day. As I approached the subway entrance, yawning, I noticed Rocko standing near the door with a group of kids. He noticed me and came up to me, his tongue flicking like an Iguana.

'Hey sir, wanna see some of these?' He flashed a set of cards in his hand.

'What have you got there, Rocko?'

'Nice, eh?' He started peeling the deck, card by card.

There were various shots of nude women smiling and pinning their labia against their legs.

'Donchya wanna see some more?' Rocko asked gleefully.

'Sorry Rocko,' I said.

Rocko shrugged. 'See you at mass on Friday, sir.'

To breach classroom instruction was to thwart an obligation or un-written contract with Christ and constituted a fundamental immoral act. More passive resistances occurred obliquely and figuratively through streetcorner argot (e.g. whatever slang was *de rigeur* in order to be a 'cool guy'). Gestures of resistance included clenched fist, pursed lips, and arms folded defiantly across the chest. These gestures did not symbolize student 'interiority' (as if thoughts somehow precede gesture). Gestures are not (following Merleau-Ponty) weak translations of thoughts. Gestures of resistance *are* student anger, fear and refusal expressed in an incarnate or corporeal mode. *The aim of the breach was to fight to establish the streetcorner state inside the suite* (whose precinct is the student state). The most common instances of resist-ance were: leaning back on chairs so that students nearly fell over (and often did); knocking each other on the backs of the knees and other forms of 'masculine' jostling; leaning over the desk and talking

to other students; lollingly sitting at your desk and looking around
the room with a bored expression; insurrectionary posing such as
thrusting out the chin and scowling at the teacher; being in a
restricted space without permission (such as a hallway or washroom)
during a classroom lesson or activity; obeying a teacher's command
but performing the required task in slow motion (symbolic stalling);
'horsing around' or fighting in class; and wearing 'intimidating'
clothing. Occasionally students would wear stained sweatshirts with
sleeves ripped off over the shoulders as forms of stigmata or symbols
of self-exile. They would affect the bravado and histrionic self-
consciousness of the aggressive and 'macho' male.

> *Teacher*: There is really nothing wrong with sitting and doing
> nothing, the question is sitting there and doing nothing for how
> long. And at what point does it become inappropriate behaviour?
> It's the same thing as going to the washroom. How long before one
> should ask? How long can a person sit without doing anything?
> *Peter*: Can you think of any others [acts of resistance]?
> *Teacher*: They constantly change. What you have with one
> group and what one group figures they can get away with is
> different from another group. For example, this year there is
> a lot of kicking each other in the back of the legs. That never
> happened before and it is something I have difficulty dealing
> with here because it is not something we are used to. Everyone
> is doing that and because it is so prevalent it's hard to stop it.
> It's just fooling around but it does get serious sometimes. Where
> does it become inappropriate? There is a great big area, to be
> perfectly honest. I felt that I managed to deal with it. I said to
> one of the boys: 'Franko, I want you to keep your hands to
> yourself for the rest of the day or you're going to get a deten-
> tion!' That worked for the rest of the day.
> *Peter*: Can you see different forms of resistance?
> *Teacher*: OK, putting one's hands up. In some group there is
> a lot of shouting out. Other groups are hesitant. That could,
> in some cases, be a form of resistance. To refuse to put your
> hands up shows resistance. Or leaning back in chairs and
> shouting out answers. Again, it's sometimes hard to condemn
> them when they are showing enthusiasm. Other things, lean-
> ing back in chairs, chewing gum, are all forms of resistance . . .
> There are limits to the resistance that they [should be] allowed
> to show. My discomfort in sitting in this chair causes me to

lean back and sit properly again – totally acceptable. I'm not going to make any comments about it. The person who leans back in their chair and stays that way – well, I'm going to point it out to them.

Seldom would physical violence erupt during the frequent and overt displays of odiousness and scurrilousness among the students, although tempers would routinely and uncomfortably flare. Natural bodily functions – such as farting ('honking') or belching – became a popular method of extending the streetcorner state into the oppressive confines of the student state.

Other instances of breach reported to me by students included: stealing the supply room keys when the teacher was absent; plugging the toilets with paper towels or stolen clothes; and vandalizing the washroom walls and ceiling. A favourite trick involved putting a full garbage can on the lever that releases water into the sink. While the water was running, students plugged the sink with toilet paper and fled the washroom. Fifteen minutes later there was a flood.

Student: Sir, did you hear what happened in the washroom? Someone broke the tank. There's about an inch of water. The teachers think some guy in my class did it.
Peter: I never heard about it. What other things do people do?
Student: Where we wash our hands, people put a garbage can there and it fills up with water.
Peter: How does that happen?
Student: They take paper and plug the drain holes.

A mini-crisis occurred when I intervened in a fight after school in which a gang of 'cool guys' were pummelling a student about the head and kidneys for telling the administration the name of the washroom vandal. I was surrounded by a group of very big 'cool guys' who asked me how well I could defend myself. When I told them I had studied martial arts and offered them the name of a well-known martial arts club, their provocation ceased as suddenly as it had begun, and I left the scene unchallenged.

MONDAY, 26 JANUARY

Just as I was concluding my fieldwork for the day, Eddie came into the hall crying. A teacher told him to go to the office. I followed him to the office where he told the secretary that he was beaten by some students for telling the vice-principal who broke the tank in the washroom. The vice-principal called him to his office. I returned to the suite to pick up my tape recorder and notes. About ten minutes later, I left the building. I noticed the vice-principal was standing by the edge of the yard, looking down the street. I said goodbye to him.

Minutes later, as I was walking towards the subway, I noticed a group of kids who had surrounded Eddie about fifty yards down the street. I picked up my pace and soon made out what was happening. Eddie was being kicked and punched by a group of about ten students. I intervened as quickly as possible. Eddie was leaning against a car, crying.

'Are you all right?' I asked.

Eddie nodded.

'Did you tell the vice-principal that you were beaten up earlier?' I asked.

'Yeah,' he said. 'The vice-principal said he was gonna see me home but he didn't!' I asked him if he would like me to walk him home. He shook his head. Suddenly about six boys – I recognized two from the suite – came up to me. Their arms were resting defiantly on their hips. They sneered belligerently at Eddie.

'Jeez, sir. What happened to him?'

'You tell me,' I answered.

'He fell over a car,' one of them laughed.

'Yeah,' another chimed in, 'he fell over this car.'

I broke in angrily. 'I know what happened. I saw you boys beating him up.'

'Did I beat you up?' one of the boys asked Eddie.

Eddie shook his head.

'Did I beat you up?' another boy asked.

Again Eddie shook his head. The rest of the boys went through the same routine, one by one.

'Come with me Eddie,' I said. 'Let's go home.'

Eddie looked at the sneering boys and shook his head.

Suddenly one of the boys (who was probably bigger than I was) said to me, 'You know karate, man?'

I paused. 'Kung-fu.'

'Hey, man. That right?'

'That's right,' I said. I wasn't really lying, because I had studied martial arts years ago. But I didn't think it would help me much in this situation. However, I continued my bluff. I took refuge behind a line Robert De Niro used in *Taxi Driver* when he was talking to his reflection in a mirror. 'You lookin' at me?'

'No,' one of the boys replied. I turned to another.
You lookin' at me?'
'No,' came the reply.
'Are you trying to mess with me, man?' I said, trying to appear larger in my leather jacket than I really was.
'So what belt have you got?' one of the boys said.
'Black,' I answered. This time I was lying.
Once again I turned to Eddie. 'Let's go home.'
Once again he shook his head.
'We'll look after him, man,' said the biggest boy in the group. Suddenly several of the boys put their arms around Eddie and began walking him down the sidewalk. One of the boys turned to me and remarked with a smile like splintered glass, 'Yeah, we'll look after him all right.'
'Are you sure you don't want me to go with you Eddie?' I asked.
'No,' Eddie whimpered.
I watched helplessly as Eddie was led away by his captors.

Possessing a major status relative to the students, the teacher was able to use his surplus of meaning (as shamen, entertainer or overlord) to fill the symbolic vacuum in the lives of the students. On the more positive side, he provided them with the symbolic skills necessary to read and write (which enabled students to 'magically' decode cultural meanings), and helped them to create some kind of rational order out of the flux of existence. What the 'resisters' tried to do was to disassemble, dismember and refashion pedagogical symbols: to turn the teachers' sacred symbols into defeatable ones. Resistance was a symbolic raid against consensus. Resisters challenged the legitimacy of the social pressure which read 'You must do this' or 'You must do that'. Resistances often provoked fulminations from the teachers, forcing them to abandon their function as priest or shaman and take on the oppressive side guise of the policeman. If a teacher wanted to keep control (and ultimately her job) she was forced to compel rebellious students to desist, pay recompense and penalty, or make restitution for their profane antics. Redressive measures within the social drama involved expelling the occasional offender, trying to find a more 'appropriate' programme for the student in another school, and administering detentions. The redressive actions usually ended the crises but did not end the instances of breach. There was usually a limit or tolerance level (which the teachers refer to as 'drawing the line') beyond which redressive action was taken. Instances of resistance were often ignored by teachers, but when they were officially acknowledged, they constituted what Goffman has called a 'frame break'.

When a frame break occurred in an instructional ritual through the perforation of resistance, teachers found the dissonance between their roles as teachers and their expectations of student behaviour to be intolerable. Their positions were thus threatened. In most instances of severe breach, the lesson was halted and the offending students were ceremoniously marginalized, ridiculed and punished in order to serve as an example to the rest of the class. Often, instances of breach were handled on the spot by a curt verbal admonishment from the teacher. Students were usually aware when the teacher's saturation or tolerance level was reached (it varied with the different teachers) and would often try to keep the teacher at a pitch below her breaking point.

Student: You can really get a teacher . . . make him go nuts. Sometimes you can get the vein in their forehead to pop out.

The reintegration stage of the social drama was never complete. Students continued to resist on a daily basis.

Surprisingly, many of the teachers expressed bewilderment at the fact that their carefully constructed instructional rituals spawned numerous instances of counter expectational conduct among students. Yet they continued to remain unaware of the oppressive nature of the instructional rituals, partly because of their conceptual confusion regarding youth culture in general and Portuguese culture in particular. Consequently, the classroom became a setting which could be described as a culture of truncation, fragmentation and displacement: in short, a culture that was certainly disempowering from the point of view of the students.

TUESDAY, 22 DECEMBER

A festive and communicative event, the mass is the heart of the Church's life, the fulcrum of the Church's ministries and apostolates. Containing a power and significance born of centuries of hallowed worship – like the Passover meal – the celebration of the Eucharist is both sacrifice and sacred meal. It functions to shrink the range of one's world in order to keep one's mind focused on particular sacred or transcendental symbols. In the way that it selects or 'brackets' a particular segment of the symbolic universe, the mass somewhat resembles Husserl's 'drive' towards consistency.

The schoolwide Christmas mass certainly did not appear to capture the attention – let alone the commitment – of a large number of students. In fact, this mass was one of the shallowest I have ever experienced; it utterly failed to engender feelings much different than the most perfunctory instructional rite.

Student: What a bore, man. We might just as well have been doing math.

A sombre, highly structured occasion, with teachers 'scanning' the aisles and watching for students who were moving or talking, the mass became a forum of student resistance. Students laughed, joked, discussed the latest drug deals and bumped into each other. During the sign of peace, hands were squeezed hard; some students even tried to pull each other over the pews – all this despite the strict controlling forces of the teachers. Resistances were 'variations' within the liturgy – indexical indicators of the present commitment of the students to this particular orchestration of religious meaning.

Carol singing was led by a sister who told the students when to lower their pitch and when to raise it. Verses to the carols were projected on to a screen from an overhead projector. During the sermon, the priest spoke condescendingly to the students using a vituperative rhetoric. He upbraided them for not attending mass with greater regularity. He spoke to the students as if they were toddlers; the message of the sermon was presented as a pathetic analogy about travelling on the road to salvation and driving to Lisbon in a car: if you stop the car and leave it unattended while you stroll on foot somewhere to enjoy the scenery, thieves will undoubtedly notice your absence and steal the tyres of your car. The message was: do not get out of the car; you must stay on the road and avoid distractions at all costs, so that you can get to heaven. The sermon constantly went over the same points again and again until the priest's voice became, in T.S. Eliot's words, like 'the rattling of dry bones'. It is no wonder the students avoided attending Sunday mass. Some students felt, however, that mass was even more important than school: 'It's where we can talk to God quietly – not like at school.' However, many of the students saw the mass as 'just another boring lesson'.

It appeared that, for many students, there was little response to what was usually an evocative display of language, gesture, and symbolism. There was almost no engagement of the students at a level of felt and intuitive meaning – despite the presence of the Portuguese priest who presided. On this occasion, the dominant symbol was not the sacrifice of Christ on the cross but the lectern from which the priest 'lectured' to the students about their inadequacies. (It is rather ironic that there were four school lecterns in the church on the day of the schoolwide confession.) Responses from the students appeared to confirm Scheff's notion of ritual overdistancing.

> *Student*: I believe in Jesus and all that but in Church I just can't concentrate. Like it gets too distracting all the time.

The students could hardly be faulted for their apathy. Indeed, the majority of the students had yet to undergo Confirmation. In addition, the overall performance of the mass was made oppressive by the structure of unconscious coercion manifest in the control functions of both priests and teachers. One of the most telling moments for me was when a teacher, standing with his legs apart and his hands on his hips, 'guarded' the entrance to the aisle where the pupils genuflected towards the alter as they filed into the pew. In effect, the students were literally kneeling submissively at the feet of the teacher, who wore a look of unmistakable self-satisfaction. Whom were the students really prostrating themselves before at that very moment? To which God(s) were they paying greatest homage? Was it the bureaucracy of the Separate School Board, or Christ – or both? Instead of becoming a celebration in the temple of God, mass became just another 'subject' in the pedagogical repertoire of the schooling process (process in the sense of being 'processed'?). Teacher patrols flanking the pews invoked a feeling of restrictedness and confinement: it was like being in a prison instead of the house of God. To construct such ambience constituted a type of 'forced feeding' of sacred symbols.

However, teachers felt that it would be more beneficial for the students to attend mass rather than not attend at all.

> *Teacher*: It's important for students to attend mass. They learn the proper responses and also learn how to act appropriately. But they also need to communicate with the Eternal. They need the forgiveness that the mass provides.

It was as if the mass were supposed to spiritually soak up sins on contact – with an absorption capacity of a transcendental sponge.

The usual sense of union, intimacy and affirmations of faith were absent from this particular celebration of the mass. In fact, the entire performance was immersed in a sense of bathos. The richness, depth and mystery of a potentially magnificent event – perhaps one of the most hallowed events known to man – was reduced to no more than a shallow lecture. At its height, the mass resembled a dithrambic eulogy more than an inspirational event. What was potentially a privileged moment became an abortive one.

Classroom rituals possessed a collective function other than simply fostering a sense of organic solidarity. As both organized and spontaneous opposition to instruction, rituals of resistance served both to flush out dead symbols from the clotted cultural conduits of the ritual system – those which had grown ossified and retarded and which no longer provided channels for addressing the needs of students – and replace them with more meaningful symbols, those that lay a 'fiduciary hold' (Turner's words) on the student. For instance, symbols of prime ministers, saints and historical figures were ignored in the streetcorner state in favour of the motorcycle rider, the hockey hero, 'Mr T', the cool guy and the 'break dancer'.

THURSDAY, 19 FEBRUARY

Today was the first dance of the year. It was a spontaneous, festive and carnivalesque event – a wildly beautiful display of the street-corner state freighted with symbolic overload and a surfeit of signifiers. As opposed to the sporadic episodes of institutionalized communitas occasionally experienced during a rare engaging lesson, this was a paradigmatic instance of spontaneous communitas. The paradox of freedom co-existing within structure became temporarily resolved for a number of students:

> *Student*: School's not so bad when they let you have fun. Hard work makes more sense when you get some time to laugh and have fun. That's what working is all about, I guess.

While the dance was structured through the orchestration and sequencing of songs by a West Indian disc-jockey, it was more novel than formulaic; both students and teachers unashamedly tapped the vitality of the streetcorner state. The dance allowed for emotional contagion and status inversion; it was one of the few occasions during which students could display their superiority: through movement. While bodies were on sexual display during the fast dances, there remained a sense of sanctified prurience. Some teachers admitted feeling threatened by the fluidity, pleasing eurhythmics and unrestrained indulgences of student performances. Laughter was explosive and feet tapped the ground in a delicate frenzy. Several students started to emit wild groans and before long the whole gym was an orgy of pre-verbal utterances. Students formed small circles and danced around the gym. Some bodies joined together in contagious hysteria: writhing, twisting and sliding across the floor in a human snake. Boys slow danced tenderly with girls although girls usually danced with other girls. One teacher admitted being 'shocked' and 'horrified' at witnessing some boys dancing with other boys.

Several other teachers were affronted by the screaming, the sweat, the shrieks and the gutteral groans emanating from the dance floor. One athletic-looking male teacher danced with an attractive female student during a slow dance – much to the delight of the students who whistled and cheered them on. Time collapsed into the strains of the music: 'When you get into the music you forget you're in school or what time it is.' A student exclaimed: 'The dance made me feel a part of everything.' It was good 'to not think all the time in your head'. Another student remarked: 'I wouldn't mind learning so much if we could just feel good about living. You gotta have some fun.' Students lamented the fact that there were so few dances. And so the dance ended with teachers clutching each other minuet style, their arms moving mincingly while their students swirled around them with unfettered gusto.

The dance echoed Worgul's assertion that a social structure high in communitas will survive whereas social structures with diminished communitas will be vulnerable to challenge and to dissolution (1980, p. 216). It would appear that events such as the school dance are more important for sustaining the school system than one would otherwise think without being adequately informed by theories of ritual.

THURSDAY, 26 FEBRUARY

On the way to the subway I stopped to break up a fight between two youths. Fists were swinging furiously while blood sprayed the sidewalk. I tried to physically separate the antagonists and the one who was getting the worst of it squirmed free and ran down the subway entrance. Suddenly I was pushed aside by the other youth as he ran in pursuit of his victim.

A crowd of teenagers who had gathered to watch laughed and jeered at my feeble attempts to handle the situation.

'Hah!' one of the students cried out. 'Lookit the teacher trying to break up a fight. He's gonna get himself punched out!'

THE UNTAMED EYE

Student: I like to pretend that I'm workin'. Like move my pencil and that kind of thing. But I'm really outside [of the class] in my head ... you know ... I'm makin' my moves but I'm not movin' but my body can still feel the muscles workin'. .... The teacher sometimes catches you because she sees you starin' at the wall. Then she screams at you: 'Eyes on your work!'

Refusing to do work was one of the most formidable methods of resistance; it was a scandal of absence, a silent insurrection, a withdrawal into the dark interiority and ludic caverns of imagination. Sitting motionless and pretending to be thinking about an assignment was more than just a policy of clandestine provocation, it was fundamentally an ontological rebellion, a breaking free from a constrictive and crippling moral perfectionism divested of the liminal attributes of the streetcorner state. To be 'on task', as the teachers call it, was to be preoccupied with the known, the tangible, the safe.

The silence and stillness that was part of the refusal to work was a feedback-seeking pause which acted as a form of 'zero sign' that signified by the absence of movement (cf. Poyatos, 1981, p. 153). To refuse to work was to exist beyond the frontiers of subordination by locating human agency and individual volition in the vesperal and chthonic antistructure of the mind where the rational gives way to the surreal, the indicative to the subjunctive, the metonymical to the metaphorical. Staring straight ahead into blank space was not vegetative. Rather it became a mental mutiny, an inert agitation, a silent upsurge against the extermination of the corporeal being: it was to shriek soundlessly against the betrayal of the mind and flesh.

The eye, as a mirror of the mind, was the most phenomenologically subversive organ of student resistance. To be faced with an 'untamed' eye was, in mythological terms, to confront the Medusa-like horror of raw being: it was to confront the enfleshment of oppositional power.

The wandering eye meant a mind disembodied from the rational discourse of assignments: a mind detached, and critical, and therefore threatening. The wandering eye promoted the incantation of the eternal teacher retort: 'Keep your eyes on your work!'

Refusing to work was subversive in that it altered the rhythm of the instructional rite, effectively bringing it to a halt. It was the inchoateness, the formlessness, the not-yetness surrounding the refusal to do work that competed with the redundancy and certainty of the instructional rite.

It was a rather girm paradox that when students were not working, they became active participants in resistance, and when they were at the mercy of the bleak self-effacement of instruction, they remained, for the most part, passionless observers and passive recipients of over-packaged (and over-cooked) information.

THE CLASS CLOWN: ARBITER OF PASSIVE RESISTANCE, INVERSION AND META-DISCOURSE

Situated in the context of more passive ritual resistance to the normative order of the school was the class clown.

> *Peter*: We've talked about the different types of students. Barbie was talking about the 'clown'. How would you describe the clown, Brock? Is there a type?
> *Brock*: The class clown would be someone who is a verbal clown who is fairly witty and can see certain things that you might be saying or doing and see the humour in it or the different side of it and can make a fool out of you on occasion and on the other hand can really add something to the lesson. It depends on the situation and your attitude towards it but I don't think we have too many of those kinds of kids; we don't have many kids who have a quick wit. What we have are more active-type clowns who act out that side of themselves and maybe Vinnie might be an example of that, but I don't think he is a witty clown. It is interesting that I was talking on the weekend, actually on Thursday, to a last year teacher who told me what a nice kid he is which is interesting in that he apparently got in trouble constantly last year. And yet the teacher's impression of him was really nice and yet he was constantly getting detentions

so there seemed to be a frustration on the part of the teacher last year with him because I guess Vinnie disrupted the class, disrupted the instruction, but at the same time, after it is all over, the teacher's impression is: 'He's a nice kid.'

Throughout the course of my fieldwork, I identified several class clowns (one of whom I shall call Vinnie, a student in Brock's class). Vinnie was capricious, vacillating and frequently obstreperous. His behaviour could be described in terms of the way it changed the context of the classroom setting which was shaped by the instructional rituals. Without the benefit of pratfalls, custard pies or *commedia dell'arte* masks, class clowns arrogated to themselves – often unconsciously – the function of deconstructing the familiar. They achieved this through sarcastic comments, a Trickster-like prankishness, buffooning the teachers, parody and burlesque.

Punning, facetious and irreverent, Vinnie would shift vagariously from farce to satire, and even to mawkishness. Like a character in one of Genet's play, he was the epitome of pure, stylized action – a performer of wordless skills in the tradition of the *mimus*.

Watching Vinnie act in non-accordance with the school norms made me aware of just how boring school really was. He also revealed the tenuousness and arbitrariness of the codes that prevented possible chaos from breaking out in the suite. Thus, Vinnie's task was not solely buffoonery, but teaching.

Vinnie nearly always smiled, despite the various degrees of seriousness of the occasion, and despite continued admonishments from the teacher. Although Vinnie was often ignored by his classmates, a large number of students either wilfully followed his antics or else they were engagingly distracted by him.

Vinnie would do zany things when the teacher's attention was somewhere else: he would roll his eyeballs sarcastically, throw a pen in the air or joke with his friends. He would frequently make bizarre faces – always incorporating some type of twisted smile. On numerous occasions I watched him gingerly roll a baseball across the floor, between the desks, while others were hard at work or at prayer.

Vinnie's performance as the class clown appeared to be consistent with Bouissac's (1982) observations that the actions of the clown constitute an 'acted meta-discourse' on the tacit rules of the social order. In other words, they mirrored or expressed 'the basic but unwritten rules' on which our construction of a culturally bound meaningful universe depends. Along these lines, it could be said that the classroom clown trivialized instructional transactions and demonstrated the arbitrariness of the 'sacred' cultural axioms and enshrined protocols that held together the symbolic universe of the suite. This profanation of the sacred rules by the clown was more than just the breaking of classroom decorum; it was the blatant exposure before all of the classroom's cultural code – the Rosetta Stone which revealed the hallowed and revered rules – the 'tacit axioms or silent dogmas' from which all the other rules were derived. The sacred binding axiom of the suite could be stated thus: 'Whatever your individual inner beliefs and/or quality of faith may be, never betray any disrespect for what your teachers regard as useful or sacred.' It was not the break-ing of the code itself which was important (everybody at least intuitively knew what the sacred rules were), but the knowledge that the clown knew and could communicate through satire and humour what the rules were – and that he understood the secret of their arbitrariness and the fact that they were not handed down from the heavens.

Like the dadaists and surrealists, his counterparts in the world of art, the clown changed the meaning of conventional axioms by dramatically shifting the context. The antics of the clown became a Damoclean sword continually poised above the teacher's head; it threatened at any moment to swoop down and cut through the teacher's 'bullshit', forcing the teacher to keep 'honest'.

One of Vinnie's methods of abrogating convention was to silently mock the prayers. With Thespian expertise he would at first appear splendidly indifferent, then suddenly crack a smile and cross himself perfunctorily. Sometimes he would prefer to play with a pen or inspect his lapel while the rest of the class stood with bowed heads. He would, on occasion, clasp his hands in front of his face as if in prayer, and then vigorously explore his nostrils with his index finger while licking his lips. This was a signal to the other students that he could slip out of the sacred shackles of the 'sanctity state' whenever he felt like it: for Vinnie, his performance was invariably a 'high' – a demiapotheosis. Another one of Vinnie's tricks was to knock over all the chairs that had been placed on top of the desks at the end of the day. Once, during mass, I observed several class clowns (including Vinnie) pull each other over the pews during the sign of peace. Class clowns that I witnessed were invariably male.

As he mocks, scoffs, lampoons and parodies the foibles of both teachers and fellow students, the class clown may be said to 'play' with the internal inconsistency and ambiguity of the ritual symbols and metaphors. He amusingly bridges the gap between the world of classroom life and the inversion of that order. Possessing a disproportionate zeal for 'being an ass', the class clown symbolically undoes or refracts what the instructional rituals work so hard to build up – the student state and its concomitant reification of the cultural order; indeed, he tacitly de-reifies the cultural order. The clown serves to attentuate the rootedness of classroom reality: he diminishes the authoritative hold which the master symbols have on the students. Unable to maintain equanimity in the culture of the student state, the clown inverts the classroom *Lebensraum*. What distinguishes the class clown's actions from more typical forms of resistance are his amusing methods of rule profanation, his ingenuous personality, and his often outrageous flouting of the ordinary canons of moral conduct. The clown is a rupture in the classroom social system, Derrida's *aporia* somaticized metaphorically. He is a minus sign placed before expected classroom protocol.

While the clown manipulates the context of classroom life, he never becomes fully reified above context to the extent that he becomes, in Grathoff's (1970) terms, a 'symbolic type'. Although he resists transmogrification into a symbolic type, Vinnie's antics would seem to support the notion set forth by Handleman and Kapferer (1980) that ritual clowns are liminal figures and thus can be transformative and retransformative of context.

Students did not have to be informed of the unstated, sanctified rules of the suite beforehand in order to know what they were. For instance, no student ever hung a crucifix upside down in Black Mass fashion or painted a moustache on the picture of the pope. Students did not wear the sacrilegious fashions of the public school punk rockers (who occasionally sported priests' collars worn with swastikas or inverted crucifixes). They did not repair to the washrooms to smoke dope and abjure the Trinity. Desecrating holy images was too blatant an act of profanation. Respect for the sacred was too strong among students (including the clowns) – or the fear of punishment too great – to test it outright. And thus the power of the sacred embodied in prayers, in religious symbols and in the religious studies curriculum continued to force consistency upon the context of classroom events. The most that the clowns achieved was to reduce this consistency and further endow these sacred symbols and

themes with ambiguity. In short: they symbolically 'lightened' the
dead weight and oppressive themes of the dominant ritual relations.
They softened the 'certainty' of the moral order and opened the
suite to oppositional meanings. Most of the clowns' profanations
were so understated and so subtle that the teacher could shrug them
off more often than take action against them.

In terms of the instructional activity in the suite, the clown
offered more than just comic relief. He was threatening in the way
that he symbolically stripped the teacher naked and demythologized
the classroom power structure. Every morning the classroom clown
symbolically sat in the boardroom of the Ministry of Education
and wagged his tongue (at a risk, perhaps, of being streamed into
a basic level programme). Because he was often amusing, the clown
was not perceived as a direct threat, yet his antics could not go
totally unpunished. He was sometimes described by teachers as 'a
bit of a nut' – a label which conveniently permitted teachers to
place him outside the context of the 'normal student', so that the
punishment meted out to him need not appear as severe as that
which was inflicted upon the rank-and-file deviant. The clown
demanded that the teacher laugh at himself or herself and all that
the teacher represented. To a certain extent teachers met this
demand (by often engaging in some self-effacing humour) for fear
of incurring extended antics from the clown or reprisals from other,
more dangerous students. The only way a clown could be severely
punished was if the teacher was not at all capable of laughing at
himself or herself. If the teacher believed with his indomitable soul
that the clown was actually dangerous, that he was working to
effectively contravene the ordinances of the school, then the teacher
would be forced to take whatever measure was necessary to curtail
the clown's antics.

THE LAUGHTER OF RESISTANCE

The laughter of resistance is unlike any other. It occurs when the
entire class – or a significant number of students within the class
– spontaneously turn against the teacher. Usually the students wait
patiently for an opening – a 'slip up' on the teacher's part (however
slight) – and, when the time is right, they begin to howl with
laughter. Yet the laughter that is directed against the teacher is
qualitatively different from other forms of laughter. For instance,
it is different from the laughter that follows the antics of the

clown: a communal laughter that signals approval; a sign of social solidarity which states that the class is 'with' the clown. And unlike the laughter of merriment, which brings the body into a state of unalloyed euphoria, or the laughter of the saint, which fills the universe as it celebrates a sense of certainty hiding behind the randomness and tenuousness of worldly events, the laughter of resistance serves to mock and denounce. It is a hostile act, an insurgent symbol, one which inscribes the *via rupta*. There is a vicious harmlessness about it. It starts high in the chest, shudders forth from the throat like sparks from an engine, and curls around its victim like wafts of thick smoke. It envelops the power of the teacher and neutralizes it. It forces the teacher to question – and abrogate – her self-typification as leader. Nothing can erode self-confidence more profoundly than the banshee-like laughter of resistance that chillingly penetrates the teacher's sense of sacral self.

The laughter of resistance reflects Mish'alani's remark that 'the demonstrative material of laughter, the open mouth, the exposed teeth, the spasmodic contractions, the roar or chuckle, always reproduces an aspect or phase of predation, conquest, and even ingestion . . . (1984, p. 151). It further echoes Mish'alani's description of the sneer and jeer as 'contemptuous because it renounces the possibility of actual harm to its victim by way of commenting on his insufficiency to merit the expenditure of force, as if the text of its self-referential comment were: "The strength brandished herewith is not being hereby deployed because you are too insignificant to merit its use"' (p. 152). For the teacher who is at the mercy of the laughter of resistance, 'the mocking jeer, the cackle of ridicule, does not lose force by distance, but persists in the imagination of its victim, pursuing him wherever he flees, haunting him, insinuating itself into him, undermining his self-complacence' (p. 153).

Yet it is important to understand the laughter of resistance as more than wanton cruelty on the part of the students. It is not some form of jocular blood lust. It is, in its essence, a form of redefining the power structure of the class. It is a way for the students to reclaim their sense of collective identity. The laughter of resistance takes on the force of a group exhortation. It is an 'argument' that cuts across class and gender boundaries yet remains culturally tied to whatever group employs it. Victims of the laughter of resistance are placed in a no-win situation. If a teacher reacts against it, or tries to deny it, then the students can prolong its effect. If the teacher acknowledges it, then he or she only confirms or reinforces the collective power behind it.

The laughter of resistance can flail and bludgeon the spirit and can only be deflected when the teacher 'goes' with it. Brock was able to survive the laughter of resistance by laughing at himself or even responding with a one-liner that the class found amusing. Penelope, however, found it difficult to protect herself from the laughter of resistance and would only prolong her agony through her attempts to force the class into silence.

RESISTANCE AND THE CULTURE OF PAIN

A highly significant concept surrounding the instructional rituals of the suite was the cultural use of pain. My use of the word pain in this context does not refer to the self-abnegation, the mortification or the bizarre vilification of the flesh that was once – and to a certain extent still is – part of the liminal journey of some religious pilgrims. The pain I refer to is far subtler than this, and, paradoxically, is apt to prove more debilitating. In some respects the pain experienced by students at St Ryan was not that far removed from the notion of wilful suffering.

Pain was present in the suite in a variety of permutations and levels. While in one sense the students were hardly burdened by a Sisyphean workload, to describe the pain of being a student as if it were simply a mild discomfort or aggravation would be a sociological euphemism or a case of analytical faint-heartedness. All of us bear symbolic wounds incurred when some form of ritual process in which we were pedagogically engaged ruptured our normal or usual reference points for anchoring our identity.

The suite was spacious and clean. Nevertheless, there were the hard plastic surfaces, the bland colours, the oppressive functionalism of the furniture, the cinderblock and masonblock walls, the rows of desks, and, with the exception of a few narrow windows, the indirect fluorescent lighting. The surroundings were not only an aesthetic judgment, but a moral one as well. Students did not just reside in this concrete and formica womb – they were 'processed' through it.

The pain of being a student was often considerable – manifested in the bland, dreary impotency of instructional rituals and routines, the grinding, drudging familiarity, the deadening, mechanical applications of instructional rites, the unremitting banality of the subject matter, the unemotional, generalized stream of boring events, the bleak inevitability of repetition and invariance, the tedious succession of unrelated episodes, and the wearisome wait for instruction to end. Students 'wore' the hegemonic culture of the school in their very beings; in their wrinkled brows, in their tense musculature, in the impulsive way they reacted to their peers, and in the stoic way they responded to punishment. There was the pain of enduring the hours spent hunched over a desk, and the pain of censure if one requested to attend to one's bodily functions at an inappropriate time (e.g. in the middle of a lesson). In fact, sitting through an entire macro ritual could be described as a type of symbolic cicatrization or scarification of mind and body. For students enmeshed in classroom ritual, there was the manifestation of a more 'abstract' and 'existential' pain resulting from the thematization and simplification of emotions which had been abstracted from physical conduct and experience (e.g. 'today's lesson deals with kindness', 'tomorrow's lesson deals with vandalism'). In addition, there was the pain of 'keeping things to oneself'. No official criticism of classroom rules was sanctioned. Pain, therefore, was endemic to the student state. Drudgery engaged invariance in a lifeless adagio.

It should be pointed out that simply because teachers do not punish students in the form of malfeasant thrashings or physical mutilations, or because students are ostensibly permitted to exert their free will in a variety of circumstance, this does not obviate the fact that students experience strong debilitating feelings of enchainment. Students often appeared as anguished configurations against the sterile landscape of formica and cement. They were transformed into bodies subjugated and fragmented, distilled to spectral shadows, and pushed to the margins of acceptability. Pain was made legible in the body postures and facial expressions of the students; it was inscribed in the tight mouths, clenched jaws, hunched shoulders and angry glares – typical gestures of the student state. Student gestures had become so highly reflexive that they had inverted themselves and had begun to wither. Brenneman *et al.* call such gestures 'industrial' or 'scientific' (e.g. as in the gestures of a factory worker, assembly line worker or laboratory technician). They had become quick and impulsive.

Commenting on the qualities of gestures, Brenneman *et al.* write:

We have all raised our hands at some time in our academic careers, in an effort to be recognized or to indicate a yes or no decision. Perhaps we have shaken our fists to amplify a point or scratched our heads to convey either deep thought or confusion. All of these actions are very close to us, but they must be properly understood as gestures found on the same continuum of power as the most profound religious rituals. (1982, p. 114).

Student gestures had become reified into intercorporeal manifestations of hegemony and could be described, in the words of David Michael Levin (1982), as a 'hostile, calculative, reductively mechanistic re-presentation of the body . . .' (p. 287).

By observing the cramped, defensive posturing of the students and the brusque, authoritative gestures of the teachers, one could see how relationships of power were grafted on to the medium of living flesh and marrow. Power and privilege became 'somaticized'. The body served as both a mirror of state oppression and an instrument for resisting domination. It was also a locus of moral and political transformation, an 'enfleshment' of state power.

Feldstein writes that imprinted upon the body is its entire past:

A silent witness to numberless influences, the body records its every experience as a nuance, gross or subtle, upon the idiosyncratic rhythms of each person's physique. It manifests its history as physiognomic clusterings of those rhythms. Those clusterings present themselves as symbolic representations of body's encoded secrets. . . . As lived body, human body – the physique – is the locus of reflective activity. As such, the body mirrors its own processes; it reflects an 'imagio' of its contours into itself. (1976, pp. 136–7).

Every body carries a history of oppression, a residue of domination preserved in stratum upon stratum of breathing tissue. The bodies of the students are pervaded by symbols which are swollen with meaning and which are infolded in the musculature, pressed into the tendons and encased in the meshwork of bone and sinew. Symbols, claims Dixon (1976), are part of human physiology. Hegemony, which is inscribed in the physiognomic symbols of the students' bodies and compressed into gestures, is an act of corporeity. It is laminated over the students' skeletal and muscular structures. Resistance among the students is a resolve not to be dissimulated in the face of oppression. It is a fight against the

the erasure of their streetcorner gestures and rhythms; it is to ritually construct a transitional world that can erase the past and deconstruct present psychosocial adaptations in order to forge new self-presentations of greater potency. It is to enflesh a loyalty to hope.

School resistance became the discipline of 'using' pain which was otherwise unendurable and irremediable. Resistance was inextricably linked to the quality of the students' forebearance in the midst of what they considered to be oppressive circumstances. Students adhered to the unwritten rule that stressed the admirable – even heroic – nature of maintaining self-composure under stress and teacher harassment. Equally admirable from the students' perspective was to react or 'hit back' against an oppressor. The determining factor in how the students chose to resolve this conflict dwelled within the status of the inflictor. For example, if the students felt that the teacher was 'one of them', or at least sympathetic to their lived cultural forms (e.g. pop music, streetcorner codes), then the students were less likely to resist. This was most evident in the case of Brock, by far the most popular teacher. Resistances were least evident in Brock's class and, when they did surface from time to time, they were much more subtle and less threatening. Observations of Barbie's and Penelope's classes revealed resistances to be more overt – and much more disturbing to the teachers.

Liminality is more than a marginal sanctuary for the creation of warm feelings and creative insight – it can also provoke anger and engender resistance. Student resistances appear to support the notion of Bilmes and Howard (1980) that pain is a form of 'cultural drama' which is associated with increased liminality and changes in status on the part of the victim or recipient of pain.

The inflictor of pain (the teacher) stands as a representative of the social category to which the victim is either being assimilated (in the case of elevation) or contrasted (in the case of degradation). What is important is that the inflictor's own status is on the line together with that of the victim.

Teacher: If you decide to punish a student, you'd better know what you're doing. If it's not effective you'll just make the situation worse for yourself.
Peter: Why is that?
Teacher: For one thing you get a reputation for being too soft and the kids will take you for a ride.

Because pain promotes the perception of the victim's liminality, and hence the victim's marginal – often 'heroic' – status, pain was sometimes self-inflicted. Students frequently engaged in subversive behaviour that was assured to bring them swift and sometimes severe punishment. Pain and punishment took various forms, and graduated in severity. These consisted of receiving a poor report card, getting a detention, writing out lines, receiving reprimands from the teacher, or having a teacher or principal call your parents to the office for a meeting (the Board supplies an interpreter in the case of non-English-speaking parents). By bearing up under punishment – by experiencing the 'holy' pain of resisting – the victim takes on a liminal and quasi-sacerdotal status. Resistance thus became a form of crypto-religion. It is perhaps significant that Turner compares liminality to the experiential notion of Christian 'grace' (1982a, p. 45).

Students who kept their composure under vituperation and accusatory procedures from teachers were exercising a spiritual or oral power – a power which is rarely recognized as such in traditional examinations of 'deviant' school behaviour. When a victim who was being degraded bore himself or herself admirably against all expectation, he called into question the teacher's interpretation of the transgression.

Through resistance, the offender extrudes himself from his corporate identity as a student and substitutes himself as a crucial ethical unit. Swollen with symbolic significance, his suffering and humiliation become the suffering and humiliation of his race. He is linked to his people and identifies with their marginality – their alien status outside of their ethnic enclave. When the punishment of a class-room offender was perceived as just by both teachers and students alike, the image of Christ as Divine Judge, which had been deconstructed and tarnished by the offender's behaviour, became reconstituted and repaired. When teachers appeared to be cruel and/or unjust, the liminal status of the victim was enhanced. Just as liminality is a menace on the factory assembly line (e.g. workers might decide to join a union to fight exploitation) so, too, is it a threat to teachers who attempt to legitimize and normalize the inferior status of the student. One function of liminality, to my knowledge not mentioned in the literature, is the forging of what used to be called 'Dutch courage' (i.e. when a stimulant such as alcohol enables an individual to do things he would normally resist). The liminal status of resisting teachers appeared to evoke some kind of stimulus or power along this line.

Student: Sometimes you get a buzz – like a high, getting on the teacher's back. It's a sort of a kick when the rest of the class gets off on what you do.

In this context, it is significant that bearing up under degradation as a form of 'macho' resistance could represent, for the students, being in a state of grace. To resist 'like a man' was to be in a hallowed state – it was to exculpate oneself from the label of 'inferior'. To endure mindless instructional rituals was to be weak and 'feminine'. The only way to go through your daily rounds as a student was to take the punishment of school 'like a man'. Following this kind of logic, one could only achieve ultimate peer status – which at times appeared to partake of a quasi-religious aura of veneration – when one was being punished. The same ideology held true for some of the female students. Masculine traits were often adopted by females as a method of resisting the prevailing norms of the school (cf. McLaren, 1982b).

A student in Brock's class – Carlos – frequently served detentions after school for various transgressions. I would sometimes chat with Carlos during his detentions. On such occasions, we would talk about his passion for automobiles. Detention time afforded Carlos about the only occasion during the school day in which he could get any kind of positive relationship going with an adult. There was time during a detention for a one-to-one relationship – something impossible to establish during class time. In the case of Carlos, punishment served a dual function: it conferred the masculine status of receiving a detention (a symbolic beating), and it permitted Carlos a closer and more intimate rapport with Brock. In one bizarre instance, a student named Eddie expressed a desire that I be his teacher so that I could get 'physical' with him. Having discovered that I had once studied martial arts, he welcomed the possibility that I would 'beat the shit' out of him and other students instead of giving detentions.

Student: Hey, we should have this guy for a teacher! We'd like him better. If we were bad, he'd beat the shit out of us – not give us a stupid detention like Mr ____!

Eddie (who was not nearly as verbally articulate as Carlos) regarded physical pain to be some kind of reward – a punishment higher in status (more masculine) than a detention. Since most 'resistance leaders' were unable to effectively challenge the authoritative codes of the suite through dialogue, debate or the foolery of the class clown, they were left with only their macho symbolic power base from which to draw their strength.

The effects of classroom discipline and punishment corresponded to Mercurico's (1974) concept of corporal punishment as a process capable of establishing a semi-mystical, ritualisic bond that ties students to their teachers. What Mercurico says about caning could be applied to the less severe or less overt forms of punishment which we have been considering.

> *Student*: I hate getting called down to the office . . . [but] I guess if the teachers didn't care about the class, then they wouldn't punish us. . . . A lot of kids goof around because it's the only way they can get attention from the teacher and the rest of the class.

Could it be that students achieved the status and strength to overcome the alienation of the student state through public ordeals? Could the prototypical cultural drama in the Catholic school (or public schools for that matter) be grounded in the way in which students bear pain?[1] Could this cultural drama be disguised in various and yet undeciphered ways? Certainly the 'suffering Christ' crucifixes which are mounted in the suites, the emphasis on the work ethic and the religion classes which stress self-denial contribute in no small way to the nexus of such cultural dramas. Perhaps this has been unconsciously recognized by some Catholics who wish the (Good Friday) traditional corpus which depicts the crucified Christ partially clad, crowned with thorns and nailed to the cross to be replaced by the (Easter Sunday) corpus which is fully clothed and risen from the dead. The latter style of crucifix resides only in the office of the principal. Certainly the crucifix of the suffering Christ plays an important role in Azorean Catholicism. Indeed, a staff member remarked that the bloodied, wretched, and emaciated figure of Christ crucified represented the world view of the Azorean people.

Generally speaking, it would seem that when the behaviour of the victim is consistent with the cultural objective of instruction, then peace and order prevail. The cultural objectives of the instructional forms of the suite are, as I have already noted, Calvinistic in tone and instrumental in design: 'Work hard because that's what the real world outside is all about. The less trouble you have inside the school, the less trouble you're bound to have on the outside.'

Teachers fully believe this. It is expressed in a 'you've got to be cruel to be kind' philosophy:

> *Teacher:* Well . . . these kids have to learn that when they go to work they can't run around and make all this noise. They've got to learn which kind of behaviour is appropriate at work . . . and which isn't. I mean, if they can't learn to distinguish this, then they'll get fired and that's all there is to it.

The cultural objectives of the instructional rites were often in conflict with those of Azorean streetcorner behaviour. For instance, conflict and obsequiousness in responding to authority are not traits that fare well in the streetcorner state – yet these are the traits which teachers regarded as highly desirable in their students. Teachers were rarely successful in confronting this dilemma:

> *Teacher:* They might not be geniuses, but at least they can try to leave here with good manners and a healthy respect for the Church and what its teachings are.

School punishment often operated at the symbolic level to give the student a foretaste of what lies ahead for those impudent enough to transgress the rules of the factory, the office or any other workplace. From yet another perspective, methods of inflicting punishment could be seen as a non-discursive externalization or theatrical display of the school's ethos. Punishment, however, was not always obvious. Tacit methods of inflicting pain can come from other domains of varied structures, e.g. insults or caustic comments from teachers, ignoring students' raised hands, or sombre or blank facial gestures when speaking to a particular student. By far the most common tactic employed by teachers in the suite was that of embarrassing the students (cf. Woods, 1975). Concerted attempts at embarrassing the students took the form of reprimands aimed at deflating them, chipping away at their sense of security or identity. For example, on one occasion I heard a teacher say to a student who was preoccupied during a lesson: 'Do you always think with your mouth open!' Another example of verbal tyranny occurred when a teacher announced to a class after they had misbehaved in front of school visitors: 'You are all ignorant!' I personally committed a variation on the punishment via embarrassment theme during a period in which I was asked to 'Keep an eye on the kids' while the teacher ran an errand. I began to panic when, in the teacher's absence, one of the students began acting rather obstreperously (which I interpreted as a challenge to my authority). In retaliation, I called the student a 'creep'. His face instantly turned red and he leaned back in his chair and sneered. Finally he buried his head in a book, humiliated, depersonified. I felt terrible about my outburst and after class conveyed my concern to the student.

I have spoken of a 'culture of pain' not out of mere cynicism, or a desire to turn phrases, but in order to gain some kind of purchase on the motivations of both teachers and students. Student resistances indicated that a rupture existed in the instructional rituals between meaning and intent, between language and metalanguage, between communication and metacommunication in general. Rebels who defied the legitimized and credentialized moral and behavioural codes of the school tacitly recognized the contradictions and incoherence of the pedagogic vision that had been systematically constructed from the variegated dimensions and complex skeins of sacred/secular symbols and metaphors. They recognized – though not always consciously – the pronounced dissymmetry and disjunction between instructional messages. Consequently, work was not always tolerated as sacred. Prayers and religious rites no longer seemed absolutely necessary for success in the world of work. What was perceived by the teachers to be a mission of sanity and love (their sacred duties as teachers) was perceived by some students to be a ritual pathology. The students witnessed the incongruity between the educational objectives which sanctioned current educational practice and the 'lived experience' that students embodied in the streetcorner state. This was the heart of the problem with the school curriculum. For the Azorean students, the suite was not a collegial community composed of benevolent priests and pedagogues but a symbolic terrain where they had to ritually affirm countercultural identities. Students didn't want to dutifully recite 'texts' – they wanted to create them.

Where the conflict most frequently and abrasively manifested itself in the suite could be observed in the contradictory notions surrounding what kinds of ceremonies the rituals of instruction really constituted. Were they ceremonies of elevation or degradation?

Student: I guess I keep quiet because I don't want to be told off in front of everybody. Some of the cool guys can take it – but they're pretty tough. Not me.

TUA, VITA MEA

From the perspective of the teachers, many of whom were convinced of the intellectual obliquity of the Azorean student, instructional ceremonies attempted to elevate the Portuguese student from the status of illiterate, belligerent immigrants to well-mannered, literate, middle-class Canadians. The untransformed and unelevated residues of the streetcorner knowledge of the uninstructed were to be replaced by academic knowledge. Minds tenacious of age-old superstition and ignorance were to be opened. Attitudes towards learning which were supposedly built on archaic presuppositions were to be radically reshaped. Instruction became the secular corre- lative to Kenneth Burke's theological formula of victimage and redemption: the unfortunate Portuguese are degraded (failed and/or punished) as part of their transformation into docile, well-mannered citizens.

> *Teacher*: We try to get them through. Even if only a few of them become doctors and lawyers – it's at least a start.

Through the coldly efficient and hyper-rational rites of instruction, teachers attempted to transform the behaviour of their students from what they perceived as stubbornness, impudence and resistance into docile, pliable, volitionless, obedient and beneficent behaviour which enable students to be easily conditioned to the mind- deadening and spirit-breaking norms of the factory, machine shop or fast food establishments. Students were made, like Christ, into criminals, underlings; they were mocked and abused. And then, once vilified, these 'primordial victims' were to be raised out of their material and cultural poverty and redeemed into the sanc- tified world of the educated. The persistent failure of many woebegone Azorean students served as a sacrifice that purged the school community of its academic ills and helped to ensure that students from non-working-class cultural strata would avoid contagion. To fail the student is a ritual vaccination against a larger outbreak of anti-colonialist malaise. The sacrificial aspect of the rites of instruction can be lucidly summed up in a teacher's remark:

> *Teacher*: It would be ridiculous to imagine every student here making as far as a corporate executive. How many teachers make principals or VP? Somebody's got to do the dirty work.

It appeared to one teacher only 'natural' that the Azorean students should be sacrificed for at least another generation:

> *Teacher:* It will probably take a few generations before we see a greater influx of Azorean lawyers and doctors and what have you. . . . It's the same situation with any immigrant group. You can't expect them to step right in and take over.

Not only were Azorean students victimized, but they were blamed for their own victimizaiton – a key scenario in the apologetics of capitalism (cf. Ryan, 1976). The pervading assumption that working-class students were only intermittently creatures of reason became transmuted into educational ideology through the setting up of basic level programmes to accommodate such underlings. By blaming the academic failure of the Azorean student on her individual deficiencies, the teachers further turned the tables on those who were suffering because of their class and ethnic location in the larger society by implying that they were the cause of their own misfortune. The ideology of blaming the victim views student insolence and provocation as solely gratuitous – not as actions which are mediated by wider relations of class, authority and power. This is a continuation of the Renaissance tradition of individual achievement which fails to see the larger sociocultural context which the individual inhabits.

Observations that Azorean students were sacrificed to the system strangely mimic Girard's argument that all institutions (including modern ones) grow out of the body of the victim and that the surrogate victim is 'the ideal educator of humanity . . .' (1977, p. 306).

The sacrificial dimension of schooling functions as a type of purity rite: a social mechanism which protects the educational system by projecting its excrement on to its enemy or those who in some way are perceived to be threatening or jeopardizing the system. Sacrifice permits aggression to be deflected from more dominant social groups while allowing them to retain their privileged sphere of colonial domination. The academic failure of the Portuguese student becomes a form of expiation for the 'good of the system' (whatever benefits the white, Anglo-Saxon population). But why is this so? Why should the victims pay for this injustice?

I believe that the answers lie in the deep-seated conviction on the part of many members of the dominant class that the social system would somehow malfunction if everyone had the same chance for academic success. Not only would the powerful lose their power to dominate the poor, but society would somehow grind to a halt. The standards and quality of our schools (and by implication, our society) would decline appreciably – some would argue drastically – in an attempt to accommodate 'inferior' races. The failure of the disempowered thus becomes, for the ruling class, a crucial factor in the maintenance and evolution of the social order. This perspective provides the ideological base that allows the inferiority of the Azorean immigrant to become part of the social heredity of the dominant white supremacist culture.

Purgation through victimage is part of the ritual of school instruction and in a multicultural society there exists an abundance of victims to help cleanse the system of its foreign impurities. Not surprisingly, these victims are often the children of the poor, and usually from minority backgrounds. Put less functionally, sacrifice is part of the social logic of schooling that is inscribed not only in the residues of social Darwinism but also, more alarmingly, in the current resurgence of neo-Conservative discourse. The social logic of sacrifice works through educational rituals as it seeks to manifest itself materially in the failure of minority students. As long as educators refuse to interrogate this colonialist logic and the ways that it contributes to the failure of minority groups, the general populace can rest comfortably in assuming that the system must continue to exclude the indigent and disaffected if our educational standards and way of life are to persist and evolve productively.

The ritual frame that is constructed around the sacrifice of the working-class immigrant student is one that can be described as follows: 'Knowledge acquired through the instructional rituals (the cultural 'sacra') amounts to power – the key to becoming the successful working Catholic. We, the teachers, are the dispensers of that knowledge. Just as "many are called but few are chosen", not everyone is worthy of receiving the sacred wisdom imparted by the teacher. If we watered down the curriculum so every group could succeed, schooling would lose its present status and power.'

Given the somewhat cynical attitude of the teachers in the suite towards the capabilities of the Portuguese student, and given the rather dull, busy work the teachers often administered to the students, it could be argued that the teachers were simply reinforcing the academic competencies which the students already possessed and which the teachers felt would be adequate for the type of job the students would most likely seek. This would account for the pronounced isomorphism between the suite and the factory.

Teaching to the lowest common denominator of the academic programme further reinforced student apathy, since the students could not help but wonder why they were not moving 'upstream' as opposed to floundering in the stream in which they were placed by the teachers at the beginning of the year – one that meanders through the basic level groups and basic level courses and ends up eventually in the reservoir of despair known as the factory floor.

Regrettably, most parents accepted the fate of their children whom they fully entrusted to the teachers.

Parent: Look, the teachers know the best thing for the students. The students got to work in Canadian society so they must do as the Canadian teachers say. But the teachers aren't as strict as they were back home and that's the problem here.

Parents were generally conformist-minded, urging a 'no-frills' core curriculum which stressed maths and reading. They wanted their children to achieve high standards but this desire was clouded in a value system which stressed strong teacher control.

Parent: Portuguese students are used to being pushed. If teachers don't push them, then they turn out to be lazy. They hang out at the plaza with those big radios and don't think about their responsibilities ... [to] ... their families.

The reaction of most parents to the prospect of economic advancement was one of a passive acceptance of their lot in life.

Parent: Not too many Portuguese can become rich here in Canada until they've been here three or four generations. It takes that long before you're accepted by the Canadians.

Several months after completing my observations at St Ryan, a number of grass roots Portuguese began to mount a public protest against the fact that their children were outranked in the competition for academic rewards. For these fledgling critics of the system, school was hypostasized as an antagonist to the future success of their children in the labour market.

Parent: Our kids don't get the same breaks as Canadian kids. They stream our kids into low-level programmes that don't lead to university. They look at us as less intelligent just because we don't come from an industrialized country. So our kids pay for it here.

Chapter 5

Making Catholics

Guiding the direction of daily instruction was the root paradigm which I have called 'becoming a Catholic'. That there is a root paradigm or cultural model for behaviour known as 'becoming a Catholic' may not come as a surprise to many readers, especially given the fact that the fieldsite under investigation is a Catholic school. And it may even be argued that, as in the case of the prevailing and secular root paradigm of 'becoming a worker', I am merely theorizing a commonplace. Be that as it may, it is supremely evident that these two paradigms are intractably linked, and it is this linkage which directs the course of this chapter. As I shall argue in the pages that follow, both root paradigms are coincident with each other. Their referents are more than partially synonymous; in fact, they freely interpenetrate one another.

The paradigm of 'becoming a Catholic' is given amplification by the refraction of educational reality through the lenses of strategically located icons and religious artefacts which wrap the students in an ideological miasma heavily laden with Catholic significance and meaning.

THE MANIPULATION OF THE SYMBOL

One of the most powerful means of both symbolizing and sustaining order in the suite was through a sacerdotal profusion of religious icons and symbols – an ensemble of messages, thick with meaning. Religious symbols are powerful precisely because their inherently ambiguous nature renders them susceptible to many meanings (c.f. Murphy, 1979, p. 319; Cohen, 1979, p. 103; Duncan, 1968, pp. 7–8; Lukes, 1982, p. 279; Eco, 1982, pp. 28–9; Lewis, 1976, p. 145). Meanings attributed to symbols are not to be understood as the random choice of individuals. They are not grasped adventitiously: there is a cultural tendency at work. Even the most idiosyncratic thoughts and gestures are rarely of one's own making but rather belong to the culture. Culturally derived symbols are employed by isolated individuals in the articulation of their most private thoughts and actions.

The dispersion of religious symbols throughout the suite and the school served as visual renderings of powers or external entities that were collectively thought to exist beyond the ordinary dimensions of space and time – usually as part of some heavenly community. Religious symbols are a form of concretizing the transcendent qualities of God; they provoke students to 'take notice' – to apprehend reality in a special way – yet a way which remains susceptible to a cargo of nuances and interpretations (unless such symbols happen to be caught in the grip of oversanctification).

While religious symbols serve as continuous purveyors of messages, they are not likened to some sort of celestial emissary from God and the prophets, as in a form of sacerdotal telex. Yet because of their structural characteristics of multivalency, multivocality and polysemy, symbols are able to point to a reality beyond that which they signify and thus enable students to participate in that reality (cf. Tillich, 1956, pp. 41–54.).

Religious insignia function in a variety of ways depending upon the context and location in which they appear. For instance, they may support or add weight to the prevailing paradigms of 'becoming a worker' or 'becoming a Catholic'; or else they make these dominant epistemes problematic by throwing them into states of contradiction or conflict. In the later instance, ambiguity may arise with respect to how the classroom culture is to be defined – a situation which has both functional and dysfunctional implications in terms of maintaining and preserving the symbol systems within the hierarchical and institutional framework of the dominant parent/teacher culture.

Religious insignia included the following: a large photograph of the pope (in the main hall), a painting of the religious founder of the school (in the main lobby), a plastic statue of Mary (in the library), crucifixes (in every classroom amd office), the logos of the Separate School Board (on stationery and official documents) and school crests and uniforms which were worn by high school students who shared the building with the students from St Ryan.

In Brock's class, a handwritten Act of Contrition and the words to 'O Canada were mounted on the wall beside the crucifix.

Students were easily able to identify the religious symbols in the school. Written responses from the students revealed a varying valence regarding their significance: some students appeared to be overwhelmed by the superordinacy of the symbols while others maintained that they were not influenced by the symbols at all. The majority of the students testified that the symbols merely served to remind them that 'they were Catholics'. However, a significant number of students remarked that they felt Christ was present 'in' the religious icons, that he was 'watching to see how we behave'.

'The crucifix is there to keep us all holy and to keep the school holy'.

'They [the religious symbols] mean that God is here with us.'

'What they mean to me is what God's done for us and every time I look at the cross I always feel that Jesus is staring at me telling me to behave.'

It is significant – if not disconcerting – to cite a remark made by a staff member who claimed that the 'bloodied and emaciated' figure of Senhor Santo Cristo represented 'the general outlook of the Portuguese on the world'. The description of the Azorean crucifix provided by this teacher reminded me of images of the tortured Saviour frequently found on crucifixes from the fifteenth century.

Staff member: Life is hard . . . it's drudgery for them. They distrust institutions just like they distrusted the government of Portugal. They won't believe you if you tell them learning can be fun. They only understand things that are tough, hard and practical. Just look at their crucifix. . . . The first thing that I noticed was that strange attachment they had to this emaciated figure of Jesus Christ, whom they call Senhor Santo Cristo. It was a blood-spattered, disfigured Christ, and he symbolized much of their lives. And they basically see life as tough, harsh and unrewarding . . . . The other side of life is going to church and seeing these beautiful, paradisical images of an afterlife – the Virgin Mary with candles – and it's kind of dreamy. . . . But all this comes as a reward for toughing it out in this life.

The rules surrounding the 'correct' interpretation of the religious symbols were provided by the exigetical authorities of the suite:

the teachers and administrators (and, to some extent, the priests who occasionally came into the class to speak to the students). The teachers constructed the pre-established codes and stringent stipulations for interpreting the symbolic order of the school. In other words, teachers 'nudged' connections between symbols and referents – connections that must be made if one is to be considered a good student and good Catholic. Because of the natural ambiguity of the symbols (e.g., Christ as humble saviour, or rebel, or ethereal spirit), teachers could unconsciously manipulate symbols to serve the interests of the dominant order.

On one occasion a staff member chastised a number of boys who had laughed and jeered at a visiting administrator from a nearby high school.

> *Staff member:* Some of you were just awful. But there were a few of you who behaved – God bless those who listened!

Misbehaviour was regarded as sacreligious and students who behaved 'like good Catholics' earned a blessing from the teacher. When the teacher blessed good behaviour, she not only employed the sacred status of the Church to reinforce her remarks but she also aligned the sacred domain with the teacher's policing function. While teachers obviously did not go so far as to proclaim themselves a type of educational National Guard or Christian militia, blessings nevertheless took the form of an invisible truncheon used to symbolically club students into line – to dragoon them into an agreed-upon sense of propriety and respect for classroom law and order. Blessings, like symbols, were convertible to many uses, some of them invidious.

By ordaining symbols with specific meanings (e.g. God loves good listeners; Jesus likes neat work; Mary appreciates politeness), teacher remarks often served as a pestle which pulverized the connotative power of the symbol into a sterile powder. We must question a culture that permits recourse to God's authority through an aggressive – and sometimes unconscionable – manipulation of referents. Once the most banal secularization was accorded almost sacerdotal significance when the image of the Pac Man video game monster was put up on the wall adjacent to the crucifix – a situation which appositely summed up the uncomfortable syncretic nature of the classroom symbology. Given this juxtaposition, this incursion of the absurd, this distilling of discomfort into a vision of holiness, what are the students to think? I'm reminded of a portrait painted by Salvador Dali which depicted a beautiful blond baby clenching a sewer rat between his teeth. But classroom life is not part of some surrealistic drama – or is it?

There was an inescapable 'ought' or hortatory prescriptiveness bound up with the sacramental symbols. Symbols often carried with them ethical purports. This was, in part, due to their opacity and multivalency. The characteristic of multivalency permitted religious symbols to serve both as instruments of social control or as instruments of liberation. Christ could, for instance, be described as a conservative who supported the existing power structures, or else as an activist who desired the government to be overthrown. Through the operationalization of sacred symbols, instructional rituals could partake of both hegemonic and utopian dimensions.

Overall, a broad range of Catholic symbols were translated by classroom rituals into graphic and readily comprehensible messages which constituted a compelling way of viewing reality and the student's location within that reality.

If, indeed, all symbols possess great connotative power by being fissile, ambiguous, multivalent, incongruous and polysemous, one could reasonably and legitimately ask: if reality is, in effect, 'up for grabs' in the sense that everybody interprets reality through symbols in different ways (echoing Vico's 'verum ipsum factum'), then how do symbols motivate groups of individuals in systematic ways? Turner answers this question by maintaining that the mixed feelings of dominant religious symbols (via the functions of the orectic and ideational poles) are 'averaged out into a single ambiguous quantum of generalized affect' which is 'deflected to . . . more abstract values and norms . . .' (1978, p. 575).

Religious symbols and religious instruction focused preponderantly on self-denial, on endurance, and on one's individual faults and inadequacies. Through the simple rituals of entry and departure – paying respect to the Supreme Deity (morning offering); saying thank-you for both material sustenancy (grace before meal) and spiritual sustenance (Act of Contrition) – the students participated in an event which further established the generalized tone and atmosphere of respect for the teacher, contributed to the sanctification of instruction, and evoked co-operation in the varied academic activities that were undertaken within the 'sacred' workplace of the school.

The opening prayers and class rituals emphasized 'work', 'suffering' and 'sinfulness'. Following the morning offering, brittle voices unaccustomed to the measure mouthed the words to 'O Canada':

O Canada!
Our home and native land,
True patriot love
In all thy sons command
With glowing hearts
We see thee rise
The True North strong and free!
From far and wide
O Canada
We stand on guard for thee
God keep our land
Glorious and free!
O Canada we stand on guard for thee
O Canada we stand on guard for thee.

Using Grimes's terminology (1976, p. 43), we have a marriage between a symbol of civilitas ('O Canada') and that of ecclesia (morning offering).[1] Another linking of symbols of ecclesia with civilitas occurred on a bulletin board, half of which was devoted to the theme 'confederation' (of the provinces) and half to the Catholic rite of 'Confirmation'.

Consider, as well, the closing prayer of the day which was repeated by Brock's class: the Act of Contrition:

O my God, I am heartily sorry for having offended you, and I detest all my sins because of your just punishments, but most of all because they offend you my God, who art all good.

In this passage there was, again, an emphasis on individual sinfulness and offending God. Also made manifest in the phrase 'just punishments' was the concept that punishment may be legitimate and may be sanctified by authoritative fiat. Prayers such as the Act of Contrition often partook of an uncanny and primordial sense of sanctity:

Student: Prayers are ways that human beings first talked to God. If it's a prayer, God listens to you. ... School teaches you the prayers you need to know before you get to go to Confirmation classes.

Jesus was always symbolically present in the suite: he constantly peered down at the students from crucifixes mounted on the walls; his teachings were continually discussed in religion class; and his name was invoked during instances in which teachers blessed students for striving hard, for postponing gratification, or for exhibiting a sense of academic stoicism in the midst of the discomfort of tests and assignments.

As part of a questionnaire, a large number of students reported that Jesus would not approve of their conduct in school. Consequently students exhibited frequent – and sometimes intolerable – feelings of guilt. This guilt prompted students to submit more readily to the forces of control – and, if necessary, the forces of punishment – meted out by Christ's educational representatives, the teachers and priests.

'I feel Jesus would sometimes like our performances but at other times not like them.'

'I think Jesus would feel sorry for me.'

'I think Jesus feels that I am rude and I like to fool around a lot.'

'I feel that Jesus would be mad at me.'

'He would not like it [the way the students behave] because of all the answering back, all the foul language and all the fighting. Also because he sees no love between the students.'

'I feel that Jesus would think we are terrible.'

'I think Jesus would feel unhappy. I feel that at home I am a very different person than when I'm at school.'

'Well, I think if he was my father, He would slap my face, because that's what my father would do if he ever saw how I act in school (which isn't so bad). But at lunch I talk to guys and my father doesn't like that and I sometimes act weird around my friends, and I don't think Jesus would be too pleased.'

CREATING THE CONFORMING CATHOLIC:
A DIALECTICAL INTERPLAY OF ROOT PARADIGMS

The daily prayers and religious activities served to metaphorically link Catholic ideologies to real 'material' events (the instructional rituals and follow-up activities). They 'spiritualized' the ordinariness of the plodding school day and served to sanctify the temporal order of the suite. Paradigmatically (the subsuming of symbols within a frame or the vertical dimension of selectivity – 'what goes with what'), the prayers located the students meaningfully within the Catholic world view. Syntagmatically (sequentially, continuously, or the horizontal flow of messages linked one after the other – 'what follows what') they established the religious/secular context for the instructional rituals that followed. Clearly, the prayers and religion classes defined a distinct cosmology for the students which – given the daily repetitiveness and formality of the rituals – the students were powerless to reject. This was, however, a cosmology riddled with and fraught by contradictions.

A contradiction was implied in the fact that students were encouraged to feel joyful and thankful for being loved by God and saved from eternal damnation – yet at the same time were exhorted to accept their sinful nature, be prepared to suffer and endure the banality of life, and accept the pains and sorrows that accompanied material existence. The religious symbols, replete with ambiguity, and the contradictory messages inherent in the religious aspects of life in the suite (prayers, religion classes, religious icons, informal remarks by teachers, visits by priests, etc.) became desituated from their respective sacred domains and *relocated* alongside the secular aspects of classroom culture which included the highly valued domain of work with its emphasis on academic subjects and concomitant work habits. Meanings recurrently shifted between these seemingly unbridgeable or ostensibly distinct domains through a dialectical traffic of symbols. The interfacing of these two systems of signification (the secular and the religious) saw them partake of each other's characteristics – in a reciprocal or even osmotic fashion (as if there were only a semi-permeable membrane separating them) – and served to bend the ritual codes into a single stream, forcing them to evoke messages in a select context and making them appear as integrally linked. Symbols and paradigms thus partook of somewhat *contrapuntal* characteristics. Though they signified distinct kinds of meanings, symbols from these two domains managed to 'play off' each other in a harmonious fashion. The power of this union was the annulment of the distinction between sacred and secular domains.

The academic objectives nested in the instructional rituals (i.e. the behavioural objectives of the lessons) were directed – and for the most part were successful – at creating student behaviour that was most concordant with the manifest or 'official' doctrines of the suite (embodied in the formal academic aims of the school and ultimately in the curriculum guidelines of the Separate School Board and Ministry of Education). The rituals succeeded in building authoritative structures which dispensed rewards to those students who were the most passive, pliable, straightforward, predictable and well-mannered, and who exhibited compliance toward adult authority, punctuality, dependability and acceptance of the daily routines and rituals – all qualities endemic to the middle-class codes of propriety belonging to the teachers and administrators. Students were induced to perceive, and therefore interpret, the world in a way that sustained the joint principles of 'being a worker' and 'being a Catholic'. The rituals of instruction amplified and maintained systems of representation furnished by the Church and state rather than imposed a specific construction of reality.

For the most part, instructional rites were directed to militate against the development of intense peer bonds. The opaque juxta-position and entanglements of sacred and secular symbols and paradigms which were linked to both the content of the rituals (formal curriculum) and their morphogenic characteristics (struc-tural characteristics of the rituals) created a type of unholy alliance which gave greater power to both the sacred and secular dimen-sions of school culture, ultimately enhancing the teachers' control over the students.

Welded together and rendered primordially relevant, the root paradigms were mediational of all instruction. Essentially, the mean-ings which constituted the two root paradigms became emanations and refracted images of one another. Through the commutative relationship between these two domains, the norms and values of secular work habits were saturated and ennobled with spiritual legitimation and certification, while the spiritual values embodied in religion class and the material symbols (the imposed artifacts and religious paraphernalia of crucifixes, statues of Mary, emblems, etc.) were given a secular, practical, 'down-to-earth' valence. There was, in Turner's terms, a movement from optation to obligation. The messages conveyed by the root paradigms were magnetized, given a visceral charge, a valency, a deep code. Thus, the root para-digms became co-constituting phases in an unbroken circle of tauto-logical power. And hence, they sustained immunity from question.

The coupling or primary fusion of religious and secular domains served to create the general 'ritual charter' of the school. This charter comprised the groundwork for the school's 'civil religion' of 'becoming a citizen'. 'Becoming a citizen' reflected the importance of student self-governance and the stewardship of the soul. To become a citizen meant being both a good Catholic and a good worker. Thus, the problematicity inherent in the 'abstractness' of Catholic dogma was diffused by locating sacred symbols in a nucleus of concrete events (classroom lessons), and the problematicity of the drudging concreteness of schoolwork was diffused by locating it within the cosmology of Roman Catholicism – thereby universalizing the overall 'truth claims' manifested in the instructional rituals. The instructional rituals 'naturalized' or 'legitimized' the religious cosmology, collapsing the hostile polarity traditionally ascribed to sacred and secular domains, while the religious cosmology sanctified the vulgar instructional domain. In this way, the secular function of schooling (that of social control and preparing students for the workplace) remained cloaked in religious meanings.

Yet there was another twist in the intercalibrations of secular and religious complexes which had to do with the mirror-like relation of homology between root paradigms. While it was true that religious symbols and activities conferred a sense of sanctity and transcendent meaning upon the vulgar aspects of the Calvinistic work ethic evident in the suite, it was also true that both religious and secular motifs repeated the same messages. For instance, the spiritual values stressing sorrow and suffering were linked – in fact, reified – through the day-to-day secular drudgery of the schoolwork. Both the sacred and secular domains invited a parallel inventory of values and characteristics, with no one domain preponderating over the other. Catholic values such as denial of the body, endurance, deference to the authority of the priest and Church, hard work and struggle (and these values are especially true of Azorean Catholicism) paralleled the secular values inherent in the ritualized instruction (e.g. hard work, endurance, sticking to the task, deference to the authority of the teacher). Together, these value domains simply mirrored each other at different symbolic junctures, or in different tacit dimensions of meaning. In fact, they were practically convertible into one other. At the level of power they were functionally identical, and thus their preeminence was rendered as natural and beneficent. It would appear to be in the very nature of Catholic instructional ritual to homogenize the sacred (Catholic) and secular (corporate capitalist) cultural capital of the dominant society. The efforts of Catholic schooling in helping the poor and oppressed are spiritualized away when Catholic values are themselves invisibly linked to a culture of domination and exploitation.

The interdictions, elicitations, preachments and imprimaturs of the teachers took on greater force when teachers were seen to dispense both the wisdom of the tables of Moses and the tables of multiplication. Therefore, the manifest intentions of both the school curriculum (e.g. the avowed commitment of the educational system to make workers) and the Church (the avowed intentions of the Church to produce Catholics, were objectified, concretized, ethicized and reified into a unified context. This conjoint relationship between sacred and the secular contexts of schooling presented – rather, 'created' – a cultural milieu which managed to convey to the students a legitimate rationalization for the world the way it was. The instructional rituals implicated and insinuated the students into a world of hard work – yet a world where hard work was sanctified and suffused with Christian morality and where credence and legitimacy were given to being an 'under socialized', 'dull-normal', or 'level four' student with not much to look forward to in the future but the shopfloor.

Enactment in the instructional rituals of the suite purported to be the solution to the problem of life's contingencies and contradictions. For most teachers and some students, affirming oneself in the rituals of the suite was the highest good – the quintessential act of being a 'good Catholic' and a 'good worker'.

In addition to bringing powerful binding sanctions to bear on the enforcement of school values, the concatenation of symbols and paradigms presented background relief for the emergence of countercultural forms and ritual dramas. It is the phenomenon of ritualized student 'resistances' to the canonical codes embedded in the instructional rites that makes it difficult to provide a balanced assessment of the consequences of ritual action. For rituals both evince deference to authority and enhance formal goal attainment and at the same time bifurcate and rupture the symbolic bonds that hold together the heterogeneous and interdependent classroom whole. They also occasionally serve as pivotal agents of social change and isotopes of creativity within the social order.

Generally speaking, there was little collective solidarity or effervescence evoked by the macro or micro rituals. In fact, these rituals served to dismember whatever minimal communitas already existed (usually left over from the streetcorner state). Communitas was diminished by the strict quotidian control over students via stock reprimands and disciplinary phrases, especially when there were strong peer bonds growing – or threatening to develop – in the suite. In other words, the rituals operative within the suite possessed the nature of a two-edged sword: they could be used as instruments either of liberation or of oppression. This latter effect often led to co-operative resistance to the school-sponsored norms and class-room system of scruples. When ritual forms were oppressive or bifurcating, there were important sociological implications. When, for instance, students created their personal constructs about schooling (cf. Kelly, 1963), they did so as if their metaphysical assumptions surrounding the bifurcated school world were true. In response to this bifurcation, new ritual metaphors emerged from the antistructure and inherited reenactment as rituals of resistance. While on the surface, the rituals of the suite appeared to cohere around the dominant symbols of the parent culture, binding the students together and creating an *in loco uteri* – a type of womb which nurtured the students' already predisposed religious and worker values – there were many instances of ritualized rebellion. Students who did not wish to resist the permeation of a Catholic worker world view (the 'browners') remained comfortable members of the *sensus ecclesiae* – the tightly knit moral community or assembly of students and teachers. Such a seemingly integrated community nevertheless invites a close comparison to Goffman's asylum or 'total institution'.

MONDAY, 14 DECEMBER

I arrived just as classes were parading out the door. The grade 8s were making their way to the nearest church (run by Italian, not Portuguese priests) for Confession. I joined up with Penelope's group.

I asked the students how they felt about the entire suite going to church for Confession; Rocko looked at me and sneered:

'Hey, man. Do you believe in priests, man?'

'Well,' I said, 'that depends on what you mean.'

'Well, I don't believe in them, man.'

'Why?'

'Wanna know somethin'?'

'Go ahead.

'Even a bum can be a priest. All a bum's gotta do is take a bath for a week. Then he can be a priest.'

I looked hard at Rocko. 'Are you telling me that you think priests are bums?'

'Hey, man, what I'm saying is that nobody can take God's job.'

'Do you believe in God, then, Rocko?'

'Sure man. But not priests. Bein' a priest is just a job - like a teacher, man.'

WEDNESDAY, 13 JANUARY

I went into the washroom to find out the extent of the damage. It was considerable. The washroom walls were decorated with graffiti, and the ceiling looked as if it had been punctured by numerous objects. The majority of toilets were unflushed and the sight of stools floating about on top of the water was enough to curb the most insistent peristaltic invitation. A student came into the washroom and pointed to the jutting pipes that marked the spot where the tank had perched over the urinals.

'Ain't that too bad about what happened?' he smiled.

'Yeah,' I replied. 'Too bad.'

'Musta been a big kid who done it, sir,' he said with more than a flicker of mischief in his eyes.

The kid continued. 'Musta been a big, strong kid. A big, tall, strong kid. Not like me - right?'

I looked at him sternly. He smiled right back defiantly.

'Couldn'ta been me, sir, could it? I ain't big enough ta rip off those pipes.' His eyes widened and he shook his head in a sense of mock outrage.

'Jeez, I hope they catch whoever done it,' he said sarcastically. 'Whoever it was should be punished.' At the last remark he left, shaking his head and clicking his tongue.

FRIDAY, 15 JANUARY

During Confession, while the students filed up to the priests on the cue of the teachers, the students remaining in their pews became so noisy that teachers were compelled to quiet them down. Some kids were talking about the movie *Christina F* which they had seen recently, a German docudrama about teenage heroin addicts. I noticed one student lean over a pew and rifle through the personal belongings of a student who was in the confessional. Another student screamed out when she twisted her leg underneath the pew.

Four or five students from another class came in and sat down behind a row of students who were in fervent prayer. A kneeling bench was brought down sharply on the floor. Rocko and his friends leered and smacked their lips at the protruding buttocks of girls kneeling in the row directly in front of them. As Franko was about to rise to make his confession, he turned to me and blurted: 'Hey man, nice haircut you got!'

I could see the priests making the sign of the cross over the heads of the students as they pronounced absolution.

TUESDAY, 27 JANUARY

Another ritual of revitalization occurred in the form of St Ryan's 'day of recollection' – an annual event which was held this year at a downtown Catholic institution. The event was essentially a professional development day combined with a religious service. Phase one consisted of listening to a keynote speaker and engaging in a series of workshop activities. Phase two was a mass celebrated together by the staff and presided over by a guest priest.

The keynote speaker and workshop leader was an extremely interesting, if somewhat overbearing, teacher. As Gestalt therapist and professor of education (and a Catholic to boot), he came well equipped to engage the staff in what he referred to as a spiritual 'imagistic voyage'.

Speaking through a wagging beard and splayed teeth, Dr Jungmann (not his real name) began his talk by referring to neuro-linguistic programming techniques, and techniques developed by Fritz Perls and other members of the spiritual mafia of Esalen, California. Next, he showed us a film on biofeedback featuring the work of Hans Selye.

I was able to engage in a private discussion with Dr Jungmann during the break. He caught me by surprise with the candid remark that he had nearly died twice, and had been clinically dead once.

Dr Jungmann: 'Since my clinical death, I have subsequently left my body a number of times ... but I don't talk about those experiences very much – it almost destroyed my career. People thought I was nuts.'

After the break, Dr Jungmann talked about various 'stressors' involved in teaching. He said that some of the worst stressors he had seen listed (such as 'abrasive language', 'breaking up fights', and 'abusive behaviour') were advanced by teachers in a workshop that he had held in North York's Jane Finch Corridor – the area in which I had spent nearly five years as a teacher.

After a short break, we made our way to the upstairs chapel where we celebrated mass. It was an emotional service: there was a strong presence of communitas among the teachers. Two teachers carrying lighted candles followed the priest into the chapel. One of the vice-principals volunteered to do the reading. As the service progressed, several teachers barely managed to hold back tears – a difficult feat after a particularly engaging mass. During the ceremony, I felt that the mass was somehow holding together the world like some sort of spiritual glue – keeping humanity from coming apart at the seams, or sinking into vortex of nothingness. What a difference between this mass and the one that the students had to suffer through before Christmas! We took communion in both species, and I supped the chalice held up to my lips by the principal. During the sermon, the priest spoke about stress and teaching and we offered prayers for our fellow teachers. Then came a most remarkable moment: a nun asked that we, as teachers, be forgiven for the ways in which we may have caused the students to suffer through our lack of love, concern and our performance as teachers. Many of us were visibly moved by the nun's gesture.

After mass we ate lunch and then listened to Dr Jungmann's tape which featured a lengthy discussion by Dr Robert Ornstein about the two hemispheres of the brain. After the film, Dr Jungmann tried to integrate Ornstein's work into a Catholic framework. His discussion of cerebral styles of dominance appeared to coincide with aspects of the ritual states of interaction which I had been uncovering. The streetcorner state appeared to be linked to right-minded characteristics (e.g. intuition, subjunctivity) while the student state appeared to represent more left-minded characteristics (e.g. logical and categorical thinking). Dr Jungmann then put us all in a mild hypnotic trance and took us on a 'visualization voyage' through imaginary gardens where we met spiritual guides in the forms of various animals. A number of teachers maintained that they were greeted by deer guides. Guides such as a yearling calf, a lamb, a mountain goat, a wolf, a dog, a horse, and a bird of prey were also encountered by various teachers. Deer, Dr Jungmann informed us, are the guides of those who are spiritually inclined (and are frequently cited by those in training for the priesthood or preparing to become deacons). Then

Dr Jungmann told us that our animal guides were really manifestations of the Holy Spirit. He concluded the workshop by asking us
to remember him in our prayers.

The professional development day mass could be termed a ritual
of revitalization which affirmed the dominant values of the Catholic
community. Dr Jungmann's talk was, essentially, a rite of intensification since many of his ideas were, in the words of one teacher,
'too far out' to be countenanced as legitimate Catholic doctrine.
But many teachers agreed that they needed some new ideas to keep
them inspired as teachers.

> *Teacher*: We should have more days like this a year. It gives you
> a chance to hear what other teachers are doing. But the public
> sees them [professional development days] as just time off for
> the teachers.

WEDNESDAY, 25 MARCH

Today the students participated in a schoolwide Confession. The
Church teaches that it is necessary for all to confess their sins
before God. The Church also believes that there are temporal
punishments for sin, pointing to the fact that a just and merciful
God requires that a penitent sinner atone for his sins. The sinner
will receive punishment for them either now – in this life –
or after death in purgatory, unless he takes punishment for his
sins upon himself by making some form of reparation. After
Confession, sometimes known as 'the second baptism', the
penitent student must complete his penitential act by doing some
form of 'penance' imposed by the priest. In earlier days, penance
was often severe. Today it consists of a relatively slight act of piety
– the recitation of certain prayers assigned by the priest after the
penitent has confessed his sins. Perhaps this can be looked upon
as the sacred analogue of 'writing lines'. The Church teaches that in
virtue of the authority given it by Christ, it may grant sinners forgiveness of their sins. The sacrament of Confession (now frequently
referred to by Catholics as Reconciliation) was administered to all the
grade 8 students and was celebrated by six priests in the same church
where the students attended the Christmas mass. Some priests
administered the sacrament in the open (and out of earshot) of the
rest of the congregation. Other priests used the private confessionals,

four priests had to administer penance in front of the alter, in which case the backs of the penitents faced the congregation). Before the sacrament of penance was carried out, hymns were sung and scripture readings took place to bind the students together as a community of Catholics. During the culmination of the rite, the priest put his hands over the head of the penitent while saying the words of absolution:

> God the Father of mercies,
> through the death and resurrection of his Son
> has reconciled the world to himself
> and sent the Holy Spirit among us for the
> forgiveness of sins;
> through the ministry of the Church may God give you pardon and peace
> and I absolve you . . .

Compared to the Christmas mass, the schoolwide sacrament of Reconciliation was the more effective ritual. Students appeared to appreciate the individual participation that Confession afforded them (e.g. in the recitation of their sins and the personal forgiveness administered by the priest).

> *Student 1*: At least in the Confession you get to talk to the priest . . . He's pretty nice most of the time and doesn't yell at you. He forgives you. And he knows who you are because he can recognize your voice.
> *Student 2*: In the mass you can hide with your friends. But at Confession you can't hide your sins from God.

TAKING THE 'ID' OUT OF IDEOLOGY: TOWARDS A CONCEPT OF RITUAL KNOWLEDGE

Ritual space

The spatial characteristics of the classroom were crucial for promoting effective ritualized communication during instructional rituals and constituted an institutional subset of the ritual codes themselves.

There were incessant complaints among the staff about the open area or 'open plan' design of the suite. Open plan schools were controversial throughout the 1960s and into the 1970s.

Originally designed as arenas of flexible 'multipurpose space' in which desks, blackboards and walls could be moved and adjusted, open area schools were supposed to usher in a wide range of pedagogic options and teacher styles. I can recall writing papers about the benefits and liabilities of open plan classrooms as far back as 1972 when I attended teachers' college. In addition, I had taught in an open plan classroom during my first year as a teacher and had engaged in almost identical debates to the ones which I frequently heard at St Ryan.

> *Teacher 1*: Well ... I'd like to teach in a closed classroom. Frankly, I've had it.
> *Teacher 2*: I don't mind it. Although I agree it's not for everybody. It depends on the kids. It's good for some kids and bad for others. The same can be said for the closed classroom, so what do you do?

While the suite assumed some of the attributes of a sacred space (through the presence of religious symbols, etc.), the feeling of sanctity was undeniably eroded by the constant noise. The sonic level of the suite was extremely high – even at the best of times. Makeshift barriers consisting of cupboards on rollers and study carrels simply marked off territorial space between the separate classes – they did nothing to combat the noise itself.

The only positive feature about the open area that I ever heard voiced by the teachers was the fact that it gave them a chance to work together. They all agreed that their philosophies were similar – the *sine qua non* for team teaching. They seemed to enjoy each other's company, even during breaks and after classes were dismissed for the day.

Although the suite had superb potential for flexible teaching arrangements (after all, that was one of the reasons open area style schools were designed in the first place) the arrangements were largely those of a standard classroom: the teachers' large metal desks ominously faced the students, who were seated in straight rows; and the blackboards were located right behind the teachers' desks. The spatial arrangement of the suite was *sociofugal* as opposed to *sociopetal* – that is, the arrangements of the suite were designed to inhibit social interaction rather than promote it (cf. Calitri, 1975; Sitton, 1980; Lewis, 1979). Students occupied their own desks (some of which were study carrels) and were restricted to them for most of the day. The lockers and desks were the only items which the students could, in any sense, feel that they 'owned'. In Brock's class, there existed a single table at which three or four students occasionally worked.

The teachers' desk and supply cupboard were 'off limits' (to use Goffman's terminology). So were the teachers' planning room, the staff room and the library. Occasionally students went to the library as a class, but they rarely went on an individual basis. Generally speaking, those areas which were 'off limits' to the students were much more physically comfortable than those that were not 'off limits' (cf. Sitton, 1980).

Students were allowed to go to the washroom only when teacher permission was granted – which was not always the case. Teachers preferred that students regulate their bowels and bladders so that they could be emptied before, after or between classes. To go to the washroom too frequently was allowing the 'streetcorner state' to invade the boundaries of the 'student state'.

The suite's 'high surveillance context' – wide, straight and uncluttered halls – provided a clear view of student transactions (cf. Sitton, 1980).

> *Brock*: There's a nice control here [near the cupboards] where over there [near the teacher's desk] there's less control.
> *Peter*: A surveillance factor.
> *Brock*: I can keep an eye on my books. If I'm over there at my desk I don't have control over this alcove as much. When some kid comes up to get a dictionary – even if I don't know he's come up to get a dictionary – he thinks I've noticed him; therefore, it's more likely that he'll put it back. He's had to pass me. Well . . . if I was sitting over there anybody could come here to take a dictionary and could take it home, leave it in their desks, leave it lying around. It's more likely that they'll return it this way.
> *Peter*: It's amazing how you've thought all this stuff out.
> *Brock*: Well, I've been here a long time and I've had my desk in various places and I think this is the best place to have it.

Open spaces of 'low surveillance' included only the washroom and, to a certain extent, the school cafetorium. In the cafetorium, the streetcorner state prevailed – but it was assiduously kept in 'check' by patrolling teachers on lunchroom duty. The washroom, on the other hand, bore the symbolic scars of the streetcorner state: walls were tattooed with graffiti; frequently used toilets remained unflushed; sinks were plugged and tissue paper littered the ground.

There was a moratorium placed on high surveillance spaces between periods when the streetcorner state was made legitimate for several minutes while students changed classes or got ready for their next subject. During these times of rearrangement and readjustment, students were in control of their spatial contexts and symbolically 'won' the suite temporarily. As the students left for lunch, the halls, too, became 'open spaces' for about ten minutes.

The semi-fixed seating arrangements in the three classes of the suite enhanced – even forced – student interaction with the teacher and his/her dissemination of the content (e.g. they served as 'soft cops'). In addition to serving as a structural lubricant for the smooth delivery of the content, the spatial arrangements of the suite also promoted the ability of the teachers to effectively generate a successful frequency and polarity for interaction rhythms. The only blemish on this achievement was the noise level which often served to 'jam' the teachers frequency and inhibit the efficacy of the instructional rites. This often resulted in an attempt by the students to set up their own frequency.

Teacher: Sometimes the noise builds up and you can hear it grow louder, class by class, building on itself.

One of the most interesting ritual uses of space occurred just before I began my field studies. During Thanksgiving week there was a mass held in the suite. It was interesting to fathom how the very same space that housed the students' desks stuffed with comic books, car magazines and the occasional porno clippings could one day be *transformed into a consecrated space* for the holy sacrifice of God's Son. In the same area where a student was 'chewed out' for not doing homework, the priest reverently chews the sacred host.

Figuring prominently in the instructional rites were the spatial positions that the teachers took during the delivery of the content of the lessons. Each teacher occupied what I half-jokingly referred to as their 'power spot'. These spots represented a ritual space which the teachers felt offered them the most advantageous position for instructing the class. Once, when I was asked to take over the class for one of the teachers, I decided to move towards that teacher's 'spot'. The instant I entered it, one of the students remarked: 'Are you the teacher now?' The power spot of the teacher was sacred space. Only the teacher was allowed to spend any amount of time in it. It was the spot where the transformation from ignorance to knowledge – from lethargy to good Catholic busyness – occurred.

Ritual time

Ritual time does not simply refer to the sounding of church bells calling you to mass. It is a dimension that impinges on the very way we articulate our humanity.

Schools are temporally insulated just as they are spatially insulated from the rest of society. The operative time system in the school was similar to what Hall (1973, 1984) prosaically named M-time (monochromatic time: emphasizing schedules, segmentation and promptness). During the streetcorner state, however, P-time (polychromatic time) was operative (emphasizing personal involvement, completion of transactions, and several things happening simultaneously).

In the polychromatic time/space continuum of the streetcorner state, many events happened simultaneously: students might have been playing with several different classmates, or groups of students, while engaging in a number of activities all at once. Time passed quickly. There was little sense of grinding endurance (such as you experienced in the student state) due to increased flow. Time 'dissolved' into whatever activity the students happened to be engaged in. Students tended to lose track of time when in the streetcorner state.

> *Student*: At lunchtime you just start getting involved with things and the time gets used up before you know it. The bell rings and it's just like you can't believe lunch is over.

During the student state, the segmentation of time into 'units' or 'periods' influenced the students' perception of work such that work became time spent 'doing one thing over and over' until the period was over. Time literally became 'death' – an enemy to avoid. This led to the propensity of many students to want to 'waste time'. When one 'wastes time' one actually 'lays waste' to time.

In the suite, time was 'owned' not by the students, but by the teachers and administrators. One of the biggest complaints from the majority of the students was the lack of time for lunch. Students had less than an hour to eat. It was perhaps noteworthy that they were given less time to fuel their bodies than they were given to attend mass (mass was usually about an hour).

> *Student*: The lunch hour is so short that we hardly have no time to do anything. We're not even allowed to go to the washroom after we're finished eating our lunch. We're not even allowed

to go to our lockers if we forget something. I hate these school rules.

The ritual content

Both secular and religious teachings were codified and translated into curriculum objectives, materials and various rubrical books for teacher use. These curriculum materials were then transmitted to the students by the body of ritual officiants – the teachers – in a manner generally binding to the students.

The content of school subjects was deeply influenced by the prevailing form of the instructional rites. In fact, the content of the instructional rituals took a position secondary to the exigencies of the structural attributes of the rituals themselves.

Subject matter was divided up into different subject areas. One teacher instructed students in level five maths, level three language and history; another taught level four maths, level four language and science; while a third took groups in level five language, level three maths and geography. Each teacher taught religion, physical education, health and current events to the students in his or her home room. The 'specials' were industrial arts and home economics and these were taught by different teachers who specialized in those areas. (Interestingly compartmentalization in subject matter began with Catholic schooling during the thirteenth century when the bishops' schools evolved into our first universities which were given over primarily to the study of the liberal arts: the trivium of grammar, dialectic and rhetoric; and the quadrivium of astronomy, arithmetic, music and geometry.)

The formats for administering the instructional rites were, for the most part, formal and invariant. Students were primarily taught through the use of a future-focused image. They were exhorted to be good students for the advantages that it would afford them in the future:

> *Teacher*: If you expect to do well later on outside of school, then I'd try a little harder.

Once students were slotted into 'categories' such as level three or level four, little could be done to change their status. During a workshop on grading and promotion, a guest speaker set up a simulation game on student placement. He gave several groups of teachers a number of fictional report card ratings from a make-believe staff concerning a make-believe student named Jason. On the basis of these fictional reports, the staff members were to rank the student and decide whether or not to promote him. They were also asked to suggest a proper 'placement' for the student. Each group, therefore, had identical information from which to base their collective decision. While all the groups decided to pass Jason, each group differed on where Jason was to be placed. A number of teachers appeared shocked when they heard the workshop leader tell them that, as a result of conducting the same simulation game with dozens of teacher groups from all over the province, Jason was placed 'anywhere and everywhere' from a class for TMR (Trainable Mentally Retarded) students to an advanced level six class. Promoting or failing students was thus arbitrary and less scientific than most of the teachers were willing to believe. In fact, the speaker mentioned that when the fictional character was made into a female black student, the results were a great deal worse.

Those students who learned to disconnect or 'abstract' school knowledge from the everyday realities of experience were channelled or streamed into an appropriate (higher status) track. All students in the suite were streamed or 'tracked' in maths and language and it was obvious that these were the two most important subject areas. I found it surprising that the teachers were expected to 'promote' all the students on the basis of half a year's work. In other words, the teachers were expected to have their promotion forms filled out and distributed to the office well in advance of the termination of the year. In order to facilitate the administrative workings of the Metro Separate School Board, teachers were asked to track their students into levels three, four or five programmes for the following year (grade 9) *before Christmas*. And what if a student miraculously changed categories before the end of the year? In that case the teacher could fill out another form and the computer system would register the alteration. Choosing the appropriate stream for the students was supposed to be done in consultation with the parents. However, the final decision about where the student was to be placed rested with the teacher.

This method of labelling and streaming students turned the students into static 'products'. Because of the bureaucratic design of the school system and the philosophical premises upon which the curriculum was based, the teachers could not work with students as if they were continually changing persons.

The symbols used in instructional rituals were mainly discursive and aggressively antiaesthetic. That is to say (following the distinction between discursive and non-discursive symbols made by Phenix (1964) and Langer (1957) instructional symbols communicated mainly facts. There was little use of non-discursive symbols (such as found in poetry, art, drama and music) that communicated intimate experience, emotions and motivations rather than objective thoughts. The rich multivalency of the symbol – which could easily engulf the sensibilities of the student – dissolved into a dissolute literalism and facticity. An inordinate emphasis was placed upon the digital dimension of assignments (univocality, precision, logic) as opposed to the analogical dimension (equivocation, ambiguity, description). Students were trained in a *post hoc ergo propter* (after the fact, therefore because of the fact) manner. This practice was in accord with the feeling among teachers and administration that Azorean students 'live in the world of hard, practical facts'. Digital tasks revolved around applying pre-given sets of logical operations such as one would find in standardized worksheets and workbooks (e.g. fill-in blanks, match items, choose correct response).

Ritual knowledge: learning 'viscerally'

Ritual knowledge is more than just the solipsistic tingle we sometimes experience when genuflecting before a church altar or some type of transcendental rapport with a distant being. One does not have to ascend Mount Carmel, descend into Dante's pit or warm one's thoughts in the reflective fire of Plato's cave to acquire it. It is a knowledge that cannot be appropriated theoretically or by meditating on some incommensurable mystery. It is a form of articulating our humanity by negotiating with and embodying the various ritual exigencies of the sociocultural order. That is, it is primarily a bodily form of knowing as opposed to a cognitive skill (cf. Jennings, 1982). In order to undertake analysis of ritual knowledge in school settings, it is imperative that we consider both the surface structure and deep structure messages of ritualized instruction and note how rituals transmit the deep codes that provide the blueprints for how students come to know and react to various situations. That is, in order to come to understand ritual knowledge, we must focus on the genealogy of the socio cultural world of the classroom and interrogate the processes by which rituals contribute to our taken-for-granted knowledge.

An exploration of ritual knowledge in the classroom enfranchises on the following questions: How do rituals influence the development of the dominant cultural epistemes that form the social recipes (or recipe knowledge) of the classroom culture? Do the ritual patterns that merge in the suite entail as a necessary postulate the existence of a unique style of knowing?

The staple repertoire of rituals enacted in the classroom provided students with unique conditions for structuring and codifying often paradoxical cultural information. The ritualizing 'moment' was an incarnate mode of knowing through which was welded the indicative and the subjunctive, the literal and the parabolic.

When taken together, the peculiar characteristics of ritual space and time, the morphological qualities of the instructional rites (the invariance, formality, punctiliousness, and the use of performatives and creedal statements), the style of performance by the teacher (who controls the speed, sequencing, and content of the lesson), and the prevailing root paradigms with their symbolic entailments, added up to a distinctive politics of communication that may be said to have both influenced and shaped the dominant epistemes through which Catholic students made sense of their phenomenal world. Many of the overall characteristics of this 'ritual knowledge' were derived from, or 'invented by', the unique conflation and coalescence of all these dimensions of instruction – a process which resulted in the creation of both an inordinate amount of symbolic power on the part of the teachers and a unique conceptual grammar and cognitive style on the part of the students. Knowledge that was held as valuable (even hallowed) proved, in essence, to be a public fiction created and refined – and ultimately mystified – by the ritualized form of its presentation. Nevertheless, the ritual appurtenances of instruction imbued this knowledge with a sense of sanctity. Therefore, the instructional rituals were only tangentially part of the instrumental act of teaching; rather, they were more important in creating a cultural world, a moral order.

By virtue of the inner circuitry of the ritual symbol (with its normative and physiological poles), the ritual exigencies of instruction constituted a 'deep coding' of information wherein the mental templates of the students were galvanized by the alloy of conventional educational thought. Ritual knowledge goes far beyond the notion of customs, morals or ideas; it is embodied in the morphology of the instructional rites and, in a broader sense, through the symbolic configurations within the various ritual systems. Ritual knowledge helped to produce an inventory of taken-for-granted values and a framework of linked presuppositions and propositions about the way things are which, over time, became sedimented into a rigid ideological sytem – into commonsensical components of day-to-day activities and classroom exchanges. At an even broader level, ritual knowledge consisted of both bodily memory and instinct as well as the particular cognitive 'alignments' of the students. It was as intramuscular as it was cerebral.

While the morphological characteristics of the instructional rites were often rigid, metallic and mechanically repetitious, the form of discourse that resulted from engagement in these rites was all-pervasive; it suffused the students' symbolic and corporeal world like an ether. The instructional rites contained, in codified form, the whole structural logic of ideological domination which is at the heart of the modern technocratic state. In fact, instructional rites worked through the bodies of the students with such subtle ferocity that drudgery and hegemony became flesh.

The failure of the working-class immigrant was unconsciously built into the curriculum structures: futility disguised as opportunity. Tired and static educational symbols had congealed into hollow rituals. The frail character and operative sterility of the 'hyper-cognitive' classroom rituals paled in comparison to the 'bodily' characteristics of working-class cultural forms. Students became fed up with passive modes of interacting with experience during the student state – with learning things hypothetically and inter-acting in a milieu of ersatz feelings. They wanted to embody knowledge viscerally and experience a style of knowing that was devoid of excessive abstraction and doctrinal baggage. My stress on visceral understanding is not meant to horrify the neo-Platonist; nor is it an attempt to argue for a post-Tridentine anti-intellectualism à la Thomas à Kempis, a return to a 'paleolithic revival' (to use Bellah's term), the recovery of an alchemical world view, or a determined effort to create a class full of 'peakers' (in a Maslovian sense). Moreover, to underscore the importance of visceral understanding is not an unqualified endorsement of the streetcorner state or the youth counterculture, or a romantic yearning for the primeval or the atavistic. Abandoning the structures of modern civilization can, after all, lead into the heart of darkness or the worship of the Beast, as Joseph Conrad and William Golding have all too clearly shown us. The values that I attribute to street-corner culture are meant to be an antidote to the technocratic consciousness and the vocationalization of student character – not ends in themselves.

From the perspective of the students, the rituals of the suite constituted degradation ceremonies that, in the end, involved an ultimate hoax. Students baulked at satisfying themselves with metaphysical categories (such as heaven and purgatory) when they realized that all the metaphysics in the world wouldn't feed their families or help their parents pay the rent. Nor would the pain and suffering from enduring the boredom of schooling necessarily grant them decent jobs. The pain of schooling was real; the manifest claims of the educational system to bridge the chasm of opportunity between the rich and the poor through a good education was more of an illusion. Trapped between a concentrated onslaught of boredom and a dim hope for a better future, Portuguese students reacted much the same way as other working-class students: they dropped out.

Ritual knowledge gained through the streetcorner state was qualitatively different from that gained through the instructional rituals of the student state. Ritual knowledge in the student state was often sullied by an inflated rationalism whereas in the street-corner state the students made use of more bodily exploration and organic symbols. Ritual knowledge in the student state was more symbolically sophisticated; but because such knowledge was discarnate and not a 'lived' engagement, it remained distant, isolated, abstract. As well, the numinous and ludic aspects of Catholicism were often reduced to rationalistic, univocal concepts.

For the Azorean students, bodily participation was necessary for knowledge to be real. The eye of the flesh had to be opened. Meaning, in order to be considered authentic, had to be 'enfleshed' (to cite a term used by the early Church Fathers). Classroom knowledge must be resurrected to the status of 'visceral' under-standing to be appreciated by the Azorean students. Rituals do not press their unique pattern on to the cognitive stock of participants the way a seal imprints its image on melted wax; acquiring ritual knowledge is more complex than this. It is a process in which the body becomes the ultimate symbol.

Ritual knowledge is not something to be 'understood'; it is always, whether understood or not, something we feel and to which we respond organically. Ritual knowledge is epistemologically disparate from traditional conceptions of school knowledge. It is a type of *mimesis* or visceral/erotic identification in which students are in touch with the '*Ding an sich*' (the thing-in-itself). It is also akin to the Italian concept of *gioco* which is a playful and informal means of indirect learning (cf. Kohl, 1984, pp. 144–5). Broadly speaking, ritual knowledge can be conceived as interaction between the form and content of curriculum and the lived culture of the students. The streetcorner state offered a more vital form of ritual knowledge since it permitted closer correspondences between the social body and the physical body. The mechanical formality, regimentation and invariance which were part of the instructional rites to a large degree stripped the classroom cultural landscape of its organic symbols.

Ritual knowledge possesses an incarnate character; it is acquired noetically and inheres in the 'erotics of knowing' (Dixon, 1974). It is both reflective and pre-reflective (Zuesse, 1975, p. 518). As students acquire information 'viscerally', the distinction between themselves and their actions become nominal: the ritual participant becomes both the means and the end of the ritualizing act. Thus, to speak of creating rituals is somewhat misleading. Rather, it is better to say that rituals create us by providing the gestural metaphors and rhythms through which we engage the world. Considered as a form of symbolic action, rituals are better understood as 'verbings' rather than the frozen accounts that one might find in the logbook of an anthropologist.

The strength of ritual's ideological force is that it often erases its traces from that which it effects – a process that enables us to understand how hegemony works invisibly through the bodies and subjectivities of students. As enacted metaphors, rituals embody what they mean (cf. Grimes, 1984a). At St Ryan, the students enacted the metaphors and embodied the rhythms that were embedded in the cultural capital of the ruling class and transmitted through the rites of instruction.

Throughout the process of schooling culture is continually made and remade without revealing the source of its legitimatizing power: it remains a smile without a face; a kiss without lips.

An understanding of the dynamics of ritual knowledge uncovers possibilities for understanding how hegemony does its 'work' through both dominant structural arrangements (e.g. architectural) and through human agency. Hegemony is not a form of uni-directional domination; it is not simply a system of ideological constraints imposed from above. Rather, it partakes of the many outcomes resulting from (often antagonistic) negotiations between symbolic meanings – meanings which are continually mediated by structural conditions, relationships of power, and the multifarious ways in which we rhythmically and gesturally engage the world.

Hegemony gives birth to itself somewhere 'between' the contradictory axes of structural domination and the self-production of subordinate groups. At the ideological level, it is embedded in a welter of contradictions: between the anger of the factory worker who has been fired from his job but who remains tenaciously loyal to the political party whose economic restraints cost him his job; between the sham of unemployment and the freedom of criticizing the system that robs you of your dignity; between the pain of an empty stomach and the kindness of an agency worker who offers to feed you from her own pocket; and between the developer who forces out low-income tenants in order to build a new highrise and his belief that he is actually creating better living conditions for the population at large.

At the level of human agency, hegemony is both sustained and contested through our 'style' of engaging the world and the ways in which we ritualize our daily lives: through our gestural embodiments, our rhythmical practices and our lived forms of resistance.

While hegemony is embedded in structural relations and the mediation of class and culture, it is sustained through the contradictions embodied not just in the way we think but in the way we attend to the world through our lived engagement with it. Although hegemony shrouds the body and dampens the will through an intricate web of symbols and root paradigms mediated by capitalist relations of power and privilege, we must remember that in the process of domination, human agency is always alive, rupturing the unitary pervasiveness of structural, sedimented oppression and allowing for liminal possibilities of emancipation.

IDEOLOGICAL STYLE: OPPOSITIONS VERSUS DISTINCTIONS

One important aspect of ideological style was the tendency of teachers to divide their opinions regarding students into binary oppositions (cf. Wilden, 1972, 1980b). For instance, Azorean students were viewed by teachers as 'working class Portuguese' as opposed to 'normal' middle-class students.

Teacher: Students here have special needs that we try to fill. Part of their needs have to do with their family background and their immigrant status. Teaching here is different from teaching in an affluent area where the students really compete . . .

Students were perceived as needing discipline because, given their 'special' backgrounds, and their cultural backwardness, it was unrealistic to expect them to co-operate during instruction.

Teacher: These students only understand it when you come down in a firm manner. They're used to firm discipline at home. They don't respond well to the whole business of 'relating' in the manner of the more middle-class school.

Play was looked upon as *opposed* to work:

Teacher: The students have to learn that you have to buckle down in the adult world. They have to understand that acting the way they do [playing] is not acceptable in a job situation.

Looking at the world through antithetical oppositions can prove to have unintentionally invidious consequences, as we have seen in our discussion of the two prevailing root paradigms: 'becoming a worker', and 'becoming a Catholic'. These two paradigms were sutured together in the instructional rites – as evidenced by the way prayers punctuated the daily 'secular' timetable to strengthen the envelope or ambience of sanctity and unquestionability already present in the instructional rites (e.g. through their morphological characteristics of invariance and performative force). Locked in the minds of the teachers as binary oppositions were other attendant ritualized classroom paradigms: 'being at play' and 'being a non-Catholic'. 'Being at play' was associated with anything that didn't have to do with doing schoolwork. Since 'being a good worker' was associated with ' being a good Catholic', there was a tendency to view 'playing' as anti-Catholic.

Teacher: A lot of the students' behaviour is unacceptable. There's too much fooling around and not enough work gets done.

Teacher: You can't earn a living later on in life by goofing off. Employers don't pay people to fool around.

Teacher: The kids weren't very well behaved at mass. Part of this has to do with the way they're taught at home. They just don't bring with them the right understanding to approach religion.

Rather than viewing 'work' and 'play' as 'distinctions' or 'contradictions', teachers and students saw them in terms of warring oppositions. Thus, to work and to be a Catholic were considered to be in opposition to play. Play was viewed as pathological or a form of deviance when engaged in during class.

Concurrently, Portuguese students were viewed in opposition to an imaginary version of the 'normal' student.

> *Teacher*: This is sure different from teaching in the suburbs where you've got your so-called good students. Kids here have a host of problems at home and with the language they have to overcome. It's a challenge.

We are concerned here with the connotative field of reference surrounding the ethnicity of the Azorean student. The Portuguese student was viewed as 'working-class' and thus 'culturally deprived'. He was described as a 'little helot', as more 'physical' or 'obstreperous' than his middle-class counterpart and given to deception, carnal appetites and unrestrained libidinal expressions. Not yet 'adequately' socialized, he appeared to be naturally divested of an innate access to intelligence. His many deficiencies were associated with his home background and language problems. These, in turn, accounted for the fact that he was most often a 'level three' student. Furthermore, he was viewed as a student who responded best to the crack of a teacher's verbal whip:

> *Teacher*: The kids understand strict discipline because they can relate it to the way they're brought up at home.

The physicality of the Portuguese student was often perceived as threatening. One staff official said that he could tell whether or not a Portuguese or Italian student had been involved in a fight by the nature of the teacher's description of the incident. If the fight was a bloody combat, then the culprits were more likely Portuguese students. If the fight was mostly verbal and gestural 'display', then the culprits were likely to be the 'more sophisticated' (i.e. closer to middle-classs Italians. The attributes of the Portuguese were thus located in an abusive semiotic system used by the management (the teachers) against the students – a system which included teachers' perceptions of their charges as the 'opposite' of ideal-typical (imaginary) middle-class students – thus collapsing a social contradiction between real levels of power into a war between imaginary opposites. The collapsing of a contradiction into oppositions was an example of what Anthony Wilden calls a 'tangled hierarchy'. The oppositions operated in the suite as conflicting poles along an ideological continuum which existed 'in the heads' of the teachers. This type of ideological structure confused the logical typing of power (since the teachers were not aware of how the middle-class social hierarchy constrained the working-class student, in terms of power and privilege), and became an 'ideological cover' for what Wilden calls a 'symmetrized social contradiction'.

We do not live – as the vulgar structuralists would have us believe – in a static and frozen world of classical science where the realities of power, domination and symbolic violence do not exist. As we have seen in the forgoing analysis, binary oppositions play not only a cognitive role but a political role as well.

Teachers unwittingly accepted the restricted contexts in which they located the Portuguese students while they flagrantly ignored the larger political contexts of society, those that revolved around the realities of symbolic power and domination. Teachers had become, in Giroux's words, 'clerks of the empire' who had taken on the 'dead weight of warehouse knowledge'.[2]

Teachers had assimilated the prevalent ideology of 'psychologizing' the failure of students. The practice of 'psychologizing' student failure amounts to blaming student failure on an individual trait – or series of traits – belonging to the student (e.g. lack of motivation or low self-concept). Teachers located the source of school failure within the student and usually such an aberration – when associated with class and ethnicity – is looked upon as so ingrained that it will allegedly endure forever. This attitude is frightening not only because it is self-evidently vile, but because it is often unconscious to those who hold it. Psychologizing school failure relieves teachers from the need to engage in a form of pedagogical self-scrutiny or a serious critique of their personal roles within the school, and the school's role in the wide society (cf. Ryan, 1976). For teachers, student failure became a function of a personalized dissociated agency rather than the structural location of an oppressed social group.

In sum, becoming a Catholic did not mean belief in a particular creed. We are far from the days when the Athanasian Creed provided eternal damnation to every man and woman who refused to accept Catholic dogma. Rather, to be a Catholic student meant to acquire the ideology of the professional (educational) ruling class – an ideology 'trapped' in the symbolic traffic of the ritual structures.

CONSTRAINTS ON THE TEACHERS

The performance of the teachers was mediated by the existence of nearly insuperable constraints placed on their role. There were, of course, the political and ideological constraints that operated from the school administration and the community at large. The most immediate constraints on the teachers in the suite were the large numbers of students per class (thirty-four) and the physical layout, especially in the way they affected the sonic environment. In addition, the teachers were always in constant demand, at the behest of the bureaucracy, to fill out forms, to attend weekly meetings for the discussion of programming or promotion, to take courses to upgrade their skills, to keep their classes quiet and problems at a minimum, and to promulgate the manifest goals of the Board of Education (which were written into the rubrics of the formal curriculum and proclaimed publicly from the offices of the Board episcopate). Far from fitting into the portrayal of the average classroom teacher as an uncaring despot – a gratuitous passing of judgment and form of intellectual target practice aimed at practitioners which, in the past, many radical educators have been guilty of committing in their classroom analyses – the teachers in the suite were exceptionally hard workers, cared deeply for their students, and grew despondent when they felt they could be achieving more with their classes. The teachers frequently took work home to mark each night and arrived at the school early the next morning. I had the distinct impression that their social life was minimal. And yet teachers continue to be chaffed by public critics for caring more about their wages than their charges. And the media keep prattling on about the illiteracy of high school graduates due to selfish and unmotivated teachers.

The tremendous support the teachers received from the administration was very heartening. However there was an inordinate emphasis on 'strictness' and rigid rule enforcement which became necessary in order to create an atmosphere, rich in disciplinary ambience, in which the teachers didn't 'always have to be down every kid's back'.

The type of 'help' requested from the administration by the teachers often required the principal to punish troublemakers (either by talking to the student's parents or by expelling the student). None the less, the prevailing attitude or motivating factor on the part of the teachers was one of concern:

Teacher: We try to teach these kids enough skills so that they can survive out there in the market. We don't go in too much for extras, because what these kids need is a core curriculum.

While teachers were not pressured to any great extent by the Portuguese community to improve programmes, this did not prevent them from constantly trying to improve the quality of instruction in the suite. Therefore teachers were not speaking pharisaically when they said that they really were trying their best:

Teacher: We must teach these kids to survive out there. Or else we're going to lose a generation of kids.

Teacher: We try to do what we can under the circumstances and it isn't easy. We don't exacty get the best of support from the Board.

The basic problem with the teachers was that they were encouraged by the bureaucracy to discover everything but themselves.

TUESDAY, 23 JUNE

All the graduating students assembled in the nearby church to celebrate mass in the swelter of a summer evening. Hundreds of students, parents and teachers filed into the poorly ventilated church with dozens of people moving periodically from the pews to the entrance where the open doors helped them to escape the heat.

The students were dressed in their finest apparel. Girls who normally appeared younger were transformed by make-up and clinging dresses into young women. Some young people not participating in the mass hung around the entrance. One young punk rocker sporting implausibly spiked hair and wearing a strategically ripped tee-shirt, black skirt and pirate belt, sauntered back and forth on the outside steps, rhythmically shaking the sweat from her brow.

A Portuguese priest, speaking in English, exhorted the students to build the rest of their lives on the rock of faith – a rock that would last a lifetime. Students enthusiastically participated in the readings and prayers and the mass progressed smoothly until the sacred hosts were about to be distributed. Suddenly a man with a stubbled face and red nose, wearing stained street clothes, and sweating profusely, entered the church howling. Eyeballs rolling in their sockets, spittle streaming from his lips, he began to mock the proceedings, an angry logorrheic banter giving rise to a series of guttural and garbled exclamations:

'Truth . . . what truth! Love . . . what love!

He then began tearing at the curtains of the confessional.

Parents and students sitting in the rear of the church stared in shock and horror at what was so evidently an act of blatant sacrilege. I rushed over to the man and quietly told him to leave. He simply sneered at me and said, 'I like it here.' A Portuguese parent came over and spoke to him in Portuguese. Suddenly the man started to yell and scream in Portuguese, flailing his arms in the direction of the altar. The vice-principal – a stocky man with a prognathous jaw – came barrelling down the aisle. There were now three of us surrounding the man. We could all smell the alcohol on his breath. Suddenly the man dropped to his knees and started to pray and cross himself in a highly exaggerated way. Then he leapt to his feet and left the church screaming in Portuguese. A man standing next to me bent over and whispered into my ear:

'A crazy . . . a Portuguese crazy!'

The service continued as if nothing had happened.

Students made their way to the altar to receive the Body of Christ. Outside the madman was talking to passing cars.

I retreated to the entrance of the church to get some fresh air. Suddenly the madman bolted up the steps, screaming at the parents. I tried to block the entrance and was assisted by one of the parents – a small, bespectacled man who spoke to the madman in Portuguese the madman cried: 'Speak English!' the parent spoke English. 'Speak Portuguese!' the madman laughed, his eyes on fire. I whirled and faced the madman, warning him of my impatience. He replied, wagging his tongue, that he would rush to his doctor to get me some pills for my impatience. He left and fortunately never returned, although I thought I heard him howling somewhere outside after the mass had ended.

To me, the madman presented the other side of the sacred: the dark; the ambivalent; the unpredictable – the frightening side of existing somewhere between the beast and the angels. The intruder represented reality crashing in on the divine – a reminder of our frailty, of our weakness and estrangement before God. The students would never forget this madman; he unwittingly reminded us all of how close the real is to the surreal and how easily the dark side of ordinary life can radically assault consensus and ambush the sacred.

Wet with perspiration, but undaunted in their enthusiasm, the students poured out of the church and made their way to the school for the awards ceremonies.

Medals and scrolls were given out for science projects, public speaking contests and other areas of academic achievement. The final award was for the student with the 'nicest Christian attitude' and 'who had the most sunshiny face'. In addition, the student receiving this award was 'kind to others, obedient, and always co-operative'. Teachers spoke of the values and advantages of schooling in an idealistic – even romantic – light. School was described as the great equalizer of society, the foundation of culture, the shaper of great minds, and the creator of the future generations of citizens. This gave the ceremony a ghost-dance quality where attempts were made to magically restore the dreams of the past.

After the awards, the students and parents made a beeline for tables loaded with fruit punch and cake. A number of students told me that they were thinking of leaving school to go out to work. Others were looking forward to learning a trade in high school. Thrilled parents took photos of their children standing beside the teachers, who were trying their best to smile. The students left the school buidling clutching tiny scrolls bound with red ribbon – symbolic reminders of their achievements and passage to grade 9.

The graduation ceremony was a ritual of revitalization celebrating the end of the school year. As soon as the students clasped their diplomas, they were instantly transformed into high school students. Catholic values (symbolized by the mass and the award for the best Christian attitude) were formally sutured to the more secular values of academic excellence (symbolized by the awards for academic achievement).

Domination was complete. There would be no more popular resistance, except perhaps later in high school, or on the shop floor. Milked of their dialectical potential to transform both Word and world, the instructional rites had calcified into a dry husk of pedagogical formalism and had impaled students upon its brittle essentialism, its alienating subjective idealism. The differences that distinguish the oppressor from the oppressed had been convivially put aside now over a cup of hot punch and ceremonial chitchat. For the graduates, objective reality would appear the same once they left the school. They would go forth and uncritically embrace the ideology of domination with the heartfelt approval of the Church, 'a church that forbids itself the Easter it preaches'

(Freire, 1985, p. 127). Students' subjectivities were now fully inscribed in the hegemonic articulations and social logics of Late Capitalism. Asymmetrical relations of power and privilege will be reactivated through their lives without them even knowing the difference. Freedom will become an acquired taste or mechanically reproduced mood.

The Word of God which they shall carry in their hearts will be a structured silence in the face of the world's injustice and oppression. The figure of Christ has been transformed into a Divine Guidance Counsellor or Metaphysical Banker who will remind them that their failures are psychological aberrations, or ethnic traits, or lack of industriousness.

I bid farewell to the students, wishing I could offer a world beyond 'the banality of rituals and profane simulacra' (Baudrillard, 1983, p. 7). The world they inherit from school is based on forms of idolatrous, acquisitive, and mimetic desire that sacralizes greed and power. It appeared doubtful if Catholic schooling could discursively 'hitch' the symbol of Christ to a project of self and social transformation without simply cannibalizing the construction of faith in the interests of furthering an economy of flexible specialization and profiteering on behalf of the rich.

Chapter 6

Summary, recommendations and reflections

> A public celebration is a rope bridge of knotted symbols strung
> across an abyss.
>
> Ronald Grimes

SUMMARY

Schools, as we have come to understand them in the preceding
pages, are intricately structured and ritually saturated institutions
serving as repositories of complex symbol systems. Whether a
particular school caters to students from opprobrious high-rise
ghettos, blighted inner city tenements, suburban redoubts, affluent
subdivisions, depressed rural landscapes or a clapboard shack in
some provincial backwater, rituals possess a privileged sphere of
articulation. They play an important role in the pedagogical
encounter and appear to be as fundamental to the classroom
curriculum as the subject matter of the lessons themselves.

While the ritual demeanour of schooling at St Ryan was found
to be considerably more muted than, say, the dramatic panoply
of ritual symbols in the Catholic mass, a complex ritual system
consisting of a medley of ritual forms was nevertheless in play.
Instructional rites carried or 'nested' the dominant epistemes, root
paradigms and symbols which gave birth to and sustained the world
views of the students. The symbols and paradigms of instruction
were found to oscillate between two general states: the physicality
of the 'streeetcorner state' and the cognitive inhabitancy of the
'student state'. A good part of the students' day was spent
negotiating among the experiential contradictions embodied in these
two states. In the streetcorner state students related to each
other emotionally, viscerally; in the student state, students were

encouraged by the teachers to develop relationships which emphasized 'rationality'.

The instructional rites functioned to communicate to students codifed messages which, in turn, served both to promote normative behavioural functions and to fashion dominant epistemological frames for the students. In short, the instructional rites provided blueprints for both 'thinking' and 'doing'. Through this pedagogical engagement, students were structured to think of the world in certain ways; they were motivated to act upon their world according to prescribed symbols and in their arbitrary or calculated juxtapositions.

While classroom rituals embodied and transmitted ideological messages, they were recuperative to the extent that they additionally served as conduits of power and creativity (which had a revivifying influence on the students). Regrettably, the latter function often became overshadowed and subsumed in the calculus of school rituals which exemplified and exonerated rationality, progress and technicism.

Classroom rituals were found to be neither enslaving nor liberating in their own internal logic; while participation in the processual dimensions of ritual altered the sensibilities of the participants (e.g. the way they codified reality), the creation of meaning was always subject to the ideological and material constraints and contexts surrounding the ritual.

Instructional rituals functioned mainly to sanctify the work-place, to hedge the cultural terrain with taboos, to shore up the status quo, and to create a student body conditioned to accept such a state of affairs. Ritualized classroom lessons tacitly created dispositions towards certain student needs while simultaneously offering to fulfill those needs. For instance, students were made to feel inadequate due to their class and ethnic status and hence the school offered to help socialize them into the 'appropriate' values and behaviours by tracking them into designated streams and basic level courses.

There was a strong tendency for both student and teachers to accept the drudgery of schoolwork. At the same time, laudable attempts were made by at least one teacher to develop in students a critical stance towards suffering and evil in modern society – attempts which usually came about during religion class. However, because religion class represented only one subject in a day filled with many subjects, the explicit teachings on religion tended to be seen as removed from the rest of the academic subjects. Yet the pervading tendency to accept what transpired throughout the instructional rites as sacred and unquestionable occurred not just in religion class but in the teaching of all the academic subjects.

The structural and ideological elements of classroom rituals – which were supplemented by prayers and reinforced by concatenations of religious symbols – were manifested in modes of cultural reification and the unproblematic acceptance on the part of a large number of students of their own domination. (This is, I'm sure, hardly what Dewey or Whitehead had in mind in referring to education as 'religious'.) Instructional rituals were experienced as part of the natural order of things, as part of the socially acceptable framework of schooling. This made it difficult for the students to perceive the relativity of the rites and of the symbolic and epistemic codes that informed their obligatory and commonsense nature.

Through the scrupulous formalization, repetitions and predictability of the student state, the daily instructional rituals transmitted messages which were not only singularly undialectical but also clearly overdistanced (and, with very few exceptions, less than charismatic). For the most part, means and ends of the ritual performances were interchangeable and the beginnings and endings were transposable. While a sense of certainty was evoked there was little room for joy and exultation. What counted was that students always appeared busy, hard at work, and 'attending to the task' – the creation of a situation to which the term 'banquet of boredom' would not be an exaggeration. While some students become engrossed in the processual accretions of the ritual proceedings – despite their instructional brittleness and the stultifying effects of their didactic invariance – others simply became detached and chose to merely 'go through the motions'. Educational ideals (curriculum guidelines) were constantly sabotaged and overturned by the invisible (taken-for-granted) structural integuments and ideological contexts of the instructional rites which superseded the academic content. In time, students came to regard work as so much boondoggle.

The Azorean students were billeted in a world of symbols ripe for manipulation and neglect. Too often ludic and inspirational symbols became twisted to organizational advantage, numbered by intrusions of the bureaucratic mentality, and lost in the mechanics of the centralized co-ordinating forces of school administration.

The teacher, as a choreographer of symbols, became a little like Goethe's sorcerer's apprentice: he could not escape from his own inventions. In the final analysis students were left to follow the vapour trails left by eroding symbols which the teacher had let fall to neglect – symbols which ceased to illuminate and which had been given over to the twilight of entropy.

A predominant function of the instructional rituals was the reification of the classroom culture. Reification, as I have defined it, basically refers to treating abstract concepts as things. What was also striking about the Catholic school setting was the treatment of things as embodied spirits or powers, a factor which served as a modest counterbalance to the process of reification. This was most evident in the regard the students had for the representative power of the crucifix and the statue of Mary which were taken as literal representations of objective supernatural entities and which sprang into action in the minds of students *as if* they were living and breathing entities. These icons carried out their work of restructuring the imagination (cf. Baum, 1975) – thus, in a sense, they *became* real, spiritual benefactors for the students. However, this somewhat animistic move from reification to deification, from immanentism to transcendentalism, did little to counter the technocratization of instruction.

The assignment of overmuch importance to the role of the teacher as the ultimate authority and the fact that religion class was taught as a separate subject (and accounted for only a fifth of the day's work) added to the technocratic nature of instruction. Religion classes represented only one cog in the gearwheel of the schooling process: a process which pumped out an endless stream of broken and tarnished symbols and ultimately conveyed to the students a clichéd model of man. Like products churned out mechanically on conveyor belts, the students were processed and standardized. And religion class proved to be the only occasion during which society and culture were problematized.

The overall lack of ritual alternatives and flexibility in the implementation of curriculum objectives underscored the tendency of Catholic schooling to arrogate 'truth' and 'normalcy' to the idealized version of the 'the obedient Catholic worker'. Instructional rituals became useful adjuncts in the moulding of student characters and in the ingraining – both bodily and cognitively – of certain 'acceptable' dispositions and demeanours which were linked to the cultural capital of the imperturbable ruling class.

Within the rituals of instruction, the role of religion – and education in general – was more one of control than liberation. The root
paradigms of the schooling process were forged within what I have
called a 'culture of pain'. In the seemingly comfortable milieu of
the suite, rituals functioned to shape and determine the conceptual, temporal and spatial contours of the students' experiences –
as well as other constellations of meanings.

There was a distinct eros-denying quality about school life, as
if students were discarnate beings, unsullied by the taint of living
flesh. Feeling as though they were entombed in a shroud of dead
skin, students put their bodies symbolically 'on hold' upon entering
the school at the beginning of the day. It was as though saturating
the senses was equivalent to alienating the intellect. The ritualized
practices of school research have, throughout history, overlooked
the fact that the body plays an important part in the acquisition
of knowledge. (Part of this betrayal of the flesh was personified in
the celibacy of the priest.) To exalt mental computation – the ability
to name and classify – as the only significant dimension of the
learning process is to wrestle with a dark angel; it is to invoke the
wrong god, or at the very least, to mistake God's reflection for God
himself. Not only was the body ignored as a vehicle for acquiring
legitimate knowledge but it also became a matrix for reflecting and
sustaining hegemonic relationships. Hegemony was not realized
solely through the mediations of the sociocultural order but through
the enfleshment of unequal relationships of power. Hegemony was
manifest intercorporeally through the actualizations of the flesh
and embedded in incarnate humanity. Yet the body also served
as the temple of human interiority and the locus of human
agency.

The political and cultural characteristics of the student state left
physical as well as psychic marks upon students. The rigid,
mechanical, invariant and eros-denying gestures of the student state
mirrored the essential ideology transmitted through the root
paradigms of 'being a good worker' and 'being a good Catholic'.
While listening to the daily 'lecture-style' instructions, students
would sit up straight and tall, their eyes frozen on the teacher. When
working on an assignment, students fixed their eyes to the opened
books or sheets of paper on their desks. Slouching or leaning
back on chairs, interrupting a lesson with a raised hand, standing
up during a seatwork exercise, or staring out of the window
for more than a few minutes invariably incurred strict reprimands

from teachers. As well, moving outside of one's 'student space' was strictly prohibited.

The rites of instruction could have offered students the potential to experience 'visceral understanding' in which they surrendered to mimesis, participation, spontaneous feeling and bodily contact; however, these characteristics of ritual were beyond the instrumental and utilitarian purview of what teachers felt school was designed to accomplish: 'We've got to teach the kids to survive in the world outside – in offices, in factories or wherever.' To deny the importance of 'bodily knowing' through the engrossment in ritual symbols and gestures was to eviscerate the liminal attributes of rituals whose meanings resided in the antistructure – the crucible of creativity. It was also to deny the students respect for their own style of learning and their own cultural capital.

Teachers in the suite laboured constantly and doggedly in a pale, monochromatic environment. Tightly organized, the classroom culture was appropriately objectified: every element had its 'natural' or 'ordained' place within the hierarchy, a hierarchy composed of a proffered reality which was structurally ordered for the most efficient functioning of the whole. To contest this order would at once be obscene, incongruous and sacrilegious and would make one a 'polluter' (to borrow a term from Mary Douglas (1970)). It would also invite a defilement of the sacrament of learning and a malfunctioning of the bureaucratic order.

For some students, the rituals which so rigidly reified the social world were nurturant and protective, providing them with a sense of order and security; for others, these same rituals summed up the very fears which the rituals were designed to alleviate in that the classroom rituals came to be seen as a structural imposition, a manifold and unified system of oppression and condemnation. Thus, while a ritual may be considered the ordering of the inchoateness of immediate experience, and the transformation of entropy into coherence – it can also rupture and tear apart.

For the Portuguese immigrants, many of whom were meeting the urban industrial environment head on for the first time, the rituals of classroom life initially provided a sense of stability and solace in the heterogeneous and unfamiliar milieu of the school with its multiplex relationships and conflicting values and principles. While undeniably providing students with such a sense of ontological security in the face of chaos, the instructional rites also served to reinforce dominant middle-class values, values which proved to be both alien and impractical. Understandably, a large proportion of students frequently disengaged themselves from the daily ritualized lessons and, in both subtle and demonstrative ways, would ritually resist what Jacques Derrida has termed the 'monological arrogance of official interpretations'.

The participation of Azorean students in the process of schooling constituted a shorthand story of the entire Azorean immigrant experience in Toronto – an experience which saw the immigrant worker entrapped in the lowest tier of the class system and which confirmed the fact that a nation's educational system is subservient to both its economic and symbol systems.

The daily lessons may indeed be considered as ritual events if we acknowledge that they derived their legitimacy from the mass itself. In the case of the instructional rituals, what was being offered up for the 'pathetic' human condition of the Azorean student was revealed knowledge – a sacred commodity necessary for material salvation and entrance into a commodity-filled heaven. In this (albeit exaggerated) sense, the rituals of the suite were but ritual modules or ritual units deriving from the ultimate Catholic teaching act – the celebration of the Eucharist.

The feelings which frequently surfaced from the students' engrossment in the instructional rituals were those of hostility and indifference. After all, a major purpose of the instructional rituals was social control. Rituals shored up a wall of densely packed symbols covered with barbed wire behind which instructional alternatives were kept in check. Instructional rites served as bureaucratic vehicles for teachers who were pressured to cover reams of preordained content; they were managerial rather than educative. In fact, they did educate – but did so tacitly and unconsciously.

The rigidity and painful endurance that constituted the ritualized life of the suite would sometimes spawn instances of counter-expectational conduct, the forswearing and rejection of established institutional values and the flouting of conventional maxims. On such occasions, resistances served as a symbolic routing of the root paradigms of instruction. Such routings of conventional norms often took the form of a reritualization of student behaviour where the accepted order was turned upside down and destructured, and where teachers were ritually abased. Symbolic inversion and status turnabouts were reactions to the unauthenticity of the meanings embodied in the instructional rites and the feeling on the part of students that they were constantly buffeted by the wider society.

The liminal frames of ritual resistances provided for students one of the few opportunities for the devestiture of subordinate status and the assumption of a superordinate one. To those denizens who comprised the Azorean working-class counterculture – the 'cool guys' who looked disdainfully at mental labour – the students who conformed to the rules of the school were known as the 'wrist-guys', 'sucks', 'queers' and 'browners'.

The class clown, too, contributed to some of the resistances among students. It was discovered that the clown possessed an ability to frame classroom experience in such a way that the tacit, unspoken or 'sacred' principles that held the suite together were laid bare and exposed through buffoonery as arbitrary.

The dominant social drama appeared as a form of resistance to the instructional rites and was referred to as 'working the system'. The dramatic tension arose from student attempts to prolong the 'streetcorner state' throughout the school day. Occasionally this agonistic social drama resulted in scattershot violence, but most often the distinctive engrossments of those engaged in the drama took the form of an innocuous 'goofing off' that drew its strength from symbolic displacement as opposed to outright physical confrontation. Resistances which made up the social drama served to engender strong feelings of antisocial vitality in the suite (what Stivers would call 'wild communitas'), characteristic of the 'street-corner state'. In fact, next to the Christmas dance, the Litton factory protest and the occasional lesson (usually in religion class) – which served to evoke a definite sense of élan, if not full-fledged spontaneous communitas – the resistances to the instructional rituals promoted the strongest sense of community and bonding in the súite.

The strategies and tactics chosen by the teachers to enforce the symbolic order of the school were those that corresponded most closely to middle-class mores. This reaffirmed the cultural differences in the suite and served to mediate class divisiveness.

One of the contributing factors to the difficulty of the school in adequately serving its Azorean clientele was the contradictory notion the Azoreans held towards work. Many Portuguese from rural areas considered the task of doing homework and studying a leisure activity. It was also a 'sign of hubris' – an attempt to escape the social conditions. While Azorean parents usually modified this attitude slightly on arrival in Canada, many still pressured their children to leave school at 16. Tension arose when something that was considered superfluous (schoolwork) became, in their new country, a very difficult task for Azorean students to master. While on the one hand schoolwork was considered a leisure activity, on the other hand it was also acknowledged as a necessary vehicle for learning English well enough to secure steady future employment. As members of the working class, however, Azorean parents had come to realize that a diploma from a classical high school would not necessarily give their children a chance for more than a blue-collar job. While many Azorean parents had high aspirations for their children to succeed, their own struggles as semi-skilled labourers and unemployed workers served as a tacit message to their children that instructed them not to depend on school as a way out of their poverty. Success in school did not necessarily mean that life as adults would be any less harsh or conflictual (cf. Ogbu, 1979, 1981).

The instructional rites contributed to the complex function of sanctifying the workplace (the workplace referring at present to the school and in the future most probably to the assembly line or shopfloor) – and served to reflect, create and reinforce social stratification. Sanctification of the classroom was made possible by the communicative properties of the sacred and secular domains of classroom life. The rites of instruction were sanctified, in fact, through the coincidence of these two domains. Following the formulation laid down by Rappaport, sanctity was also discovered to be inherent in the morphology of the instructional rites themselves. The central questions concerning domination and oppression revolve, then, around the collective characteristics of the instructional rites; their morphological properties; their performative characteristics; their coercive power; and the way in which they are embedded in systems of mediation that reproduce the symbols, meanings and relationships of privilege of the larger society. The teacher, as a prescriber of arbitrary meanings and guardian of the hegemonic boundaries of knowledge, assumes the position of affirming, and to a lesser extent manufacturing, the dominant cultural forms of the social order.

It is no understatement to say that in many ways the classroom at St Ryan mirrored the workplace of the factory; there was a distinct isomorphism between the use of space and time in the school and the daily itinerary of the factory worker. Instructional rituals were orchestrated by the teachers to facilitate (whether consciously or not) the inculcation, legitimization and credentialization of specific modes of work skills among students. As one staff member announced in a rather stentorian voice: 'Given the rural environment that these kids grew up in, they only understand work if it's hard, practical – a kind of drudgery. We, as teachers, have to be sensitive to their cultural background.' It is one thing, of course, to say that the Portuguese students' inurement to drudgery is natural – it is quite another to attempt to reinforce this world view through the daily rounds of school life. While I would argue that Catholics are called to experience the pain and humiliation that goes along with taking up the cross of Christ, the cross must also be witnessed as a symbol of joy and transcendence – a metaphor to inspire working-class students to surpass their hardships and fight against their lived subordination.

In addition to confirming hard work as an *ipso facto* proof of moral worth, instructional rites could also be interpreted as the ritual enactment of a pedagogical model that subscribes to a consensual image of working-class students as a 'they'; it is a mode of instruction which maintains that since Azorean children are 'from the hills' and find it too hard to adjust to the 'civilized world', they are incapable of becoming self-directed learners. Therefore, the best one could do (in the words of one teacher) was to 'teach them to write a business letter or something to get them a job'. Adherence to the commonplace assumptions surrounding the concept of Azorean students as 'deprived' served as an unconscious rationalization for the failure of the school to educate the Portuguese student. This model of cultural deprivation was what Ortner (1973) would refer to as a 'key scenario' – a symbol or paradigm that has action-elaborating power.

Commonly shared assumptions of 'the way things are' took the form of imaginary binary oppositions in the heads of the teachers. These dyads presented a model of the social structure of the school which corresponded to the ideological conditions conducive to maintaining the stratification patterns of the wider society. The major oppositions may be summarized as follows: Portuguese students are 'practical thinkers' and middle-class students are 'abstract thinkers'; strict discipline works, while freedom always gets abused; working-class students are courteous, well-mannered, and law-abiding; work is necessary and valuable if the student is to cope with the 'real world', while play is frivolous, threatens discipline, and must be kept hermetically sealed off from work.

The important work of Anthony Wilden provided a means of effectively mapping the ideological orientations of the teachers in order to understand how these orientations often worked against the students. Binary distinctions such as middle-class/working-class, delinquent/normal, work/play, and Portuguese/Anglo-Saxon were often collapsed, symmetrized and incorporated as binary *oppositions*. In reality, many of these classifications were not oppositional but merely *contradictory* and were made into *imaginary oppositions* in the minds of teachers. For instance, if we take the binary distinction between middle-class and working-class, we discover that the first term constrains the second in terms of actual power. The same situation arises in the contradiction between a delinquent student and a normal student. Those who are deemed normal possess the authority to define and punish those who are deemed delinquent. While many of these dyads do identify a locus of conflict, to view them as oppositions tends to collapse an important contradiction. In Wilden's terms, this reduces a real conflict between levels to an imaginary conflict between 'opposites' at a single level only. The typical result in teacher thinking was that a real conflict between social levels (defined as a contradiction), and notably between levels of power, was symmetrized – and thus neutralized.

As agents of class domination, school rites courted catastrophe: they appeared to be a crucial contingency in the reproduction of inequality. This conclusion, of course, needs to be investigated further, but it is admissible if we accept the fact that the rites of instruction reified the classroom world according to the tenets of an oppressive dominant culture. Forms of instruction and teaching practices generally constituted an inadvertent ritualized reaffirmation of ethnic stereotypes and the daily remaking and reconfirmation of class division. This was accomplished by the ritualized stress put on Spartan forbearance and middle-class cultural capital, i.e. modes of behaviour and values constituting docile and co-operative workers. Large numbers of students naturally resisted the dominant forms of cultural capital and developed their own countersymbols and rituals of resistance. However, by undergoing reritualization, they consequently foreclosed their future educational options – such as going to a level five or six high school – by opting out of taking schoolwork seriously (cf. Willis, 1977). In the final analysis, however, it must be admitted that St Ryan did function beyond the maintenance of its own institutional power – especially during religion class when students were provided with the opportunity to question the social order and when 'radical' interpretations of Christ's teachings were introduced.

But teachers could be seen as unwitting accomplices in cultural and social reproduction in a number of contexts. Their failure to take into consideration the class/cultural differences and competencies of the Azorean student in the instructional rituals shaped tacit messages which read: 'This is the kind of people *we* are and, to the extent that you differ from us, this is the kind of behaviour we expect of *you*'. These messages infused the ethos of the suite, shaped the ideologies behind the rituals, and constituted the alloy from which symbolic violence was forged. The patently processed instructional rituals served, in a sense, as icons of the school's cultural character. However, we must guard against the simple blaming of teachers for these and other baneful situations besetting St Ryan, just as we must guard against labelling the Azorean student body as slow-minded, pathological dopes from the hills.

From the teacher's perspective, a central curricular concern was the cultural background of the Portuguese student; because she was supposedly raised with extreme harshness and exigence at home, teachers believed her to be socialized against the more liberal and 'humane' values of the school. However, the real issue is more than one of simply socialization: it has to do with issues surrounding class stratification and the unequal distribution of both economic and symbolic power. The smoke from the salvos fired at the alleged deficiences of the Portuguese student obscured the fact that the teachers themselves used the 'deficit theory' of the immigrant student as a rationalization for their failure to teach. The tendency of teachers to 'blame the victims' contributed to a high body count of Azorean student drop-outs. While there was a certain amount of freedom for the teachers to use discretionary behaviour in planning tasks, the institutional constraints impinging on the teachers played an overwhelming role in influencing the pedagogical, epistemological and physical idioms upon which their rituals were built. There were the constraints of the open area with its oppressive noise; the demands of the school Board and the administration; and the pressure of tracking students into an 'appropriate' programme – before Christmas! Without question, innumerable ritual forms could have been devised by the teachers to meet the individual needs of the students, but this would have meant more work and toil on the part of the teachers, some of whom already perceived themselves as martyrs: 'This is the toughest school in the Catholic system and I wonder how anybody expects us to survive.' But it cannot be denied that the teachers cared deeply for the students and expended a great deal of physical and emotional energy trying to succeed in their jobs. Therefore they should in no way be seen as mendacious, Goffmanesque con men inhabiting the shadowy back rooms of educational programming who, in fits of self-serving blindness, are planning strategies to cut off the educational opportunities of Portuguese students. Their actions do not constitute an 'invisible hand' that orchestrates the purposeful destruction of the working-class intellect.

Students were generally rewarded when they exhibited the approved form of ritual knowledge: appearing busy and abstaining from questioning the authoritative tenets which controlled the suite; thinking componentially or mechanistically; separating mind from body (as if knowledge were extraneous to the body); and responding to knowledge as if it were something 'out there' – something that could be objectively grasped. Students were encouraged to embrace the concept of autonomy only when it didn't threaten the social order of the suite – a situation from which we can forecast a continuing diminution of their freedom.

A conglomerate of supporting instructional material, which included religious symbols and icons, helped link together the composite nature of the core paradigms of instruction. With their stylized, routinized and formalized characteristics, and daily reinforcement through sacred emblems, verbal interdictions, creedal statements and imprimaturs from the staff, the instructional rituals helped to legitimize the roles and statuses of the teachers. And although teacher-sponsored rituals were sometimes met with a variety of ritualized resistances, these frequent impediments to maintaining the system of social control were often overcome by rigidifying the already existing institutional rituals, a situation that is not uncommon in modern institutional life.

Issues raised by this study are sympathetic to the critical stance of educational revisionists who maintain that we inhabit an oppressive, class-stratified society in which the school reinforces the psychological and social implications of this dictum. None the less, there are also a number of implications contrary to the notion of class domination which emerge from this investigation and which merit discussion. At times throughout the instructional rites, there was an important stress on the concepts of spiritual growth and social reconstruction. On the surface, this would appear to contradict the teachers' emphasis on creating docile workers. Within the setting of religion class, a concept of Catholic charity developed which stressed the important values of love, kindness, justice, generosity, self-denial and social action. These values provided the context for questioning one's self, and for plotting the direction of one's spiritual life. And they were best realized when the teacher taught as a liminal servant. In and of themselves, these values are important, and certainly possess an autonomy of their own. According to one teacher, they 'served to neutralize capitalism'. However, these values were too often superseded by those which were located in the root paradigms – values which stressed subservience and subordination. The power of the root paradigms operative in the daily instructional rituals – 'becoming a worker' and 'becoming a Catholic' – lies in the fact that, as part of the ritual process, they are symbiotically and incorrigibly entwined in such a way that hegemony is both inwrought and invisible. Although these paradigms may be distinguishable, they are virtually inseparable. During the instructional rites, these associative chains of meanings converge and are activated simultaneously. The *polysemy* and *ambiguity* that are part of the religious symbols permit them to be perfectly suitable for the perpetuation of Catholic values *and* corporate capitalist secular values to the extent that *one set of values co-implies the other*. These two paradigms support and validate one another through the prevailing ideology of 'becoming a citizen'. (This could perhaps explain why, in the 1960s, so many recent high school graduates in the United States willingly, even supererogatorily, went off to Viet Nam to fight 'with God on their side'.) The coupling of academic and religious teachings (including their dense array of concomitant symbols and metaphors) created an exchange which oscillated between religious and secular values. The effect of such an exchange served to accommodate a world view which unproblematically accepted order, inequality, oppression and deference to authority. Power and legitimacy were symbolically linked to 'our forefathers', 'our country', 'our God'.

One of the major problems with religion class other than not taking more of its momentum from some of the more recent writings in Curial neo-scholastic theology or liberation theology, was that its instructional rituals were couched in the cultural forms of the technocrat. When symbols grow weak and detached from the lives of learners, revelation becomes threatened. While the contents of the religious lessons were often unmistakably Christocentric, the lessons were technocratic in form, taught as a 'subject', and relegated to a 'slot' in a timetable. There is nothing wrong with formally teaching Christianity as an academic enterprise (this has been going on since the thirteenth century when theology became a distinct academic subject) as long as it is done reflectively, and as long as there is no loss of synthesis between religious studies and the street-corner state. However, given the educative ambience in the suite, is it any wonder that religious teachings, when they are turned into dreary utilitarian exercises, are prone to miscarriage? One teacher admitted (albeit *sotto voce*) that formal religion classes should be abolished in school. He also maintained that since prayer was really just a technique to get students to settle down before the lessons, formal prayer should be replaced by silent prayers which could be repeated spontaneously throughout the day. The dilemma surrounding the teaching of religion was summed up in an *obiter dictum* from another teacher who was amazed that more members of the Portuguese community didn't send their kids to the public schools where there was lower pupil-teacher ratio and where the resources were far superior. After all, he said resignedly, 'We only have three periods of religion a week. For all that matters, the parents can teach their kids religion.'

Catholic schooling did show 'flashes' of progressivism and emancipation in its religious teachings. That certain factions of the Catholic Church constitute a radical force devoted (sometimes feverishly) to social reconstruction cannot be questioned, especially when we consider the growth and popularity of liberation theology and, more recently on our home front, the stance taken (in the spirit of Pope John Paul II's *Laborem Exercens*, 1982) by the Roman Catholic Bishops of Canada with respect to the immoral aspects of capitalism.[1] Since Pope John XXIII's encyclical, *Pacem in Terris* (1963), and Vatican II, the Church has been brought back into the contemporary world. The fight for social equality, then, is not new to the Catholic Church, especially today. Interestingly, no less a radical than Gramsci admitted (however grudgingly) that the Church has always resisted serving only the elite (Harrington, 1983, p. 213).

The spirit of problematicizing the existing social order with the intent to reform it was often evident in the religious teachings of the suite; yet this spirit was frequently contradicted by the ritualized structural relations through which these lessons were transmitted.

For the most part, the teachers were constrained by class size and evaluation techniques handed down from the administration, and were constricted by curriculum materials that did not take into account the class/cultural background of their students. Consequently, the orchestration of the instructional rites was commensurate with patterns that could be termed 'survival strategies'. The demands of the inner city school environment necessitated authoritative role characteristics. Strict roles and rigid rituals best suited the managerial and control necessities of classroom practices. Needless to say, these were not the 'ideal roles' which teachers aspired to after completing their teacher training – they were the 'survival' roles which experience had taught them. Many teachers expressed disappointment at the prospect of spending the remainder of their teaching careers locked into such roles. In fact, such dictatorial and inquisitorial roles were, by their own terms, antithetical to the development of a teacher's own individuation. But one could not 'keep one's sanity' without them.

Not only did teachers in the suite frequently 'act' at teaching, but students also 'pretended' to learn. This was, primarily, a function of the *overdistancing* of instruction. While overdistanced rituals enabled both teachers and students to become dangerously detached from the content of the lessons and overly self-conscious of their roles, aesthetically distanced instruction (to use Scheff's (1977) term) enabled the students to be absorbed in the lessons, and at the same time provided them with the opportunity to reflect on the meta-meanings of their actions. Aesthetically distanced instruction occurred most often when teachers enacted the role of liminal servant.

It is hard to resist the notion that, at a fundamental level, the schooling that I witnessed was oppressive and could be improved substantially by a greater understanding of the ritualized relations inherent in classroom interaction. I feel strongly that, in the confines of school life, the necessity for traditional pedagogical rituals vanishes; they become extrinsic to what the students feel is the 'real' meaning of their lives, their 'lived sense of difference' from the dominant codes of middle-class propriety.

In summary, we have discovered that the rituals of instruction served as recursive mediative devices that continually recapitulated the objectification of the secular and sacred domains of school life yet paradoxically provided some 'openings' or 'avenues' for creative endeavour and reflexive change. These latter effects could be called the 'propitiatory function' of classroom rituals. Through the missions of icons, metaphors, metonyms and symbols, ritual both broadens and limits human agency in the classroom. Ritual structures are both enabling and constraining: they simultaneously endorse and restrict particular actions.

What is of ultimate importance with respect to the instructional rites is how they are put into effect, predicated or 'bodied forth', and how well their 'missions' are carried out and made relevant for the youth of today. We must discern just how pedagogical rituals are affecting students. To what extent are they alienating and anxiety-producing? To what extent do they muffle communitas and reproduce the division of labour in the wider society?

Analysis of the instructional rites of the schooling process underscored the importance of creating a 'felt context' between the transmission of knowledge and the embodiment of that knowledge. Congruent with our conception of ritual knowledge is the belief that knowledge is more than just words – more than just being told something. Practical experience also plays an important part in learning. This view supports Dewey's notion that knowledge is not acquired independently of the means of instruction. Learning includes a physiognomic/somatic meaningfulness – a 'postureful-ness' as well as 'mindfulness.'[2]

RECOMMENDATIONS

I do not intend to offer here detailed suggestions for the classroom planning, some type of ritual cookbook for the multicultural classroom. To offer step-by-step solutions would be to extend the technocratic mind set that this book has devoted itself to criticizing. The following suggestions are to be seen simply as guideposts for the teacher or researcher who wishes to come up with his or her own solutions, according to his or her own particular classroom situation.

One directive emerging from this study is the need for greater interdisciplinary collaboration in the study of classroom culture. As an emerging discipline which mounts a formidable challenge for curriculum theorists and planners, ritology puts at the disposal of both educational reformer and researcher its heuristic utility as a 'conceptual lens' for understanding and evaluating the symbolic dimensions of schooling. In this regard, the specialized knowledge of the ritologist can assist the teacher in understanding the corporeal and cognitive nature of ritual knowledge, thus increasing the likelihood that the teacher will be able to discover ways of problematizing the reified and hegemonic systems of thought that tacitly unfold in his or her classroom. Grimes has warned us that 'Rituals and symbols can become sick, just as organs can. In fact, some psychologists, along with a few anthropologists and religionists, have suggested that symbolism and ritual ... [can be] ... pathological' (1982a, p. 130). Consequently, the quixotic educator will want to reritualize and thus reinvigorate the educative setting. One way of achieving such reritualization can come from a greater understanding of the power of ritual to shape and mould world views and actions within a cultural milieu. Another way is to make the most of the power of ritual by appropriating classroom approaches that make use of bodily engagement and spontaneous drama. Drama is the whetstone upon which we must sharpen the blade of school reform to excise the curricular cancer of current anti-incarnational educational programming.

In palmier days of educational research and programming – referred to by the ancient denizens of our classrooms who taught in the decade of the 1960s as 'the golden years' – addressing ourselves to questions about ritual, bodily knowing, affectivity and spontaneous drama and the arts would perhaps not have appeared so removed from the concept of education. On the question of the present role of the dramatic arts in the schools, Carla de Sola and Arthur Easton write:

> Is it an accident that when a budget crisis arises in schools, public or private, the first subjects to be eliminated have to do with the creative in life? Courses in music, art, and dance are early casualties when administrators – generally linear, left hemisphere types – are allowed to have the final decision about priorities given. Perhaps we need committees to make such decisions, with weight given to the less vocal viewpoint of those whose speech is not primarily verbal, but who speak the language of the sour – those whose language is organized on the mystical, intuitive, musical, and imaginative elements of life. (1979, p. 78)

Further criticizing the propensity of curriculum planners to overlook the value of the arts and bodily engagement in education, McGregor *et al.* remark that:

The arts, both inside and outside education, have tended to be seen as recreational, as something to do when we have time off from the business of the world. They are relaxing, even stimulating but they are not quite so important as getting on with the 'real business' of life. But if relaxation were their only purpose then going to sleep would be a much cheaper and less strenuous alternative. The persistent influence of the arts suggests that they fulfill a much more basic need. They are the product of a compulsion to make sense of, express and communicate from, the inner world of subjective understanding. (1977, p. 16)

Why the arts continue to be marginalized in our society is a curious if not perpetually depressing question. What does all this mean in relation to ritual? First of all, a stronger link must be made between ritual studies and drama theorists. While this is currently being pursued by, among others, drama theorists Richard Schechner and Richard Courtney, more substantive work in this area is needed.

Herewith my more fundamental recommendations, involving general suggestions for some restructuring of the classroom rituals. Before I begin, I wish to interject one caveat by reminding the reader that any recommendations surrounding classroom rituals can never fully take into account the awesome multireferentiality of any major ritual system or its ancillary symbols. Just as the analysis of the root paradigms took hermeneutic precedence over sociologically conceived covariants, so must any recommendations yield to the subject matter (as research can never vie with life itself). It is difficult to make *a priori* predictions of student behaviour in terms of how students will react to particular symbols or in what fashion they will enact or embody ritual meanings. However, that does not prevent our making suggestive or educated guesses. The best an educational investigator can do is develop a pedagogical night vision in the hope that he or she will somehow be able to penetrate and eventually illuminate the dark side of the schooling process otherwise known as the hidden curriculum.

Having said this, I would argue that the instructional rituals must be approached with the realization that they overwhelmingly influence the development of school spirit and the orchestration of the symbolic tonalities, chords and modulations which comprise the overall ethos of the school. A poor choice of ritual orchestration evokes a cacophony of discomfort among students. School instruction should – and here I can go no further than programmatics

– become more of a celebration than a painful rite of passage and should attempt to incorporate some of the cultural forms of the streetcorner state which, after all, belong to the phenomenal world of the students themselves. The administration of St Ryan saw fit to hold only one dance before Christmas, as if a homeopathic dose of popular culture is all that is necessary. Sanctioning the occasional popular event is a little like vaccinating the school against street-corner culture by injecting it with a watered-down version of the 'virus'.

David Davies notes:

> When the school recognizes the existence of, for example, popular music, dance and style (as it sometimes is forced to), it relegates these to the periphery of school life (lunch-time discos) or characterizes them as merely shallow and transient. School culture does not penetrate the subjective experiences of its pupils as 'a whole way of life'. It does not *validate* the symbolic and expressive forms through which subjectivity and 'self' are defined and lived out by contemporary youth. More often than not, it anathematizes them. School culture values very specific and selective discourses and languages. Popular culture, as a working-class-based phenomenon, is not characterized by the abstract language and formality of the school. Quite the reverse. Thus, in expressing self-consciousness and subjectivity, quite different forms of discourse can be expected from working-class youth. Clothes, music, 'styles' are thus invested with symbolic and oppositional meaning. The conventional language and discourses of schooling represent a dominant culture that specifically excludes working-class youth, except at a subordinate or epiphenomenal level. (1981a, p. 85)

Here I would like to sound a caution. While praising the attributes of Portuguese streetcorner culture, there is always a danger of falling into a form of neo-paternalism or a romantic identification, especially when describing the richness of working-class cultural forms. An uncritical ennobling of victims can amount to a type of sociological voyeurism. We must remember that the working-class, as members of an oppressed group, suffer serious economic – and sometimes considerable emotional – privations. Accordingly, we should disembarrass ourselves from being overly sentimental in our accounts of streetcorner life. With this is mind, I would point out that the failure of incorporating celebration motifs into school programming is nowhere more evident than during the school mass. The mass should not be an occasion for teacher foot patrols, but for communitas. What prevents teachers from participating with the students in the masses? Could they not become *co-celebrants* with the students rather than security guards? How can you 'enforce' a mass? It is a contradiction in terms, a liturgical deceit. Students should be given the choice as to whether or not they wish to attend the mass.

THE MACRO RITUAL

Rituals of instruction should not be attempts to manipulate students into the student state by completely sealing off the streetcorner state. In an inner city classroom, a macro ritual whose student state is 'top-heavy' often lends itself to the creation of an over-routinized and instrumental school culture. I am not suggesting that order, routine, and redundancy be given short shrift by teachers. After all, chaos and order are ritual correlatives and we all need some predictability in our day-to-day endeavours in order to feel comfortable and secure. School life cannot be lived solely in a festive air or within a liminal forbearance of pain. But routine can be easily swayed to repression; we must be cautious not to surrender our routines to the contamination of oppressive constraints or transform our secure and predictable daily rounds to the tortuous pathways of regimentation. Pedagogical rituals designed to 'fill time' are wisely abjured. To reduce instructional ritual to routine is to be in thrall to empty structures.

Knowledge is 'style' of awareness, content, and cultural form. One way of incorporating the 'felt' knowledge of streetcorner culture would be to make more time available throughout the day for arts activities. However, creative drama is not something that should be relegated to a slot in the timetable like religion class. It should be used as a valuable pedagogical or instructional technique open for use by teachers in the teaching of all subjects. The full potential of using arts activities in general instruction could be approached through in-service workshops by drama teachers, drama theorists, ritologists, performance theorists and other experts in the arts.

It would appear to make more sense if individualized instruction were emphasized to a greater degree, along with a more critical monitoring of the values associated with the school's expressive culture (activities, procedure and judgments involved in the transmission of values and their derived norms). Classroom control could be modified and made more flexible and interpersonal by permitting more student-generated rituals. This would more readily contribute to the therapeutic transmission of the expressive culture (cf. Bernstein *et al.* 1966). The social order would therefore rest more on cooperation than domination.

The weakening of the expressive culture of the school is no doubt linked to the differing values of the school system and the Portuguese community, especially with respect to the relationship between schooling and future employment. A stronger link between the school and the community must be facilitated by a willingness on the part of the teachers to incorporate more distinctive Portuguese cultural forms, symbols and rituals into the classroom setting (e.g. in the forms of folk tales, myths, religious celebrations, plays, dances). These need to be re-situated outside of a discourse of colonialism and imperialism and linked to creating a critical citizenry that is able to bend reality in the interest of a greater socialist democracy.

THE MICRO RITUAL

The micro ritual, which is adult-imposed and overly regulated, must be made flexible enough to include student-generated and student-regulated rituals. A greater awareness of the characteristics of the streetcorner state may give teachers a clue as to how to monitor for unique cultural participatory structures. In other words, interaction rituals (which exist between high 'liturgy' and low 'ritualization' poles on the ritual continuum) with specific indigenous ethnic characteristics could be identified by trained teachers. A knowledge of unique forms of ethnic and/or personalized interaction styles could then be utilized by the teachers in developing their 'high' or liturgical aspects of instruction. The liturgical forms should take into account how students encode their personal and class/cultural habituations. Liturgy (which deals with the transmission of power) should always take into account student interaction (or streetcorner state) rituals.

Students should also be given the opportunity to plan their own time, find their own ritual rhythms, and discover ritual spaces in which they feel comfortable. The creation of sound-proofed study centres in which interaction between students is encouraged would be one way of achieving this. Students would then have the opportunity to work alone at their own pace or with partners.

Either the sonic environment of the suite should be remedied by a different approach to programming (as I have suggested) or else walls should be erected despite their financial cost. Ultimately, the question must be raised: What is the price the pupils must pay if the noise level remains the same and is not improved by reprogramming or, even better, by 'replay'? For those students who find the noise oppressive, opportunities should be provided so that they may work in areas which are presently 'off limits': the library, the teachers' planning room, the halls or the supply rooms.

The problem with the micro rituals as they presently stand is that they lack the prescribed movement of the classic ritual process. In classical terms, initiands move from the indicative mood (preliminal) to the subjunctive (liminal) to the indicative again (although this recovered mood has, in Turner's terms, been 'tempered, even transformed, by immersion in subjunctivity'). This process has been severely ruptured – even reversed – throughout the instructional rituals of the suite. Once the students enter the school, they are symbolically stripped of whatever liminality they experienced in the streetcorner state. They move, in other words, from the 'subjunctive' mood (before class) to the 'indicative' (during class) and then back to the 'subjunctive' (either through the spontaneous communitas of resistance rites or when school is dismissed and the students return to the playground or street). Of course, not all activity in the playground is liminal or subjunctive, and not all activity during classroom instruction is indicative, but there is more chance of encountering these motifs or social modalities during these prescribed times and places.

Turner's theories imply the reinstatement of the charismatic character of the teacher and the power of intimacy and liminality. They bespeak the need for students to occasionally confront atavistic, chthonic or subterranean symbols (such as those found in modern punk or rock music) as well as images of transcendence. After all, the person of Christ, who spent much of his time with thieves, prostitutes and lepers, cannot be dragged by the sandals out of the antistructure and inspected solely under the fluorescent lights of the antiseptic school lab. Urban T. Holmes has said, after M. D. Chenu, that 'good liturgy borders on the vulgar' (1980, p. 19). Too often it seems that what we, as teachers, in assuming the right and 'fit' role of the pedagogue, may accord as much to a fear of getting our hands dirty as to a loss of pedagogical nerve and vision. The teacher intent on developing ritual literacy might consider employing symbols of mirth, sexuality and darkness ('low' symbols) in conjunction with more clinically pure ('high') symbols of truth and transcendence (e.g. the Sacred Heart of Jesus, Mary Queen of Heaven). We might consider, along with pseudo-Dionysius, Teilhard de Chardin or Jung, whether or not Christianity requires a return to a certain pantheism in order to revitalize its roots.

Students could be 'resuscitated' by employing non-discursive language and motorically expressive activities through play and replay. Spontaneous drama and creative arts should form the nub of the multidisciplinary curriculum. It is extremely important that the structural attributes of the micro rituals do not foreclose responses from the students. What is important is the creation of an 'intuitive engagement' between teaching and the embodiment of what is taught. We must avoid becoming like Plotinus and feeling ashamed of being in the body. There must not be such a wide disjunction between the generative mode of ritual knowledge which entails exploration and discovery and the pedagogic mode of ritual knowledge (cf. Jennings, 1982).

Clearly, an important direction in which the instructional rituals should proceed is in the creation of situations destined to spawn liminal zones of learning in the form of either spontaneous or institutionalized communitas. Myerhoff and Metzger (1980) announce that since liminality is not only 'reflexive' but 'reflectiveness', it is fundamental to the teaching act. In fact, they describe it as 'the great moment of teachability ...' (p. 106).

Urban T. Holmes (1977a and 1978), to whom I owe the term 'liminal servant', reminds us that liminality and communitas describe an existence outside the hierarchical constraints of society. For this reason, liminars are open to a reality that is not controlled by societal constraints. As Holmes puts it: '*The imagination is freed!*' (1977a, p. 95). Furthermore, Holmes writes that communitas is a 'generative centre' which is the goal of pilgrimage; it is the antistructure in which we can discover our humanity (1977a, p. 83). Needed, then, is an instructional approach that is able to find the correct balance 'between communitas, the trip into the world of symbols, and the social structures, life amid the univocal signs' (1977a, p. 95). The individual who can best determine and orchestrate the correct balance between communitas and structure is the teacher acting in the role of liminal servant. Knowledge gained in class through a liminal engagement could replace the linear, positivistic and pathogenic literalism of mainstream schooling with metaphoric knowledge (the kind which Schechner describes as being released through engagement in the arts). Eventually this could lead to a knowledge that is 'danced' – to 'qualities of postmodern subjunctivity' such as multicentricity (no single-point perspective), rhythmicity and holism (Schechner, 1982, p. 120) yet a knowledge linked to a wider project of social change.

Rituals, as Turner has shown, operate as a dialectical relationship between flow and reflexibity. Too much flow can lead to a sterile anti-intellectualism whereas too much relexivity can lead to the overdistancing of emotions followed by an intellectual aloofness. On the question of reflexivity, the point must be made that it is not reflexivity itself that contains the seeds of a counter-hegemonic discourse, but the quality of that reflexivity. Reflexivity can do its 'work' to create a liberatory pedagogy only when we begin to 'unthink' the past (Heidegger, 1972) and when we begin to grasp a 'reciprocity of perspectives' (Merleau-Ponty, 1975, p. 314). This also means that tough questions must be sanctioned by the ritual officiants – such as those dealing with relations of power and privilege.

One of the consequences of Turner's doctrine of liminality can be neatly summarized in a contradiction: rituals can help dismember group cohesiveness or promote a creative unity. We can thus look to Turner's theories as a new avenue for approaching the concept of teaching – especially as a means of adjudicating the issue between teaching for transformation and teaching for oppression.

A further suggestion for the improvement of instruction would be replacing the image of the student as a passive receptacle for depositing facts with the paradigm of the student as pilgrim. Holmes has described the characteristic stance of the pilgrim as one of 'active, waiting, hopeful expectation, power in innocence and weakness, and acceptance of strangeness of others as a possible source of transcendence' (1973a, pp. 63–4). The pilgrim

> is an incongruous, ambiguous person, for whom no category fits. To be a pilgrim means to move out of the institutional structures and their roles and statuses that define the person and to free the imagination for the discovery of what is new. (p. 64)

A pilgrimage is a journey into normative communitas where the pilgrim withdraws to the periphery of the social structure and into the land of symbol and myth known as antistructure. However, pilgrimages themselves are far from unstructured. As Holmes reminds us, 'Pilgrimages require the organization of symbols or rituals, for it is the ritual that carries the pilgrims through the ambiguity and risk of a world of symbol and myth' (1976, p. 126).

Pilgrimage could be undertaken by students in the form of out-door excursions into the wilderness such as in camping or canoe trips (popularized by Anglican boys' schools), or visits to holy shrines. These could be accompanied by periods of fasting, singing and chanting. But to engage in a pilgrimage does not necessarily mean leaving the confines of the school. One could, in effect, 'dramatize' a pilgrimage to the Holy Land. Or students could create a miracle play and invite the community. Perhaps a school procession could be orchestrated in which students would proceed from a nearby parish to the school (perhaps carrying a statute of the Virgin); the statue could then be rotated among the neigh-bouring schools and kept in each school for a month. Students could make moral and/or academic pledges during the time the statue resided in the school. At the micro level, it is also possible to plan single lessons on the model of pilgrimage – a journey designed around the embodiment of knowledge. Instruction in a subject could take the form of different tasks designed to take groups of students on liminal 'voyages'. (For those interested in reading about one American minister's attempt to construct initiation rites for the youth in his congregation, see William O. Roberts, Jr., 1982.)

Unfortunately, students will often uncritically accept theatrical antics from teachers as a surrogate for true instructional liminality; students become inured to the teacher as a prison guard or hegemonic overlord rather than experience the shamanic dimen-sions of the pedagogical encounter. As a whole, students appear to be sufficiently critical to accept, but not criticize, the dominant modes of pedagogical discourse.

It is unfortunate that teacher roles too often manifest an 'improper use of impersonation'. Courtney tells us that

> under certain conditions identification can degenerate into pseudo-roles: the individual who surrenders to a role acts according to the image he would like to maintain. He is guided by role expectations rather than the demands of the situation and his own Being. He 'pretends' to be a teacher or a student; he gestures and postures. The student pretends to pay atten-tion. The teacher pretends to teach. Then schooling becomes an elaborate game and dramatization has got out of hand.

Neither must submit to their roles. Their authentic pedagogic relationship is an encounter where they *acknowledge* each other. That is genuine drama. (1982, p. 151)

Instruction that amounts primarily to the recitation of facts by teachers too often amounts to a pseudo-ritual bereft of organic symbols and gestural metaphors. Knowledge of this sort remains unembodied and hence removed from the student's corpus of felt meanings. The student's path to knowledge should be an incarnate, bodily journey, rich in gesture as well as contemplation. The seed of each student's creative liberation requires liminality for successful germination.

Considering the dramatic qualities of ritual, it would appear instructive for both drama theorists and ritologists to begin to forge connections between ritual and drama applicable to the creation of improved curricular programming. Curriculum planners could also derive benefits from a dialogue with ritologists. Programming should ultimately allow solutions to be posed to the practices of teachers who continue to coerce reality for students through calcified and consensually shallow forms of ritualized instruction. Grimes writes that

> the road to ritual lies through drama. When the lights go out and the masks are donned, I bathe in the mystery which I cannot find in churches, synagogues, and temples. I could go to African and Brazilian jungles, but the way of the tribe only takes me farther away from placing my body in the midst of a ritualistic performance. I am not a preindustrial tribalist. Neither nostalgia for the rituals of my childhood nor longing for the moities, paints and sacrifices of other peoples can locate my body in ritual space and time. When longing and nostalgia fail, imagination, I hope, can succeed. Drama is the ritualizing of imagination, and my imagination, unlike my body, is not sitting under a tree taking notes. If my body is ever to unlearn its boredom and find its ritual rhythm, it will do so dramatically. It will do so by pretending and imagining.[3]

Given drama's historical roots in ritual, it would seem improvident for the curriculum planner not to consider the drama teacher as an invaluable aid in employing ritual to shape learning potential in the classroom. What is needed is not simply more time for drama and the related arts in schools, but the orchestration of the entire school day as a series of ritualized events – events that truly nurture and celebrate the potential for human freedom instead of fulfilling an Apollonian passion for order and control. To what extent this can be deliberately strategized as a project of self and social transformation remains to be seen.

Teachers could draw upon the works of Stanislavski, Bolton, Brecht and Grotowski in order to promote an awareness in students that they are active body-subjects that engage the world not just in their heads, but in their hands, their heart, their guts and their loins. Educational literature could include the writings of Bellah, Grimes, Turner, Goffman and Schechner in order to lay the groundwork for an emergent epistemology of learning theory by way of ritual embodiment.

A focus on forms of ritual which best provide the liminal loam for creative growth could change the 'work' (*magnum opus*) of instruction from drudgery to exploration. Describing the nature of 'work' in the dramatic arts, McGregor *et al.* write that:

> To work in the arts is to tackle problems of understanding through representing them in symbolic forms. This revolves around a dialogue between the content of the expression and the form in which it is made. The symbolic form encapsulates the meaning. The symbols chosen critically affect the nature of the understanding which develops during the work. (1977, p. 19)

Special occasions could, for instance, become forums for celebration. The end of exams, the end of school, birthday parties, Saints' days or special holidays could be incorporated into the school calendar of ritual events. They should be flexibly planned, allowing for input and orchestration by the students themselves. More time should be afforded to the creation of communal ritual forms that will engender communitas. Spontaneous and nascent ritual forms should also be appreciated, including – if not especially – symbols that arise from the meaning structures of the student themselves.

Since many symbols are polysemous and their interpretations and meanings are negotiable or 'up for grabs', teachers are thus challenged to repattern their classroom symbols so that they speak to the 'here and now' of their students – so that these symbols revealingly and magnetically relate to the students' life-world infusing them with a sense of hope and providing them with the ability to take control of their lives and relativize their condition of inequality.

As a rule, teachers should be more dexterous in their orchestration of instructional rituals – especially with regard to the home cultures of their students. For instance, not once during my classroom observations did I hear a teacher mention anything about the Azores or Azorean culture. And yet the vast majority of the student body was Azorean. The flat, homogenizing influence of the dominant culture of the student state had brought about a cultural chauvinism, an inward-looking parochialism, an ethnocentric consciousness.

Herbert Thelen notes that

> differences between the culture of the teacher and that of his students result in a truce rather than in the emergence of a more adaptive way of life. Diversity is seen not as a source of strength but as deviancy, and is punished. In short, conflict in the classroom is suppressed as wrong rather than taken as the beginning of insight-stimulating inquiry and growth. The teacher's opinion is regarded as the judgement of Solomon, and conformity is the *sine qua non* of achievement. (1970, p. 5)

As a way of severing the suffocating tendency of schools to foster dependence in students, David Norton, an educator, has proposed 'the desirability of reintroducing within our culture public *rites of passage*'. For Norton,

> These ceremonies are, among primitive peoples, a universal means for marking the transition from childhood to adolescence. By their public and dramatic character, they serve to put the community on notice that the manner in which it has been accustomed to treat the initiates must now be abandoned in favour of a different manner. By thus publicizing the necessity for change, I believe that so-called primitive peoples exhibit a wisdom surpassing our own. (1970, p. 23)

Just as churches are seeking liturgical renewal to increase the membership of young people – to add to the numbers of those loyal patrons of the pews who sport blue hair or wield canes – so too must schools begin to create renewed sense of instructional delivery; they must revitalize their tiresome and archaic rituals or they will lose – as they have been doing – the motivation of the students.

To what extent ritology, as an interrogative discourse, is destined for deployment in the schools for the purposes of social reconstruction or cultural edification is better left for future researchers to decide. However, in a more circumspect and *ad hoc* sense, some of the critical ramifications of using a ritual focus to map the classroom culture imply an immediate responsibility on the part of the educational researcher to begin to problematicize the symbolic dimension of the schooling process. Having said this, I wish to sound another caution. It is vitally important for teachers to be wary of the dangers of creating liminal conditions in the classroom. Since, as Holmes warns, liminality 'feeds the vision of revolutionaries, reformers, and prophets' (1977a, p. 95), there is certainly a danger that the efforts of teacher-ritologists will be lost in premature revolutionary praxis. There is, undeniably, a need to undertake more minute vivisections of the ritual process, to bring into relief dimensions of ritual which will better determine its processual characteristics. More typologies of classroom events are needed in order to invoke some kind of comparative analysis between the rituals of Catholic and other types of schools (e.g. public schools, parochial schools, Montessori schools, alternative schools). Yet typologies and criteriologies are not substitutions for the development of theory.

Many of the concepts such as ritual, symbol and metaphor still remain, to a certain degree, imprecise. To capture ritual completely in a definition is well-nigh impossible because individual rituals have such a diverse assemblage of ingredients, components and functions – and the functions are primarily determined by the contexts in which the ritual appears. However, once we disabuse our thinking of the specious and circulatory definitions of ritual that continue to have currency in the social sciences, we may extend the heuristic usefulness of the concept to further research in education. This investigation, then, best serves as a proto-theory or forerunner of what I hope will be more substantive developments of classroom ritology. It is illustrative rather than systematic.

Ritology appears to possess a rich future in connection with what Dilthey calls the cultural sciences (sociology, psychology, anthropology, etc.). Personally, I foresee ritology's greatest critical direction to be in forging theoretical connections with the sociology of knowledge. Ritology's methodological underpinnings in the analysis of symbol and metaphor as well as its recent links with performance theory could provide pivotal theoretical tools for decoding and rendering problematic the political sphere of schooling as it pertains to topics such as inequality, cultural reproduction and technocracy. Any development of ritual theory, to be truly liberating, must, however, be linked to a formal theory of hegemony and resistance. Whether the path to knowledge is paved with quotes from Christ or Marx makes little difference if we fail to consider the systems of material and symbolic mediation that help 'suture' the subjectivities of students and create sovereign regimes of truth.

LIMITATIONS OF ANALYSIS

I do not foresee ritology as providing insights which will lead to the *new* theoretical elixir, metalanguage or single all-encompassing theory for classroom instruction. Theoretical perspectives take time to gather momentum and it is unrealistic to assume that they will generate any type of pendulum swing of educational opinion, something that might eventually lead to a contagion of reform.

This study has been primarily concerned with an exploration of the symbolic interstices of meaning and action in the instructional rituals of schooling. It is important, therefore, that in the process of analysis the researcher does not succumb to the temptation of over-interpretation – the comparative symbologist's occupational disease and the ritologist's Achilles' heel. Hidden meanings can be wrung out of the most recalcitrant symbol if interrogated with sufficient indulgence. It is therefore questionable to proceed on the methodological presupposition that all rituals can be explained by symbolic analysis, i.e. that every act, every gesture, every speech and every word is seen to be pregnant with a deep symbolic significance. It is equally shortsighted to harbour the corollary of this proposition – namely that all symbolic behaviour is ritual behaviour. Interpreting symbols involves a tacit knowledge of their contexts and since there exists no one school to instruct researchers in such arcana, we must sound a caution against over-extended interpretations of ritual symbols. Nor should we, in the final analysis, be deflected from a more sustained and serious understanding of gestural metaphors.

What has been offered herein has been the task of recognizing the teaching act in light of the heuristic power of cultural and performance study. This heuristic power must be measured against the degree to which an analysis of instructional rites contains the possibility of galvanizing modes of collective self-reflection and political struggle. Once the possibility of collective self-reflection is established, the terms ritual and performance become more than just heuristic tools but concepts that have the power to shift classroom analysis to entirely different – and illuminating – realms of discourse. I would assert that the potential of ritual to assist teachers in the classroom hinges conceptually on two accounts: (1) whether or not the teacher is willing to draw upon his shamanic roots and embrace the role of the liminal servant; and (2) whether or not the root paradigm of the teaching act becomes more like a pilgrimage directed towards experiencing knowledge, with all due nuances, in a felt context, rather than filling up students-as-empty-containers with numerous facts. We need the ideals surrounding the teacher as liminal servant to be re-embodied in the characters and actions of future generations of teachers. We also need our curriculum planners to deliver an apologetic suited to the realities of our times. We must accept the fact that many of our traditional instructional forms have died of exhaustion. Misguided but undaunted, we continue to embalm them with sterile enthusiasm, paint them in gaudy colours and dress them in the latest pedagogical finery. We have become trained morticians of the mind who make pitiful attempts to give our corpses the illusion of life. We would serve our students far better if we would prop up our tired symbols and rituals and dance them one last jig over their graves. Then we should dismiss them on the grounds of their patriarchal and colonialist assumptions.

It is time that we acknowledge the uncomfortable reality that our present rites of instruction are more than antidiluvian answers to the challenge of modern education; they are age old ways of providing for the containment of counter-ideologies which germinate in the streetcorner cultures of the working class. Today more than ever before, the importance of understanding the dynamics of contemporary cultural forms cannot be underestimated. Such an understanding cannot with impunity be excluded in our attempts, as educators, to come to terms with instruction and resistance. The streetcorner state embodies characteristics that are linked to what has become known as informal or popular culture. Informal culture relates to the everyday rhythms of our existence, our lived encounter with our world, our daily engagement with a multitude of symbols and icons, and the informal patterns that make up our shared community of meanings. It is unfortunate that the 'official' culture of the classroom and the informal culture of the street mix about as well as oil and water. The fractious antipathy between these two cultures lies at the very core of student alienation. The fact that our curriculum planners still largely ignore popular culture

– particularly the culture of the streets – augurs poorly for the creation and development of a liberatory pedagogy.

REFLECTIONS

We have strayed far from the historical/mythological purlieus of ritual in order to locate its dynamics in the cultural setting of a contemporary Catholic school. Similarly, by eschewing early psychoanalytical associations which linked ritual to private pathology, we have shown that ritual also exists ouside of the simplistic preserve of perfunctory habit, routine and neurosis.

While we may agree with contemporary scholars that the overarching primordial myths and rites that once welded together the world views and beliefs of pre-industrial man have been severely attenuated, we must nevertheless be cautious not to interpret this as the death-knell for the existence of modern ritual. While it is true that ritual in contemporary society has little to do with Dionysian festivals, Bacchanalian revels, saturnalias, or the sacred rituals of the Oglala Sioux it must in no way be considered an anachronistic remnant of earlier stages of culture. The weary and downtrodden poor rarely troop from their homes to be regaled by street processions celebrating saints and the sacred; but many of them join the middle class during Saturday afternoon supermarket christenings where they can shake hands with their favourite soap opera star. Rituals continue to have fundamental implications in the everyday events of our cosmopolitan existance, whether they are related to the the synthetic pageantry of a supermarket opening or the rhythms we embody in our ritualized encounter with everyday school life. Secular rituals of today have assumed prismatically, in play, theatre, art and everyday institutionalized life, many of the functions once served by Church and state.

Through millennia, we have existed as cultural beings. Since much of modern cultural life ramifies from the root process of ritual, then ritual must be considered the very core of our social existence. The fact that we no longer live cheek by jowl with our neighbours in small, pre-literate tribes does not negate the daily reality of communicating with each other ritualistically and symbolically. To indiscriminately argue that rituals not longer exist in modern society – or to underestimate by several orders of magnitude the role that ritual plays in schools – only underscores the conceptual parochialism of many mainstream social scientists.

While it is undeniably the case today that religious ceremonials no longer serve as the obligatory structural foundations of the cultural system, and priests no longer serve as the architects, and while it is true that we have modernized the communal-religious celebrations of the past with hockey games, Miss Canada pageants, Front Page Challenge and other media charades, the fact that these system-wide rituals have been transmuted does not mean that they have been extinguished. Instead, one must ask whether or not early rituals have been replaced by rituals more domesticated, secular or private – what Turner refers to as 'ritualized progeny' – which, by their own unique structure and logic, perform similar functions and possess similar powers (1980, p. 159).

Despite the fact that industrial life creates a very different ambience than that which was created at Delphi to consult the future, or at Stonehenge, where Druid priests in brilliant robes festooned with Zodiacal signs danced eastwardly around a sacred dolmen, ritual should be acknowledged as part of the contemporary cultural garment; it must avoid being trapped in a reductive misidentification with cultural artifice – a perspective that subsumes ritual under the rubric of 'symbolic slag'. The study of contemporary ritual cannot afford to be shunted to the periphery of scientific respectability. Clearly, rituals are more than sociocultural embellishments, more than irrelevant, theoretical toys created so that anthropologists and academics exegetes can amuse themselves while studying exotic cultures. The pervading use of ritual in its colloquial sense – which is made evident in such partially synonymous descriptions as stereotyped behaviour, habit and gesture, the stillborn image of someone perfunctorily going about a simple routine, or the naive identifying of ritual with neurosis – not only does violence to the work of contemporary ritologists, but continues to prejudice the use of ritual as an important variable in scientific research. As well, the view that considers ritual a mere epiphenomenal expression of basic structural determinants of social life is but a further step in the deracination of ritual's analytic utility and must therefore be abandoned.

If these misconceptions surrounding ritual remain as unrecognized and unconscious as they have hitherto, they will continue to serve as serious impediments to further research into the symbolic dimensions of schooling. While more than a single study is necessary to break the anti-ritual Zeitgeist that has plagued educational research over the years, this study has at least attempted to serve as a modest counterbalance to some of the more maladroit formulations of ritual used in current investigations by bringing into relief some of the perspectives of the new ritologists.

At the core of recognizing the importance of understanding school culture and performance exists a radical reappropriation of the term ritual itself, one in which ritual is recognized as being grounded in hegemonic symbol systems operating at various levels of institutional life. Any culture – and this includes the academic one that nurtures educational research – which ignores or deprecates the importance of ritual unwittingly excludes an important factor in human interaction, the analysis of which can assist the investigator to interpret data, pose alternatives and create solutions to existing societal pathology and injustice. The consequences of ignoring the importance of ritual ramifies into many directions. Most important, it permits educational theorists to overlook a variable *par excellence* – one that is worth pondering rather than dismissing out of hand as a contrivance, cultural artifice or form of sociological dross. To consider ritual as foam on the surface of the vast ocean of culture only echoes the positivistic ideological cant of mainstream educational research. Attention to ritual as a significant social variable in the course of formulating substantive generalizations about institutional life would seem an expedient direction for future ethnographic studies of schools. Concurrently, a defective awareness of classroom rituals can only damage the quality of educational ethnography. As ethnographers, it would serve us well to take seriously Turner's remark: 'When we act in everyday life we do not merely re-act to indicative stimuli, we act in frames we have wrested from the genres of cultural performance' (1982a, p. 122).

I trust that an emphasis on the performative and cultural nature of classroom instruction as put forward in this study, serves to counter the reductionist tendencies, whether from the pundits of anthropology, comparative religion, the social sciences or educational research, that would de-emphasize the importance of the symbolic and dramatic dimensions of learning.

Yet we must always remember that while rituals may be symbolic phenomena *sui generis*, this does not mean that they are sovereignly independent of how others define and manipulate them. Like technology, ritual is neither good nor bad by virtue of its own properties. Those who ultimately control and shape the rituals – the ritual officiants – have a powerful two-edged sword that can either sever our day-to-day lives from the symbols which nurture us or carve out new liminal spaces for the development of more adaptive ritual forms. Ritual therefore stands in relation to the classroom as half progenitor, half monster. It can be variously felt as hostile or nurturing, repressive or enabling, dangerous or beneficient. It is simultaneously poison and its own antidote. It can both sanctify and criminalize, illuminate and befog, engage and estrange, immure and liberate, belie and strengthen, empower or take away, wreak havoc or confer grace. These are the stark antipodal attributes of any ritual which must neither be deplored nor applauded but rather accepted as a concrete state of affairs. All rituals thus function in the manner of Shiva, the God of Shivaite Hindus – they both pollute and purify, destroy and create. Rituals, to be sure, have holocaustic as well as whole-making potentialities. Rituals are used for healing the sick and yet Hitler used Nazi rituals to help proclaim himself the Holy Ghost. We celebrate in the ludic rites of Mardi Gras, and yet shudder at the military power of the Soviet civil ceremonies (*Sovetskaia grazhdanskaia obriadnost*) such as the Great October Socialist Revolution (cf. McDowell, 1974). Ritual works for both weal and woe.

An important question has come to the fore throughout our discussion of ritual and schooling: do classroom rituals implacably control our destinies and those of our students? Though a definitive answer to this question is not yet possible we must nevertheless recognize that students are harmed less by classroom rituals than by their being persuaded that these rituals are natural and inviolable.

Rituals are not unlike the connective tissue of an organism, miraculously holding the frame in shape, yet disguised under layers of smooth skin. Most of us enjoy living in a world of surfaces, as long as they are smooth and unblemished; we prefer not to think about the structure of bones and sinew beneath our skin – that is something for medical vivisectionists and dissectors to probe with their scalpels and electric saws once we are gone or for artists to painstakingly reproduce for their anatomy instructors. The educational ritologist must be like the artist or anatomist; she must render articulate the frame under the surfaces and probe beneath the classroom's outer tissue to its viscera.

To enable the teachers to solicit the loyalty of more students, the rituals of instruction must be changed drastically, at least until the worst encroachments are done away with. To say as much is not to malign or denigrate the achievements of Catholic schooling, which have been outstanding, particularly with regard to preserving an enclave for the exercise of care and compassion in an often indifferent society. Nor can the schools be held solely responsible for the malaise of religion and the muted motivating power of sacred symbols in the lives of Catholic youth.

The quality of our everyday rituals, including, if not especially, our classroom rituals, is critically important and needs realistic and sensitive consideration, especially in terms of ritual's relationship to the learning process. We need to incorporate ritology into a pedagogy of liberation, a pedagogy whose heterodoxy is informed by a resolve to scrape through the coagulation of oppression and despair that lies at the heart of the capitalist state. A new approach to schooling is required that refuses to humanize inhumanity or spiritualize injustice. We must strive to keep our classrooms from becoming cuspidors for castaway symbols – symbols that benumb our spirits and which no longer remain linked to the universe of meanings embedded in the codes of contemporary youth culture. We must deplore the waning power of religious symbols to inspire our youth because, in that diminuition, students' access to political and spiritual transformation is lost. The symbols that we seek must be, of necessity, curative and whole-making. We need to develop within schooling a rhetoric of playful and fictive religiosity, one which will enable us 'to construe the universe "as if" it were humanely ordered and meaningful, even though we know these construals are "not really" true' (Kleiver, 1981, p. 665) and in doing so contest the ubiquitous deference to white Anglo partriarchy.

POSTSCRIPT

Though the scholar of religion may still consider the word ritual to be too profound to be hitched to the lexicon of educational researchers, and while the psychologist may consider classroom rituals to be a form of pathological illness linked to learning, we must not cease our efforts to increase ritual's currency in educational research.

While we can, according to Chapple, only 'speculate on the next state of symbolic and ritual crystallization, and how soon it will appear' (1970, p. 324), we must nevertheless remain resolute in our determination to help teachers increase their efforts to become ritually literate. Ritual literacy implies that we radically change our model of the teacher and the pedagogic encounter. It directs

the teacher to shed his or her subaltern custodial role and embrace
that of the liminal servant or mana-person, who is 'able in himself
to strike a creative compromise between the conscious world of the
ego and the antistructural world of symbol and myth' (Holmes,
1976, p. 222).

Given the arguments presented in this study, and the continuing
work of ritologists in a number of academic disciplines, we can
dispense with the glib belief that ritual belongs only to the realm
of the exotic, the anomalous, the marvellous, the bizarre, or that
the ritual participant, possessed with the liminal capabilities of self-
transcendence, belongs only to a certain small class of strange
persons, including priests, mystics, cabalists, hermetics, anchorites
and augurs, but not to ordinary people, and surely not to
schoolteachers and their students.

I hope that this investigation has given educators a greater
realization of the power of their choices for ritualizing their
classrooms. These choices are fateful and important for the future
of education while an ignorance of the consequences of these choices
continues to pockmark the performance of our schools. Without
a greater understanding of the importance of the ritual dimensions
of instruction, we will continue to demand that our students yield
to our mechanical classroom arrangements, to our didactical and
rigid teaching styles, or insist that they genuflect before a phalanx
of sclerotic, saprogenic, and petrified symbols – symbols knotted
into restraints which lash us to the chariot of the power elite. We
must at all costs decry the fettering of the human spirit in our
classrooms. Only by including an exegesis of the symbolic and
performative characteristics of instruction, and the help of scholarly
fools, will we be able to mine the rich veins of both sacred and secular
symbols which disclose the multiplicity of relationships and
transactions of power that exist in our classrooms.

It is crucial that we continue to explore how Catholic schooling,
by virtue of its ineffably vast and unique universe of signifying
structures, plays a fundamental role in the socialization of students
and in the production of dominant cultural formations. With respect
to the constitutive powers of the root paradigms of classroom
instruction, we have seen how what were once thought to be
asymmetrical – the 'sacred' associations of 'becoming a Catholic'
and the 'profane' associations of 'becoming a worker' – are
in reality conjoined and de-differentiated through the processual
dimensions of ritualized instruction. What were supposedly

two separate rationalities or discourses can now be considered as indissolubly intermingled, serving to strengthen the paradigm of 'the good citizen' who does not oppose the 'friendly fascism' of the capitalist state.

Teachers borrowed freely values and attributes such as docility, predictability, obedience, and respect for authority, etc., from both the religious and secular dimensions of classroom life and syntagmatically combined them into a strong unified message which served as a blinkered code of belief and conduct. At the paradigmatical level, the multireferentiality of the symbol allowed the figure of Christ to be substituted at will for the image of the punctual schoolboy who dutifully attends mass, addresses his teachers in a respectful tone, and completes his homework.

By undertaking a critical examination of the synonymity between the cultural capital and recipe knowledge required for being a worker and being a Catholic, we can begin to explore the role of instruction as a regulatory mechanism which provides students with a complement – a repertory so to speak – of rhythms, gestures, and meanings that they must incorporate into their daily lives if they are to achieve adaptive regulatory functioning as adult Catholic workers. The comparability between these two root paradigms should, I think, create a further mandate for examining the role of religious and secular symbols in school instruction. It is important that we continue to examine how rituals – despite their own inner logic and autonomous circuity – are linked to larger systems of mediation such as relationships of class, capital, ethnicity, gender and power. We must investigate the commensurability of symbolic structures from the discourse community of the streets and that of the classroom.

Classroom ethnographers must always remember that rituals never convey meaning in a vacuum or outside of history. They are not transparent or vitrescent. They never communicate outside of specific cultural systems of discourse. Rituals are wrapped in skeins of symbols with each layer intertwined in its own history, culture and social relations. As carriers of culturally and politically coded meanings, rituals are never self-evident or unproblematic. Rather, they channel meanings contextually, so that power and domination are rendered transparent or ex-nominated (cf. Barthes, 1972). They rarely escape the historically determined legacy of sedimented oppression and anomie that have been the hallmarks of life under capitalism. It is imperative that we continue to interrogate the process by which symbols working collectively within a ritual system become rubricized into unswervable, unbridled and unassailable educational dogma. We must explore how the over-sanctification of classroom symbols serves as an ideological cover or protective vault for the status quo. Classroom symbols must be freed from the prison of dead convention. Of critical importance will be our ability to determine whether or not particular symbols have died a natural death or have lost their place in the syntagmatic chain of meaningful classroom signifiers. In other words, is our choice of pedagogical symbols at fault or the way we combine them in instructional discourse?

A ritual studies approach to understanding schooling has important implications for interrogating oppositional student behaviour and discourse. At the cynosure of such an approach is the examination of resistance as a liminal cultural form that is generated in the antistructure. Resistance, we have noted, takes place outside the normative constraints of bureaucracy and social structure through the inversion and rupture of the dominant order and the way the cultural terrain is recombined. The form and content of resistence were discovered to be entropic: student reactions to dominant messages generated by teachers were rendered less predictable, less redundant, and less recursive. The canopy of sanctity created by the invariance of instructional forms was punctured by embodied symbols which dead time and boredom in school had slowly whittled into oppositional weapons. But resistance must be seen as more than a capricious quest for novelty that leads students into the cavernous antistructural realm of oppositional discourse. Stepping outside the margins of consensus-validation and bureaucratically mandated norms proves to be both personally and collectively liberating in the sense that it creates a new discourse and politics of cultural self-affirmation, one that provides students with the metalingual ability to destabilize the 'text' of instruction and to invert and recombine dominant modes of representation.

Classroom researchers should recall that resistance underscores the difference between how cultural knowledge is appropriated. For instance, streetcorner knowledge among the Azorean students partook of a generic religiosity and involved a visceral *knowing* (related to bodily knowledge, ritualization, mimesis, and the rhythms of the street) as distinct from *knowledge* (analytic exposure to facts and empirical information). Participation in rituals of resistance involved an enfleshment of whatever symbols – or combination of symbols – were necessary to counter the bland redundancy and oppressive systemacity of classroom instruction. Students who participate in rituals of resistance become liminars and culture bricoleurs who attempt to find meaning outside the ritualized discourse of despair that constitutes the signifying practices – the 'imperative text' – of the dominant pedagogy. Given this context, classroom educators would do well to reconsider their traditional views of student misbehaviour. From a ritual studies perspective, resistance becomes a crude but effective means of cultural dissidence, of siphoning away the potency of dominant interpretants and myths from the semiotic reservoir of the state.

Into the well from which capitalist rationality and the logic of consumption draws its life-sustaining signifieds, students pitch rotting vermin: subterranean symbols of an oppositional nature which have surfaced from the repressed unconscious of the state. Accepted meanings promulgated – often trumpeted – by the state through its pedagogical rituals become, for a limited time at least, contaminated. Master symbols are fissured and the regularity of the frames that establish classroom discourse ruptured. Resistance not only decentres the teacher as the subject, producer and communicator of shared meaning, it virtually pulls the syntagmatic carpet of classroom discourse out from under the teachers' feet, catapulting the teacher into the unfamiliar and baleful Other.

Students who indulge in new systems of signifying proscribed by teachers are exercising a fight against the forced enclosure and institutionalized censorship of their streetcorner society. And occasionally the gatekeepers of cultural consensus get piked on the school fence, so to speak.

The reform that I am suggesting is more than the creation of liminal classrooms where students can cavort in an unalloyed, unfettered state of *communitas*. On the contrary, it is rooted in the inexorable exigency for building a more just and humane world and calls for teachers to critically engage students at the level of their own cultural literacy. The formations of popular youth culture, in all their complexity, radical variousness, and subterranean potency, must be seen as valuable by the teacher but must not be unqualifiedly endorsed. These cultural formations must also be interrogated for their racist, sexist, and sometimes fascist dimensions (as found, for example, in some recent rock video productions). Resistances that emerge from the antistructure of streetcorner culture can sometimes derail into serving the interests and discourse of the worst aspects of capitalist rationality such as intolerance of minority groups and the poor, and violence against women (cf. Giroux, 1983; Willis, 1977). I am arguing for the creation of an emancipatory politics of culture which will help to render problematic the meanings embedded in the cultural forms and content of classroom instruction. This emancipatory politics repays further elaboration. Such a political project carries with it the implicit injunction to foster critical thinking among students; it also carries the twin imperatives of rethinking present paradigms of teacher professionalism and developing new alliances with popular constituencies such as women's movements, gay rights, the peace movement, and the workers' movement.

The conceptual core of the analyses undertaken by radical scholarship over the last decade has involved unpacking the relationship between schooling and the economic sphere of capitalist production; yet all too often this has been done at the expense of understanding the role of symbol and ritual in the colonization of student subjectivities and proletarianization of teachers. Although mainstream studies of ritual (including anthropological and liturgical traditions) often fall prey to hegemonic instrumental rationality and are imprisoned in a discourse in which positivism bcomes the theoretical centre of gravity, this must not prevent radical educational researchers from adapting some of the contributions of ritual scholars into their work. Scholars such as Victor Turner, Ronald Grimes and Abner Cohen have helped us to understand that rituals are not to be disparaged as encumbering social residue, as simply decorative, gesturally superfluous, or forms of corporeal embellishment. Ritual understanding involves knowledge somaticized metaphorically and symbolically. Wielded by saints and madmen alike, rituals serve as swords sheathed in the symbolic scabbard of social life; they both challenge and defend the sovereign power of dominant cultural meanings. In Giroux's terms, rituals shape the discourses of critique and possibility. Seen in this light, rituals are not less than means to cultural power. Manifested within the awesome referentiality, irreducible plurality and variability of associations surrounding collective symbols, cultural power can be harnessed for freedom or destruction. Once we understand the classroom as an embattled symbolic arena where classroom and streetcorner discourses collide and where teachers and classroom peer groups struggle over how reality is to be signified, and in what manner and style the cultural terrain is to be engaged, then we, as teachers, can begin to situate classroom reform in both the fight for material equality and the forging of a new symbolic sphere.

Unless we begin to act on the moral imperative of creating pedagogy for the opposition (cf. Giroux, 1983), we run the risk of becoming hagiographers of Marx and of his intellectual custodians and critical allies; we place ourselves in peril of becoming curators of antiquarian socialist dreams. It is one thing to lionize the writings of Gramsci and Althusser in the academic halls and quite another to act on the wisdom they have bequeathed to us. To remain revolutionary, radical educators must do more than reformulate, reconstitute or simply abandon various doctrines from the decomposing body of orthodox Marxism; radical pedagogy must prevail against its reification into a cult of saints. But a laicization of the Left need not mean that educators must cease to dream. Not only must we dream a better world, but we must muster the civic courage which requires us to act 'as if' we are living in a democratic society (cf. Giroux, 1983, p. 201). Within the tensions and conflict that exist between radical critiques of schooling and Catholic education I am confident that, in the long run, a vision of social justice and emancipation can be won. More important, I am confident that educators will begin to take a more active role in the fight for equality and liberation.

The task ahead for constructing an emancipatory curriculum is as promising as it is formidable; and in the creation of such a curriculum of discernment, we can expect ritual studies and cultural theory to play important roles. We can look ahead to more productive attempts at constructing a reconciliatory framework for examining the constitution of the subject and the ways in which students construct their significative world. New advances in discourse theory will enable curriculum theorists to appropriate the works of Marx, Gramsci, Foucault, Derrida, Barthes and post-Althusserian writers with more telling results. Growing interest in comparative symbology, radical constructivism, ecological epistemology, semiotics, reception theory, performance studies, ritual studies and post-critical theology will further tighten the conceptual stranglehold on metaphysical realism or the existence of some extra-discursive domain of reality. Not to mention advances in 'postmodern' anthropology.

The development of deconstructionist hermeneutics will continue to challenge the tyranny of the literal, to victimize received texts, and to splinter the syntax of positivist discourse. The mirror that intellectual tradition has poised between reality and the symbolic will be irrevocably shattered. And a growing emphasis on the ideological context of mimesis will help to bury essentialist interpretations of performance. The era of universal or normative epistemologies of symbol and ritual has, I trust, come to an end. Under these influences, the discipline of curriculum theorizing must be transformed into a liminal genre so that it will be able to advance along the margins, the seams, and the interstices of a critical pedagogy of hope and transformation.

Yet gains made in our theorizing about how culture is invented, how reality is constrained by our signifying construction, and how the signified is greatly dependent on the signifier must be accompanied by advances in the role that cultural studies will play in the schools. The focus of the new post-critical curriculum should centre around the importance of providing students with the theoretical equipment for dismantling the discourses and deconstructing the textualizations that are produced in the matrix of mass, popular and 'high' cultures. A theory of cultural analysis – which I refer to as cultural cartography – must go beyond the superficial level of locating penises in the ice cubes of liqueur advertisements or marvelling at the reasons why Arabs like to stand closer than Americans during informal conversations. Cultural cartography must engage students – by way of 'semiotic guerilla warfare' and 'hermeneutical combat' – in a penetrating critique of the culture industry that will have the effect of an unassimilable 'dialectical shock'. Contemporary social life in all its cleavage and continuity, rupture and bland consensus, provides a fecund arena for undertaking such a critical enterprise. The bottom line for theorists of culture must be summed up thus: what good is a politics of representation and performance if we cannot, in some pragmatic sense, provide oppositional curriculum instruction in schools which will turn classrooms into laboratories where hegemonic apparatuses and regnant discursive practices can be critically unravelled?

Cultural cartography must, of political necessity, be committed to mapping the construction of meaning in contemporary social formations by paying precise and consistent attention to the ways in which larger representations of power – those which exist at various levels within the state – are inseparately bonded to rituals and institutionally honed. Upon such rituals the habits, gestures, and signifying constructions of the action subject are semiotically impaled. Cultural cartography must be constituted such that, as it strives to locate itself among a plurality of emancipatory discourses, it provides for the interrogation of its own discursivity. Radical educators must take precautions not to foreclose the kind of critical discourse and contextual exegesis that ritual studies can bring to ethnographic accounts of schooling.

In conclusion, it remains the task of Catholic schooling to decry the mythological abuse (in Barthes's sense of the term) that has rendered working-class students as inferior beings in the minds of many educators. If Catholic schooling persists in remaining tributary to the political project of social justice by holding at arm's length critical social analysis and practice – history may one day record this quietistic detachment as a deep moral stain in the Christian soul. Schools must begin to give measurable shape to our dreams for a more just society by becoming not only laboratories for critique, but also strongholds for purposeful and life-giving symbols. The realm of school ritual must illuminate these symbols, fire them in the crucible of wisdom, and shape them on the anvil of liberation. Only then will we move confidently towards the brink of the fearful abyss that Victor Turner calls the antistructure, grab hold of that rope of snarled symbols, and propel ourselves to the other side where knowing and action meet in the struggle for liberation and the passion for social justice.

WEDNESDAY, 28 JUNE

The school stands empty. The doors are bolted and the grounds are bare. Yet nearby the sidewalks are alive with people. With brisk strides, they make their way from the subway exits and disappear down the narrow streets. Several young women from the Hairdressing School, resplendent in their stained white smocks and overly rouged faces, order coffees and cigarettes at the donut shop. Rust-splotched cars with metallic impressions of Senhor Santo Cristo dangling from the mirrors wind their way through the growing traffic. In the distance the procession of Mary, Queen of Angels, solemnly winds its way to the Iglesa Santa Cruz, led by an out-of-tune brass band. A statue of Our Lady is reverently held aloft on the shoulders of stocky men in oversized grey suits. At the far end of the procession the madman begins to howl, then stumbles and falls to the ground. And all around the pilgrims, children cry and tyres screech and sirens wail. And church bells sound the mass.

Coda

Collisions with otherness; the politics of difference, and the ethnographer as Nomad

The spirituality of Oliver North, for example, who prays regularly, is bogus because, like the pious imperialists in whose footsteps he stands, his politics are in the service of global plunder and greed.

Joel Kovel, 1991, p. 235

My life does not belong to me. I've decided to offer it to a cause. They can kill me at any time, but let it be when I'm fulfilling a mission, so I'll know that my blood will not be shed in vain, but will serve as an example to my *compañeros*. The world I live in is so evil, so bloodthirsty, that it can take my life away from one moment to the next. So the only road open to me is our struggle, the just war. The Bible taught me that. I tried to explain this to a Marxist *compañera*, who asked me how could I pretend to fight for revolution being a Christian. I told her that the whole truth is not found in the Bible, but neither is the whole truth in Marxism, and that she had to accept that.

Rigoberta Menchú, 1984, p. 246.

There are indeed good reasons to accept prophetic Christian claims, yet they are good not because they result from logical necessity or conform to transcendental criteria. Rather, these reasons are good (persuasive to some, nonsense to others) because they are rationally acceptable and existentially enabling for many self-critical finite and fallible creatures who are condemned to choose traditions under circumstances not of our own choosing. To choose a tradition (a version of it) is more than to be convinced by a set of arguments; it is also to decide to live alongside the slippery edge of life's abyss with the support of the dynamic stories, symbols, interpretations, and insights bequeathed by communities that came before.

Cornel West, 1991b, pp. xxix.

Calling it your job don't make it right, boss.

Cool Hand Luke

In order to understand the intensity of ritual forms, one must rid oneself of the idea that all happiness derives from nature, and all pleasure from the satisfaction of a desire. On the contrary, games, the sphere of play, reveal a passion for rules, a giddiness born of rules, and a force that comes from ceremony, and not desire.

Jean Baudrillard, 1990, p. 132

DISJUNCTURE AND THE RESEARCH MOMENT

Engaging in deconstructive anthropology is an inglorious enterprise. If other anthropologists aren't always perched on one shoulder like plump little dybuuks, homunculus heads reminding you of the interpretive functions of their various schools and their special claims to pedigree, then the participants are sitting on your other, challenging conceptual dysesthesia and ethnocentrism with frequent sharp (and, I might add, frequently deserving) blows to the side of your head. Anthropology, if nothing else, teaches through jolts, tremors, rifts, irruptions, concatenations and cleavages, as ideas are gently sifted from tears in the fabric of our cultural world, semiotic ruptures that stretch like Munchean screams over the canvas of the ordinary. The ideas themselves are appurtenances to the epistemic ruptures that occur when cultures collide; when multiple regions of being perforate the hegemony of sameness; when contesting epistemes collude in each other's own invisibility; when differences peel against the grain of predictability; when meanings can no longer be contained or deferred and begin to haemorrhage.

Scholars like to stylize their characterizations of reality into neat, packaged paradigms suitable to all. However diligent, rigorous and noteworthy the research effort to systematize social life into dogma and doctrines, reality always gets stuck somewhere in the act of naming, most often as a lump in the anthropologist's gullet. It is held there as a stammer of repressed complicity in splitting off the 'native' from the 'civilized' world; or dissolves into a silent yawn of cultural forgetfulness, the brief and innocent interval of social amnesia that unwittingly opens the floodgates of cultural violence or invites the 'repressive desublimations' (Marcuse's term) characteristic of the present age's drive towards *bourgeois gentilhomme* political sensibility (not to mention the gentrification of political anthropology). Anthropology is an act of desperation, a dangerous and murky occupation, whose office of theory is to identify reality by inventing or dismembering it – or worst of all, choosing not to take notice of it all.

Having created 'the native' or 'primitive' societies (*Naturvölker*), anthropology continues to succor this myth, refusing to disinter its practices from the worst aspects of the romantic tradition and failing to recognize that its own illusions have been conjured not just in fieldsites but within a field of competing discourses that help structure a variegated system of socially constituted human relationships. I have tried to show in *Schooling as a Ritual Performance* that the fieldsite can no longer be considered simply the physical or geographical location of the study; it also is the place where geopolitical vectors of power crosscut the cultural terrain in the investigation. Fieldsites are real places, but they do not exist simply in a manner which makes knowledge pre-ontologically available to various schools of anthropologists in order that they may give different readings of the same reality. Rather, the discourses that inform the problematics of anthropologists constitute the very reality that they are attempting to understand. The fieldsite is the site of the researcher's own embodiment in theory/discourse and her own disposition or 'place' as a theorist, within a specific politics of location or positionality. Here it should be recognized that 'place' plays an important role in situating field analysis. I am not simply talking about the physical or temporal place where one conducts research but also the textual space one occupies and the affective space one creates. In other words, the discursive practices of 'doing' anthropology do not simply reflect the fieldsite as a seamless repository for transcriptions of a pristine, prefigurative 'source' of cultural authenticity, or the anthropologist as an objective observer without residue, but are constitutive of such a site.

Unless one is able to make one's home in the permanent thrall of Zen-like satori, or the mystical instant that Ernst Bloch calls the *nunc aeternum*, participating in daily life is always already an act of interpretation (and this is as true for washing socks as it is for doing anthropological fieldwork). Constructing reality is unavoidable. However, claiming that one has 'discovered' it is an inevitable act of forgery, a conjuring trick of logocentric scholarship. Often we don't acknowledge when we are making such claims; yet it is an enterprise in which all of us, however reluctantly or unwittingly, participate.

Recognizing that our explanations are inventions or that our experience is always reality's surrogate does not, however, always mean that we must falsify the real – that we must ambush reality and rob it of all meaning. Agreeing that meaning is always in transit, (and not necessarily through a linear temporalization or a theory of *éternel retour*) and that facts possess no veridical status apart from the language forms available to us for validating our assumptions, does not mean that we should abandon ourselves to a postmodern textualism. As Christopher Norris (1991) claims, reason is not altogether powerless in the face of uncertainty.

The apparent smudging of distinctions between rationality and rhetoric or fact and fiction that characterizes our so-called postmodern condition need not hold the multiple voices of reason hostage. Simply because language does not give us unmediated or transparent access to the world should not leave us tethered to despair nor give us cause to abandon ethical and political projects. We don't need an ontological commitment to a classical realist philosophy in order to struggle for a better world. While we can never escape from the language of ontology even as we try to deconstruct it (except into the gaps along the signifying chain) we must, I believe, follow Emmanuel Levinas (1969) in placing our ethical relation to the Other prior to our ontological, cosmological, and epistemological relation to ourselves. Part of such an ethics involves an attempt not to camouflage ourselves in our statements about the Other or to impose upon the 'native' text the taxonomic nature and ethnocentrist assumptions of our encounter with Otherness.

ETHNOGRAPHY AS NOMADOLOGY

I do not pretend that my own work is anything more than a form of poetic invention as the starting point for cultural criticism. But in saying this I am not arguing for an escape from reason or an anti-empiricist attempt to avoid all forms of theoretical totalization. While I am sympathetic to the enterprise of Taussig (1980, 1987) and Clifford and Marcus (1986) in decentring traditional forms of ethnographic authority, I will argue that critical ethnography, of which this analysis is certainly a part, embodies an intent that moves beyond the epistemic murk of the postmodernists, whether spectral (see Lash, 1990), ludic (see Ebert, 1991) or sceptical (see Rosenau, 1992). 'Ludic' or 'spectral' postmodernists invoke reality in a frenetic avoidance of mimetic inscription (representation);

displace the historical subject by rendering human agency merely in more abstract terms; reflect an ontological or explanatory agnosticism, an epistemological or ironic scepticism, and aesthetic historicism; and disperse authorship in a way that implodes object into subject so that desire become locked into the sign-value of the spectacle, thus prohibiting the researcher from conducting her work in a way that might be defensible in scientific, ethical, or political terms. I also wish to argue that treating lived experience simply as 'text' poses some real problems in situating anthropological research in a project of possibility.

The explanatory nihilism (especially that associated with the *post-historie* of the French Nietzscheans) that often infects postmodern themes of otherness and difference must be supplanted by a politics of the concrete that links modes of intelligibility and economies of affect to the commodification of labour and capitalist accumulation (West, 1991b). That knowledge might be radically undecidable is an important postmodern qualification we should take to heart as researchers but, as Dean MacCannell (1992, p. 6) makes clear, instead of 'worrying endlessly about minute alternative possibilities (deconstruction)' it would serve us well to 'affirm the *speculative* nature of theory as the real ground of freedom', become attentive to the obverse of undecidability which is *possibility*, and attempt to 'bridge or tunnel the impossible (which I take to be "reality") and reach for possible truth'.

On this more optimistic note, the goal of *Schooling as a Ritual Performance* has, in part, been to defang naïve empiricism when it has proved disabling to an emancipatory praxis, to provide provisional, anti-foundational grounds for launching a politics of hegemonic refusal, one that menaces the modernist notion that research can – and should – be separated from forms of advocacy. Furthermore, the goal has been to provide communities of resistance with the capacity for assuming more semantic authority in making their own decisions should their own indigenous idioms of analysis prove insufficient for contesting the cultural dominance of late capitalist exploitation, and for authoring their realities from a perspective that is able to locate its source of hope not in the solemn, sovereign chamber of certainty but within the more expansive terrain of contingent possibilities.

Schooling as a Ritual Performance adopts the position that we are unable to grasp ourselves or others introspectively without social mediation through our positionality with respect to race, class, gender, and other configurations. But what does this suggest for the ethnographic researcher? William Connolly's (1992) discussion of Todorov's *The Conquest of America* is instructive. Todorov's critics have chastized him for not trying to 'enter into' the internal codes of 'discovered peoples' (such as the Aztecs). But Connolly suggests that Todorov was trying to highlight the dangers of transcending western codes by trying to establish a pure contextualism of local knowledges. At the same time Todorov recognizes, in Connolly's view, the dangers of a pure universalism, rationalism or empiricism. Rather, Todorov's text adopts a 'problematizing stance to its own mode of inquiry'. In other words, Todorov engages in a research practice that contestably and fugitively ambiguates its own grounded assumptions, entrenched antimonies and contingencies – a practice that creates a 'pathos of difference' in that it recognizes the creative tension among contrary perspectives that are embodied in the interdependence of self and other. Connolly writes,

> In place of trying to understand the other (the Aztecs) within a universal code or as they understood themselves, he [Todorov] explores how fixed patterns of encounter available to the western invaders forced some priests into moments of self-doubt, confusion, and creative thinking as they pursued their encounters with the other . . .
>
> Todorov treats Aztec culture, on the other hand, mostly as if it were an undecipherable, resistant, and inexhaustible text upon which representatives of the west reinscribed their own stories and in which, when pushed to the limits of their own cultural resources, they encountered the enigma of otherness in the other and themselves. (1991: 41, 42)

The cultural cartography of Todorov's work points to the importance of understanding both the researcher and the research participants as constituting indentities that are historically contingent and relational and of resisting institutional and academic attempts to establish their fixity and definition through the inscription of teleotranscendental assumptions of good/evil, normal/abnormal, male/female.

The cultural cartography that constitutes this research does not promise, or even try, to transcend western codes of rationality even as it attempts to instantiate an eschatological hope in a heteronomous future of democratic possibility, a leap into epistemological blasphemy and a journey into radical Otherness. But it does attempt to disidentify with their founding binarisms in order to lay bare some of the linkages between knowledge and power, discourse and authority.

Times have changed since work first began on *Schooling as a Ritual Performance* nearly a decade ago. They have appreciably worsened. I have been residing in the United States since the publication of the book, and so on the one hand, my outlook has invariably been colonized through particular forms of ideological production to which no one – perhaps especially anthropologists – is ever completely immune. On the other hand, I dare say that my perspective on domination and resistance has been sharpened by the changing tides in world events and shifting geopolitical configurations. In the USA – as in most centres of western imperialism – the 'new times' are growing more pock-marked with racism and violence.

It is clearer to me that we live in a pathological age, one in which madness has been granted the dark illumination of reason and has become for many a reasonable option in the face of the corporate and fetishistic logic of contemporary dominant cultures. Such cultures are accompanied more and more by social chaos, bureaucratic terrorism, assaults on people of colour, gays, lesbians, and the aged, not to mention increasing violence directed against women in general. Cultural critics have called it the 'society of the spectacle', the 'Kingdom of Fakes', the 'World of Pseudo Events', and the 'Culture of the Simulacrum', a weld of simulated values, of copies without originals, of bodies without organs in which 'image' and 'persona' have become the prime arbiters of value.

The fortified, postmodern *noir* metropolises of the *fin de siècle* have grown more Latinophobic, homophobic, xenophobic, sexist, racist, and bureaucratically cruel. Much of this is due to the post-cultural production of a cannibalized reality of simulacra that accrues to itself only its own detritus, that wallows in its own its dregs, that secretly cossets whatever it purportedly disavows. It is simply wrong to blame the general public who, Marx noted, exercise considerable agency but in conditions not of their own making. I prefer to raise the following question: What are the underlying conditions – both discursive and material – out of which the present social crisis has emerged?

The now apocalyptic urgency among corporations to maximize profits at the expense of the already exploited and marginalized coupled with new forms of surveillance and bureaucratic control, have led to insidious forms of exploitation previously unimaginable.

Of course, with profits come not only profiteering but prophecy. Electronic prophets who manufacture personalities and manage corporate images have turned wimp presidents into wrathful avengers and a frustrated citizenry into phallo-military warrior citizens, who are being conditioned to turn a media-instilled hatred of 'Sadd'am' against a new enemy within its own ranks: the poor, the homeless, those who comprise the detritus of capitalism, who are disadvantaged by their race, gender, caste or circumstance. What is postmodernity if not the triumphalistic attempt to privilege differentially the colonized and the colonizer, to turn the whole of culture into a pleasure palace for the rich while mortgaging the hopes and dreams of the powerless and disadvantaged? What is the mission of postmodernity if not the construction of a global theme park for recreationalizing white racism? What, indeed, is postmodernity if not the attempt to 'Americanize the un-American' by assimilation through diversity and through particular forms of cultural assertion linked to capital and patterns of consumption but also on a grander scale to interlocking international networks of finance and surveillance. What can we say of the zombified citizens of these 'new times' except that they have been manufactured as the functional correlation of a service economy and decentred, and refractory, subjectivity?

Realizing that we are currently positioned in the twilight of certain manifestations of postmodernity that have abetted a politics resting on a discourse of nihilistic grandeur, a politics that has thrown Enlightenment dialectics back upon its own negations, I want to stress the importance of working within the interstices that exist between and among discourses of power. I highlight this because no discourse of power is absolutely totalizing; all sprout leaks and produce fissures into which seeds of resistance may be scattered and cultivated. The dominant social order cannot arrogate to itself the full capacity for the production, classification, hierarchism, and distributive management of subjectivity. It is therefore absolutely necessary that our scholarly exactitude and academic situatedness do not displace the urgency of our critical practice; it must not deflect us from our interventionist project as active collaborators in social change. We must not distance ourselves – or allow ourselves to become distanced – either in our disquisitions or our deconstructions from a politics of the concrete, from shaping existing material practices or installing new ones.

As critical practitioners and agents of menace we need to make certain our work does not lapse into a formalistic effacement of the suffering of humanity either by silencing the oppressed who are attempting to make themselves heard, by assuming an anarcho-bohemian posture that affords the illusion of intervening in relations of domination through clever double readings of social texts, or by speaking for those who are attempting to win a space in order to speak for themselves. Rather, we are implored to labour in order to recentre ourselves through the moralized order of subject positions made available to us as researchers, to construct new positions from which to view the contemporary scene, and to see spaces heterotopically as well as forge utopian visions of a better world.

I do not want to make pretence to the availability of critical postures that are untouched by the stain of ideology. Sometimes ethnography needs to be a place where we can lose our voices not to the indeterminate sensations of experience but in the sense of letting go of our unified, fixed, position of enunciation. This is not an argument for ethnographers to enter into fractional relation-ships with those whom they research, or for celebrating the mutable, ersatz, multiphrenic identity or pastiche personality (see Gergen, 1991). Rather, it is an invitation to claim a nomadic subjectivity in order to assume a position of coevalness with the people one studies (Fabian, 1983), a call for researchers to abandon escapades into modernist critiques of apocalyptic preformulation in order to assume border identities that can better enable them to address the historical topicality of the present through detours and diver-sions – within counteracting 'heterotopic' spaces.

Foucault described heterotopias as 'counter-sites, a kind of effectively enacted utopia in which the real sites, all the other real sites that can be found within the culture, are simultaneously represented, contested, and inverted' (cited in Soja, 1991, p. 7). Whereas utopias represent 'at once a placeless, virtual, unreal place in which I see myself where I am not, over there where I am absent', a heterotopia represents 'a real, counteracting space in which I discover my absence from the place where I am since I see myself over there, a realization that makes me come back toward myself, to reconstitute myself there where I am' (Soja, 1991, p. 8). There is a tension – a formidable disjunction – between heterotopias and other 'real' sites and a 'different interpretive analytics' is required to see them and grasp their meaning or 'revealing genealogies'. Schools have the capacity to become heterotopias in the ways that they take on the qualities of human territoriality, with its surveillance of presence and absence, its demarcation of behaviours, its protective definition of the inside and the out. Implicit in this regulation of opening and closing are the workings of power, of disciplinary technologies. (Soja, 1991, p. 10).

How can we read schools *heterotopologically*, as a cultural logic, as a spacialization and concretization of power? How have schools become cultural bunkers, encampments of greed and competitiveness, fortresses of acquisitiveness and citadels of colonial domination – the social will and cultural logic of capitalism compressed into a "hyperspace" of mystification? In what manner do schools structure a disavowal of cultural heterogeneity, historicize desire, spacialize history, and organize subjectivities through particular geographies of the will? How have schools positioned the body/subject, territorialized pleasure, mapped perceptions, and created cognitive templates stamped in the mint of colonialism that ready us through the politics and practices of normalization for our engagement with both the word and the world? How are they incommensurable spaces of 'fragmentary possible worlds' that both constrain and enable a politics of emancipation (Harvey, 1989, p. 48)? How have dominative practices been mapped on to liberatory ones, and how can we discern which worlds we are living in, legitimating, and reproducing?

Schooling as a Ritual Performance has initiated an analysis of the relationship among space, time, and power but current work by Mike Davis and Edward W. Soja that apply a Foucauldian reading of heterotopia to postmodern geographies will be able to give educational researchers a closer and more profound reading of school sites as *l'espace vécu* – as real, lived spaces that are heterogeneous and relational. It is especially important that critical scholarship such as this cease to be ghettoized, that it remain resistant to absorption by the status quo, that it does not unwittingly conspire to contain rupture and contestation by reproducing those same structures of power and knowledge it seeks to displace, and reinscribing the oppressed within the discourse of neo-colonialist instruction.

BODY DOUBLES: RESEARCH AND THE THE POLITICS OF ENFLESHMENT

Like the figure on the right panel of Francis Bacon's *Three studies for figures at the base of a crucifixion* (1944), the modernist dream has collapsed the human spirit into ice-cold will, compressed the human agent into compound of organs and bone, into a sinewed mass of bodily torment, reflecting a deep psychological wounding. Every pleasure and pathology imagined can somewhere be reflected in the mirror of human flesh. The hierarchy of pain and pleasure lived through the economy of human tissue knows no summit. Pain and pleasure are experienced in socially and culturally specific ways. This is most readily visible through posture and behaviour – through individual and group comportment.

In *Schooling as a Ritual Performance* I argued that the ritualization of desire through institutionalized and pedagogical practices could be seen in the coded gestures and interactive patterns of the Azorean and Italian students. This was, I reasoned, reflective of how late capitalism has transformed 'ethnic' bodies into incubators for specific forms of desire. What I did not explore were the ways in which capitalism itself has become parasitic on desire. In an era of post-Fordist economic transmutations, we can expect such desires to be more specialized and designed to target specific ethnic populations. Schools, of course, are interested in turning bodies into desiring machines that feed upon consumer longings which in turn feed the hydra-headed beast of capitalism. For this reason we need to understand the process of normalization through which rituals are able to constitute subjectivity and regulate the insatiability of the consumer citizen through the theological doxa of capital.

Desires are nomadic and atopic. However, they can be frozen, territorialized, regimented, and coded. In short, they can become invested in meaning, situated in discourse. In principle, desire can be coded in an infinite number of ways, but in practice is always coded in *some* way. Without such a coding, nothing would be possible. Yet because of this desire is always experienced as reified. In this way, bodies can be seen as meaning-systems that need to be renegotiated. One of the main themes of my research has been to explore how meaning is linked to desire. I have tried to raise the question of how ritualized knowledge is tacitly embodied and made sense of through the investment of bodily pleasure. I refer to this as the enfleshment of meaning, particularly the formation of the specific type of practical consciousness that Raymond Williams referred to as ideology.

By enfleshment I mean the mutually constitutive enfolding of social structure and desire; that is, it is the dialectical relationship between the material organization of interiority and the cultural modes of materiality we inhabit subjectively. The idea here is that dreams are not only about flesh, as Freud would lead us to believe, but the flesh also *dreams*. Further, it is enfolded within its own architecture of desire. It dreams not simply through the teleologies of western narratives – masculine dramas in the form of detective stories and knockabout transatlantic spy thrillers. It dreams through counter-narratives and anti-narratives. It dreams outside the classical epic forms, literary devices, and metropolitan tropes hewed in the drawing-rooms and rooming houses of our *modernista* mega-fathers. It is dreamed in the language of Borges and Lispector. Gestures and comportment are desire's hieroglyphs. We can read desire and how it has been ideologically produced by paying attention to students' bodies and how they have been produced both to conform and to resist.

Schooling as a Ritual Performance raises the question: If discourses are not grounded transcendentally, and if they are not entirely trackable or even mappable by intellection or meaningful narrative emplotments within modernist epistemes (and that includes post-Kantian interpretive dialectics), how, in fact, are they grounded? Recent research on the body suggests that knowledge is grounded through forms of embodiment.

The concept of the body as a site of cultural inscription is growing in prominence as a topic of investigation among contemporary social theorists. For instance, efforts are being made to uncouple the idea of the feminine body/subject and the black and Latino body/subject from the negative and unspoken Other and to recognize the body as a site of enfleshment, that is, as a site where epistemic codes freeze desire into social norms. Enfleshment is the 'quilting point' that results when the radical externality of the body/subject as surplus to our volition welds or sutures the pure interiority of our own subjectivity. Thus it involves both the entextualization of desire and the embodiment of textual forms. The body is the site of learned narratives that are spatio-temporally constructed at the intersection of desire and meaning. Bodies are becoming recognized and explored as both instruments and victims of ideology, socially situated and incarnated (not to mention incarcerated) social prac-tices that are semiotically alive.

The 'text' of enfleshment is the body/subject which, properly speaking, constitutes the space of ultimate intertextuality. The body/subject is the site of the dialectical re-initiation of desire and signification. All meaning is, therefore, material yet exceeds codification. It is at once transgressive of social norms and situated in socially sedimented discourses of desire. Enfleshment is that meeting place of both the unthought social norms in which meaning is always already in place and the ongoing production of knowledge through particular social, institutional and disciplinary procedures. Enfleshed knowledge is not the matching of information to external reality but rather the building of discursive positionalities and economies of affect from the discourses and material practices available and the histories and regulatory practices of their operations. Broadly speaking, enfleshment refers to the patterns of interaction between mind and nature, patterns which are not only localized in the body. Enfleshment refers to inscriptions of patterns of difference which operate at different hierarchical levels – at the level of habits and habitus, for instance.

However, I should add that the importance of understanding the body is not so that researchers can turn it into a textualized semiotic laboratory, but rather to recognize knowledge as a typography of embodiment; that is, to recognize the body as the grounds for all our intersubjective relationships with the subjects of our investigations and for our affective investment in our own research projects. We cannot separate the body from the social formation, since the material density of all forms of subjectivity is achieved through the 'micropractices' of power that are socially inscribed into our flesh.

As Allen Feldman reports in his brilliant ethnography of political terror in Northern Ireland, *Formations of Violence* (1991), the body is 'the factored product of the unequal and differential effects of intersecting antagonistic forces' (p. 176) that 'coheres onto an economy of the body' (p. 177). Although the body is the product of history, it is, through the workings of the subject, also the shaper of history. Ethnography in my estimation should help produce those forms of agency necessary for the transformation of historical forces and structures of oppression. Feldman's formulation of agency is important.

> Exteriority folds the body, but agency, as a self-reflexive framing of force, subjectivates exteriority and refolds the body. It is not only a matter of what history does to the body but what subjects do with what history has done to the body. (p. 177)

It is important that ethnographers engage the means by which discourses 'live' inside both 'us and them' as linguistic and

extra-linguistic mediations. Our capacity as researchers to understand the body as an effect of power–knowledge relations and also
as a site of their articulation can help us to escape the political
paralysis that often accompanies the post-structuralist recognition
that values, desires, and practices always originate elsewhere in
pre-disclosed structures and in conditions not of our own making.
In other words, while it is true that our desires and intentions and
those of our subjects never can be completely mapped or made
conscious, this should not compel us as researchers to assume a
passive, passionless, and politically inert role. Nor should it be an
occasion for a voluntaristic denial or abandonment of hope – a
sanctioned refusal to upstage despair in the face of the dominant
culture's persistent demonization of the Other. Hope can be
frustrated; it can be diminished, but it cannot be eliminated. For
this reason we must always remain loyal to hope.

If the objectivist programme in the social sciences was grounded
in empirical studies, the postmodernist approach to research is
grounded in the metaphoricity and tropicity of all discourse.
Metaphor and polyseme form the cornerstones of what George
Lakoff calls 'experiential realism' and what Mark Johnson calls
'embodied, nonpropositional, and imaginative meaning' (cited in
Frank, 1990). Metaphor and polyseme are constituent not only of
speech but also of thought, and we can trace our embodiment in
knowledge preverbally to our early experiences of balance, containment, forces, cycles, and so forth, which become our image
schemata and which in turn inform our propositional logic (Frank,
1990, p. 158). As Arthur Frank notes, understanding and knowledge
are projections of embodied image schemata that are multivocal,
yet can form the basis of mutual understanding, since bodily
experience is shared. Cartesian philosophy managed to overlook
the fact that validity claims no longer can afford to exclude the body.
In fact, I would go so far as to say that theoretical knowledges
constitute externalized metaphors of the body; they form the discursive protheses of the body, artifacts that offer strategies of desire.
As embodied metaphors, metonymies, and images based on experience; they solicit; they seduce; they hypnotize; they advocate;
they cannot be considered lifeless nor objective. Ann Game (1991,
p. 192) puts it exeedingly well when she writes that 'the body provides the basis for a different conception of knowledge: we know
with our bodies. . . . In this regard . . . if there is any truth, it is
the truth of the body.'

Recent post-structuralist investigations have revealed how the body has been produced by the carceral machine of corporate capitalism, that is, by contructing bodies 'incorporally' through the commodification of signs and within social formations that serve to regulate the production of desire and that organize and align the heterogeneous regimes of discourses of the flesh. In their steely resolve as custodians of reason, educators have hacked away at the tendons that connect meaning and the body. They have done so to the detriment of their pedagogies and at their own peril as producers of historical agency. This is most damagingly evident in 'official' school practices where we witness in oppositional student behaviour what Terry Eagleton (1990, p. 13) calls 'the body's long inarticulate rebellion against the tyranny of the theoretical'.[2] My concern is that the school curriculum needs to draw upon the affective economies situated within what Paul Willis (1990) calls 'common culture', in order to render such economies problematic, and eventually to find ways of transforming them into a larger political project and social vision. Only in this way can liberating pedagogies be developed that will enable students to construct meanings that are lived in the body, felt in the bones, and situated within the larger body politic in the form of public meta-narratives (as distinct from master narratives) aimed at increasing social justice and emancipation. Of course, in our studies of meanings as they are lived through the body, we must be careful not to bring the autonomy of experience back into the debate through the back door. This can occur, as Ebert (1991, p. 129) notes, by essentializing resistance in the subject of the body. Such an essentializing can resurrect the illusion that experience is devoid of ideology and is undertaken as a form of free choice by independent subjects. Ebert warns that this can cause the 'subject' to be seen as 'merely an updated nomenclature for the old humanist individual rather than the mark of the post-humanist theory of the social construction of individuals' (pp. 129–30).

Here I must also underline the importance of understanding the body as the site of embodiment of racist discourses. As David Theo Goldberg (1990) has so brilliantly pointed out in his Foucauldian analysis of racism as socio-discursive praxis, the discourse of the body reflects particular ways of seeing (e.g. classifying, ordering and valuing) that have been produced through institutional, economic, and ethical practices situated within particular technologies of power. Specific forms of subjectivities and otherness are produced through discourses of the body, and this was certainly evident in the way in which the teachers classified themselves in hierarchical orders of purity, with the Anglo teachers and students on top, followed by the Italians and Azoreans.

The way in which racist discourses are produced by the body as well as the manner in which they have become conjoined with discourses of class, gender, and nation need to be interrogated by educators in their understanding of how historical agency is determined. It is also important to understand and struggle against those presuppositions of racial differences that in educational research unwittingly perpetuate research efforts that serve the current history of racist expression and formation.

Needed is a critical pedagogy that moves beyond the (albeit important) domain of relevance and into the arena of a trans-formative social practice through the struggle against multiple forms of oppression and multiple determinations of racial discourse. This means, following Teresa de Lauretis (1990, p. 138), 'giving up a place that is safe, that is "home" – physically, emotionally, linguistically, epistemologically – for another place that is unknown and risky, that is not only emotionally but conceptually other; a place of discourse from which speaking and thinking are at best tentative, uncertain, unguaranteed'. This 'theory in the flesh' involves 'a constant crossing of the border' and 'a remapping of boundaries between bodies and discourses, identities and communities'.

As educators, we need to address the issues of gender, race, class, and sexuality as cultural and social determinations that are lived within multiple forms of subjectivity (e.g. as emotional differentia-tion and sensibility, see Heller, 1989); further, we need to see them as social constructions that are formed within official, alternative, and oppositional cultural formations and readings. With teacher education programmes there are too few opportunities for teachers to understand how student identities become 'locked' into certain behaviours, desires, and visions of the past, present, and future (i.e. how they both adapt to *and* resist western hegemonic arrange-ments of knowledge and power). Unless we take seriously as educators the various cultures out of which student identities are formed, we are inviting students to view schooling as little more than a form of cultural imposition.

Our research agendas with their accompanying theoretical formulations must be situated within the borders defining their respective projects. A project is more than a subjective disposition, but rather constitutes a political imperative grounded in an ethical discourse (Giroux and McLaren, 1991). The ethical project known as critical ethnography is one that does not emerge transcendentally in textual forms detached from perception, bodily experience, and the friction of social reality. It is an ethics that emerges from the body, is situated in the materiality and historicity of discourse, in the call of the flesh, in the folds of desire (McLaren, forthcoming). It is an imperative that presupposes an answer, in a response from the other. If the way in which metaphors are grounded in bodily experience become part of the theoretical structures through which we perceive the world, then it is important for critical ethnographers to utilize an ethics fully grounded in the body (see Chambers, 1990; McLaren, 1989b). And such an ethics must take into consideration how bodies are regulated, become policed through machineries of surveillance and inspection, experience pleasure and pain, and how they are produced discursively through material struggles, power–knowledge relations, and often through capitalism's catachrestic relationship to democracy.

Schooling as a Ritual Performance did not adequately address the gendered characteristics of identity formation (including that of the ethnographer) through the inscription of the body/subject by patriarchal discourses and social practices. This was brought to my attention by a number of feminist readings of my text. Such readings have essentially redirected the focus of my more current research. One particular feminist insight that has recently been articulated by Patricia Ticineto Clough (1992) deserves attention by ethnographers in particular and social scientists in general. According to Clough, research constitutes a particular disciplining of reading and writing. In the case of ethnographic analysis, she has brilliantly identified a function of narrative desire in such a disciplining. More specifically, Clough argues that the narrativity one discovers in ethnography constitutes an oedipally organized logic and scenarios of desire that configure a unity of identity in the masculine subject. She traces this to the existence and preponderance of realist narrativity that legitimates the patriarchal authority of empirical representations. Consequently, ethnographers are depicted as assuming patriarchal heroic stances and making 'uncritical use of an oedipally organized logic of sexual difference' – which is disavowed – and reconstituting 'empiricism for sociological discourse in terms of various writing technologies of the subject' (1992, p. 9). What would have benefited *Schooling as a Ritual Performance* would have been an attempt to uncover its writing technologies of the subject – the unconscious desire that reproduces particular forms of authority and modes of narrative address. It is in the domain of gender research and in analysing social science as a particular narrative construction of authority that the fluorescence of future liberatory struggles will take root. I would encourage multiple readings of cultural texts outside a masculinized discourse of social efficiency, patriarchy and class privilege that are non-absolutist, encourage alternative interpretations, and reject essentialist views of truth and human agency.

Another way that ethnographers and field researchers can begin to think of the 'truth' of their work is not to render knowledge as something ultimately to be discovered, but rather as social texts that are relationally produced in a multiplicity of mutually informing contexts. When such truths become official, when they are presented as discourses of sanctioned legitimacy, then they often serve as an impediment to further truth and must therefore be deformed – even perverted – by rhetorizing moves on the part of the researcher that deconstruct their metaphysical bearings. Representation is always re-presentation within particular ideological configurations. If every signification constitutes a mask (Levinas, 1969; Patterson, 1990), then the way to truth becomes the absolute pursuit of alterity – to probe the totality of Otherness.

THE POLITICS OF DIFFERENCE

There's room for all at the rendez-vous of victory.

Césaire

The concept of 'otherness' is becoming a crucial category for educators, especially given the new constructions and concentrations of state power within the current historical juncture, and attempts to disrupt and contest such power among growing social movements organized around ethnicity and nation. The politics of difference that was at work at St Ryan in terms of differentially constituting students as Azorean, as Italian, as Catholic, as workers, and as male and female, was undoubtedly racist and sexist and grounded in bourgeois classificatory systems. This could be seen in some of the primitive biologistic notions of race held by certain teachers, the Manichaean thinking undergirding the racial categories that were used to define 'civilized' and 'deviant' behaviour, and the social relations within the school which were largely determined by economic and political forces at work in the larger society.

The analysis proferred in *Schooling as a Ritual Performance* needs to be seen in light of the current debate over the meaning of difference and how it might figure in a renewed struggle for democracy. A key question that emerges from *Schooling as a Ritual Performance* (one that was not adequately addressed in the original analysis) is how to develop a multicultural curriculum that is attentive to the specificity (historical, cultural) of difference (in terms of race, class, gender, sexuality, etc.) yet addresses the commonality of diverse Others under the law with respect to universal principles of equality and social justice. The liberal and conservative attacks on multiculturalism as separatist and ethnocentric carry with them the erroneous assumption that North American society fundamentally constitutes social relations of uninterrupted accord and a space of analytical and political guarantees. This view furthermore underscores the idea that North American society is largely a forum of consensus with different minority viewpoints accretively added on. It presupposes harmony and agreement – an undisturbed space in which differences can coexist. It assumes that a steady accretion in the repertoire of cultural viewpoints is axiomatically a development welcomed by a democratic order. It is a call for a discursive symbiosis and de-differentiation under the guise of pluralism. Chandra Mohanty (1989/90) notes that difference cannot be formulated as negotation among culturally diverse groups against a backdrop of presumed cultural homogeneity. Difference is the recognition that knowledges are forged in histories that are riven with differentially constituted relations of power; that is, knowledges, subjectivities, and social practices are forged within 'asymmetrical and incommensurate cultural spheres' (p. 181). A dialogic society is agonistic and is informed not by a fusion of horizons but a conflict over differences. There are no easily discernible or stable links between antagonisms and social struggles but rather radically contingent hegemonic articulations within a plurality of social, cultural and political formations and constituencies.

The conservative view of multiculturalism assumes that justice already exists and needs only to be evenly apportioned. However, both teachers and students need to realize that justice does not already exist simply because laws exist. Justice needs to be continually created, constantly struggled for. The question that I want to pose to teachers is this: Do we have a language of analysis that is adequate to create alternative social figures or simply to preserve the status quo in which the illusion of democracy 'covers' injustice and inequality – an illusion that blinds democracy to its constitutive outside? Democracy, in the terms I use (after Laclau, Mouffe, and Žižek) means continually suspending the habitual, undoing associations that bring closure to, that 'quilt', 'suture' or complete the subject/ citizen within the discourse of racial/cultural apartheid and other forms of domination specific to North American geopolitical locations.

One of the crucial distinctions teachers need to explore is that made by Homi K. Bhabha (1990) when he talks about 'difference' and 'diversity'. The notion of diversity is a mainstream liberal one that speaks to the importance of plural, democratic societies. But with diversity comes a 'transparent norm' constructed and administered by the 'host' society that creates a consensus. A normative grid locates cultural diversity while at the same time *contains* cultural difference. The 'universalism that paradoxically permits diversity masks ethnocentric norms' (p. 208). Differences, on the other hand, do not always speak to consensus but are often incommensurable. Culture, as a system of difference, as symbol-forming activity, must be seen as 'a process of translations'. Culture in this view never really exists fully formed in the sense that it possesses 'a totalized prior moment of being meaning – an essence' (p. 210).

Otherness in this sense is often internal to the symbol-forming activity of that culture and it is best perhaps to speak of the 'hybridity' of culture. There exists a 'third space' that enables other positions to emerge (Bhabha, 1990). This 'third space' opens up possibilities for new structures of authority, and new political vistas and visions. Identity from this perspective is always an arbitrary, contingent, and temporary suturing of identification, of meaning. Bhabha's distinction between difference and diversity makes it clear to me why prominent US critics such as Ravitch and Bennett are so dangerous when they talk about the importance of building a common culture. Who has the power to exercise meaning, to create the grid from which otherness is defined, to stipulate the identifications that invite closures on meanings, on interpretations and translations, to showcase Otherness in Euro-America's *cabinets de curiosités?*

In order to ascertain better what a politics of difference might look like, it is productive to follow Bhabha (1990, p. 293) in recognizing the 'metaphoricity of the peoples of imagined communities'. This 'requires a temporality of representation that moves between cultural formations and social processes without a centred causal logic'. We need to give credence to a new 'ambivalent' or 'disjunctive' temporality in order to give 'lived historical memory and subjectivity their appropriate narrative authority' (p. 293). That is, more attention must be directed towards the 'contingent and arbitrary signs and symbols that signify the affective life of the national culture' (p. 293).

While the master narratives of culture are usually the master's narratives and belong in the master's house, even such narrative as that of 'the nation' is not as unproblematically dominative or reproductive as one might think. As Bhabha points out, such narratives exist in a state of tension between the pedagogical (historical sedimentation) and the performative (the loss of identity in the signifying processes of cultural identification): a tension which makes 'the people' into a problem of knowledge and authority. Bhabha is instructing us that narratives are constituted in both indicative and subjective modes (as models of and models for). The pedagogical gets its narrative authority from its situatedness in linear historical time. But the performative ruptures the self-generation of the pedagogical by introducing the 'in-between' of the liminal – the 'emptiness' of the signifier (p. 299). Bhabha's notion of the subject's agonistic double inscription as pedagogical objects and performative subjects, his stress on the instability and supplementarity of cultural signification, and his assertion that the liminal character of performance can function as a counter-narrative to rupture the essentialist identity of the state, are analogous to the argument that I tried to raise in *Schooling as a Ritual Performance* in stressing the performativity of ideology, the metaphoricity of ritual, and the mutli-valency (multi-accentuality) of the ritual symbol.

In Bhabha's terms, it is the iconicity of authority and the perpetual sliding of the signifier that produces spaces of resistance at the margins of convention (i.e. in the horizontality of community and the homogeneous time of social narratives). It is here that minority discourses can assemble their counter-narratives of resistance. According to Bhabha, 'minority discourse acknowledges the status of national culture – and the people – as a contentious, performative space of the perplexity of the living in the midst of the pedagogical representations of the fullness of life' (p. 307). Understanding narrative identity this way can help us to dismantle those representations of social life that speak the language of permanence, continuity and self-generation, and to reveal the hybrid character of identity formation.

While Bhabha's interest is the study of the nation through its forms of narrative address, his insights, in my opinion, are also pertinent to understanding both the constitution of the national or sovereign subject – and also of the popular subject; they are both tied to the closure or totalization of the discourses of selfhood and citizenship. It is the practice of understanding how narratives of the self become constituted in contexts of colonialism, post-colonialism and neo-colonialism that can lead to a new politics of difference and identity. This, in turn, can bring about a new subject-space of meaning construction and praxis. To reveal the fissures in the continuity of the narrative self is to contest claims to domination by groups on the basis of race, class privilege, and gender and other interests. For Bhabha (1990, p. 6) it is also 'a challenge to relativistic notions of the diversity of culture'. It provides a place where we can 'begin to write histories of peoples and construct theories of narration'. For teachers, it can be a place of hybrid pedagogical space where students do not need the colonizer's permission or approval to narrate their own identities, a space where individual identities find meaning in collective expression and solidarity with cultural others, where mimetic, Eurocentric time recedes into the lived, historical moment of contemporary struggles for identity – to 'women's time' (Kristeva) or a time of 'occult instability' (Fanon).

For me, a space for rewriting dominant narratives comes into being by the very fact of the patience of infinity, the diachrony of time that, observes Levinas, is produced by our situatedness as ethical subjects and our responsibility to the Other. Because we are temporal beings, self-identity is impossible. We are always in motion conceptually and affectively – a motion striving towards infinity. For here the 'other' always exists beyond totalization in a positive relation to the Other. The problem, of course, is that the remaking of the social and the reinvention of the self are too often nonsynchronous occurances. However, Bhabha (1991) notes that there exists a 'postcolonial' time lag between the event of modernity and the contingency of the present. This could be described more specifically as the interruptive temporality of the sign of the present. In other words, there is a blockage in the totalization of the site of social utterance. This is due to the gap between the pedagogy of symbols of progress and the signs of the present and the ethics of self-enactment or the performativity of discursive practices.

We don't need prefigured and unitarily assigned symbols of identity to which selves must conform. Rather, Bhabha advocates a form of self and social transformation through establishing new conditions of enuncation at the level of the sign where the inter-subjective realm is constituted. That is, we need to redefine signifying relations to a disjunctive present. For Bhabha, this involves a cultural translation through minority subaltern discourses. In Bhabha's thesis, signs become 'performers' that point to the paradoxical nature of modernity through their process of 'time-lagged signification'. They possess the power to make visible a 'postcolonial contra-modernity'. In MacCannell's terms, 'a thinking being that receives a *sign* must think again. A sign informs the thinking being of the existence of another mode of thought' (1992, p. 7).

In light of these issues, how can we further conceptualize the concept of multiculturalism and difference? This study suggests that liberal multiculturalism is really about the politics of assimilation. It assumes we really do live in a meritocracy. Such an understanding of difference implies, as Iris Marion Young (1990, p. 164) notes, 'coming into the game after the rules and standards have already been set, and having to prove oneself according to those rules and standards'. These standards are not culturally and experientially specific, as one would hope, because within a pluralist democracy privileged groups have occluded their own advantage by invoking the ideal of an unsituated, neutral, universal common humanity of self formation in which all can happily participate without regard to differences in race, gender, class, age or sexual orientation.

Difference needs to be understood, as Teresa Ebert (1991) points out, not as clearly marked zones of auto-intelligible experience or a unity of identity within a cultural pluralism. Rather, difference needs to be seen as produced through a politics of signification, that is, through signifying pracices that are both reflective and constitutive of prevailing economic and political relations. Our current ways of seeing and acting are, according to Ebert, being disciplined for us through forms of signification, that is, through ideological frames of sense-making. For instance, too many anthropological accounts of the 'other' use theories of culture that rely on a temporal distancing between the decoding subject and the en-coded object that promote a separation between knower and known – misconceptions that mask the materiality of language and the cotemporality of Self and Other (Fabian, 1983).

To make a claim for a critical multiculturalism is not, in the words of Trinh T. Minh-ha (1991, p. 232), 'to suggest the juxtaposition of several cultures whose frontiers remain intact, nor is it to subscribe to a bland "melting pot" type of attitude that would level all differences. It lies instead, in the intercultural acceptance of risks, unexpected detours, and complexities of relation between break and closure'. Multiculturalism is more about 'maximizing points of interaction rather than harmonizing, balancing, or equillibrating the distribution of bodies, resources, and territories' (Simone, 1989, p. 191). It is about constructing what Stuart Hall (1991) has termed 'new ethnicities' in which identity and difference work against the essentializing of ethnicity. It is the construction of identity grounded in memory, narrative, and history but not contained by them. And finally, it is, in the words of Cornel West (1991a, p. 15), 'not just a matter of talking about difference and heterogeneity, but difference and hetereogeneity as a matter of concrete embodiment in a certain political direction. It's not just a matter of being accused of being a metaphysician of presence, but trying to change the world'. A critical multiculturalism as part of a pedagogy of difference seeks not simply to invert dependent hierarchies of domination but rather to inflect the central categories and assumptions of western rationality towards a displacement of their oppressive political effects. Conflict is not described as a monolinear struggle between the oppressed and the oppressors but as a struggle for spaces of hegemonic rupture out of which new democratizing possibilities may be won and new articulations of identity may be constructed. Since hegemony is not seamless, we must ask: What is the stuff of agency that escapes the act of interpellation? Is it the subject of history? And, if so, whose history is being written and for whose benefit? As Lawrence Grossberg (1992, p. 65) writes, 'Declaring oneself to be on the side of the oppressed too often serves as a way of avoiding the more difficult task of locating the points at which one already identifies and is identified with those who hold power in society.' Grossberg makes some observations with respect to identity formation and historical agency that bear repeating here. First, it is crucial to recognize that the concepts of identity, difference and subjectivity are important but especially – if not mainly – in the context of 'actual historical effectivity'. Identity formation is important in so far as individual agency is contextually enacted within the tendential forces of history. What creates the economies of investment that are inscribed in the shape of the histories that we live? This, for Grossberg, is the crucial issue. How do the sites and spaces of our struggles serve as social agents? Our identity papers may, in fact, be of secondary importance to the sites and apparatuses of agency and the vectors of historically inscribed forces to which our actions are linked. (Examples of these sites, agents, and forces include capitalism, industrialism, technology, democracy, nationalism and religion.) Where are our affective investments located? To what forces are they constitutive or allied? For instance, our identities may be 'radical' or 'progressive' or 'avant-garde', but we may still be investing in the structures of tendential forces of capitalist enslavement that oppress and dominate. One direction for constructing a critical pedagogy is not only a receptiveness to Clough's advice of 'making writing visible as a desiring production, a fantasy to make the impossible a fictional possibility for living' (1992, p. 13) but also empowering particular articulations of agency in order to 'win various identities, subjects, knowledges and actors to specific commitments of agency' (Grossberg, 1992, p. 122). This means decoupling ourselves from the disciplined mobilizations of everyday life in order to rearticulate the sites of our affective investment so that we can 'reenter the strategic politics of the social formation' (1992, p. 394). Desire must be inflected into a transformative politics of hope and action.

CONCLUSION: THINKING THE UNTHOUGHT

> ... America needs a reset button. It needs to be set right.
> Ice-T, *Spin* 1992, p. 74

I would like to conclude by restating the importance of laughter as the underlying referent for a politics of refusal and reinvoking the fool and the itinerant clown as pedagogical agents of resistance – liminal figures that I tried to identify in *Schooling as a Ritual Performance*. Like Bataille (1945), I believe that laughter is a means of destroying transcendent regimes of truth. Laughter contains the germ of liberation as it constantly challenges and subverts the limits of the possible and decentres the self-engendering referentiality of logocentric consciousness. Here, I follow Derrida and especially Bakhtin in their accounts of the ontology of laughter (Kujundzic, 1990). For Bakhtin, laughter and ridicule help us to forget tradition, hierarchies, presence and logos (p. 285). For Derrida, laughter is an 'amnesic affirmation', the forgetting of classical reasoning and a reaching out towards the Other (ibid.). It is a form of writing with the body, a way of deferring closure, of keeping dialogue open in the face of the irreversible march of time.

According to Kujundzic, laughter is 'both the gesture of *reaching the other*, the force that eliminates the monologism and autocracy of logos, and, interpreted as a figure underlying writing, *the very possibility of truth and philosophy*,' (1990, p. 282). While clowns 'do nothing but mimic the masque that the language of power offers as naturalized and "normal" (p. 282), their laughter also serves to decentre power, undermining its own presence and that of the law (pp. 281–2). Laughter can provide a provisional standpoint for a pedagogy of refusal – one that cuts across all strata of social and institutional power. It can serve as a 'teratology' that destabilizes and unsettles the manageable boundaries of western rationalism that so effectively polices the unknown, the awe-full, and the deformed. Laughter conceived as a form of postmodern discourse attempts to 'blow up the law, to break up the "truth"' (Cixous, 1976, p. 288). William Connolly's words are illustrative:

> One may live one's own identity in a more ironic, humorous way, laughing occasionally at one's more ridiculous predispositions and laughing too at the predisposition to universalize an impulse simply because it is one's own. Laughing because one senses that the drive to moralize difference is invested with the wish to reassure oneself that one is what any normal being should be. Laughing at *us*, too, for the same reasons. Laughing in a way that disrupts this persistent link between ethical conviction and self-reassurance while affirming the indispensability of ethical judgement in life. Such laughter pays homage to fugitive elements in life that exceed the organization of identity, otherness, rationality, and autonomy. (1991, p. 180)

Teachers require the defamiliarizing power of laughter that deconstructs the presence of logos, reveals its rhetorical moves, and invites students to construct subjectivities formerly considered to be strange and alien. Indeed, they need this sociological laughter in order to prevent the absolutization of monologic, authoritarian and totalitarian discourses of the centre. Laughter helps to counter totalizing discourses by writing through the body as a transgressive and recusant material act; it celebrates the multiplicity of narrative paractices of the self and struggles against the givenness of the social world. But as oppositional and insurgent intellectuals and fools, teachers must not confuse their political projects with an avant-garde confrontational sensibility, an oppositional posturing or a reactionary retreat into a world of progressive liberal academicism.

The element of refusal in critical pedagogical projects must move beyond mere reformism, beyond a mere resistance to bourgeois authority structures. It must move in the direction of a transformation of our identity as practitioners and the practice of our pedagogy as historical agents for social justice. This is not simply a romantic call to create a rococo individualism out of discursive fragments culled from the consumer marketplace nor is it a call to return to a pre-modern tribalism. Rather, it is a move to decentre and displace the binary moorings upon which western modes of identity are fastened. It is a move to destabilize the dependent hierarchies which privilege whiteness over blackness, men over women, epistemology over ethics, the self over the other.

How can educators begin to map the conditions of their colonized life-worlds such that they may devise alternative conceptions of engaging otherness and new narratives of cultural meaning that rupture the homogenizing stability of a simulated postmodern world, of a social disabledness in which the ritualization of representation assumes centre stage in the theatre of the will? As they increasingly recognize modernity's 'swindle of fulfilment' and 'magnificent bribe', educators need to effect a greater critical detachment from their quest for a viable identity politics in order to acknowledge the internal rifts of bodily desire and how the particularity of individual being can become visible without giving up a common ground of struggle, of paramagnetic solidarity. Within such a common ground of struggle, as in the form, perhaps, of a reconstituted Marxism, how can educators work towards a multiplicity of justices and pluralistic conceptions of politics, ethics, and aesthetics? Joel Kovel (1991, pp. 235–6) reflects the tension of this sentiment when he writes, 'We are all fragments of nothing against the infinite unity of Ultimate Being. Yet despite this unsurpassable truth, the soul's destiny is to be a warrior – for justice, for truth, for nonviolence, for love, for solidarity, for all the manifestations of being – to be a warrior, moreover, whose struggle need have no victory.'

Teachers must work hard at displacing the tendency of schooling to become merely a ritual of self-perpetuation. Pedagogies that fashion themselves in the image of the marketplace invite a vision of citizenship that descends uncannily from the future only to unfold as the burial shroud of the historical past, casting its cold shadow over schools as possible sites for the production of possibility. Pedagogies that are constructed as rituals for the creation of reliable consumers are often adept at concealing the connections between the curriculum and its knowledge-constitutive interests and how these connections are implicated in new and insidious forms of domination. Capitalism, even its post-Fordist variants, has through the logic of consumption and privatization, transformed schools into mausoleums of dead knowledge, into stationary dioramas in which students, sheathed in reifications, are assembled and installed as immobile observers of a world 'out there'. By preventing students from being 'in' the world, educators can use prevailing forms of pedagogy to mould their own anxieties, to veil their own inscrutable desires towards the Other, to engender a mirage that leads students to misrecognize their collaboration in their own ruin, to constitute the Other as the Same. Without a politics of the possible, a social and cultural imaginary – however provisional – that is grounded in an emancipatory politics, educators are deprived of a persistence of vision and narrative path that can lead to the transformation of identities mobilely anchored in the world of publically consumed images and the referential illusion of autonomous agency. This means that educational research must carnivalize the lifeless terrain of empirical research so that the concept of agency is not reduced to frozen statistics but can be embodied in the critical affirmation of the researcher as a laughing fool who challenges the idea of the rational western self-identical subject, wrapped in reifications and rationalizations.

A pedagogy that is not grounded in a preferential option for the disempowered and disenfranchised – 'the wretched of the earth' – only transforms students into vessels for the preparation of new forms of fascism and a grand epic of destruction. This is a master narrative of absence that persists unannounced in all of our pedagogies, even those designed to challenge the cultural imperialism of the most auratic institutions of higher education – and one that cannot be overcome by merely invoking the defamiliarizing tropes and conceits of postmodern social theory.

This study began with the rituals of the Catholic Mass and those that inhere in the movements of our everyday lives. These rituals appeared not only draped in the finery of church vestments but enthroned in the pulsating rhythms of street life and the drudging banality of the classroom. The rhythms of our rituals are changing. They speak more directly to our flesh. Youth are no longer summoned solely by the sound of church bells in the distance but by polyrhythms calling us to older gods. Candles and bones in Brooklyn's Prospect Park or in the back room of a Botanica in Chicago or Los Angeles summon an Eleda. Young people dance with the Saints and Orishas to the sound of drums. The voice of La Carida del Cobre calls us back into our flesh and the drums spirit us across divine borders to rejoin our forgotten hearts.

Peter McLaren
Café Tortoni
Buenos Aires, Argentina
August, 1992

Afterword

Seven years after it first came off the press in 1986, *Schooling as a Ritual Performance* is still a very new book. Those working within critical ethnography have yet to follow McLaren's lead in developing a theory of meaning which is cognizant of insights available to us from postmodernism and yet retentive of the critical project. Because 'postmodernism' has become a bandwagon it is now relatively easy to find ethnographic works which have made partial appropriations of the Derridian and Foucaultian vocabularies. But such partial appropriations tend to be irritatingly ignorant of the consequences which a strict and honest application of the postmodern critique would entail for ethnography, if it were fully articulated within our domain. Journal articles and book chapters written about critical ethnography have been published during the last few years which in one sentence discount any effort to 'represent reality' and provide a reference to Derrida to 'back' the point up, in another sentence blast all moral discourses as arbitrary impositions of power and provide a reference to Foucault for support, and then go on to call for critical ethnography to 'reveal' the way in which cultural forms 'mask [presumably real] relations of domination' so that struggles for 'greater democracy' may be enhanced. This is not the 'active forgetfulness' celebrated by Nietzsche and taken up by Derrida – it is simply dull and embarrassing. Ethnographies, and critical ethnographies particularly, can not and do not avoid claims to represent the world, can not and do not jettison claims to present a moral position – whether they acknowledge this or not.

In light of this state of affairs, where critical ethnographies either fail to take note of what are, in fact, many important insights within the post-structuralist movement, or (much worse) contradict themselves by attempting to join the Post Modern Club while necessarily wearing the wrong clothes from start to finish, *Schooling as a Ritual Performance* stands before us today as a work seven or eight years old in its composition but still ahead of our time. In this afterword I shall attempt to intensify the light about the door McLaren has opened for us in the hopes that future ethnographies may pass through it, much as McLaren himself has done in this book, in their own various directions.

McLAREN'S ROOT METAPHOR: ENFLESHMENT

Postmodernism has provided us with insights which must be acknowledged and used, but it needs to be relocated, reworked, rethought, and, subsuming all, made more precise, if critical ethnography is to continue without contradicting itself. *Schooling as a Ritual Performance* addresses this problematic in the most astonishing ways, particularly given the fact that it was composed so many years ago. McLaren's 'root metaphor' of enfleshed meaning informs most of the other original concepts in the book and will thus be the focus of my discussion. The concept of 'enfleshment' displaces the trendy term 'sign' from a taken-for-granted background context of abstract and passive consciousness to a more convincing framework of the embodied active symbol. McLaren's core insights on embodied meaning then further articulate into an understanding of what ethnographers have long called the interactive setting as a ritually-invoked 'state', an understanding of what we customarily term social integration as 'entrainment', a reconceptualization of discourse as 'performative discourse', and an enriched grasp of cultural power as the 'culture of pain'.

THE FEELING-BODY

The central place given to the 'body' by McLaren in his discussion of meaning and ritual must not be mistaken for a crudely materialist view which reduces 'the mental' by considering it an epiphenomenon of biological processes. McLaren's 'body' is not the body as split from the 'mind', nor is it the 'mind's' projection. It is something ontologically prior to a body–mind distinction and, indeed, McLaren's point is that body does become distinct from mind in a variety of ways which cultural rituals and routines help to shape. Prior to this necessary but ideologically shaped separation is what I choose to call the 'feeling-body'. We can get a clearer idea of the insight here by noting that it combines the phenomenological body with a dialogical understanding of experience.

To grasp the dimension of the 'phenomenological body' incorporated within McLaren's theory of meaning one can refer to the field note excerpt provided in Chapter 3 (pp. 120) where McLaren's own thoughts and feelings are described in relation to the postures and gestures he was making use of when interacting with his subjects of study. Meaning is *felt* in the body, in a state coming close to a fusion of subjectivity and materiality. It is this type of state, described from a first person perspective in the passage just referred to, with which McLaren is concerned when describing the rituals and routines within his school. While the postmodern critique of signs and sign usage prioritize language in the sense of speech and writing, McLaren has relocated the primary unit of meaning in the *performing* body, where each configuration of feeling, thought, posture and motion is a symbol. Gesture and posture are McLaren's 'units' of meaning, but gesture and posture in a sense which retains their first-person, phenomenological, properties: the felt unity of emotions, desires and body position.

THE DIALOGICAL CONSTITUTION OF THE FEELING-BODY

Yet the analogy from phenomenology must not be pressed too hard, and this for three reasons. First of all, it is the feeling-body considered from first, second and third person positions which McLaren introduces us to, and not only as experienced within the first person position prioritized by phenomenology. The feeling-body is conceived of *intersubjectively* in *Schooling as a Ritual Performance*. The passages which describe McLaren's own bodily configurations and their associated feelings and thoughts work reflexively within his text to show us how first, second, *and* third person perspectives undergird the interactive settings described elsewhere from the observer position (third person) of the ethnographer. In addition, they show us how intersubjectivity actually constitutes the feeling-body, for McLaren's body movements and gestures were all constructed in reference to his audience – to the students he was interacting with. The enfleshment of meaning is dialogical; from the start it contains otherness in a primordial way.

Secondly, the body symbol is not to be conceived as a 'sign', intersubjective in origin or not, which a passive consciousness apprehends as 'present' to it, but rather as an expressive act whose impetus (desire) only exists through its articulation. Intentionality, subjectivity, and desire are not prior to the expressive act but come to be through that act. In McLaren's own words 'Gestures ... are not weak translations of thoughts. Gestures of resistance *are* student anger, fear and refusal expressed in an incarnate or corporeal mode' (Chapter 4, p. 149). This is not an entirely new idea, for it is a theme which played a major role in the expressivist reaction against the Enlightenment (as in Herder's philosophy) and a theme informing Hegel's concept of Geist and Marx's concept of praxis. It is a 'postmodern' theme in so far as it has been appealed to by those unsettled with the Enlightenment (modernist) conception of representative knowledge since the time of the Enlightenment itself. It receives a new twist with McLaren, however, through its synthesis with the idea of the feeling-body as symbol and its incorporation of Mead's dialogical theories of thought. As McLaren writes elsewhere, thought–feeling complexes can be conceived as 'virtual gestures'.

This synthesis of expressivist themes within a dialogical framework promises much for cultural and semiotic theory. For one thing, it is a way of understanding how the various *parts* of a meaningful act always implicate a *whole*. The parts of symbolic action, the particular tones of voice used, the particular words, the particular movements of eye, arm, trunk and leg, come forth together as an expressive whole. This is one reason why McLaren can call feeling-body states 'symbols'. They implicate a unity through all their diversity. And what provides them with this unity? The impetus, the motivation, the desire complex which, however, only is as it comes forth; only is as embodied. McLaren's 'unit of meaning', then, is the act which is always embodied. As he says, 'symbols perform'.

But the picture is still incomplete. The third reason we must move beyond the analogy from phenomenology is that McLaren is not writing of autonomous, self-sufficient embodiments of meaning but rather of meanings constituted by structure. We have the structuralist insight into the nature of symbols here with two added provisos: 'structure' is a set of felt relations to others (not a set of abstract relations between 'signs'), and 'structure' is the paradigmatic illocution carried by all meaningful acts. The first proviso involves the category of intersubjectivity pretty much as I have already discussed it. Gestures embody the social other within them. Feeling states are shaped by the perspectives of others taken by the actor as she acts. Otherness is felt in the body, and thus desire, as McLaren insists, will take forms shaped by social relations. The second proviso brings us back to whole–part relationships. All meaningful acts build upon primordial states of gesture and posture which they bring into being, and these states of gesture and posture *claim* an entire order of feeling-bodies, a social order with associated, holistic, views of the world. Meaningful acts are situated within social realms they simultaneously claim to create; virtual worlds open other counter-claims of others. Meaningful acts claim normative force upon others and depend upon a prescribed range of responses from others to retain themselves as valid symbols. Thus, the gesture and posture which will be found at the core of all symbolic acts are existential claims – configurations of feeling in which a risk to the self is always present. The sections of this book which discuss the paradigmatic (the whole) and syntagmatic (order of parts), the sections on ritual as 'container', and the considerations of ritual as constitutive of the 'canopies' within which they themselves reside, all express this idea.

POSTMODERN THEMES RECONCEPTUALIZED

I think I have presented key portions of the 'root metaphor' informing *Schooling as a Ritual Performance* in the paragraphs above. Now I shall briefly indicate some of the additional advances this work provides. These are many and I will only be able to mention a few. First, McLaren writes of individuals as having 'frequencies' which may become 'synchronized' in interactions. The concept of enfleshment, where social relations become 'inscribed' upon actors to produce a 'culture of pain' gives this metaphor of the oscillation potent sense. It is a refreshing and empowering view of individuality in social contexts. It captures the dialectic of agency and structure from a new angle, for the inscriptions of culture upon us only take place when we *act* to embody them.

Second, McLaren also uses the term 'states' to replace that of 'setting' or 'normative order'. Once again, it is the idea of the feeling-body which gives this new term sense. The 'streetcorner state', the 'student state', and so on, are paradigmatic realms in which a number of possible feeling states, a number of possible identities, are allowed and others excluded. Each possibility has its own implications in terms of how the actors *feel*. The worst implication for any individual is that none of the possibilities are possible *for them*. As McLaren writes in one passage, 'one can feel literally like a nothing' if a particular setting, or state, seems to offer one no place and appears to be something only for 'others' to reside within. 'States' links the insights carried by considering individuals as having 'frequencies' to the dialogical constitution of the feeling-body.

Third, rituals for McLaren are what bring about, maintain, and shift, the paradigmatic horizons within which people act and feel. His use of 'micro-ritual' contributes much to what we mean by social integration, and his use of 'macro-ritual' contributes to our understanding of system integration.

Finally, postmodern themes appear in importantly new articulations within *Schooling as a Ritual Performance*. Consider McLaren's extensive use of the concept of liminality. His deployment of this concept through the book acknowledges postmodernism's claim that all signs are polysemenous, multi-valent, etched over a gaping ontological void. It is the penetration of the social other into the heart of the impetus to act that gives rise to the perpetual ambiguity of the symbol. Each symbolic act, and all the feeling states embodied within it, indicate only possibilities and never actualities. In Hegelian or Meadian terms, it is the dependence of the self-claim, which partially motivates all acts, upon the response of the social other – and the uncertainty which must always accompany both the actor's expectations and interpretations of this response – which makes all symbols intrinsically ambiguous. They are claims to totality, to holistic views of life and the world, which yet can never be known in their totality because of the otherness with which they are infused. Like the texts produced by scholars, a drive towards totality and closure informs all social acts, but it is a drive which can never reach its goal. Rituals help to ward off uncertainty and keep forms of fear at bay by restricting the possible responses of the other and thus by restricting modes of embodying feeling and desire. But rituals never construct a totally certain, enclosed, world; they can always be refused or deconstructed, as in the case of the 'class clown', so successfully analysed by McLaren. The liminal is a sort of ontological suspicion that one may really in fact 'be nothing', that no possible worlds really have any ground, that a void does indeed underlie all the worlds we work so hard to construct and maintain. Yet it is this suspicion which serves as the well-spring for acts of creativity, and resistance.

RETAINING CRITIQUE

If McLaren's use of the concept of liminality is, as he calls it, 'Derrida's aporia somanticized', what remains of critique? If the void awaits performative discourses as much as it does linguistic ones, what ground exists for a critique of social life? This question, of course, is the problem of the day for those engaged in critical ethnography and an answer is not easily forthcoming. But McLaren's relocation of postmodernist themes is very promising with respect to this issue. When considered as bodily feeling states, symbols imply their own criteria, their own ground. Simply put, some feel better than others. In one place McLaren indicates that the streetcorner state offers a better match between the physical and social bodies than does the student state, for most of the students he studied at any rate. But the 'street state' owes its existence to other states which feel worse. Its symbols are critique, which is partially why they feel better, and provide a better match. They feel better because they point forward, to other possible socially constructed states, ultimately to a better society. The issue begs more investigation on a massive scale but McLaren provides us with a starting point, something postmodernism has failed to do in most of its other articulations.

Phil Francis Carpsecken
Houston

Notes

1 Education as a cultural system

1 While one hesitates to burden the syntax of ritual discourse with yet another neologism, Grimes's term 'ritology' – meaning the study of ritual – is a fecund one given the conceptual orientation of this study. Grimes, however, acknowledges that the word is 'a bit of rhetorical magic'. For a further discussion of ritology, see Ronald L. Grimes, *Beginnings In Ritual Studies*, Washington, DC, University Press of America, 1982.

2 Dean MacCannell, *The Tourist: A New Theory of the Leisure Class*, New York, Schocken, 1976. See also F.E. Manning, 'Cosmos and chaos: celebration in the modern world', in F.E. Manning (ed.), *The Celebration of Society*, Bowling Green, Ohio, Bowling Green University Popular Press, and London, Ontario, Congress of Social and Humanistic Studies, 1983, p. 6.

3 For an important overview of Aronowitz's position, see Henry A. Giroux, 'Marxism and schooling: the limits of radical discourse', *Educational Theory*, vol. 34, no. 2, 1984, pp. 113–35.

4 Cited in Andrew M. Greeley, *Unsecular Man: The Persistence of Religion*, New York, Schocken, 1972, p. 55. Original quote appears in Clifford Geertz, 'Religion as a cultural system', in Donald Cutler (ed.), *The Religious Situation: 1968*, Boston, Beacon Press, 1968, p. 641.

5 First and foremost, *ritual symbols* may be understood as types of mediating devices that enable individuals to shape reality. Such symbols possess a great connotative power by the very fact that they are multivalent, fissile, incongruous, polysemous, ineffable, imponderable and intangible. Rituals are able to enter into symbolic action and are able to circulate complex world views (Munn, 1973, p. 580). They are able to condense the representation of many things by a single formulation, unify disparate significata and polarize meaning into normative and psychological poles (Turner, 1979b, pp. 146–7). Through an interchange between the affective and normative poles of the ritual symbol, the obligatory is made desirable (Turner, 1974c, p. 55), the conceptual is given the power of the experiential, and the experiential is given the guidance of the conceptual (Rappaport, 1979, p. 212).

Symbols are inherently ambiguous and possess an ideological character (Cohen, 1979, p.103; Murphy, 1979, p. 319; Duncan, 1968, pp. 7–8; Eco, 1982, pp. 28–9). They often serve to integrate cultural meanings and may dominate a conceptual system by providing frames or templates for symbolic formulation in different domains. Key symbols can summarize or 'collapse' complex experience; they possess conceptual or action elaborating power (Ortner, 1973). Symbols have the power to structure the imagination (Baum, 1975) and proclaim or frame disorder as well as order by invoking a surplus of signifiers (Babcock, 1978b).

The term *ethos* is used in this study to refer to the tone, character, mood and quality of a group's life (Geertz, 1957). A symbol system refers to 'the web-like relations among symbols and between symbols and other nonsymbolic elements' (Grimes, 1976, p. 44).

Victor Turner (1979b) has given vigour to the articulation of contemporary ritual through his Van Gennepian concepts of *liminal* and *liminoid*. Liminality is the second state in Turner's basically tripartite processual structure of ritual consisting of separation, margin or limen, and reaggregation. I shall describe these two important concepts by quoting Turner directly:

> *Liminality* (From Lat. *limen*, a threshold): The state and process of mid-transition in a rite of passage. During the liminal period, the characteristics of the *liminars* (the ritual subjects in this phase) are ambiguous, for they pass through a cultural realm that has few or none of the attributes of the past or coming state. Liminars are betwixt and between. The liminal state has frequently been likened to death; to being in the womb; to invisibility, darkness, bisexuality, and the wilderness (V. Turner, 1969, pp. 94–96). Liminars are stripped of status and authority, removed from a social structure maintained and sanctioned by power and force, and leveled to a homogeneous social state through discipline and ordeal. . . . Much of what has been bound by social structure is liberated, notably the sense of comradeship and communion, or communitas. (1979b, p. 149).

Closely resembling the concept of 'liminal', the term 'liminoid' refers to particular qualities of leisure – genres and their concomitant symbolic forms and manifestations in complex industrial societies. Again, in Turner's words, the term liminoid describes:

> the many genres found in modern industrial leisure that have features resembling those of liminality. These genres are akin to the ritually liminal, but not identical with it. They often represent the dismembering of the liminal, for various components that are joined in liminal situations split off to pursue separate destinies as specialized genres – for example, theatre, ballet, film, the novel, poetry, music, and art, both popular and classical in every case, and pilgrimage. These genres develop most characteristically outside the central economic and political processes, along their margins, on

their interfaces, in their tacit dimensions. They are plural, fragmentary (from the point of view of the total inventory of liminoid
thoughts, words, and deeds), experimental, idiosyncratic, quirky,
subversive, utopian and characteristically produced and consumed
by identifiable individuals, in contrast to liminal phenomena (see
V. Turner, 1976), which are often anonymous or divine in origin
(1979b, p. 153).

Liminality and communitas are sometimes referred to as social
antistructure. The antistructure is composed of human bonds that exist
outside the structure of roles, statuses and positions within the society.
The antistructure is a state of undifferentiated, homogeneous
humankindness (Holmes, 1973b, p. 389).

Just as root paradigms or root metaphors are expansions of symbols,
social dramas are expansions of root paradigms. As 'cultural transliterations of genetic codes' (Turner, 1974e, p. 67), root paradigms
'exist in the heads' of the main actors in a social drama. Root paradigms
can also become 'enacted' as part of key scenarios or social dramas.
Holmes says that social dramas are related

> to that antistructure necessary for the production of root metaphors,
> constellations of connected symbols. The root metaphors orient the
> identity of a people ... [and are] ... consequently ... expanded,
> as I see it, into the social dramas which constitute the 'literature'
> of a people and feed the creative imagination. (1977a, p. 89).

The concept of social drama is developed by Turner as a four-phased
series of acts: breach, crisis, redressive action and reintegration or
recognition of schism; it is a type of unconscious action paradigm
corresponding somewhat to Aristotle's description of tragedy in the
Poetics. Urban Holmes offers us a pithy summary of social drama:

> In the breach the pattern of social interaction prescribed by the struc-
> tures of the system break down. The crisis that results has a liminal
> quality, which surrenders the normative patterns of social life to a
> deeper level of meaning. It is no longer 'business as usual.' In the
> redressive action some perduring resource takes over and resolves
> the failure in human interaction. As I have already suggested, this
> can be a structural resource at a somewhat deeper level or it can
> throw the culture back into the experience of communitas and mythic
> or symbolic reality in the anti-structure. At this latter, deeper level
> the ritual process is particularly important. Reintegration involves
> a reconstitution and appraisal of the structures of the society and
> should bring about change. (1977b, p. 206).

Social dramas are, reports, Turner, 'units of aharmonic or dis-
harmonic process, arising in conflict situations' (1974e, p. 37). They
constitute 'our native way of manifesting ourselves to ourselves and,
of declaring where power and meaning lie and how they are distributed'
(1982a, p. 78). In its formal development, Turner regards the social
drama 'as a process of converting particular values and ends, distributed

over a range of actors, into a system (which is always temporary and provisional) of shared or consensual meaning' (ibid., p.75). Ritual, as Holmes points out, 'is central to the articulation and formulation of the social drama' (1977b, p. 207). As such, ritual becomes a 'key to the corporate intentionality of a community' (ibid.).

The term *root paradigm* is similar to Stephen Pepper's famous concept of root metaphor. Root paradigms may be considered as types of 'master metaphors' – as expansions of symbols existing in ritualized performances and eventually forming the nodal images of the social drama.

The term root paradigm is used after Victor Turner as follows:

A higher-order concept than symbols, root paradigms are certain consciously recognized (though not consciously grasped) cultural models for behaviour that exist in the heads of the main actors in a social drama, whether in a small group or on the stage of history ... (A prime example of a root paradigm is the Way of the Cross). They represent the goals of man as a species, where they prevail over particular interests – the general good over the individual welfare. They are, as it were, the cultural transliterations of genetic codes; that is, they represent the species life raised to the more complex and symbolic organizational level of culture, and are concerned with fundamental assumptions underlying the human societal bond, with preconditions of communitas ...

Root paradigms are shown in behaviour which appears to be freely chosen but resolves at length into a total pattern. They go beyond the cognitive, and even the moral, to the existential domain, and in so doing become clothed with allusiveness, implicitness, and metaphor. They reach down to the irreducible life stances of individuals, passing beneath conscious prehension to a fiduciary hold on what the individual senses to be axiomatic values, matters literally of life and death. Root paradigms emerge at life crises, whether of groups or individuals, whether institutionalized or compelled by unforeseen events. One cannot escape their presence or their consequences .... In cultures deeply influenced by Christian beliefs and practices, for example, the *via crucis*–Resurrection paradigm seems to have affected the behaviour of a number of major historical figures ... (1979b, pp. 148-9)

6 Pioneering work being done on the topic of schooling, culture and resistance can be found in work that has been influenced by the Centre for Contemporary Cultural Studies, an independent research and postgraduate unit in the Faculty of Arts, University of Birmingham. Work published by the Open University is also excellent in this regard. One cannot ignore the pathfinding efforts of writers such as Stuart Hall, Geoff Whitty, Paul Willis, Dick Hebdige, Tony Jefferson, John Clarke, R. Johnson and others. Excellent work on schooling and culture is also being carried out in the US, most notably by Michael Apple and Henry Giroux. Giroux's work constitutes a virtuoso exposition and analysis of schooling, power and resistance. From 1985-93, Miami University of Ohio's Center for Education and Cultural Studies has developed

a body of research that has examined student resistance, identity formation and subjectivity in the context of schooling and popular culture. See Giroux and McLaren (1989, 1991).

7   Ernest Becker, *The Lost Science of Man*, New York, George Braziller, 1971, pp. 81-2. As quoted in L.L. Langness, *The Study of Culture*, San Francisco, Chandler & Sharp, 1974, p. 73.

8   Jack Goody, "Against ritual": loosely structured thoughts on a loosely defined topic', in Sally Falk Moore and Barbara Myerhoff (eds), *Secular Ritual*, Amsterdam, Royal Van Gorcum, 1977, pp. 25-35. I would like to emphasize here that anti-ritual sentiment is not a blanket category; there are few writers who attempt to marshall a 'knockdown' argument against ritual. I am not attempting to set up straw men; rather, I am commenting upon a general prejudice against the scientific study of ritual's role in industrial (secular) settings.

9   See Ronald Grimes, 'Ritual and illness', *Canadian Journal of Community Mental Health*, vol. 3, no. 1, Spring, 1984, pp. 55-65.

10   Ronald Grimes, 'Ritual studies', in Mircea Eliade (ed.), *Encyclopedia of Religion*, 1987, vol. 12, pp. 422-5, New York, Macmillan and the Free Press.

11   Ibid.

12   Ronald Grimes, 'Research in Ritual Studies: A Programmatic Essay', in the ATLA Bibliography Series 14, Metuchen, NJ, and London, Scarecrow Press.

13   Ibid.

14   For perceptive and thorough discussions of modern secular rituals, see: Ronald L. Grimes, 'The Actor's Lab; the roots of human action', *Canadian Theatre Review*, vol. 22, 1979, pp. 9-19; Barbara Myerhoff, *Number Our Days*, New York, Simon & Schuster, 1979; *Symbol and Politics in Communal Ideology*, Sally Falk Moore and Barbara Myerhoff (eds), Ithaca, New York, Cornell University Press, 1975; William Partridge, *The Hippie Ghetto: The Natural History of a Subculture*, New York, Holt, Rinehart & Winston, 1972; Barbara Myerhoff and Deena Metzger, 'The journal as activity and genre: on listening to the silent laughter of Mozart', *Semiotica*, vol. 30, nos. 1/2, 1980, pp. 97-114.

15   Conrad P. Kottak, 'Rituals at McDonald's', *Journal of American Culture*, vol. 1, no. 2, 1976, pp. 370-6.

16   The work of Roland Delattre (1978, 1979) is of major significance in contemporary ritology. Delattre argues that ritual rhythms (or motions through which individuals commonly engage the world) are paradigmatic of how human beings construct reality and develop their moral attributes. Thus, he stresses the humanity-shaping and reality-constituting powers of ritual. In Delattre's thesis, a sense of reality is articulated for individuals as they are engaged by ritual rhythms (a process which Delattre claims is as influential as being exposed to the ethos, mythology, ideology or world view of a prevailing culture). Delattre contends that ritual is an *articulation* of our humanity rather than an expression of it. More than a simplified symbolic expression or rendering of something that already exists, a ritual *brings into being*

something which otherwise would not be. Put simply, this means that a ritual cannot be said to express something precisely because there is no 'thing' that can be expressed outside of the ritual itself. When we say that a particular ritual expresses something, *we fall into the trap of trying to separate the content of a ritual from its form*. A ritual does not express; rather, a ritual *articulates*. Delattre follows Hofstadter's (1965) concept of articulation as bringing about forms and joints and building up an organized product, with interconnected members, where beforehand there was only the potentiality for it. Articulation is the process by which a living impulse works itself out (Delattre, 1979, p. 38).

17 See Grimes (1982a, p. 32). For a wide spectrum of approaches to ritual, see Richard Schechner and Mady Schuman (eds), *Ritual, Play and Performance: Readings in the Social Sciences/Theatre*, New York, Seabury Press, 1976.

18 Grimes's soft definition of ritual, which he terms 'ritualization', reads: 'Ritualizing transpires as animated persons enact formative gestures in the fact of receptivity during crucial times in founded places' (1982a, p. 55).

Other useful definitions of ritual are as follows: Ritual: '*rule-governed activity of a symbolic character which draws the attention of its participants to objects of thought and feeling which they hold to be of special significance*' (Lukes, 1975, p.291); 'Ritual is the symbolic use of bodily movement and gesture in a social situation to express and articulate meaning' (Bocock, 1974, p. 37); a ritual is: 'nondiscursive gestural language, institutionalized for regular occasions, to state sentiments and mystiques that a group values and needs' (Klapp, 1969, p. 121); a ritual is: 'the acting out of metaphoric predication upon inchoate pronouns which are in need of movement' (Fernandez, 1972, p. 56); a ritual is: 'the performance of a more or less invariant sequences of formal acts and utterances not encoded by the performer' (Rappaport, 1980, pp. 62–3); a ritual is: an 'intermediary process between analogic and digital commmunication, simulating . . . message material but in a repetitive and stylized manner that hangs between analogue and symbol' (Watzlawick *et al.*, 1967, p. 104); a ritual is: 'a relatively rigid pattern of acts specific to a situation which construct a framework of meaning over and beyond the specific situational meanings' (Bernstein *et al.*, 1966, p. 429); rituals are: 'formal behaviour prescribed for occasions not given over to technological routine that have reference to mystical beings or powers' (Turner, 1967, p. 19); rituals are: 'Those carefully rehearsed symbolic motions and gestures through which we regularly go, in which we articulate the felt shape and rhythm of our humanity and of reality as we experience it, and by means of which we negotiate the terms of conditions for our presence among and our participation in the plurality of realities through which our humanity makes its passage' (Delattre, 1978, p. 282); a ritual is: '*a means of performing the way things ought to be in conscious tension to the way things are in such a way that this ritualized perfection is recollected in the ordinary, uncontrolled, course of things*' (italics original) (Smith, 1982, p. 63); and rituals are: 'dramatic actions performed in imitation of models' (Courtney, 1982, p.23).

2 The setting

1 *Completion Campaign Handbook* of the Ontario English Catholic Teachers' Association, 1971.

2 Ibid.

3 Reverend Laurence K. Shook, 'The relevance of Catholic education in the society of today', address by the president of the Pontifical Institute of Medieval Studies delivered at the 26th annual conference of the English Catholic Education Association of Ontario, 9 April 1970.

4 Ibid.

5 Ibid.

6 Ibid.

7 D.E. Thomsen, 'The quotable pope at CERN', *Science News*, vol. 122, no. 7, 14 August 1982, p. 109.

8 Elaine Carey, 'Portuguese community struggles to eliminate its feeling of isolation', *Toronto Star*, 1 September 1983.

9 *The Globe and Mail* (Toronto), 28 April 1983.

10 Carey, op. cit.

11 John Slinger, *The Globe and Mail* (Toronto), 26 August 1971.

12 Ibid.

13 Carey, op. cit.

14 Ibid.

15 The Every Student Survey, Toronto Board of Education, 1975.

16 M. Crespi, 'Portuguese immigrants: economic strategies and the need for appropriate education', Proceedings from the Fourth National Portuguese Conference, USA, 1979.

17 Pedro da Cunha, 'The dropout syndrome among Portuguese youth', n.d.

18 Seminar report from St Helen's Portuguese Community Centre, Toronto, November 1973.

19 Da Cunha, op. cit.

20 Seminar report, op.cit.

21 Carey, op.cit.

22 Dr Wallace E. Lambert, 'Portuguese child rearing values: cross national analysis', paper given at the National Conference on the Portuguese Experience in the United States, n.d.

23 Ibid.

24 Ibid.

25 Ibid.

26 Raymond F. Bronowicz, 'Towards a Catholic identity', *Homiletic and Pastoral Review*, vol. 82, no. 6, 1982, p.68.

27 Da Cunha, op. cit.

28 Ibid.

29 Ibid.

30 Ibid.

31 Ibid.

32 Ibid.

33 *Toronto Star*, 25 April 1977.

34 Carey, op. cit.
35 Ibid.
36 Anna Maria Coelho, 'Conflicts and adjustment of Portuguese youth in school, home and community', Toronto Board of Education Library, 1977.

3 The structure of conformity

1 I am using the term liminal servant after Urban T. Holmes's description of the priest. See Urban T. Holmes, *The Priest in Community: Exploring the Roots of Ministry*, New York, Seabury Press, 1978.

4 The antistructure of resistance

1 Some of the best work on the relationship between the body and knowledge can be found in the writings of Merleau-Ponty. And few commentators are better versed in the correspondence between the body and power than Michel Foucault.

5 Making Catholics

1 The term *civitas* is used by Grimes to designate symbols of city mindedness or symbols aimed at engendering co-operation and respect among citizens. The term *civilitas* refers to symbols with governmental and political overtones. *Ecclesia* and *ethnos* are terms used to denote religious and ethnic symbols respectively. See Grimes, *Symbol and Conquest*, Ithaca, New York, Cornell University Press, 1976, p. 43.
2 Peter McLaren, 'Towards a pedagogy of liberation: Peter McLaren interviews Henry Giroux', *Borderlines*, no. 2, 1985, pp. 10–12.

6 Summary, recommendations and reflections

1 For a lucid commentary on *Laborem Exercens* and the response of the Canadian bishops to the current economic crisis, see *Ethics and Economics: Canada's Catholic Bishops on the Economic Crisis* by Gregory Baum and Duncan Cameron, Toronto, James Lorimer & Co., 1984. In this book Baum discusses public reaction to the Catholic bishops' 1983 New Year's Statement, 'Ethical reflections on the economic crisis,' and the ongoing debate that it provoked across the country. Saddled by the labels 'red' or 'Marxist' in some sectors of Canadian society, statements made by the Social Affairs Commission of the Canadian Conference of Catholic Bishops called critical attention to the structural crisis in the international system of capitalism. The bishops were strong in their insistence on the priority of labour over capital. Baum describes this event as

the emergence of a new Catholic social theory, first in Latin America and then in the world Church, which has developed its own critique of capitalism on the basis of biblical prophecy, the experiences of oppressed peoples, and traditional Catholic social teaching. This new Catholic social theory has been worked out through critical dialogue with Marxist ideas, but it has created its own independent orientation and its own original vocabulary. Its foundation is theological. Its principal bias is that the God of the Bible is partial – that God stands on the side of the poor and oppressed against the empires of this world. (pp. 65–6)

2 Victor Turner, 'Dewey, Dilthey, and drama: an essay in the anthropology of experience', in Victor Turner and Edward M. Burner (eds), *The Anthropology of Experience*, Urbana and Chicago, University of Illinois Press, 1985. For a good example of Dewey's rejection of the dualism of mind and body, see his *Democracy and Education*, New York, Macmillan and the Free Press, 1966, pp. 141–4.

3 Grimes, 'The poetics of monotony', unpublished paper. Grimes and others who have written on the topic of ritual frequently highlight ritual's dramatic and processual characteristics. But social action is not simply a 'given' but a lived historical moment. The majority of ritual scholars do not follow the tenets of critical ethnography. Their work often ignores how macro-social concepts such as class, power, and domination can sensitize the researcher to the fullest range of agenda in micro-social interaction and drama. A greater understanding and appreciation of Marxist anthropology is needed by these scholars in order to situate their work in a discourse of critique and possibility.

Coda

1 A shortened version of this Postscript appears in Peter McLaren, 'Collisions with Otherness; Multiculturalism, the Politics of Difference, and the Ethnographer as Nomad,' *The American Journal of Semiotics*, in press. The section dealing with multiculturalism may also be found in Peter McLaren, 'Critical Pedagogy, Multiculturalism and Politics of Risk and Resistance: A Response to Kelly and Portelli,' *Journal of Education*, vol. 17, no. 3, 1991, pp. 29–59. Other sections appear in Peter McLaren, 'Multiculturalism and the Postmodern Critique: Towards a Pedagogy of Resistance and Transformation, *Cultural Studies*, vol. 7, no. 1 (January, 1993), pp. 118–46 and Henry A. Giroux and Peter McLaren (eds) *Between Borders: Pedagogy and Politics in Cultural Studies*, New York and London, Routledge.

2 For a brilliant treatment of Bakhtin's work in relation to the discourse of resistance and its implications for educators, see Witkowski, 1990.

3 At a recent Umbanda ritual in Brazil – 'Roda de Exús' – I found the laughter of those possessed by spirits of prostitutes to serve as a rupturing device that ripped through the social norms and cultural proprieties of

the larger society that prevailed outside of the Favella where the ritual was held. The ceremony included the participation of many of those inhabitants who were socially marginalized – gays, lesbians, and prostitutes – and served as a liminal space where communitas occurred and affection could be displayed openly among all those who participated in and observed the ritual.

Bibliography

Agar, Michael (1977), 'Into that whole ritual thing: ritualistic drug use among urban American heroin addicts', in M. Du Toit (ed.), *Drugs, Rituals, and Altered States of Consciousness*, Rotterdam, A. A. Balkema, pp. 137–48.

Anderson, Robert (1976), *The Cultural Context: An Introduction to Cultural Anthropology*, Minneapolis, Minnesota, Burgess Publishing Company.

Anyon, Jean (1980), 'Social class and the hidden curriculum of work', *Journal of Education*, vol. 162, pp. 67–92.

Apple, Michael (1978), 'The new sociology of education: analyzing cultural and economic reproduction', *Harvard Educational Review*, vol. 48, no. 4, pp. 495–503.

Apple, Michael (1979), *Ideology and Curriculum*, London, Routledge & Kegan Paul.

Apple, Michael (1982), *Education and Power*, London, Routledge & Kegan Paul.

Aronowitz, S. (1977), 'Marx, Braverman and the logic of capital', *The Insurgent Sociologist*, vol. 8, pp. 126–46.

Aronowitz, S. (1981), *The Crisis in Historical Materialism*, South Hadley, Mass., Bergin & Garvey.

Aronowitz, S. (1988), 'Foreword', in Alain Touraine, *Return of the Actor*, Minneapolis, Minn., University of Minnesota Press, pp. vii–xx.

Austin, J.L. (1965), *How To Do Things With Words*, ed. J.O. Urmson and Marina Sbisà, Oxford, Clarendon Press, 2nd edn.

Babcock, Barbara (1978a), 'Introduction', in Barbara Babcock (ed.), *The Reversible World: Symbolic Inversion in Art and Society*, Ithaca, New York, Cornell University Press, pp. 495–503.

Babcock, Barbara (1978b), 'Too many, too few: ritual modes of signification', *Semiotica*, vol. 23, no.s. 3/4, pp. 291–301.

Barnett, Steve and Silverman, Martin (1979), *Ideology and Everyday Life: Anthropology, Neo Marxist Thought and the Problem of the Social Whole*, Ann Arbor, University of Michigan Press.

Barth, Frederick (1975), *Ritual and Knowledge Among the Baktaman of New Guinea*, New Haven, Conn., Yale University Press.

Barthes, R. (1967), *Elements of Semiology*, London, Jonathan Cape.

Barthes, R. (1972), *Mythologies*, London, Jonathan Cape.

Bataille, Georges (1945), *Sur Nietzsche*, Paris, Gallimard.

Bates J.A.V. (1975), 'The communicative hand', in Jonathan Benthall and Ted Polhemus (eds), *The Body as a Medium of Expression*, London, Allen Lane.

Bateson, Gregory (1958), *Naven*, Stanford, Calif., Stanford University Press.

Bateson, Gregory (1972), *Steps to the Ecology of Mind*, San Francisco, Chandler.

Baudrillard, Jean (1983), *In the Shadow of the Silent Majorities*, translated by Paul Fess, Paul Patton and John Johnston, New York, Semiotext(e), Columbia University.

Baudrillard, Jean (1990), *Seduction*, New York, St Martin's Press.

Bauer, David H. (1979), 'As children see it', in K. Yamamoto (ed.), *Children in Time and Space*, New York, Teachers College Press, pp. 21–58.

Baum, Gregory (1975), *Religion and Alienation: A Theological Reading of Sociology*, New York, Paulist Press.

Baum, Gregory (1979), *The Social Imperative: Essays on the Critical Issues that Confront the Christian Churches*, New York, Paulist Press.

Baum, Gregory and Cameron, Duncan (1984), *Ethics and Economics: Canada's Catholic Bishops on the Economic Crisis*, Toronto, James Lorimer & Co.

Bauman, R. (1972), 'An ethnographic framework for the investigation of communicative behaviour', in R.D. Abraham and R. Troike (eds), *Language and Cultural Diversity*, Englewood Cliffs, New Jersey, Prentice-Hall, pp. 154–66.

Beattie, J.H.M. (1966a), 'Ritual and social change', *Man*, n.s., vol. 1, no. 1, pp. 60–74.

Beattie, J.H.M. (1966b), 'On understanding ritual', in Bryan R. Wilson (ed.), *On Rationality: Key Concepts in the Social Sciences*, New York, Harper & Row.

Beck, Brenda (1978), 'The metaphor as a mediator between semantic and analogic modes of thought', *Current Anthropology*, vol. 19, no. 1, pp. 83–97.

Becker, Ernest (1971), *The Lost Science of Man*, New York, George Braziller.

Becker, Ernest (1973), *The Denial of Death*, New York, Free Press.

Becker, Ernest (1975), *Escape from Evil*, New York, Free Press.

Beidelman, T.O. (1981), 'The Nuer concept of *Thek* and the meaning of sin: expiation, translation, and social structure, *History of Religions*, vol. 21, no. 2, pp. 126–55.

Bellah, Robert N. (1970), 'Christianity and symbolic realism', *Journal for the Scientific Study of Religion*, vol. 9, no. 2, pp. 89–99.

Bellah, Robert N. (1983), 'Cultural vision and the human future', *Teachers College Record*, vol. 82, no. 3, pp. 497–506.

Benedict, Ruth (1934), 'Ritual', in Edwin R.A. Seligman and Alvin Johnson (eds), *Encyclopaedia of the Social Sciences*, vol. 13, New York, Macmillan, pp. 396–7.

Bennett, Lance W. (1980), 'Myth, ritual and political control', *Journal of Communication*, vol. 30, no. 4, pp.166–79.

Berger, Peter (1967), *The Sacred Canopy: Elements of a Sociological Theory of Religion*, Garden City, New York, Doubleday.

Berger, Peter (1979), *The Heretical Imperative*, New York, Anchor Books, Doubleday.

Berger, Peter and Luckmann, Thomas (1967), *The Social Construction of Reality: A Treatise on the Sociology of Knowledge*, New York, Anchor Books, Doubleday.

Berger, Peter and Pullberg, Stanley (1965), 'Reification and the sociological critique of consciousness', *History and Theory: Studies in the Philosophy of History*, vol. 4, pp. 196–211.

Bernstein, Basil (1977), *Class, Codes and Control, Volume 3: Towards a Theory of Educational Transmission*, London, Routledge & Kegan Paul.

Bernstein, Basil (1982), 'Codes, modalities and the process of cultural reproduction: a model', in Michael Apple (ed.), *Cultural and Economic Reproduction in Education*, London, Routledge & Kegan Paul, pp. 304–55.

Bernstein, Basil *et al.* (1966) 'Ritual in education', *Philosophical Transactions of the Royal Society of London*, Series B, vol. 251, no. 772, pp. 429–36.

Best, David (1974), *Expression in Movement and the Arts*, London, Lepus.

Best, David (1978), *Philosophy and Human Movement*, London, Allen & Unwin.

Bhabha, Homi K. (1990), 'Introduction: narrating the nation', in Homi K. Bhabha (ed.), *Nation and Narration*, London and New York: pp. 291–322.

Bhabha, Homi, K. (1991), ' "Race", time, and the revision of modernity', *Oxford Literary Review*, vol. 13, no. 1–2, pp. 193–219.

Bidet, J. (1979), 'Questions to Pierre Bourdieu', *Critical Anthropology*, vol. 4, pp. 13–14.

Bilmes, Jacob and Howard, Alan (1980), 'Pain as a cultural drama', *Anthropology and Humanism Quarterly*, vol. 5, nos. 2 and 3, pp. 10–13.

Birdwhistell, Ray L. (1970), *Kinesics and Context: Essays on Body Motion Communication*, Philadelphia, University of Pennsylvania Press.

Blackham, H.J. (1966), 'Ideological aspects: a reevaluation of ritual', *Philosophical Transactions of the Royal Society of London*, Series B, vol. 25, no. 772, pp. 443–6.

Bloch, Maurice (1974), 'Symbols, song, dance, and features of articulation', *European Journal of Sociology*, vol. 15, pp. 55–81.

Bloch, Maurice (1975), 'Introduction', in Maurice Bloch (ed.), *Political Language and Oratory in Traditional Society*, London, Academic Press.

Bloch, Maurice (1983), *Marxism and Anthropology: The History of a Relationship*, Oxford, Oxford University Press.

Bocock, Robert (1974), *Ritual in Industrial Society: A Sociological Analysis of Ritualism in Modern England*, London, Allen & Unwin.

Bogdan, Robert and Biklen, Sari Knopp (1982), *Qualitative Research for Education: An Introduction*, Boston, Allyn & Bacon.

Bogdan, Robert and Taylor, Steven J. (1975), *Introduction to Qualitative Research Methods: A Phenomenological Approach to the Social Sciences*, New York, Wiley.

Bolton, Gavin (1980), *Towards a Theory of Drama in Education*, London, Longman.

Bossard, James H.S. and Boll, Eleanor (1951), *Rituals in Family Living*, Philadelphia, University of Pennsylvania Press.

Bouissac, Paul, (1976), *Circus and Cultures: A Semiotic Approach*, Bloomington, Indiana Uniersity Press.

Bouissac, Paul (1982), 'The profanation of the sacred in circus clown performance', paper given at Wenner-Gren Foundation for Anthropological Research, Symposium no. 89, 'Theatre and Ritual', New York, 1982.

Bourdieu, Pierre (1977a), *Outline for a Theory of Practice*, Cambridge, Cambridge University Press.

Bourdieu, Pierre (1977b), 'Symbolic power', in Denis Gleeson (ed.), *Identity and Structure*, Nafferton, N. Humberside, Nafferton Books: Studies in Education Ltd, pp. 112–15.

Bowers, C.A. (1984), *The Promise of Theory: Education and the Politics of Cultural Change*, London, Longman.

Bowles, Samuel and Gintis, Herbert (1976), *Schooling in Capitalist America: Educational Reform and the Contradictions of Economic Reform*, New York, Basic Books.

Breen, Myles and Corcoran, Farrel (1982), 'Myth in the television discourse', *Communication Monographs*, vol. 49, no. 2, pp. 127–36.

Brenneman, Walter Jr *et al.* (1982), '*The Seeing Eye: Hermeneutical Phenomenology in the Study of Religion*, Pennsylvania, Pennsylvania State University Press.

Bronowicz, Raymond, F. (1982), 'Towards a Catholic identity', *Homiletic and Pastoral Review*, vol. 82, no. 6, pp. 67–70.

Brown, Frank Church (1972), 'Transfiguration: poetic metaphor and theological reflection', *Journal of Religion*, vol. 62, no. 1, pp. 39–56.

Brown, Richard, H. (1978), *A Poetic for Sociology*, Cambridge, Cambridge University Press.

Buckley, Pamela and Houston, Robert (1980), 'New insights into teaching through ethnography', *Review of Education*, pp. 43–7.

Burke, Kenneth (1965), *Language as Symbolic Action*, Berkeley, University of California Press.

Burke, Kenneth (1969), *A Grammar of Motives*, Berkeley, University of California Press.

Burnett, Jacquetta Hill (1969), 'Ceremony, rites and economy in the student system of an American high school', *Human Organization*, vol. 28, no. 2, pp. 1–10.

Burns, Tom and Laughlin, Charles C. Jr (1979), 'Ritual and social power', in Eugene d'Aquili *et al.* (eds), *The Spectrum of Ritual: A Biogenetic Structural Analysis*, New York, Columbia University Press.

Burroughs, William S. (1980), *Port of Saints*, Berkeley, California, Blue Wind Press.

Butters, Steve (1976), 'The logic of participant observation', in Stuart Hall and Tony Jefferson (eds), *Resistance Through Rituals: Youth Subcultures in Post-War Britain*, London, Hutchinson, pp. 253–73.

Calitri, Charles J. (1975), 'Space, time and people in schools', *Teachers College Record*, vol. 77, no. 1, pp. 83–97.

Callois, Roger (1961), *Man, Play and Games*, translated by Meyer Barash, New York, Free Press.

Campbell, Jeremy (1982), *Grammatical Man: Information, Entropy, Language, and Life*, New York, Simon & Schuster.

Carey, Elaine (1983), 'Portuguese community struggles to eliminate its feeling of isolation', *Toronto Star* (1 September).

Carnoy, Martin (1974), *Education as Cultural Imperialism*, New York, McKay.

Carspecken, Phil Francis (1991), *Community Schooling and the Nature of Power: the Battle for Croxteth Comprehensive*, London and New York, Routledge.

Cassirer, Ernst (1955), *The Philosophy of Symbolic Forms*, vol. 2, New Haven, Conn., Yale University Press.

Chambers, Iain (1990), *Border Dialogues: Journeys in Postmodernity*, London and New York, Routledge.

Chapple, Eliot D., (1970), *Culture and Biological Man: Explorations in Behavioural Anthropology*, New York, Holt, Rinehart & Winston.

Chapple, Eliot D. (1981), 'Movement and sound: the musical language of body rhythms in interaction', *Teachers College Record*, vol. 82, no. 4, pp. 635–48.

Cippolla, Richard C. (1973), 'Ceremonial and the tacit dimension', *Worship*, vol. 47, no. 7, pp. 398–404.

Cixous, Hélène (1976), The Laugh of the Medusa', translated Keith Cohen and Paula Cohen, *Signs*, vol. 1, no. 4, pp. 875–93.

Clancy, P.G. (1977), 'The place of ritual in schools: some observations', *Unicorn*, vol. 3, no. 1, pp. 36–42.

Clarke, John *et al.* (1976), 'Subcultures, cultures and class', in Stuart Hall and Tony Jefferson (eds), *Resistance Through Rituals: Youth Subcultures in Post-War Britain*, London, Hutchinson.

Cleckner, Patricia (1977), 'Cognitive and ritual aspects of drug use among black urban males', in M. Du Toit (ed.), *Drugs, Rituals, and Altered States of Consciousness*, Rotterdam, A.A. Balkema, pp. 149–68.

Clifford, Marcus and James, George (1986), *Writing Culture: the Poetics and Politics of Ethnography*, Berkeley, University of California Press.

Clifton, Rodney (1979), 'Practice teaching: survival in a marginal situation', *Canadian Journal of Education*, vol. 4, no. 3, pp. 60–74.

Clough, Patricia Ticento (1992), *The End(s) of Ethnography: Realism to Social Criticism*, Newbury Park, Calif., Sage.

Coelho, Anna Maria (1977), 'Conflicts and adjustments of Portuguese youth in school, home and community', unpublished paper, Toronto Board of Education Library.

Cohen, Abner (1969), 'Political anthropology: the analysis of the symbolism of power relations', *Man*, n.s., vol. 4, pp. 213–35.

Cohen, Abner (1971), 'The politics of ritual secrecy', *Man*, n.s., vol. 6, pp. 427–49.

Cohen, Abner (1974), *Two Dimensional Man: An Essay on the Anthropology of Power and Symbolism in Complex Society*, London, Routledge & Kegan Paul.

Cohen, Abner (1979), 'Political symbolism', *Annual Review of Anthropology*, pp. 87–113.

Cohen, Abner (1980), 'Drama and politics in the development of a London carnival', *Man* n.s., vol. 15, pp. 65–87.

Cohen, Abner (1982), 'A polyethnic London carnival as a contested cultural performance', *Ethnic and Racial Studies*, vol. 5, no. 1, p. 23–41.

Collins, Mary (1976), 'Critical studies: examining an intersection of theology and culture', in John R. May (ed.), *The Bent World: Essays in Religion and Culture*, California, Scholars' Press, pp. 127–47.

Collins, Mary (1979), 'Ritual symbols and the ritual process: the work of Victor Turner', *Worship*, vol. 50, no. 4, pp. 336–46.

Completion Campaign Handbook (1971), Ontario English Catholic Teachers' Association.

Connelly, Michael F. and Clandinin, Jean (1982), 'Personal practical knowledge at Bay Street School', paper given at the American Educational Research Association Conference, New York.

Connolly, William, E. (1991), *Identity/Difference: Democratic Negotiations of Political Paradox*, Ithaca, New York and London, Cornell University Press.

Coon, Caroline, (1977), *1988: The New Wave Punk Rock Explosion*, London, Orbach & Chambers and New York, Hawthorn Books.

Corrigan, Paul (1979), *Schooling the Smash Street Kids*, London, Macmillan.

Corrigan, Philip *et al.* (1980), 'The state as a relation of production', in Philip Corrigan (ed.), *State Formation and Marxist Theory*, London, Quartet.

Courtney, Richard (1974), *Play, Drama and Thought: The Intellectual Background to Dramatic Education*, London, Cassell; New York, Drama Book Specialists.

Courtney, R. (1978), 'The significance of anthropological thought for arts and education: (2) The anthropological perspective', paper given at the 23rd World Congress, International Society for Education through Art (INSEA), Adelaide, South Australia.

Courtney, R. (1980), 'The medium is the missile: arts therapy in the electric age', The Selwyn Dewdney Memorial Lecture, First Annual Conference of the Canadian Art Therapy Association.

Courtney, R. (1981), *The Dramatic Curriculum*, London, Ontario, University of Western Ontario; London, England, Heinemann; New York, Drama Book Specialists.

Courtney, R. (1982), *Re-Play: Studies in Human Drama and Education*, Toronto, OISE Press, Ontario Institute for Studies in Education.

Cox, Harvey, (1969), *The Feast of Fools: A Theological Essay on Festivity*, Cambridge, Mass., Harvard University Press.

Crespi, M. (1979), 'Portuguese immigrants: economic strategies and the need for appropriate education', Proceedings from the 4th National Portuguese Conference, USA.

Crocker, Christopher (1974), 'Ritual and the development of social structure: liminality and inversion', in James Shaughnessy (ed.), *The Roots of Ritual*, Grand Rapids, Mich., William B. Eerdmans, pp. 47–86.

Csikszentmihalyi, Mihaly (1975a), *Beyond Boredom and Anxiety*, San Francisco, Jossey-Bass.

Csikszentmihalyi, Mihaly (1975b), 'Play and intrinsic rewards', *Journal of Humanistic Psychology*, vol. 15, no. 3, pp. 41–63.

Da Cunha, Pedro, (n.d.), 'The dropout syndrome among Portuguese youth', Procceedings of the 3rd Annual Symposium on the Portuguese Experience in the United States.

Da Matta, Roberto (1979), 'Ritual in complex and tribal societies', *Current Anthropology*, vol. 20, no. 3, pp. 589–90.

D'Aquili, Eugene and Laughlin, Charles Jr. (1975), 'The biophysical determinants of religious ritual behaviour', *Zygon*, vol. 10, no. 1, pp. 32–59.

Dauenhauer, P.B. (1989), 'Ideology, Utopia and responsible politics', *Man and World*, vol. 22, pp. 25–41.

Davenport, Guy (1981), *The Geography of the Imagination*, San Francisco, North Point Press.

Davies, D. (1981a), 'The politics of cultural freedom', a third level course, Open University, in *Education Studies: Society, Education and the State*, Milton Keynes, Bucks, Open University Press.

Davies, David (1981b), *Popular Culture, Class and Schooling*, Milton Keynes, Bucks, Open University Press.

Davies, Robertson (1982), 'Nobility and style', *Parabola: Myth and the Quest for Meaning*, vol. 7, no. 3, pp. 15–21.

Davis, Mike, (1990), *City of Quartz: Excavating the Future in Los Angeles*, London and New York, Verso.

Delattre, Roland (1978), 'Ritual resourcefulness and cultural pluralism', *Soundings*, vol. 61, no. 3, pp. 283–301.

Delattre, Roland (1979), 'The rituals of humanity and the rhythms of reality', *Prospects: An Annual Review of American Studies*, vol. 5, pp. 35–49.

De Lauretis, Teresa (1990), 'Eccentric subjects: feminist theory and historical consciousness', *Feminist Studies*, vol. 16, no. 1, pp. 115–50.

Deleuze, Gilles and Guattari, Felix (1972), *Anti-Oedipus: Capitalism and Schizophrenia*, New York, Viking Press.

Derrida, J. (1977), *Of Grammatology*, Baltimore, Johns Hopkins Press.

De Sola, Carla and Easton, Arthur (1979), 'Awakening the right lobe through dance', in Gloria Durka and Joanmarie Smith (eds), *Aesthetic Dimensions of Religious Education*, New York, Paulist Press.

Dewey, John (1966), *Democracy and Education*, New York, Macmillan and the Free Press.

Dilthey, William (1976), *Selected Writings*, edited and introduced by H .P. Rickman, Cambridge, Cambridge University Press (first published 1883–1911).

Dixon, John W., Jr (1974), 'The erotics of knowing', *Anglican Theological Review*, vol. 56, no. 1, pp. 3–16.

Dixon, John W., Jr (1976), 'The physiology of faith', *Anglican Theological Review*, vol 48, no. 4, pp. 407–31.

Dolgin, Janet et al. (1977), 'Introduction', in Janet Dolgin et al. (eds), *Symbolic Anthropology: A Reader in the Study of Symbols and Meanings*, New York, Columbia University Press.

Donovan, Kevin (1970), 'The need for ritual', *The Way Supplement*, pp. 4–13.

Doty, William G. (1980), 'Mythophiles' dyscrasia: a comprehensive definition of myth', *Journal of the American Academy of Religion*, vol. 48, no. 4, pp. 531–621.

Douglas, Mary (1970), *Purity and Danger: An Analysis of Concepts of Pollution and Taboo*, Harmondsworth, Penguin.

Douglas, Mary (1973), *Natural Symbols: Explorations in Cosmology*, New York, Random House.
Douglas, Mary (1978), *Implicit Meanings: Essays in Anthropology*, London Routledge & Kegan Paul.
Douglas, Mary and Isherwood, Baron (1979), *The World of Goods: Towards an Anthropology of Consumption*, London, Allen Lane.
Douglas, Mary and Wildavsky, Aaron (1982), *Risk and Culture*, Berkeley, University of California Press.
Dreeben, R. (1968), *On What is Learned in Schools*, Reading, Mass., Addison Wesley.
Driver, Tom F. (1978), 'Concerning methods for studying rituals: less is more', paper given at the Ritual Studies Consultation, American Academy of Religion, New Orleans.
Ducey, Michael H. (1977), *Sunday Morning: Aspects of Urban Ritual*, New York, Free Press.
Dulles, Avery (1973), *The Survival of Dogma: Faith, Authority and Dogma in a Changing World*, New York, Image Books.
Duncan, Hugh (1968), *Symbols in Society*, New York, Oxford University Press.
Duncan, Hugh (1969), *Symbols and Social Theory*, New York, Oxford University Press.
Durka, Gloria and Smith Joanmarie (1979), 'Community: an aesthetic perspective', in Gloria Durka and Joanmarie Smith (eds), *Aesthetic Dimensions of Religious Education*, New York, Paulist Press, pp. 99–106.
Dussel, Enrique (1985), *Philosophy of Liberation*, Maryknoll, NY, Orbis Books.
Durkheim, Emile (1965), *The Elementary Forms of the Religious Life*, translated by Joseph W. Swain, New York, Free Press.
Eagleton, Terry (1990), *Ideology*, London and New York, Verso.
Ebert, Teresa (1991), 'Political semiosis in/of American cultural studies', *American Journal of Semiotics*, vol. 8, no. 1–2, pp. 113–35.
Eco, Umberto (1982), 'On symbols', *Semiotic Inquiry*, vol. 2, no. 1, pp. 15–44.
Eddy, Elizabeth M. (1969), *Becoming a Teacher: A Passage to Professional Status*, New York, Columbia University, Teachers College Press.
Edelman, Murray (1964), *The Symbolic Uses of Politics*, Urbana, University of Illinois Press.
Edelman, Murray (1971), *Politics as Symbolic Action: Mass Arousal and Quiescence*, Institute for Research on Poverty Monograph Series, Chicago, Markham.
Edelman, Murray (1974), 'The political language of the helping professions', *Politics and Society*, vol. 4, no. 4, pp. 295–310.
Edelman, Murray (1977), *Political Language, Words that Succeed and Policies that Fail*, New York, Academic Press.
Eggan, F. (1963), 'Social anthropology and education', *School Review*, vol. 65, no. 3.
Eliade, Mircea (1958), *Rites and Symbols of Initiation*, New York, Harper & Row.

Eliade, Mircea (1961), *The Sacred and the Profane*, New York, Harper & Row.

Eliade, Mircea (1963), *Myth and Reality*, New York, Harper & Row.

Eliade, Mircea (1964), *Shamanism: Archaic Techniques of Ecstasy*, translated by Willard R. Trash, Princeton, New Jersey, Princeton University Press.

Erikson, E.H. (1966), 'Ontogeny of ritualization in man', *Philosophical Transactions of the Royal Society of London*, Series B, vol. 251, no. 772, pp. 337–50.

Erikson, E.H. (1977), *Toys and Reasons: Stages in the Ritualization of Life*, New York, W.W. Norton.

Everhart, Robert and Doyle, Wayne J. (1980), 'The symbolic aspects of educational innovation', *Anthropology and Educational Quarterly*, vol. 11, no. 2, pp. 67–90.

Every Student Survey (1975), Toronto Board of Education.

Fabian, Joannes (1983), *Time and the Other: How Anthropology Makes its Object*, New York and Oxford, Columbia University Press.

Feinberg, Richard (1979), 'Schneider's symbolic culture theory: an appraisal', *Current Anthropology*, vol. 20, no. 3, pp. 541–9.

Feldman, Allen (1991), *Formations of Violence: The Narrative of the Body and Political Terror in Northern Ireland*, Chicago, University of Chicago Press.

Feldstein, Leonard C. (1976), 'The human body as rhythm and symbol: a study in practical hermeneutics', *Journal of Medicine and Philosohy*, vol. 1, no. 2, pp. 136–61.

Fenn, Richard K. (1982), *Liturgies and Trials: The Secularization of Religious Language*, New York, Pilgrim.

Fernandez, James (1972), 'Persuasions and performances: of the beast in every body . . . and the metaphors of Everyman, *Daedalus*, vol. 101, no. 1, p. 39–60.

Fernandez, James (1974), 'The mission of metaphor in expressive culture', *Current Anthropology*, vol. 15, no. 2, pp. 119–33.

Fernandez, James (1977), 'The performance of ritual metaphors', in J. David Sapir and J. Christopher Crocker (eds), *The Social Use of Metaphor, Essays on the Anthropological Use of Rhetoric*, Philadelphia, University of Pennsylvania Press, pp. 100–31.

Feuerbach, Ludwig Andreas (1957), *The Essence of Christianity*, translated from the German by George Eliot, New York, Harper & Row.

Finnan, Christine Robinson (1980), 'The emergents of policy statements from ethnographic case studies', paper given at the American Educational Research Association annual meeting, Boston, Mass.

Finnegan, Ruth (1969), 'How to do things with words: performative utterances among the Limba of Sierra Leone', *Man*, n.s. vol. 4, no. 4, pp. 537–52.

Fischer, Edward A. (1973), 'Ritual as communication', *Worship*, vol. 45, no.2, pp. 73–91.

Fitzer, Joseph (1973), 'Liturgy, language and mysticism', *Worship*, vol. 47, no. 2, pp. 67–9.

Foster, Herbert L. (1974), *Ribbin', Jivin', and Playin' The Dozens: The Unrecognized Dilemma of Inner City Schools*, Cambridge, Mass., Ballinger.

318 Schooling as a Ritual Performance

Foucault, Michel (1977), *Discipline and Punish: The Birth of the Prison*, New York, Pantheon.

Foucault, Michel (1980), *Power/Knowledge: Selected Interviews and Other Writings*, ed. Colin Gordon, New York, Pantheon.

Frank, Arthur W. (1990), 'Bringing Bodies Back in: a decade review', *Theory, Culture and Society*, vol. 7, no. 1, pp. 131–62.

Frank, David A. (1981), ' "Shalom Achshav" – rituals of the Israeli peace movement', *Communication Monographs*, vol. 48, pp. 165–82.

Freire, P. (1973), *Pedagogy of the Oppressed*, New York, Seabury Press.

Freire, P. (1978a), *Pedagogy in Process: The Letters to Guinea-Bissau*, New York, Seabury Press.

Freire, P. (1978b), *Education for Critical Consciousness*, New York, Seabury Press.

Freire, P. (1985), *The Politics of Education: Culture, Power and Liberation*, South Hadley, Mass., Bergin & Garvey.

Freud, Sigmund (1953), 'Totem and Taboo', in *The Standard Edition of the Complete Works of Sigmund Freud*, edited and translated by James Strachey, vol. 13, pp. 1–161, London, Hogarth.

Friedenberg, Edgar Z. (1980), *Defence to Authority: The Case of Canada*, White Plains, New York, M.E. Sharpe.

Gadamer, Hans-Georg (1976), *Philosophical Hermeneutics*, Berkeley, University of California Press.

Game, Ann (1991), *Undoing the Social: Towards a Deconstructive Sociology*, Toronto and Buffalo, NY, University of Toronto Press.

Gay, Volney Patrick (1979), *Freud on Ritual: Reconstruction and Critique*, AAR Dissertation Series, no. 16, Missoula, Montana, Scholars' Press.

Geertz, Clifford (1957), 'Ethos, world-view and the analysis of sacred symbols', *Antioch Review*, vol. 17, no. 4, pp. 421–37.

Geertz, Clifford (1966), 'Religion as a cultural system', in M. Banton (ed.), *Anthropological Approaches to the Study of Religion*, London, Tavistock.

Geertz, Clifford (1971), 'The Balinese cockfight', in Clifford Geertaz (ed.), *Myth, Symbol and Culture*, New York, W.W. Norton.

Geertz, Clifford (1972), 'Religion as a cultural system', in A. Lessa and Even Z. Vogt (eds), *Reader in Comparative Religion: An Anthroplogical Approach*, New York, Harper & Row.

Geertz, Clifford (1980), 'Blurred genres, the refiguration of social thought', *American Scholar*, pp. 165–79.

Geertz, Clifford (1983), *Local Knowledge: Further Essays in Interpretive Anthropology*, New York, Basic Books.

Gehrke, Nathalie J. (1979), 'Rituals of the hidden curriculum', in K. Yamomoto (ed.), *Children in Time and Space*, New York, Teachers College Press, pp. 103–27.

Genet, Jean (1970), *Our Lady of the Flowers*, translated by Bernard Frechtman, New York, Bantam.

Gergen, Kenneth J. (1991), *The Saturated Self: Dilemmas of Identity in Contemporary Life*, New York, Basic Books.

Gerth, Hans and Mills, C. Wright (1953), *Character and Social Structure: The Psychology of Social Institutions*, New York, Harcourt, Brace & World.

Gill, Sam D. (1977), 'Prayer as person: the performative force in Navaho prayer acts', *History of Religions*, vol. 17, no. 2, pp. 143–57.

Girard, Rene (1977), *Violence and the Sacred*, translated by Patrick Gregory, Baltimore, Johns Hopkins University Press.

Giroux, Henry A. (1981a), 'Hegemony, resistance, and the paradox of educational reform', *Interchange*, vol. 12, nos. 2/3, pp. 2–27.

Giroux, Henry A. (1981b), *Ideology, Culture and the Process of Schooling*, Philadelphia, Temple University Press and London, Falmer Press.

Giroux, Henry A. (1983), *Theory and Resistance in Education*, South Hadley, Mass., Bergin & Garvey.

Giroux, Henry A. (1984), 'Marxism and schooling: the limits of radical discourse', *Educational Theory*, vol. 34, no. 2, pp. 113–35.

Giroux, Henry A. and Aronowitz, Stanley (1985), *Education Under Siege*, South Hadley, Mass., Bergin & Garvey.

Giroux, Henry, and McLaren, Peter (1989), 'Introduction,' *Critical Pedagogy, the State and Cultural Struggle*, Albany, NY, State University of New York Press.

Giroux, Henry, and McLaren, Peter (1991), 'Radical pedagogy as cultural politics: beyond the discourse of critique and anti-utopianism', in Donald Morton and Mas'ud Zadarzadeh (eds), *Theory/Pedagogy/Politics: Texts for Change*, Urbana, Ill. and Chicago, University of Illinois Press, pp. 152–86.

Glaser, Barney (1978), *Theoretical Sensitivity – Advances Made in the Methodology of Grounded Theory*, Mill Valley California, Sociology Press

Glaser, Barney and Strauss, Anselm L. (1965), *Awareness of Dying*, New York and Chicago, Aldine.

Glaser, Barney and Strauss, Anselm L. (1967), *The Discovery of Grounded Theory: Strategies for Qualitative Research*, New York and Chicago, Aldine.

Glaser, Barney and Strauss, Anselm L. (1971), *Status Passage*, Chicago, Atherton.

Glaser, Robert (1982), 'The future of educational research by a panel of AERA's past presidents', *Educational Researcher*, vol. 11, no. 8, pp. 11–19.

Gluckman, Max (1963), *Order and Rebellion in Tribal Africa*, London, Cohen & West.

Goethals, Gregor T. (1981), *The TV Ritual: Worship at the Video Altar*, Boston, Beacon Press.

Goffman, Erving (1961), *Asylums*, Garden City, New York, Anchor Books, Doubleday.

Goffman, Erving (1967), *Interaction Ritual: Essays on Face-to-Face Behaviour*, Garden City, New York, Doubleday.

Goffman, Erving (1974), *Frame Analsyis*, Cambridge, Mass., Harvard University Press.

Goffman, Erving (1981), *Forms of Talk*, Oxford, Blackwell.

Gold, R.L. (1958), 'Rules in sociological field observations', *Social Forces*, no. 36, pp. 217–23.

Goldberg, David Theo (1990), *Anatomy of Racism*, Minneapolis, Minn., University of Minnesota Press.

Goodin, Robert E. (1978), 'Rites of rulers', *British Journal of Sociology*, vol. 29, no. 3, pp. 281–9.

Goodlad, J.S.R. (1971), *A Sociology of Popular Drama*, London, Heinemann.

Goody, Jack (1961), '*Religion and ritual: the definitional problem*', British Journal of Sociology, no. 12, pp. 142–64.

Goody, Jack (1977), ' "Against ritual": loosely structured thoughts on a loosely defined topic', in Barbara Myerhoff and Sally Falk Moore (eds), *Secular Ritual*, pp. 25–35.

Gramsci, A. (1971), *Selections from the Prison Notebooks*, London, Lawrence & Wishart.

Grathoff, R. (1970), *The Structure of Social Inconsistencies*, The Hague, Martinus Nijhoff.

Greeley, Andrew M. (1972), *Unsecular Man: The Persistence of Religion*, New York, Schocken.

Greenfield, Thomas B. (1980), 'The man who comes back through the door in the wall: discovering truth, discovering self, discovering organizations', *Educational Organization Quarterly*, vol. 16, no. 3, pp. 26–59.

Grimes, Ronald L. (1976), *Symbol and Conquest: Public Ritual and Drama in Sante Fé, New Mexico*, Ithaca, New York, Cornell University Press.

Grimes, Ronald L. (1978), 'The rituals of walking and flying: public participatory events at Actors Lab', *The Drama Review*, vol. 22, no. 4, pp. 77–82.

Grimes, Ronald L. (1979a), 'The Actor's Lab: the roots of human action', *Canadian Theatre Review*, vol. 22, pp.9–19.

Grimes, Ronald L. (1979b), 'Modes of ritual necessity', *Worship*, vol. 53, no. 4, pp. 126–41.

Grimes, Ronald L. (1982a), *Beginnngs in Ritual Studies*, Washington, DC, University Press of America.

Grimes, Ronald (1982b), 'The life blood of public ritual; fiestas and public exploration projects', in Victor Turner (ed.), *Celebration: Studies in Festivity and Ritual*, Washington, DC, Smithsonian Institute Press.

Grimes, Ronald (1984a), 'Rituals and illness', *Canadian Journal of Community Mental Health*, vol. 3, no. 1, pp. 55–65.

Grimes, Ronald (1985), 'Research in ritual studies: a programmatic essay' ATLA, Bibliography Series 14, Metuchen, N.I., and London, Scarecrow Press.

Grimes, Ronald (1987), 'Ritual studies', in M. Eliade (ed.), *Encyclopedia of Religion*, vol. 12, New York, Macmillan and the Free Press.

Grimes, Ronald (n.d.), 'Ritual: the poetics of monotony', unpublished paper.

Grossberg, Lawrence (1992), *We Gotta Get Out of This Place: Popular Conservatism and Postmodern Culture*, London and New York, Routledge.

Grotowski, Jerzy (1968), *Towards a Poor Theatre*, New York, Simon & Schuster.

Grotowski, Jerzy (1973), 'Holiday: the day that is holy', *Drama Review*, vol. 17, no. 2, pp. 113–19.

Grotowski, Jerzy (1978), 'The art of the beginner', *International Theatre Information*, Paris, International Theatre Institute, Spring/Summer, pp. 7–11.

Grove, Cornelius Lee (1977), 'Six non-language related problems facing older immigrant Portuguese students', Proceedings of the 3rd Symposium on the Portuguese Experience in the United States, Adelphi

University. Published by the National Dissemination Centre, Cambridge, Mass.

Grumet, Madeleine R. (1978), 'Curriculum as theatre: merely players', *Curriculum Inquiry*, vol. 8, no. 1, pp. 37–64.

Gusfield, J.R. (1981), *The Culture of Public Problems: Drinking-Driving and the Symbolic Order*, Chicago, University of Chicago Press.

Guthrie, G.P. (1981), 'Bilingual education in a Chinese community: an ethnography in progress', paper given at the annual meeting of the American Research Association, Los Angeles.

Hall, Edward T. (1973), *The Silent Language*, Garden City, New York, Doubleday.

Hall, Edward T. (1984), *The Dance of Life: The Other Dimension of Time*, New York, Anchor Press.

Hall, Stuart (1977), 'Culture, the media and the "ideological effect"', in James Curran *et al* (eds), *Mass Communication and Society*, London, Edward Arnold, pp. 315–48.

Hall, Stuart (1991), 'Ethnicity: identity and difference, *Radical America*, vol. 23, no. 4, pp. 9–20.

Hall, S. *et al*, (1978), *Policing the Crisis: Mugging the State and Law and Order*, London, Macmillan.

Hammer, Rhonda (1982), 'The pattern which connects: towards an understanding of a communicational approach', unpublished thesis, Simon Fraser University, British Columbia.

Hammer, Rhonda and Wilden, Anthony (1987), 'The chorus line, in Anthony Wilden, *The Rules Are No Game: The Strategy of Communication*, London, Routledge & Kegan Paul.

Handleman, Don (1977), 'Play and ritual: complementary frames of metacommunication', in A.J. Chapman and H.C. Foot (eds), *It's a Funny Thing, Humour*, New York, Pergamon Press, pp. 185–92.

Handleman, Don (1981), 'The ritual clown: attributes and affinities', *Anthropos: International Review of Ethnology and Linguistics*, vol. 76, nos. 3/4, pp. 317–66.

Handleman, Don and Kapferer, Bruce (1980), 'Symbolic types, mediation and the transformation of ritual context: Sinhalese demons and Tewa clowns', *Semiotica*, vol. 30, nos. 1–2, pp. 41–71.

Hargreaves, D. (1967), *Social Relations in a Secondary School*, London, Routledge & Kegan Paul.

Harrington, Michael (1983), *The Politics at God's Funeral: The Spiritual Crisis of Western Civilization*, New York, Holt, Rinehart & Winston.

Harris, Marvin (1979), *Cultural Materialism: The Struggle for a Science of Culture*, New York, Random House.

Harrison, Robert (1979), ' "Where have all the rituals gone?" Ritual preserve among the Ranau Dunsun of Sabah, Malaysia', in A.L. Becker and Aram A. Yengoyan (eds), *The Imagination of Reality: Essays in Southeast Asian Coherence Systems*, Norwood, New Jersey, Ablex, pp. 55–74.

Harvey, David (1989), *The Condition of Postmodernity*, Oxford, Basil Blackwell.

Hebdige, Dick (1979), *Sub-Culture: The Meaning of Style*, London, Methuen.

Heidegger, M. (1972), *What is Called Thinking?*, translated by J. Glenn Gray, New York, Harper Torchbooks.

Heller, Agnes (1989), 'Are we living in a world of emotional impoverishment?', *Thesis Eleven*, vol. 22, pp. 46–60.

Hermanson, George, 'Towards a process theory of action', unpublished doctoral dissertation, Faculty of Theology at Claremont, Vermont.

Hextall, Ian (1977), 'Marking work', in Geoff Whitty and Michael Young (eds), *Explorations in the Politics of Social Knowledge*, Nafferton, N. Humberside, Nafferton Books, pp. 65–74.

Hine, Virginia H. (1981), 'Self-generated ritual: trend or fad?', *Worship*, vol. 55. no. 5, pp. 404–19.

Hofstadter, Albert (1965), *Truth in Art*, New York, Columbia University Press.

Holloman, Regina E. (1974), 'Ritual opening and individual transformation: rites of passage at Esalen', *American Anthropologist*, no. 5, pp. 265–80.

Holmes, Urban T. (1973a), 'Revivals are un-American: a recalling of America to its pilgrimage', *Anglican Theological Review*, supplementary series, no. 1, pp. 58–75.

Holmes, Urban T. (1973b), 'Liminality and Liturgy', *Worship*, vol. 47, no. 7, pp. 386–99.

Holmes, Urban T. (1976), *Ministry and Imagination*, New York, Seabury Press.

Holmes, Urban T. (1977a), 'What has Manchester to do with Jerusalem?' *Anglican Theological Review*, vol. 59, no. 2, pp. 79–97.

Holmes, Urban T. (1977b), 'Rituals and the social drama', *Worship*, vol. 51, no. 3, pp. 196–213.

Holmes, Urban T. (1978), *The Priest in Community: Exploring the Roots of Ministry*, New York, Seabury Press.

Holmes, Urban T. (1980), 'Theology and religious renewal', *Anglican Theological Review*, vol. 62, no. 1, pp. 3–19.

Honda, Robert W. (1982), 'Liturgy as Kingdom play', *Worship*, vol. 56, no. 3, pp. 261–3.

Huizinga, J.H. (1955a: orig. 1944), *Homo Ludens*, Boston, Beacon Press.

Huizinga, J.H. (1955b), *The Waning of the Middle Ages*, Harmondsworth Press, Penguin.

Hymes, Dell H. (1972), 'The use of anthropology: critical, political, personal', in Dell Hymes (ed.), *Reinventing Anthropology*, pp. 20–6.

Hymes, Dell H. (1977), 'Qualitative/quantitative research methodologies in education', *Anthropology and Education Quarterly*, vol. 8, no. 3, pp. 165–76.

Hymes, Dell H. (1978), 'Educational ethnology', *Anthropology and Educational Quarterly*, vol. 11, no. 1, pp. 3–8.

Hymes, Dell H. (1981), 'Ethnographic monitoring', in G.P. Guthrie (ed.), *Culture and the Bilingual Classroom: Studies in Classroom Ethnography*, Rowland, Mass., Newbury House, pp. 56–68.

Ice-T (1992), 'Police on my back', an interview with Ice-T and Jello Biafra by Karen Woods, *Spin*, Sept., pp. 73–5.

Illich, Ivan (1970), 'Schooling: the ritual of process', *New York Review of Books*, vol. 15, no. 10, 3 December, pp. 20–6.

Inglis, Fred (1975), *Ideology and the Imagination*, London, Cambridge, University Press.

Jameson, Fredric (1989), 'Afterword-Marxism and postmodernism', in Doug Kellner (ed.), *Postmodernism/Jameson/Critique*, Washington, DC, Maisonneuve.

Janulin, Robert (1970), *La Paix Blanche*, Paris, Seuil.

Jennings, Theodore (1982), 'On ritual knowledge', *Journal of Religion*, vol. 62, no. 2, pp. 111–27.

Johnson, Nels (1978), 'Palestinian refugee ideology: an inquiry into key metaphors, *Journal of Anthropological Research*, no. 34, pp. 524–9.

Johnson, Norris Brock (1980), 'The material culture of public school classrooms: the symbolic integration of local schools and national culture', *Anthropology and Educational Quarterly*, vol. 11, no. 3, pp. 173–90.

Jung, C.G. (1953), *Psychology and Alchemy*, London, Routledge & Kegan Paul.

Kamens, David H. (1977), 'Legitimating myths and educational organization: the relationship between organizational ideology and formal structure', *American Sociological Review*, vol. 42, pp. 208–19.

Kapferer, Judith L. (1981), 'Socialization and the symbolic order of the school', *Anthropology and Educational Quarterly*, vol. 12, no. 4, pp. 258–74.

Katz, Michael (1968), *The Irony of Early School Reform*, Boston, Beacon Press.

Katz, Michael (1975), *Class, Bureaucracy and Schools*, New York, Praeger.

Kavanagh, Aidan (1973), 'The role of ritual in personal development', in James Shaughnessy (ed.), *The Roots of Ritual*, Grand Rapids, Mich., William B. Eerdmans, pp. 145–60.

Kelly, George A. (1963), *A Theory of Personality*, New York, W.W. Norton.

Kenny, Michael and Hatfield, C.R., Jr. (1973), 'Introduction: no longer at ease', *Anthropological Quarterly*, vol. 46, no. 1, pp. 1–6.

Kett, Robert (1981), 'The cultural anthropology of advanced industrial society', *Canadian Journal of Political and Social Theory*, vol. 5, nos. 1/2, pp. 208–15.

Kilbourn, Brent (1980), 'Ethnographic research and the improvement of teaching', in Hugh Munby *et al.* (eds), *Seeing Curriculum in a New Light: Essays from Science Education*, Toronto, OISE Press (Ontario Institute for Studies in Education), pp. 162–81.

Kimball, Solon T. (1960), 'Introduction', in Arnold van Gennep, *The Rites of Passage*, London, Routledge & Kegan Paul.

Kimball, Solon T. (1972), 'Series editor's foreword', in Thomas A. Leemon (ed.), *The Rites of Passage in a Student Culture*, New York, Teachers College Press.

Kimball, Solon T. and Partridge, William L. (1979), *The Craft of Community Study: Fieldwork Dialogues*, Gainesville, University Press of Florida.

Klapp, Orrin E. (1969), *A Collective Search for Identity*, New York, Holt, Rinehart & Winston.

Kliever, Lonnie D. (1981), 'Fictive religion: rhetoric and play', *Journal of the American Academy of Religion*, vol. 49, no. 4, pp. 657–669.

Knight, Tony (1974), 'Powerlessness and the student role: structural determinants of school status', *Australian and New Zealand Journal of Sociology*, vol. 10, no. 2, pp. 12–17.

Kohl, Herbert (1984), *Growing Minds: On Becoming a Teacher*, New York, Harper & Row.

Korzybski, Alfred (1933), *Science and Sanity – An Introduction to Non-Aristotelian Systems and General Semantics*, Lancaster, Pennsylvania, International Non-Aristotelian Library Publishing.

Kottak, Conrad P. (1978), 'Rituals at McDonald's', *Journal of American Culture*, vol. 1, no. 2, pp. 370–6.

Kovel, Joel (1991) *History and Spirit: an Inquiry into the Philosophy of Liberation*, Boston, Mass., Beacon Press.

Kuhn, T. (1962), *The Structure of Scientific Revolutions*, Chicago, University of Chicago Press.

Kujundzic, Dragan (1990), 'Laughter as Otherness in Bakhtin and Derrida', in Robert Barsky and Michael Holquist (eds), *Bakhtin and Otherness*, special issue of *Social Discourse*, vol. 3, no. 1–2, pp. 271–93.

Laing, R.D. (1966), 'Ritualization and abnormal behaviour, *Philosophical Transactions of the Royal Society of London*, Series B, vol. 251, no. 772, pp. 331–5.

Laing, R.D. (1983), *The Voice of Experience: Experience, Science and Psychiatry*, Harmondsworth, Penguin.

Lakoff, George and Johnson, Mark (1980), *Metaphors We Live By*, Chicago, University of Chicago Press.

Lambert, Wallace E. (n.d.), 'Portuguese child rearing values: cross national analysis', paper given at the National Conference on the Portuguese Experience in the United States.

Lancy, David F. (1975), 'The social organization of learning: initiation rites and public schools', *Human Organization*, vol. 34, no. 4, pp. 371–9.

Langer, Suzanne K. (1957), *Philosophy in a New Key: Study in the Symbolism of Reason, Rite, and Art*, Cambridge, Mass., Harvard University Press.

Langness, L.L. (1974), *The Study of Culture*, San Francisco, Chandler & Sharp.

Lash, Scott (1990), 'Learning from Leipzig . . . or politics in the semiotic society', *Theory, Culture and Society*, vol. 7, no. 4, pp. 145–58.

Larsen, Neil (1990), *Modernism and Hegemony: A Materialist Critique of Aethestic Agencies*, Minneapolis, Minn., University of Minnesota Press.

Lawler, Michael G. (1979), 'Right lobe religion: theology and religious education', in Gloria Durka and Joanmarie Smith (eds), *Aesthetic Dimensions of Religious Education*, New York, Paulist Press, pp. 167–84.

Lawler, Thomas et al. (1976), *The Teaching of Christ: Catechism for Adults*, Indiana, Our Sunday Visitor.

Leach, Edmund (1968), 'Ritual', in D.L. Stills (ed.), *International Encyclopedia of Social Sciences*, New York, Macmillan, vol. 13, pp. 520–6.

Leemon, Thomas A. (1972), *The Rites of Passage in a Student Subculture*, New York, Teachers College Press.

Leslie, Charles (1970), 'Review of *The Ritual Process*', *Science*, vol. 8, no. 168, pp. 702–4.

Lessing, Doris (1972), *The Golden Notebook*, St. Albans, Granada.

Lester, Marilyn and Hadden, Stuart C. (1980), 'Ethnomethodology and grounded theory: an integration of perspective and method', *Urban Life*, vol. 9, no. 1, pp. 3–33.

Levin, David Michael (1982), 'Moral education: The body's felt sense of value', *Teachers College Record*, vol. 84, no. 2, pp. 283–300.
Levinas, Emmanuel (1969), *Totality and Infinity*, Pittsburgh, Pa., Duquesne University Press.
Lévi-Strauss, Claude (1967), *Structural Anthropology*, translated by Claire Jacobson and Brooke Grundfest Schoepf, Garden City, New York, Doubleday.
Lewis, B.H. (1979), 'Time and space in schools', in K. Yamamoto (ed.), *Children in Time and Space*, New York, Teachers College Press, pp. 128–69.
Lewis, Gilbert (1980), *Day of Shining Red: An Essay on Understanding Ritual*, Cambridge, Cambridge University Press.
Lewis, I.M. (1976), *Social Anthropology in Perspective*, Harmondsworth, Penguin.
Lincoln, Bruce (1977), 'Two notes on moden rituals', *Journal of the American Academy of Religion*, vol. 45, no. 2, pp. 147–60.
Lorenz, Konrad (1966), *On Aggression*, translated by Marjorie Latzke, London Methuen.
Luckmann, Thomas (1967), *The Invisible Religion: The Problems of Religion in Modern Society*, New York, Macmillan.
Lukes, Steven (1975), 'Political ritual and social integration', *Sociology: The Journal of the British Sociological Association*, vol. 9, no. 2, pp. 289–308.
Lukes, Steven (1982), 'Relativism in its place', in Martin Hollis and Steven Lukes (eds), *Rationality and Relativism*, Cambridge, Mass., MIT Press.
Lutz, F.W. (1981), Ethnography – the holistic approach to understanding schooling', in Judith Green and Cynthia Wallat (eds), *Ethnography and Language in Educational Settings*, Norwood, New Jersey, Ablex, pp. 51–63.
Lutz, F.W. and Ramsey, Margaret A. (1973), 'Nondirective cues as ritualistic indicators in educational organizations', *Education and Urban Society*, vol. 5, no. 3, pp. 345–65.
MacCannell, Dean (1976), *The Tourist: A New theory of the Leisure Class*, New York, Schocken.
MacCannell, Dean (1992), 'Introduction', *Empty Meeting Grounds*, London and New York, Routledge.
McDowell, Jennifer (1974), 'Soviet civil ceremonies', *Journal for the Scientific Study of Religion*, vol. 13, no. 3, pp. 265–79.
McGregor, Lynn *et al.* (1977), *Learning Through Drama*, Report of the Schools Council Drama Teaching Project (10-16), Goldsmiths' College, University of London, London, Heinemann.
McLaren, Peter (1978), 'Back to the basics; not enough for inner-city classrooms', *Catholic New Times*, 22 October 1978.
McLaren, Peter (1979a), 'Back to the basics; consequences for inner-city kids', *Educational Courier*, vol. 49, no. 3, pp. 11–13.
McLaren, Peter (1979b), 'Immigrant children in the schools', *Centrefold*, vol. 4, no. 1.
McLaren, Peter (1979c), 'Teaching in the suburbs: the new reality', Canadian Educational Association National Newsletter.
McLaren, Peter (1980a), *Cries from the Corridor: The New Suburban Ghettos*, Agincourt, Ontario, Methuen.

McLaren, Peter (1980b), 'The corridor kids', *Replay: A Canadian College Reader*, Agincourt, Ontario, Methuen.

McLaren, Peter (1981), 'They called it Metro's worst school', *Mudpie*, vol. 2, no. 2.

McLaren, Peter (1982a), *Cries from the Corridor: The New Suburban Ghettos* (revised with new Afterword), Markham, Ontario, PaperJacks.

McLaren, Peter (1982b), 'Bein' tough: rituals of resistance in the culture of working-class schoolgirls', *Canadian Woman Studies*, vol. 4, no. 1.

McLaren, Peter (1984a), 'Victor Turner: in memoriam', *International Semiotic Spectrum*, no. 1.

McLaren, Peter (1984b), 'Rethinking ritual', *Etc. A Review of General Semantics*, vol. 41, no. 3., pp. 267–77.

McLaren, Peter (1985), 'A tribute to Victor Turner', *Anthropologica*, 27(1/2), pp. 17–22.

McLaren, Peter (1985a), 'A prolegomena towards establishing links between ritology and schooling', in Judith Kase-Polisini (ed.), *Creative Drama in a Developmental Context*, Washington, DC, University Press of America, pp. 209–51.

McLaren, Peter (1985b), 'Towards a pedagogy of liberation: Peter McLaren interviews Henry Giroux', *Borderlines*, no. 2, pp. 10–12.

McLaren, Peter (1989b), 'Schooling the postmodern body: critical pedagogy and the politics of enfleshment', *Journal of Education*, vol. 170, pp. 53–8.

McLaren, Peter (ed.) (1992), *Postmodernism, Postcolonialism and Pedagogy*, Albert Park, Vict., Australia, James Nicholas Publishers.

McLaren, Peter (1992), 'Collisions with otherness; "traveling" theory, post-colonial criticism and the politics of ethnographic practice – the mission of the wounded ethnographer', *International Journal of Qualitative Research in Education*, vol. 5, no. 1, pp. 77–92.

McMannus, John (1979), 'Ritual and human social cognition, in Eugene d'Aquili *et al* (eds) *The Spectrum of Ritual: A Biogenetic Structural Analysis*, New York, Columbia University Press, pp. 207–32.

McRobbie, A. (1980), 'Settling accounts with subculture', *Screen Education*, vol. 34, pp. 37–49.

Madaus, George F. and Linnan, Roger (1973), 'The outcome of Catholic education?', *School Review*, pp. 207–32.

Malinowski, B. (1922), *Argonauts of the Western Pacific*, London, Routledge.

Manning, Frank (1983), 'Cosmos and chaos, celebration in the modern world', in Frank E. Manning (ed.), *The Celebration of Society: Perspectives on Contemporary Cultural Performance*, Bowling Green, Ohio, Bowling Green University Popular Press and London, Ontario, Congress of Social and Humanistic Studies.

Marcuse, H. (1964), *One Dimensional Man*, Boston, Beacon Press.

Marsh, Peter *et al.* (1978), *The Rules of Disorder*, London, Routledge & Kegan Paul.

Martin, Richard J. (1974), 'Cultic aspects of sociology: a speculative essay', *British Journal of Sociology*, vol. 25, no. 1, pp. 15–31.

Marx, K. (1972), *Capital*, Book 1, London, J.M. Dent.

Marx, K. (1973), *Grundrisse*, Harmondsworth, Penguin.

Maslow, A.H. (1971), *The Further Reaches of Human Nature*, New York, Viking Press.

May, Rollo (1961), 'The significance of symbols', in Rollo May (ed.), *Symbolism in Religion and Literature*, New York, George Braziller, pp. 11–49.

Mead, Margaret (1966), 'Ritual and the expression of the cosmic sense', *Worship*, vol. 40, no. 2, pp. 67–72.

Menchú, Rigoberta (1984), *I Rigoberta Menchú: an Indian Woman in Guatemala*, London and New York, Verso.

Mennen, Richard (1976), 'Jerzy Grotowski's paratheatrical projects', *Drama Review*, vol. 19, no. 4, pp. 58–69.

Mercer, Kobena (1990), 'Welcome to the Jungle; identity and diversity in postmodern politics', in Jonathan Rutherford (ed.), *Identity: Community, Culture, Difference*, Lawrence & Wishart, pp 43–71.

Mercurico, Joseph E. (1974), 'Caning: educational ritual', *Australian and New Zealand Journal of Sociology*, vol. 10, no. 1, pp. 49–53.

Merleau-Ponty, Maurice (1962), *Phenomenology of Perception*, translated by Colin Smith, London, Routledge & Kegan Paul.

Merleau-Ponty, M. (1975), *The Primacy of Perception*, ed. J.M. Edie, Evanston, Illinois, Northwestern University Press.

Metcalf, Peter (1977), 'Meaning and materialism: the ritual economy of death', *Man*, vol. 16, no. 4, pp. 563–78.

Metropolitan Toronto School Board (Intermediate Division) (1972), 'Liturgy is life', Religious Education Department, September.

Meyer, John W. (1977), 'The effects of education as an institution', *American Journal of Sociology*, vol. 83, no. 1, pp. 55–77.

Meyer, John W. and Rowan, Brian (1977), 'Institutionalized organizations: formal structures as myth and ceremony', *American Journal of Sociology*, vol. 83, no. 2, pp. 340–63.

Minh-ha, Trinh T. (1991), *When the Moon Waxes Red: Representation, Gender and Cultural Politics*, New York and London, Routledge.

Mish'alani, James K. (1984), 'Threats, laughter and society', *Man and World*, vol. 17, pp. 146–56.

Mitchell, Douglas E. (1980), 'The ideological factor in school politics', *Education and Urban Society*, vol. 12, no. 4, pp. 436–51.

Mitchell, Leonel L. (1977), *The Meaning of Ritual*, New York, Paulist Press.

Mohanty, Chandra (1989/90), 'On race and voice: challenges for liberal education in the 1990s', *Cultural Critique*, Winter, pp 179–208.

Moore, Alexander (1976), 'Realities of the urban classroom', in J.I. Roberts and S.K. Akinsanya (eds), *Schooling in the Cultural Context: Anthropological Studies in Education*, New York, McKay, pp. 238–55.

Moore, Alexander (1980), 'Walt Disney World: bounded ritual space and the playful pilgrimage center', *Anthropological Quarterly*, vol. 53, no. 4, pp. 207–18.

Moore, Robert L. *et al.* (1983), 'Introduction', *Zygon*, vol. 18, no. 3, pp. 209–19.

Moore, Sally Falk (1975), 'Epilogue: uncertainties in situations, indeterminacies in culture', in Sally Falk Moore and Barbara G. Myerhoff (eds), *Symbols and Politics in Communal Ideology*, Ithaca, New York, Cornell University Press, pp. 111–39.

Moore, Sally Falk and Myerhoff, Barbara (eds) (1977), *Secular Ritual*, Assen/Amsterdam, Royal Van Gorcum.

Moore, Sally Falk and Myerhoff, Barbara G. (1977), 'Secular ritual: forms and meanings', in Sally Falk Moore and Barbara G. Myerhoff (eds), *Secular Ritual*, Assen/Amsterdam, Royal Van Gorcum, pp. 3–24.

Moran, Gabriel (1974), *Religious Body: Design for a New Reformation*, New York, Seabury Press.

Moran, Gabriel (1979), 'Teaching within revelation', in Gloria Durka and Joanmarie Smith (eds), *Aesthetic Dimensions of Religious Education*, New York, Paulist Press.

Munn, Nancy (1973), 'Symbolism in a ritual context: aspects of symbolic action', in John J. Honigmann (ed.), *Handbook of Social and Cultural Anthropology*, Chicago, Rand-McNally, pp. 597–612.

Murphy, Robert E. (1972), *The Dialectics of Social Life: Alarms and Excursions in Anthropological Theory*, London, Allen & Unwin.

Murphy, Ronald G. (1979), 'Ceremonial ritual: the mass', in Eugene d'Acquili *et al.* (eds), *The Spectrum of Ritual: A Biogenetic Structural Analysis*, New York, Columbia University Press, pp. 318–41.

Myerhoff, Barbara G. (1974), *Peyote Hunt: The Sacred Journey of the Huichol Indians*, Ithaca, New York, Cornell University Press.

Myerhoff, Barbara G. (1975), 'Organization and ecstasy: deliberate and accidental communitas among the Huichol Indians and American youth', in Sally Falk Moore and Barbara Myerhoff (eds), *Symbols and Politics in Communal Ideology*, Ithaca, New York, Cornell University Press, pp. 33–67.

Myerhoff, Barbara G. (1977), 'We don't wrap herring in a printed page: fusion, fictions and continuity in secular ritual', in Sally Falk Moore and Barbara Myerhoff (eds) , *Secular Ritual*, Assen/Amsterdam, Royal Van Gorcum, pp. 199–224.

Myerhoff, Barbara G. (1979), *Number Our Days*, New York, Simon & Schuster.

Myerhoff, Barbara G. (1982a), 'Rites of passage: process and paradox', in Victor Turner (ed.), *Celebration: Studies in Festivity and Ritual*, Washington, DC, Smithsonian Institute Press, pp. 109–35.

Myerhoff, Barbara G. (1982b), 'The transformation of consciousness in ritual performances: some thoughts and questions', paper given at Wenner-Gren Foundation for Anthropological Research Symposium, no. 89, 'Theatre and Ritual', Asia Society, New York.

Myerhoff, Barbara and Metzger, Deena (1980),'The journal as activity and genre: on listening to the silent laughter of Mozart', *Semiotica*, vol. 30, nos. 1/2, pp. 97–114.

Nagendra, S.P. (1971), *The Concept of Ritual in Modern Sociological Theory*, New Delhi, Academic Journals of India.

Neale, Robert E. (1969), *In Praise of Play: Toward a Psychology of Religion*, New York, Harper.

Neiburg, H.L. (1970), 'Agonistics – ritual of conflict', *Annals of the American Academy of Political and Social Science*, no. 391, pp. 56–73.

Norris, Christopher (1991), 'Deconstruction versus postmodernism: critical theory and the "Nuclear Sublime"', *New Formations*, vol. 15, pp. 83–100.

Norton, David (1970), 'The rites of passage from dependence to autonomy', *School Review*, vol. 79, no. 1, pp. 19–42.

O'Farrell, Lawrence Patrick, (1981), 'Ritual in creative drama', *Drama Contact*, pp. 16–18.

O'Farrell, Lawrence Patrick (n.d.), 'Making it special: ritual as a creative resource for drama', unpublished paper.

Ogbu, John U. (1979), 'Social stratification and the socialization of competence', *Anthropology and Education Quarterly*, vol. 10, no. 1, pp. 3–20.

Ogbu, John U. (1981), 'School ethnography: a multilevel approach', *Anthropology and Education Quarterly*, vol. 12, no. 1, pp. 3–29.

O'Keefe, Daniel L. (1982), *Stolen Lightning: The Social Theory of Magic*, New York, Continuum.

Olson, David (1980), 'On the language and authority of text books', *Journal of Communication*, vol. 30, no. 1, pp. 186–96.

Olson, Wayne (1979), 'Ceremony as religious education', *Religious Education*, vol. 74, no. 6, pp. 563–9.

O'Neill, John (1975), 'Gay technology and the body politic', in Jonathan Benthall and Ted Polemus (eds), *The Body as a Medium of Expression*, London, Allen Lane.

Ontario English Catholic Teachers' Association, 'The Ontario Catholic school system', pamphlet.

Ortiz, Alfonso (1969), *The Tewa World: Space, Time, Being and Becoming in a Pueblo Society*, Chicago, University of Chicago Press.

Ortiz, Alfonso (1972), 'Ritual drama and the Pueblo world view', in Alfonso Ortiz (ed.), *New Perspectives on the Pueblos*, Albuquerque, University of New Mexico Press.

Ortner, Sherrey (1973), 'On key symbols', *American Anthropologist*, vol. 75, no. 5, pp. 1338–46.

Ortner, Sherry (1975), 'God's bodies, God's food: a symbolic analysis of Sherpa ritual', in C.E. Hill (ed.), *Symbols and Society: Essays on Belief Systems in Action*, Athens, Georgia, University of Georgia Press, pp. 133–69.

Ortner, Sherry (1978), *The Sherpas and their Rituals*, Cambridge, Cambridge University Press.

Paine, Robert (1981), 'Politically speaking: cross-cultural studies of rhetoric', Philadelphia, Institute for the Study of Human Issues (ISHI), and St John's, Newfoundland, Institute of Social and Economic Research (ISER).

Palazzoli, Selvini Mara *et al.* (1978), *Paradox and Counterparadox: A New Model in the Therapy of the Family in Schizophrenic Transaction*, New York, Jason Aronson.

Palmer, Richard E. (1969), *Hermeneutics: Interpretation Theory in Schleiermacher, Dilthey, Heidegger and Gadamer*, Evanston, Northwestern University Press.

Panikkar, Raimundo (1977), 'Man as ritual being', *Chicago Studies*, vol. 16, no. 1, pp. 5–28.

Partridge, W. (1972), *The Hippie Ghetto: The Natural History of a Subculture*, New York, Holt, Rinehart & Winston.

Partridge, W. (1977), 'Transformation and redundancy in ritual: a case from Columbia', in M. Du Toit (ed.), *Drugs, Rituals, and Altered States of Consciousness*, Rotterdam, A.A. Balkema, pp. 59–73.

Patterson, David (1990), 'Laughter and the alterity of truth in Bakhtin's aesthetics', *Social Discourse*, vol. 3, no. 1–2, pp 295–310.

Pedersen, Eigil (1982), 'Sociology of education: its roots and current concerns', *The Study of Education: Canada*, Ninth Yearbook, Canadian Society for the Study of Education, Faculty of Education University of British Columbia, pp. 49–62.

Pepper, Stephen C. (1942), *World Hypothesis: A Study in Evidence*, Berkeley, University of California Press.

Perinbanayagam, R.S. (1974), 'The definition of the situation: an analysis of the ethnomethodological and dramaturgical view', *Sociological Quarterly*, vol. 15, pp. 521–41.

Perkarsky, Daniel (1982), 'Dehumanization and education', *Teachers College Record*, vol. 84, no. 2, pp. 339–53.

Phenix, Philip (1964), *Realms of Meaning: A Philosophy of the Curriculum for General Education*, Toronto, McGraw-Hill.

Phenix, Philip (1982), 'Promoting personal development through learning', *Teachers College Record*, vol. 84, no. 2, pp. 301–16.

Pink, William C. (1982), 'School effects, academic performance, and school crimes: some inescapable realities of viewing schools from the inside', *Urban Education*, vol. 17, no. 1, pp. 51–72.

Piven, Frances Fox (1976), 'The social structuring of political protest', *Politics and Society*, vol. 6, no. 3, pp. 297–326.

Polanyi, Michael (1958), *Personal Knowledge: Towards a Post-Critical Philosophy*, Chicago, The University of Chicago Press.

Polemus, Ted (ed.) (1978), *Social Aspects of the Human Body*, Harmondsworth, Penguin.

Popkewitz, Thomas *et al.* (1982), *The Myth of Educational Reform*, Madison, Wis., University of Wisconsin Press.

Postman, Neil (1982), *The Disappearance of Childhood*, New York, Dell Pub.

Poulantzas, Nicos (1975), *Classes in Contemporary Capitalism*, London, New Left Books.

Poyatos, Fernando (1981), 'Towards a typology of somatic signs', *Semiotic Inquiry*, vol. 1, no. 2, pp. 136–56.

Radcliffe-Brown, A.R. (1952), *Structure and Function in Primitive Society*, New York, Free Press.

Rappaport, Roy A. (1968), *Pigs for the Ancestors*, New Haven, Conn., Yale University Press.

Rappaport, Roy A. (1971a), 'Ritual, sanctity and cybernetics', *American Anthropologist*, vol. 73, pp. 57–76.

Rappaport, Roy A. (1971b), 'The sacred in human evolution', *Annual Review of Ecology and Systematics*, vol. 2, pp. 23–44.

Rappaport, Roy A. (1976), 'Liturgies and lies', *International Yearbook for the Sociology of Knowledge and Religion*, vol. 10, pp. 75–104.

Rappaport, Roy A. (1978), 'Adaptation and the structure of ritual', in N. Blurton Jones and V. Reynolds (eds), *Human Behaviour and Adaptation*, Symposia of the Society for the Study of Human Biology, vol. 18, pp. 77–102.

Rappaport, Roy A. (1979), *Ecology, Meaning and Religion*, Richmond, Calif., North American Books.

Rappaport, Roy A. (1980), 'Concluding remarks on ritual and reflexivity', *Semiotica*, vol. 30, nos. 1/2, pp. 181–93.

Ray, Benjamin (1973), 'Performative utterances in African rituals', *History of Religions*, vol. 13, no. 1, pp. 16–35.

Regan, Patrick (1973), 'Liturgy and the experience of celebration', *Worship*, vol. 47, no. 9, pp. 592–600.

Richards, Mary Caroline (1980), 'The public school and the education of the whole person', *Teachers College Record*, vol. 82, no. 1, pp. 47–76.

Richardson, Miles (1980), 'The anthropologist as word-shaman', *Anthropology and Humanism Quarterly*, vol. 5, no. 4, p. 2.

Richardson, Miles (1982), 'Putting death in its place in Spanish America and the American South: application of the dramaturgical model to religious behaviour', paper given at Wenner-Gren Foundation for Anthropological Research Symposium no. 89, 'Theatre and Ritual', Asia Society, New York.

Ricoeur, Paul (1969), *The Symbolism of Evil*, Boston, Beacon Press.

Ricoeur, Paul (1975), *The Rule of Metaphor: Multidisciplinary Studies of the Creation of Meaning in Language*, Toronto, University of Toronto Press.

Roberts, Douglas (1970), 'Science as an explanatory mode', *Main Currents in Modern Thought*, vol. 26, no. 5, pp. 131–9.

Roberts, William O. Jr. (1982), *Initiation to Adulthood: An Ancient Rite of Passage in Contemporary Form*, New York, Pilgrim.

Rosen, David M. (1980), 'Class and ideology in an inner city preschool: reproductionist theory and the anthropology of education', *Anthropological Quarterly*, vol. 53, no. 4, pp. 219–28.

Rosenau, Pauline Marie (1992), *Post-moderism and the Social Sciences: Insights, Inroads and Intrusions*, Princeton, NJ, Princeton University Press.

Rozak, Theodore (1969), *The Making of a Counterculture: Reflections on the Technocratic Society and its Youthful Opposition*, Garden City, New York, Anchor Books/Doubleday.

Ryan, William (1976), *Blaming the Victim*, New York, Vintage Books.

St Helen's Portuguese Community Centre (1977), Seminar Report.

Salvidar, Ramon (1990), *Chicano Narrative: the Dialectics of Difference*, Madison, Wis., University of Wisconsin Press.

Schatzmen, L. and Strauss, A.L. (1973), *Field Research: Strategies for a Natural Sociology*, New York, Prentice-Hall.

Schechner, Richard (1974), 'From ritual to theatre and back: the structure/process of the efficacy-entertainment dyad', *Educational Theatre Journal*, vol. 26, pp. 455–81.

Schechner, Richard (1977), *Essays on Performance Theory: 1970–1976*, New York, Drama Books.

Schechner, Richard (1981a), 'Restored behaviour', *Studies in Visual Communication*, vol. 7, no. 3, pp. 2–45.

Schechner, Richard (1981b), 'Performers and spectators transported and transformed', *Kenyon Review*, vol. 3, no. 4, pp. 83–113.

Schechner, Richard (1982), *The End of Humanism: Writings on Performance*, New York, Performing Arts Journal Publications.

Schechner, Richard (1983), *Performative Circumstances: From the Avant Garde to Ramlila*, Calcutta, Seagull Books.,

Schechner, Richard and Schuman, Mady (eds) (1976), *Ritual, Play and Performance: Readings in the Social Sciences/Theatre*, New York, Seabury Press.

Scheff, Thomas J. (1977), 'The distancing of emotion in ritual', *Current Anthropology*, vol. 18, no. 3, pp. 483–504.

Scheff, Thomas J. (1979), *Catharsis in Healing, Ritual and Drama*, Los Angeles, University of California Press.

Schneider, David M. (1968), *American Kinship*, Englewood Cliffs, New Jersey, Prentice-Hall.

Searle, J.R. (1969), *Speech Acts*, Cambridge, Cambridge University Press.

Searle, Mark (1981), 'Liturgy as metaphor', *Worship*, vol. 55, no. 2, pp. 98–120.

Sebeok, Thomas A. (1974), 'Semiotics: a survey of the state of the art', in T. Sebeok (ed.), *Current Trends in Linguistics, Volume 12: Linguistics and Adjacent Arts and Sciences*, The Hague, Mouton, pp. 211–64.

Sharp, Rachel (1980), *Knowledge, Ideology and the Politics of Schooling: Towards a Marxist Analysis of Education*, London, Routledge & Kegan Paul.

Shils, E. (1966), 'Ritual and crisis', *Philosophical Transactions of the Royal Society of London*, Series B, vol. 25, no. 772, pp. 447–50.

Shipman, M.D. (1968), *The Sociology of the School*, London and Harlow, Longmans Green & Co.

Shook, Laurence K. (1971), 'The relevance of Catholic education in the society of today', an address by the president of the Pontifical Institute of Medieval Studies. *Completion Campaign Handbook*, Ontario Catholic Teachers' Association.

Shor, Ira (1980), *Critical Teaching and Everyday Life*, Boston, Mass., South End Press.

Simone, Timothy Maliqualim (1989), *About Face: Race in Postmodern America*, New York, Autonomedia.

Sitton, Thad (1980), 'Inside school spaces: rethinking the hidden dimension', *Urban Education*, vol. 15, no. 1, pp. 65–82.

Skorupski, John (1976), *Symbol and Theory: A Philosophical Study of Theories of Religion in Social Anthropology*, Cambridge, Cambridge University Press.

Slinger, John (1971), 'Dreams of Eldorado Fade for Portuguese', *Globe and Mail* (Toronto), 26 August.

Smith, John (1979), 'Ritual and the ethnology of communicating', in Eugene d'Aquili *et al.* (eds), *The Spectrum of Ritual: A Biogenetic Structural Analysis*, New York, Columbia University Press, pp. 51–79.

Smith, Jonathan Z. (1978), *Map is not Territory: Studies in the History of Religion*, Leiden, Brill.

Smith, Jonathan Z. (1982), *Imagining Religion: From Babylon to Jonestown*, Chicago, University of Chicago Press.

Smith, Richard (1979), 'Myth and ritual in teacher education', in M.R. Pusey and R.E. Young (eds), *Control and Knowledge: The Mediation of Power in Institutional and Educational Settings*, Canberra Educational Research Unit, Australian National University, pp. 97–123.

Smith, W. Robertson (1956), *The Religion of the Semites*, New York, Meridian Books.

Soja, Edward W. (1991), 'Heterotopologies: a remembrance of other spaces in the Citadel-LA', *Strategies*, no. 3, pp 6–39.

Staal, Fritz (1979), 'The meaninglessness of ritual', *Numen*, vol. 26, pp. 2–22.

Stivers, Richard (1982), *Evil in Modern Myth and Ritual*, Athens, Georgia, University of Georgia Press.

Stoller, Paul (1982), 'Relativity and the anthropologist's gaze', *Anthropology and Humanism Quarterly*, vol. 7, no. 4, pp. 2–10.

Sullivan, Patrick H. (1975), 'Ritual: attending to the world', *Anglican Theological Review*, supplementary series, no. 5, pp. 9–43.

Tambiah, S.J. (1968), 'The magical power of words', *Man*, n.s., vol. 3. no. 2, pp. 175–208.

Taussig, Michael (1980), *The Devil and Commodity Fetishism in South America*, Chapel Hill, NC, University of North Carolina Press.

Taussig, Michael, (1987), *Shamanism, Colonialism and the Wild Man: a Study in Terror and Healing*, Chicago and London, University of Chicago Press.

Thelen, H. (1970), 'Secularizing the classroom's semisacred culture', *School Review*, vol. 79, no 1, pp. 1–18.

Thomsen, D.E. (1982), 'The quotable pope at CERN', *Science News*, vol. 122, no. 7, p. 109.

Tillich, Paul (1956), *Dynamics of Faith*, New York, Harper & Row.

Tillich, Paul (1960), 'The religious symbol', in Rollo May (ed.), *Symbolism in Religion and Literature*, New York, Braziller.

Toronto Star (1977), 'Portuguese parents should be closer to the school system, counsellor says', 25 April.

Turner, Victor (1966), 'Anthropological postscript', *Philosophical Transactions of the Royal Society of London*, Series B, vol. 25, no. 772, p. 521–2.

Turner, Victor (1967), *The Forest of Symbols: Aspects of Ndembu Ritual*, Ithaca, New York, Cornell University Press.

Turner, Victor (1968), *The Drums of Affliction*, Oxford, Clarendon Press.

Turner, Victor (1969), *The Ritual Process: Structure and Anti-Structure*, Chicago, Aldine.

Turner, Victor (1973), 'The centre out there: pilgrim's goal', *History of Religions*, vol. 12, no. 3, pp. 191–230.

Turner, Victor (1974a), 'Metaphors of anti-structure in religious culture', in A. Eister (ed.), *Changing Perspectives in the Scientific Study of Religion*, New York, Wiley, pp. 63–84.

Turner, Victor (1974b), 'Liminal to lininoid, in play, flow and ritual: an essay in comparative symbology', *Rice University Studies*, vol. 60, no. 3, pp. 53–92.

Turner, Victor (1974c), 'Symbols and social experience in religious ritual', *Studia Missionalia*, vol. 23, Rome, Gregorian University Press, pp. 1–21.

Turner, Victor (1974d), 'Pilgrimage and communitas', *Studia Missionalia*, vol. 23, Rome, Gregorian University Press, pp. 305–27.

Turner, Victor (1974e), *Dramas, Fields and Metaphors*, Ithaca, New York, Cornell University Press.

Turner, Victor (1975a), *Revelation and Divination in Ndembu Ritual*, Ithaca, New York, Cornell University Press.
Turner, Victor (1975b), 'Ritual as communication and potency', in Carole Hill (ed.), *Symbols and Society: Essays on Belief Systems in Action*, Athens, Georgia, University of Georgia Press.
Turner, Victor (1976), 'Ritual, tribal and Catholic', *Worship*, vol. 50, no. 6, pp. 504–24.
Turner, Victor (1977), 'Process, system, and symbol: a new anthropological synthesis', *Daedalus*, vol. 1, pp. 61–80.
Turner, Victor (1978), 'Encounter with Freud: the making of a comparative symbologist', in George and Louise Spindler (eds), *The Making of Psychological Anthropology*, Berkeley, University of California Press, pp. 558–83.
Turner, Victor (1979a), 'Dramatic ritual/ritual drama: performance and reflexive anthropology', *Kenyon Review*, vol. 1, no. 3, pp. 80–93.
Turner, Victor (1979b), *Process, Performance and Pilgrimage*, New Delhi, Concept.
Turner, Victor (1980), 'Social dramas and stories about them', *Critical Inquiry*, vol. 7, no. 1, pp. 141–68.
Turner, Victor (1982a), *From Ritual to Theatre: The Human Seriousness of Play*, New York, Performing Arts Journal Publications.
Turner, Victor (1982b), 'Are there universals in performance?', paper given at Wenner-Gren Foundation for Anthropological Research symposium no. 89, 'Theatre and Ritual', Asia Society, New York.
Turner, Victor (1983), 'Body, brain, and culture', *Zygon*, vol. 18, no. 3, pp. 221–45.
Turner, Victor (1986), 'Dewey, Dilthey, and drama: an essay in the anthropology of experience', in Victor Turner and Edward M. Bruner (eds), *The Anthropology of Experience*, Urbana, University of Illinois Press.
Turner, Victor and Turner, Edith (1982), 'Performing ethnography', *Drama Review*, vol. 26, no. 2, pp.33–50.
Tyler, E.B. (1924), *Primitive Culture* (2 vols), 7th edn, London.
Van Gennep, Arnold (1960), *The Rites of Passage*, translated by Monika B. Vizedom and Gabrielle L. Caffee, Chicago, University of Chicago Press.
Vatican Council, Second (1964), *The Constitution on the Sacred Liturgy*, Commentary by Gerard S. Sloan, Glen Rock, New Jersey, Paulist Press.
Wallace, Anthony (1966), *Religion: An Anthropological View*, New York, Random House.
Wallace, Anthony (1970), *Culture and Personality*, New York, Random House.
Watzlawick, Paul (1984), 'Self-fulfilling prophecies', in Paul Watzlawick (ed.), *The Invented Reality*, New York and London, W.W. Norton.
Watzlawick, Paul *et al.* (1967), *The Pragmatics of Human Communication*, New York, W.W. Norton.
Way, Brian (1968), *Development Through Drama*, London, Longman.

Weekend Magazine (Toronto) (1973), 'They never really left home', 11 August.

Weiss, Milford S. and Weiss, Paula H. (1976), 'A public school ritual ceremony', *Journal of Research and Development in Education*, vol. 9, no. 4, pp. 22–8.

Welsford, Enid (1966), *The Fool: His Social and Literary History*, Gloucester, Mass., Peter Smith.

Wernick, Andrew (1980), 'Dionysis and the crucified: towards a left theology', *Canadian Journal of Political and Social Theory*, vol. 4, no. 1, pp. 33–58.

West, Cornel (1991a), 'Decentring Europe: a memorial lecture for James Snead', *Critical Quarterly*, vol. 31, no. 1, pp. 1–19.

West, Cornel (1991b), *The Ethical Dimensions of Marxist Thought*, New York, Monthly Review Press.

Whitehead, Alfred North (1929), *The Aims of Education and Other Essays*, New York, Macmillan.

Whorf, B.L. (1956), *Language, Thought and Reality*, Cambridge, MIT Press.

Wilden, Anthony (with Jacques Lacan) (1968), in Anthony Wilden (ed.), *The Language of the Self: The Function of Language in Psychoanalysis*, Baltimore, Johns Hopkins Press.

Wilden, Anthony (1972), *System and Structure: Essays in Communication and Exchange*, London, Tavistock; New York, Harper & Row.

Wilden, Anthony (1980a), *The Imaginary Canadian: An Examination for Discovery*, Vancouver, Pulp Press; Toronto, Virgo Press.

Wilden, Anthony (1980b), 'Semiotics and praxis: strategy and tactics', *Semiotic Inquiry*, vol. 1, pp. 1–34.

Wilden, Anthony (1982), 'Postcript to semiotics as praxis: strategy and tactics', *Semiotic Inquiry*, vol. 2, no. 2, pp. 166–70.

Wilden, Anthony (1986), 'Ideology and the icon: oscillation, contradiction, and paradox. An essay in context theory'. *Iconicity: The Nature of Culture. Essays in Honour of Tom Sebeok*, Bloomington, Indiana University Press.

Wilden, Anthony (1987), *The Rules Are No Game: The Strategy of Communication: A Scientific, Historical and Humanist Perspective*, London, Routledge & Kegan Paul.

Wiliams, Raymond (1973), 'Base and superstructure in Marxist cultural theory', *New Left Review*, vol. 82, pp. 3–16.

Williams, Robin M. Jr. (1970), *American Society: A Sociological Interpretation*, 3rd edn, New York, Alfred A. Knopf.

Wilis, Paul (1977), *Learning to Labour: How Working Class Kids Get Working Class Jobs*, Aldershot, Gower.

Willis, Paul (1978), *Profane Culture*, London, Routledge & Kegan Paul.

Willis, Paul (1990), *Common Culture: Symbolic Work at Play in the Everyday Cultures of the Young*, Boulder, Colo. and San Francisco, Westview Press.

Willower, Donald J, (1969), 'The teacher subculture and rites of passage', *Urban Education*, vol. 4, no. 2, pp. 103–14.

Winnicott, D.W. (1974), *Playing and Reality*, Harmondsworth, Penguin.

Witkin, Robert W. (1974), *The Intelligence of Feeling*, London, Heinemann.

Witkowski, Lech (1990), 'Education and the universal challenge of the border', paper presented at the Second International Symposium for Universalism, Frankfurt, Germany, Max-Planck Institute für Bilungsforschung, pp. 1–41.

Wolf, Eric (1965), 'The Virgin of Guadalupe: a Mexican national symbol', in William A. Lessa and Evon Z. Vogt (eds), *Reader in Comparative Religion: An Anthropological Approach*, New York, Harper & Row.

Woods, Peter (1975), 'Showing them up in secondary school', in Gabriel Chanan and Sara Delamont (eds), *Frontiers of Classroom Research*, Walton-on-Thames, NFER, pp. 122–45.

Worgul, George (1980), *From Magic to Metaphor: A Validation of the Christian Sacraments*, New York, Paulist Press.

Yamamoto, Kaoru (1975), *Individuality: The Unique Learner*, Columbus, Ohio, Charles E. Merrill.

Yinger, Milton (1977), 'Presidential address: countercultures and social change', *American Sociological Review*, vol. 42, no. 6, pp. 833–53.

Young, Iris, Marion (1990), *Justice and the Politics of Difference*, Princeton, NJ, Princeton University Press.

Zeichner, Kenneth M. and Teitelbaum, Kenneth (1982), 'Personalized and inquiry oriented teacher education: an analysis of two approaches to the development of curriculum for field-based experiences', *Journal of Education for Teaching*, vol. 8, no. 2, pp. 95–117.

Zuesse, Evan M. (1975), 'Meditation on ritual', *Journal of the American Academy of Religion*, vol. 43, no. 3, pp. 517–30.

Name index

Subject index